California Property Management

Donna L. Grogan, CPM

Published by the National Real Estate Institute

By National Real Estate Institute
14949 N.E. 40th Street, Suite 300
Redmond, Washington 98052
(206) 881-2517 / 1-800-221-9347

PRINTED IN THE UNITED STATES OF AMERICA

ISBN: 0-915799-56-1

CONTENTS

ABOUT THE AUTHOR

Donna Grogan has many years of property management experience. She received her Masters Degree in Property Management, Training and Education from California Polytechnic University, Pomona, in 1984. She went on to receive her Certified Property Manager (CPM) designation in 1985. She is also a Certified Residential Specialist (CRS), a graduate of the Realtors Institute (GRI), and the broker for Sunbelt Real Estate Services in Downey, California.

Donna Grogan has also taught various real estate courses at El Camino, Rio Hondo, and Cerritos Community Colleges.

AUTHOR'S NOTE

This book was designed to fill a variety of needs. Its primary purpose is to inform and inspire both novice and experienced property managers. It was also designed as the primary textbook for property management courses in California. To this end, it was developed to match the outline of the California Community Colleges Instructor and Student Study Guides as published by the Real Estate Depository.

I wish to thank all those instructors for their input into this book. The following were particularly helpful and deserve special recognition:

Dr. Gilbert McKee, Jr., Finance, California Polytechnic University, Pomona

Dr. David L. Parry, Chair, Finance, California Polytechnic University, Pomona

Dr. Djavad Kashedinejad, Finance, California Polytechnic University, Pomona

Dr. Rocky Tarantello, Adj. Assistant Professor of Real Estate, USC

Dr. Gene Six, Chair, Real Estate, Mt. San Antonio College

Phyllis Pearce, Chair, Business, Rio Hondo College

Lowell Anderson, Chair, Real Estate, Cerritos College

Frank Fowler, Chair, Real Estate, El Camino College

William Pivar, College of the Desert

But I am especially grateful to the hundreds of students who have taken my property management courses and completed the management plan project. Their feedback, comments, and support have been invaluable.

1
Overview of Property Management

Reference

Esty & Associates. *The Vocabulary of Real Estate.* 1984.

Principles of Real Estate Management. 12th ed.

Irwin, Robert. *Smart Money Real Estate for the 80's.* 1982.

Chapter Overview

In this chapter you will read about how the history of property management has influenced present day property management operations. You will also learn about the different phases of a property's life cycle —knowledge that is essential to its effective management. You will be introduced briefly to the different types of properties and their individual management needs. Finally, you will learn about the professional organizations of property management.

PROPERTY MANAGEMENT–PAST, PRESENT, AND FUTURE

Property Management in the U.S.

Managing property owned by another dates back to Biblical times when stewards cared for lands owned by Kings, emperors and other rulers. The powers, responsibilities, and compensation of property managers have changed dramatically over these thousands of years, but the need for competent, trained professionals is just as pressing.

Property Management
That portion of the real estate business involving the operations, maintenance and marketing of income-producing property according to the objectives of ownership.

The European feudal structure is the basis for today's three-party property management system. The king owned the land and transferred the daily operations of management to feudal lords. The feudal lords employed tenants to work the land.

Colonization of much of the world by European countries perpetuated this three-party system which is just as effective today: landlord, property manager, and tenant. Just as stewards leased property to shepherds for grazing on behalf of the king, modern property managers lease apartments or office space to tenants while representing property owners.

This system was also imported to the United States. The United States was founded on the ideal of preserving individual property rights. The United States Constitution upholds the right of property ownership: the right of an individual to hold title to and possess property; to make legal use of it; to pledge, mortgage or encumber it; to sell, transfer or dispose of it; to enjoy it; to exclude others from it; and to hire someone to manage it.

In the 1800's, most American property managers handled European investments on the East Coast. These "out-of-town" investors needed someone on-site to manage their properties. Multi-family residential, commercial and office space were the primary sources of management. Then, in the 1900's, residential housing standards rose, along with breakthroughs in high-rise technology—thus, greater expertise was required to manage property, even properties owned by local investors.

The demand for property management continued to grow. The advent of the automobile encouraged urban sprawl, moving owners farther from the properties they owned. Great accumulations of wealth encouraged high growth in real estate projects. Then the Depression led to mass accumulations of bank-owned, bank-managed holdings. These banks needed property managers to handle their suddenly large property portfolios.

Since the 1950's, demand for property management has varied according to regional development, economy, age of population, lifestyle, and government policies. It is estimated that by the year 2000, there will be a constant demand for management in certain American sectors, while others will have little need for it. The highest demand will be in areas of high population and property values, like the West Coast. International and multilingual firms will also be in high demand.

Knowing the market in a popular area will be a distinct plus for the up-and-coming property manager, as the national trend is towards management specialization, education, and experience.

Property Management in California

The California and southwestern areas evolved a little differently than the rest of the United States. From tribal days to present times, California has been influenced by unique cultures, doctrines, and philosophies that have carried over to shape today's property management operations. The following material is a brief summary of some of the historical highlights that have affected property management in California.

The Period Prior to 1768. The Yuma Indian tribes occupied the territory that is now California when the Portuguese explorer, Cabrillo (who was employed by Spain), discovered California in 1542. Over 30 years later, in 1579, Sir Francis Drake claimed the land for England. Thus began the first land dispute in California. The Indian Chief, the King of Spain, and the Crown of England each wanted to be landlord and wanted the others to be tenants. Since there were no established permanent structures (property improvements) to help the claims of the Spanish and English, the Indians won the first round.

The Period From 1769 to 1823. In the eighteenth century it became apparent to the King of Spain, Charles III, that the unknown lands in Alta, or Upper California might soon be settled by either Russia or England. The Russians were venturing farther south from the Bering Sea each year in their search for otter skins. The English, by recently winning control of Canada, posed an equally serious threat. To forestall the

The period prior to 1768

The period from 1769 to 1823

advance of these competing nations, Charles III gave permission to the Franciscan Order to develop missions in California.

While Spaniards had established other missions and settlements in Baja, or Lower California, it was not until 1769 that Captain Portola led the expedition that established the first presidio (military fort) at San Diego. He also established one at Monterey in 1770, and San Francisco in 1776. More missions were founded along with some pueblos (villages) near the coast. By 1823, the Franciscans had built a chain of 21 missions—the first chain of income-producing multi-family, hotel, and commercial developments in California.

The missions gave Spain some control over the land, giving rise to a right of ownership by occupation. The "occupation" (by the "landowner") required only the manpower of two padres (the "property manager") and a few protective soldiers.

The missions were to become self-sufficient after some years of receiving supplies from Spain. After training the native Indians (the "tenants") for ten years, the missions were to turn over the mission lands and improvements to the natives as self-governing Spanish subjects. The Franciscans, who wanted to save souls, and the King, who sought to secure the land, joined together in an alliance of mutual benefit. No one asked the Indians or the English for permission—they were both promptly evicted from the area. In the meantime, California was still owned by Spain. But in 1821, the property came "under new management" when New Spain (Mexico) won its independence from Spain.

The Period From 1823 to 1845. The Russians established Fort Ross in northern California in 1812. Their activity in California was one reason for the United State's Monroe Doctrine (proclaimed in 1823), which stated that all the American continents were "henceforth not to be considered subjects for colonization by European powers." This marked the arrival of the first government intervention in California housing.

In 1824, Russia agreed to limit its settlements to Alaska. In 1839, Sacramento had a population of only 16. Juan Alvarado, Mexican Governor of California, granted over 48,000 acres to John Sutter, in hopes of stopping both the Russian push inland and the arrival of eastern American trappers. This successfully stopped the Russian expansion in California in 1840, known as history's longest eviction.

The period from 1846 to 1849

The period from 1850 to 1870

The Period From 1846 to 1849. It is no wonder that the Indian tribes fled from California when another new management (John Sutter) arrived, creating more new policies and procedures. The American rebels raised the "Bear" flag in 1849, starting the Mexican War of 1846-1848. With the Gold Rush in 1849, hundreds of eastern American colonists arrived in California. Sacramento had grown to 4,000 by then (the state population was only 12,000). There were plenty of funds but little available housing—the high demand had stripped all existing supply. Little formal management was needed at this time.

The Period From 1850 to 1870. On April 4, 1850, Los Angeles was incorporated as a city and, five months later, California became the 31st state. The state's population grew from 26,000 in 1848 to 379,994 in 1860; the city of Los Angeles grew from 1,610 in 1850 to 5,628 in 1870.

When the Civil War ended in 1865, thousands of settlers came to California to buy land at low prices. With eastern investors pouring thousands of dollars into California land speculation and the railroad system (completed in 1869), land management was in high demand.

The first low-income government housing was established for the Chinese railroad laborers in the 1860's. By 1870, the state population had risen to about 560,000. Structures, even whole towns, were thrown up almost overnight to meet the needs of an expanding population, with no long range planning for public facilities, zoning, or minimum building requirements.

The Period From 1871 to 1889. For the next ten years, economic depression was widespread. The first major discrimination riots took place in Los Angeles in 1871, and in San Francisco in 1877. The cause of the riots? Workers from other countries would work for lower wages and state residents rebelled against them. Many of these workers were prudent savers and managed to pay the high rental rates, forcing prices even higher for local residents.

The first major marketing campaign took place in the 1880's, publicizing the lower real estate and rental costs in the "Sunshine State" to Easterners. Thousands came to the area during this period and the demand for property management fell because of the high supply of tenants. So many came to southern California in 1887 that agriculture, industry, and housing flourished because of the increased demand.

The Period From 1900 to 1929. These years ushered in the period of government regulation of real property. The great San Francisco earthquake in 1906 destroyed 28,000 buildings. When the city was rebuilt, building codes, ordinances, and building material regulations were welcomed by the outraged citizens.

Between 1905-1907, floodwaters from the Colorado River formed the 450-square mile Salton Sea in southeastern California. In 1928, Congress authorized the construction of the Boulder Dam, completed in 1936. The California Land Management offices had the tasks of controlling floods, providing irrigation for the vast farmlands, and distributing power to the ever growing southern California area. Farming increased. Oil, natural gas, and minerals were mined. Major shipyards were established. Because of government controls regulating land use, mineral rights, and housing, property management was in high demand.

By 1910, Hollywood had become the motion picture capital of the world, and investor funds poured into California's income-producing properties, sparking even more of a demand for property management.

The Period From 1930 to 1959. During the Great Depression of the 1930's, the economy of Los Angeles slumped, but its population grew as thousands of jobless and homeless drifted into the area. Naturally, this increased the already high demand for housing units.

Following the outbreak of World War II in 1939, yet another wave of new residents flooded into the cities of California to work in aircraft factories, shipyards, and other war-related plants. By the end of the war in 1945, Los Angeles had over 1.5 million persons. Thousands of new homes quickly covered the city's open spaces. Landlords, investors, and developers could not provide the supply of housing units that was needed by tenants, homebuyers, and commercial and industrial entities.

Property management had a low profile because of the virtual 100% occupancy, until about 1957 when an equilibrium point was reached as the supply of housing began to catch up with demand.

The Period From 1960 to 1969. Air pollution, control and distribution of water, and growing industry were initially thought to be the issues of the 1960's. By then, population of California had grown to over 2.75 million people.

Then the Watts riots broke out in 1965. After millions of dollars in damage and the death of 34 persons, the true problems of housing in southern California surfaced. The government responded to the complaints of minorities by providing increased education, employment opportunities, and affordable housing. Many government-owned or controlled units were built that required property managers. The units and their management costs were paid for by California landowners in the form of property taxes.

The Period From 1970 to 1990. In the early 1970's, the housing market was sluggish, with low demand and little turnover. High taxes and increased government spending became a major issue in the 1970's as the aircraft industry declined, brush fires rose, and earthquakes shook the very foundation of the area. Homebuyers, investors and renters were no longer able to pay the rapidly escalating prices. In 1978, Proposition 13 (which limited the increase of property taxes) was voted in to restrict government spending. The late 1970's saw the formation of tenant associations, tenant strikes, and government-imposed rent controls.

In the early 1980's, thousands of investment dollars left California, causing upheavals in the housing market. New investors were unable to afford the high prices, negative cash flows, and increasing taxes.

If current housing trends persist, by 1990 San Francisco will have enough housing for only one worker out of three. Though California's cost of living is 132.7% higher than the national average, San Francisco housing costs are even higher—223.9% higher (as of spring 1989). Skilled property managers, city planners, and business persons will have vast opportunities to meet these challenges.

Coupled with the large influx of Hispanic and Asian people into the Los Angeles, San Diego and San Francisco metropolitan areas is the ever increasing retirement population. These retired people, who have seen the values of California real estate grow tremendously, often choose to keep their property as rental-income units while they travel in their motorhomes or move out of the crowded cities. They demand professional property management.

California represents 25% of the nation's wealth. On the basis of dollars produced, it ranks sixth in the world, just behind Italy, and ahead of Great Britain. It supports one of the largest employment bases in the world. This employment base, in turn, is the foundation for an enormous financial/banking industry. This industry demands professional management for their property holdings.

Conclusion. Studies show that California is thousands of housing units short of the present market demand. Effective property management is needed to stabilize the properties that are floundering and to efficiently manage all existing real property assets. The greatest challenge, at present, is meeting tenant demands and solving the financial problems of the industry. With less funds available to support public housing, and the already deficient number of affordable units, the next several years will be turbulent times in the real estate industry.

Foreign Influences on Property Management

International investors from the western Pacific-Rim have brought large amounts of additional investment dollars into California. The influx of immigrants has changed the complexion of entire communities as ethnic mixes change. New culturally diversified interests have brought about new business opportunities. Higher demand for more affordable, smaller size living units has spurred the condo market into new heights of sales volume. Ethnic neighborhood shopping centers are in high demand to cater to local areas. Multinational and international business headquarters and regional offices are leasing California coastal and airport-convenient, high-rise office buildings. California property management now interacts with markets in every part of the world.

Anticipated appreciation due to the large influx of immigrants, many of whom are gaining citizenship, has caused prices to increase. The high price of homes in other countries makes California homes more desirable. For example, an $80,000 medium-priced United States home is $150,000 in Belgium, France, or Germany. Even worse, the same house would be $300,000 in Hong Kong.

REAL ESTATE LIFE CYCLE

People go through different phases of life, each requiring different levels of physical ability, skills, and medical attention to achieve their optimum productivity. The words infant, teenager, young married or single adult, mature, retired, and senior all have distinct connotations. Real property is much the same. To properly manage property, you must be able to identify which phase a property is in and know what needs to be done to ensure optimal productivity.

Real Estate
The land, all things permanently attached to it, and all interests, benefits, and rights inherent to ownership.
Informally: "The dirt, the bricks and sticks, the rights of the bundle."

The life cycle phases of real property improvements are initiation, introduction, growth, maturity, decline, and demise. An improved property may be in any stage at any chronological age, depending upon the management of the asset. The White House, almost 200 years old, is in better shape than new construction projects that had to be abandoned prior to completion because of lack of adequate funding. Thus, even though new, a building may have depreciated. Redevelopment and rehabilitation are as important to the life of a building as on-going maintenance programs and the materials used in the initial construction.

Life phases are handled in different ways according to the type of property managed. Agricultural property is usually managed in terms of crop productivity. Politics, rainfall, crop prices and demand are all elements outside the realm of professional property management as used in this textbook. Non-residential property management takes into account more than the life cycle of the physical structure. It also includes the general business cycle, both domestic and international, the cycle of the specific industry in the local area, and government activities affecting the structure's use. Residential property management cycles are directly tied to demand within a particular market.

The Life Cycle Phases

Initiation. The initiation phase of the life cycle is the creative period when the most choices are available and the most questions must be answered. This is the phase that includes lining up funding commitments and meeting with architects, surveyors, contractors, and decorators. The property manager must be able to accurately predict the performance on a project at this point. The construction or rehab is just beginning and capital expenditures are large.

Introductory. The introductory phase is the period of highest operating expenses. Pre-sale advertising, lease-up fees, bonuses and move-in incentives are major expenses. A high level of property management expertise is required to decrease losses from expenditures that net little results and to avoid poor marketing which leads to prolonged vacancies. Proper management ensures this phase is kept as short as possible.

Growth. The growth phase is the period of time from the first move-ins to the break-even point of the financial operations of the building. The income increases the most during this phase, when the property manager's projected rent-up schedules are met. This phase should proceed on a specific, pre-designed program, reviewed regularly with all staff members to ensure adherence to the projected targets and goals.

Maturity. The maturity phase lasts the longest. This period is when stable income flows meet on-going operational costs. This phase can be extended for many years with careful attention to complete on-going maintenance programs. Adhering to long-range ownership goals enhances the performance of a building in the maturity phase.

Decline. The decline phase of a building's life is when the majority of the building's components are so old that they are obsolete. Rehabilitation can be done only if the potential income would offset the high cost of modernization. These buildings usually attract tenants who are willing to give up amenities in exchange for lower rents. As the building continues to decline, it attracts even poorer tenants. Maintenance expenses are very high during this phase. Schematics, expertise, and parts are often lacking, so repairs are rarely possible at a reasonable cost.

Demise. The demise phase is that stage in a building's life when the value of the raw land far exceeds the cost to maintain the existing structure and its use. The property's income cannot meet its expenses. When one pipe is repaired, the next crumbles. The quality of tenants willing to live in these structures may add to the extra cost of keeping these old buildings in place. Overcrowding is common. The "slumlord" buildings often pictured in the news are generally in this phase. The highest and best use of the property is not the present structure.

Redevelopment agencies specialize in areas where demise-phase buildings exist. Rezoning, special loans to build, and other incentives are often available for these non-productive properties.

Life Cycle Phases
Initiation
Introductory
Growth
Maturity
Decline
Demise

TYPES OF PROPERTIES TO BE MANAGED

Non-Residential

Agricultural/Farm Lands. This property is easily distinguishable from city, or urban, real estate. The income from rural properties is often heavily dependent upon weather conditions, soil productivity, national and international economic sanctions, embargos and tariffs. These conditions are out of the realm of property management as referred to in this text. Special agents are trained for this field, and many colleges offer courses in managing ranches, farms, and acreage. Government agencies administer special funding programs for this segment of the economy and agents receive training to handle these operations.

Commercial Property. Commercial property is that part of the real estate industry that relates to the commerce and trade operations of a business. Office buildings, for example, were once located in the Central Business District (CBD) where most commerce was handled. Decentralization of trade areas has caused many offices to move to locations near transportation arteries. Major freeway intersections, airport hubs, and proximity to skilled employees have drawn commercial property to more outlying locations.

GLENDALE
PASADENA
ALTADENA
SIERRA MADRE
MONROVIA
BRADBURY
DUARTE
AZUSA
ARCADIA
TEMPLE CITY
SAN MARINO
EAST PASADENA
SOUTH PASADENA
SAN GABRIEL
EAGLE ROCK
HIGHLAND PARK
ALHAMBRA
ROSEMEAD
EL MONTE
BALDWIN PARK
IRWINDALE
COVINA
WEST COVINA
MONTEREY PARK
SOUTH SAN GABRIEL
SOUTH EL MONTE
BASSETT
INDUSTRY
LA PUENTE
EAST LOS ANGELES
LOS ANGELES
COMMERCE
VERNON
MAYWOOD
MONTEBELLO
HACIENDA HEIGHTS
WALNUT
PICO RIVERA
HUNTINGTON PARK
BELL
BELL GARDENS
CUDAHY
WHITTIER
LOS NIETOS
LA HABRA HEIGHTS
EAST WHITTIER
ROWLAND HEIGHTS
SOUTH GATE
WATTS
DOWNEY
SANTA FE SPRINGS
LA HABRA
BREA
LYNWOOD
WILLOWBROOK
HOLLYDALE
LA MIRADA
COMPTON
PARAMOUNT
NORWALK
FULLERTON
BELLFLOWER
GARDENA
ARTESIA
BUENA PARK
NORTH LONG BEACH
LAKEWOOD
CERRITOS
LA PALMA
CARSON
DOMINGUEZ
HAWAIIAN GARDENS
CYPRESS
ANAHEIM
LOMITA
STANTON
SIGNAL HILL
LOS ALAMITOS
GARDEN GROVE
HARBOR CITY
ROSSMOOR
WILMINGTON
BELMONT SHORE
WESTMINSTER
LONG BEACH
SEAL BEACH
MIDWAY CITY
SAN PEDRO
SANTA

Special Purpose Commercial Property. Special purpose commercial property management includes that portion of the real estate industry geared to customized expertise within a particular business area. Examples include ownership of gas stations, mini-warehouse storage facilities, day-care centers, and recreational-use centers.

Industrial Property. Industrial property is real estate used by a business entity to process, fabricate, manufacture, and/or distribute its product. The earlier multi-story loft structures are being replaced with automated, computer-assembly, one- or two-story buildings within industrial parks or within highly developed industrial cities, such as City of Industry or City of Commerce.

Industrial complexes can be private projects, municipality projects, or joint ventures between municipalities and private corporations. Important to their success are factors such as transportation arteries, water supply, labor market, maintenance costs, government regulations, and pollution standards.

Residential

More square feet of property are managed as residential than any other type and, consequently, a large percentage of all property managers handle residential property. Residential real estate includes any property unit that can be occupied as the living space of an individual.

Almost 50% of California's mostly urban population of over 20 million people are tenants. This makes the rental housing market the third largest industry in California (ranking behind only tourism and agriculture).

Single-Family Residential. A single-family home refers to a residential unit intended to be occupied by one family. It is the most spacious residential rental unit. Single-family properties often become rentals when the owner is unable to sell the house or because the owner plans to move back into the property after travelling or a temporary job transfer.

These owners often discover the benefits of owning a rental property. Single-family homes are usually less labor-intensive to manage because the tenants often carry more pride of ownership, possibly due to the higher cost of occupancy. And once the owner discovers the tax advantages of owning a rental, it is hard not to continue to be a landlord. Single-family residential housing allows more flexibility, is rarely subject to rent control, incurs fewer maintenance and upkeep costs because of tenant contribution, and is often in a positive cash flow position.

> **Example:** A person facing retirement has a home worth $160,000, with an existing loan of $50,000, payable at $500 per month (including taxes and insurance). If the person sells the home, she will have approximately $100,000 to invest after paying $10,000 in transaction costs and paying off the mortgage. A safe investment would currently give a rate of return of about 9% per year, and about $9,000 annual income would be generated. However, if she keeps the home, it will probably appreciate at about 7% a year. In addition, the rental income should generate about $5,000 positive cash flow the first year and increase each year by about $700. (Note: The general public expects home prices to increase at a pace equal to or slightly above the inflation rate for each year. This rule has held true in California's past.)

Single-family homes can usually be quickly liquidated to the tenant, relatives, neighbors, or the general market. Equity in these homes can also be used to buy additional property, or to trade up for more units.

Condominiums. Condominiums are more spacious than apartments and often attract tenants because of their amenities, more desirable interior unit features, and better neighborhood environment. Many of the neighbors are homeowners, so more overall "pride of ownership" is maintained. Some are built as resort property housing and the space is traded or rented, as in time-share property management. Coupled with enforcement of association rules and regulations, condominiums can be one of the most desirable forms of rental-income property.

Condominium management is a specialized form of property management that can be grouped with non-residential property management. It involves, however, residential knowledge and expertise since most condominiums are residential units. However, condominiums used for businesses and industry are becoming more popular in some California areas.

The structural composition of the condominium influences the functions, activities and involvement of the property manager. A planned unit development (PUD), townhouse, or other type of layout affects the type of contracts, fees, and maintenance needed.

Mobile Home Parks. Mobile home property management is a segment of the real estate industry that involves several types of management skills. Many communities have ordinances placing these parks under rent control. This came about because many owners live in a different voting district than where the parks are located. The mobile home park tenants vote in local rent control ordinances with little opposition.

The management of these parks involves marketing to a specific target segment of the population. Even though there are mixed-use parks with mixed age groups, most are geared to "Children's Complexes" or "Senior Citizen Parks", or resort communities catering to activities unique to an area or activity. The park managers also administer the sale of utilities to the tenants as a separate billing item.

Types of Residential Property
Single-Family Home
Condominiums
Mobile Home Parks
Multi-Family Housing
Motel/Hotel

The laws regulating mobile home park management are different than other residential forms of property management, especially with reference to notice time for rent increases, evictions, and changes in the terms of the tenancy. Although rents are lower, so are many of the services offered compared to other types of rentals.

Multi-Family. Multi-family residential housing is the largest segment of the income-producing residential property market. Almost 40% of all housing units are apartments. They may be owned privately, by government entities, or by institutions. The public housing authorities, collectively, are the largest landlords in the United States, controlling, supervising or regulating over one-half million units. Operations differ between public and private housing as to rents, deposits, damages, and required notice periods.

Motel/Hotel. Motel/hotel operations are another type of property management. Professionals are trained in handling conventions, large parties, and the "people" operations associated with the running of the hotel. Large chains usually establish policies and guidelines of operation and often help arrange the purchase of, and financing for, the property and the business. Colleges offer degrees in hotel and restaurant management.

Miscellaneous. Other types of residential property management include those situations where the residence is really a means to another end. An example would be a corporation-owned mobile home park in the middle of a Middle Eastern oil-producing city or dormitories on a university. There may be a convalescent or a nursing home affiliated with a religious group or hospital. These kinds of housing are referred to as "institutional housing," because the reason for their existence is the institution which owns and/or operates the housing.

PROPERTY MANAGEMENT ORGANIZATIONS

One place to start learning more about the property management profession is by taking a course such as the one this text is designed for. Interacting with other students is also informative and can even spur entry-level job offers. Instructors sometimes receive requests for job referrals from the property management segment of the real estate industry.

The **California Apartment Association (CAA)** has local level organizations that meet regularly. Helping these groups on committees is a good way to develop opportunities within the field of property management. This is especially true in the buying and selling of income property because so many owner/managers belong to this group. Excellent on-site or maintenance positions are also available from members of this group. The local CAA chapters have several advisory groups for seminars on the legal aspects and management of residential properties. They offer a **Certified Apartment Manager (CAM)** certificate for completion of specified courses taught by association members at the organization's offices or local community colleges.

The **National Association of Realtors (NAR)** group for property management is under their **Institute of Real Estate Management (IREM)** division. For property management, they confer professional designations on individuals and organizations who have met their requirements for experience, education and participation in the field of property management. Professional on-site managers can receive the **Accredited Residential Manager (ARM)** designation. IREM has awarded the designation of **Certified Property Manager (CPM)** to only 8,700 persons since it was formed in 1933 (as of August, 1988). These individuals handle a total of about 13 million apartment units. They must: 1) be a candidate, 2) manage over 300 apartments for five years (three years if working under a CPM), and 3) write a comprehensive management plan for a project. An organization can obtain the coveted **Accredited Management Organization (AMO)** designation by meeting the same criteria or having one or more CPM on staff who maintain the auditing, banking, licensing, and bonding requirements.

For non-residential organizations, IREM also awards CPM designations for those who manage 120,000 square feet of office space, or 150,000 square feet of retail space. These CPM's manage a total of over $600 billion in real estate.

Persons specializing in the management of retail space can receive the designation of **Certified Shopping Center Manager (CSM)** from the **International Council of Shopping Centers.**

The **Building Owners Management Association (BOMA)** awards the professional designation of **Real Property Manager (RPA)** to its members.

Those seeking information about groups in their area should look in the telephone yellow pages under Real Estate Management, or contact local firms. It is also helpful to call the local Board of Realtors to find active members. For additional information, write the following:

California Apartment Association
1225 Eighth Ave., Suite 101
Sacramento, CA 95814

National Association of Realtors
Real Estate Mgt.
430 North Michigan Avenue
Chicago, IL 60611

BOMA, International
1250 Eye St., N.W.
Washington, DC 20005

International Council of Institute
of Shopping Centers
665 Fifth Avenue
New York, NY 10022

CHAPTER 1–QUIZ

1. California's earliest property manager(s) was(were):

    a. King Charles III
    b. Captain Portola
    c. Franciscan padres
    d. Yuma Indians

2. An early government intervention in California housing controls was:

    a. the Indian Land Management
    b. the Monroe Doctrine
    c. the Mexican-American War
    d. the Gold Rush

3. Building codes, ordinances, and building material regulations were largely a result of the:

    a. California Statehood Act of 1850
    b. San Francisco earthquake in 1906
    c. Colorado River/Salton Sea flooding in 1905-1907
    d. Great Depression of the 1930's

4. There was little professional management in California prior to World War I because:

    a. residential property was primarily single-family dwellings
    b. society was mostly agrarian (rural/farmers)
    c. multiple housing units were rare
    d. All of the above

5. Banks and savings and loans acquired a great deal of property requiring management in the early 1930's because:

   a. they aggressively purchased property
   b. a large number of trust accounts were created at that time
   c. there were many loan defaults and foreclosures
   d. the laws were changed to allow institutional real estate purchases

6. The era when there were plenty of funds, a severe housing shortage, and high demand describes:

   a. Gold Rush (1846-1849)
   b. Spanish-American War (1846-1849)
   c. Statehood (1871-1880)
   d. Post-Civil War (1880-1889)

7. The ten-year depression that was widespread in California in the late 1800's was followed by a land boom that was a direct result of:

   a. foreclosures available
   b. high wages
   c. investment analysis consultants
   d. a marketing campaign

8. A professional designation for a property manager would be:

   a. CPM
   b. RPA
   c. ARM
   d. All of the above

9. The phase of a building's life when the most choices must be made is:

   a. initiation
   b. growth
   c. introduction
   d. demise

10. Which is not an advantage of owning single-family rental units?

    a. Less labor-intensive to manage
    b. Tax benefits
    c. Rarely subject to rent control
    d. Rent control ordinances

CHAPTER 1–QUIZ ANSWERS

1. c
2. b
3. b
4. d
5. c
6. a
7. d
8. d
9. a
10. d

2

Property Management and Real Estate Markets

References

De Carlo, J., CPM. *California Real Property Management. Study Guide.* Sacramento: California Community Colleges, 1986.

Downs, J., CPM. *Principles of Real Estate Management.* 12th ed. Chicago: Institute of Real Estate Management of National Associations of Realtors, 1980.

Last Chapter Review

The first chapter gave you an overview of the specialized area of real estate called property management. You read about how history has influenced present day customs, usage and laws in California. You learned about the life cycles of buildings and the different types of property to be managed. You also read brief accounts of today's organized property management associations.

Chapter Overview

The strength of the real estate market is vital to the successful management of property. Its income and value depend a great deal on specific events that occur within the real estate market. The effective property manager pays careful attention to the various factors that affect the market and the various indications of market strength.

The real estate market depends a great deal on local government policies, state and regional activities, the pace of the national economic growth, and the amount of available international investment dollars. All of these factors affect the performance of a specific property. To be a successful property manager, you must consider each of these factors as you analyze each property and project future performance.

THE REAL ESTATE MARKET

Like most other commodities, a property's value is affected by the supply of and demand for real estate on the market. Thus, a property manager must understand the real estate market to maximize a property's value and income.

When determining the value of property (i.e., setting rental rates), there are several factors the property manager should consider:

- money supply
- occupancy rates
- rental prices
- employment level
- family unit formation

These factors, in turn, influence the outward signs of strength in the real estate industry:

- foreclosure rates
- mortgage volume
- building activity
- sales activity

These measures of the real estate market are watched vigilantly by various organizations. For example, housing starts are watched closely by the U.S. Department of Commerce, private mortgage insurers and the FHA and VA keep careful track of mortgage foreclosure rates, and sales figures are watched by industry organizations, such as the National Association of Realtors and the Mortgage Bankers Association.

Factors Affecting the Market

Money Supply and Value. How much the dollar is worth and how available it is for use in real estate transactions has an obvious impact on the value of property. If few people are willing to invest their money in real estate, the value of real estate will decline.

Occupancy. The total number of units available for occupancy in the area and the total number of potential tenants able to pay rent for those units also affects the real estate market. This is simply the rule of supply and demand. The greater the supply and the less the demand, the less the value; the less the supply and the greater the demand, the greater the value.

Turnover
The frequency with which new tenants move into and out of a unit.

Since the real estate market is affected by the number of comparable units available, the property manager will want to determine the occupancy trend for his or her particular locale. If the trend is towards rising occupancy levels, the value of the units will increase; as space becomes more scarce it increases in value. It is during these times that managers raise rents and can upgrade the tenant mix and building character. On the other hand, if there is a growing vacancy rate, the value of the vacant units will decrease. In periods of high vacancy, the public is likely to resist rent increases and/or make more demands for services or repairs at renewal time.

Occupancy levels are constantly fluctuating. The direction and speed in which they are moving will have a significant impact on the property manager's operating and merchandising policies.

Absorption Rate
The rate at which new units are rented from the time they enter the market.

Rental Levels. Current rental rates are evidence of the economic strength of the existing real estate market. Rental rates move up and down in response to supply and demand (occupancy). A residential property manager can discover rental trends by using the Bureau of Labor statistics on rents paid for residential properties. Nonresidential property managers can read commercial or industrial association reports to obtain general rent levels. A property manager may also survey the properties that he or she is managing to determine the average monthly rental per unit or square foot. Statistics kept by individual property managers can also be combined with those of other managers in the area to get a broader perspective. Rental rates given in classified ads can also be examined. These methods give a manager a basic idea of rental trends.

Employment Trends. The property manager should be aware of local employment trends. The basic questions the property manager will want to answer are:

1) How many consumers are in the able-to-buy category?
2) What is the trend of their spending (up or down)?
3) How do they feel about spending versus saving?

Obviously, if a potential customer cannot afford the product or would rather save than spend, the product is not going to be sold. Gross purchasing power can be estimated from statistics on net income.

Family Size and Lifestyle. Family size has a great deal to do with the value of particular residential units. Assume for a moment that the average family size is three (two adults and one child). In these circumstances, five-bedroom units will have little appeal and two-bedroom units will be very attractive. Therefore, the two-bedroom units will command a higher price per square foot than the five-bedroom units. It is important that the property manager be aware of the nationwide trend toward smaller and even single-person households and also any peculiarities in local family size trends. In California, larger family units are more common due to the large immigrant population, and higher rental rates often cause unrelated persons to live together to reduce their living expenses, called doubling up.

Measures of Market Strength

As previously noted, the factors that influence the strength of the real estate market have a direct bearing on the outward signs of the market's health.

Foreclosure Rates. When real estate investments can no longer pay for themselves, foreclosure rates increase. Most foreclosures occur because the property is no longer generating enough income to meet the mortgage payments (this can be caused by increased expenses, high vacancy rates, or increasing interest rates.) An increase in the foreclosure rate is a sign of weakness in the real estate market. However, single-family residence foreclosures increase the demand for rentals.

Mortgage Volume. When mortgage loan activity increases, this is a sign that both borrowers and lenders have confidence in the real estate market. Borrowers believe that the property will generate more money than it costs to buy it, and lenders believe that the value of the property is high enough and stable enough to support the loan amount.

Mortgage volume is also directly tied to the interest rates for mortgages. If rates are low, more borrowers can qualify for the loan payments. (As more people purchase homes, vacancy rates for higher rent apartments tend to increase.)

Building Activity. Building activity measures the availability of construction funds and the projected demand for future units. Increased building activity does not necessarily bode well for the real estate market. If there is too much building activity, an oversupply results and property values stop increasing (rental rates usually decrease). On the other hand, if there is too little building activity, a shortage results and property values and rental rates increase.

Sales Activity. Brisk real estate sales indicates confidence in the real estate market. It also ensures the liquidity of real estate holdings, further increasing their appeal to investors. The price of homes, volume of sales, and future housing supply all affect the demand for rental housing.

POPULATION, POLITICAL AND SOCIAL TRENDS

The real estate market, as discussed above, is affected by local government policies, state and regional activities, the pace of the national economic growth, and the amount of available international investment dollars. All of these factors affect the performance of a specific property. To be a successful property manager, you must consider each of these factors as you analyze each property and project future performance.

The International Market

The speed of communications has made the world shrink in terms of financial markets. A shout in one corner of the globe can be heard and responded to immediately in a local market. Global economies are so intertwined that their individual independence in the 1990's is questionable. Nowhere is this more apparent than in California, especially in California's real estate markets.

California property management interacts with markets in every part of the world. The fluctuation in the price of the dollar valued against foreign currencies now affects the price of local income properties. And, of course, the price of homes affects demand in the rental market.

> **Example:** In the late 1970's, when the U.S. dollar lost value due to inflation, the demand for housing rose as people invested in real property as a hedge against inflation. This caused the price of residential property to increase. The price increase was passed along to tenants in the form of economic rent raises. All phases of property management reacted to this shift in the market.

Economic Rent Raise
Rent is raised by a property manager after determining that there is a shortage of available units in the marketplace and that the tenants have the ability to pay the rent increase.

The growing world population also affects the demand for housing in local California markets. The United States had less than 6% of the world's population in 1970, 200 million people. However, the United States has nearly one-third of the world's total land area (approximately 3.6 million square miles). As the world's population increases, overcrowding in other countries increases immigration to the United States. The need for housing accommodations multiplies at an ever-increasing rate in the clamor for more room.

San Diego, Sacramento, San Francisco, and Los Angeles are all "new" cities in comparison to the larger cities in the rest of the world: Paris, London, Tokyo, or Cairo. Their youthful image—of being less set in their ways, more adaptable to change, and more flexible in opportunities—increases their attraction to immigrants, making them the destination for large numbers of new citizens.

The National Market

From 1926 to 1966, the rural population in the U.S. decreased from 120.7 to 107.1 million, and over 50% of the United States population was living in urban developments. By 1980, this figure had grown to 70%. The United States was building 342 dwellings per 1,000 people by 1970. Twenty-six million more housing units had been added by 1980.

California has been the benefactor to the new urban population, providing many job opportunities, a desirable climate, and popular lifestyle. A slowing in the national economy increases the demand for California housing as people influx to find jobs in a bigger marketplace.

The demand for housing is directly related to the composition of the population. Figure 1 shows the national age composition for 1955, 1985, 2015, and 2035. Currently, the largest segment of the national population is between ages 20 and 39. This age group has the highest demand for rental housing. Those under 20 tend to live with their parents; the 40 and over group tend to own their own homes. Never before has the national rental market been stronger, and California is one of the strongest rental markets within this group.

The national economy also greatly influences California's investment property market. The cost of investment capital in California is affected by competition for the national supply of available dollars. The rate of national economic growth (measured by Gross National Product) influences the demand for commercial units in particular employment-base areas.

Figure 1

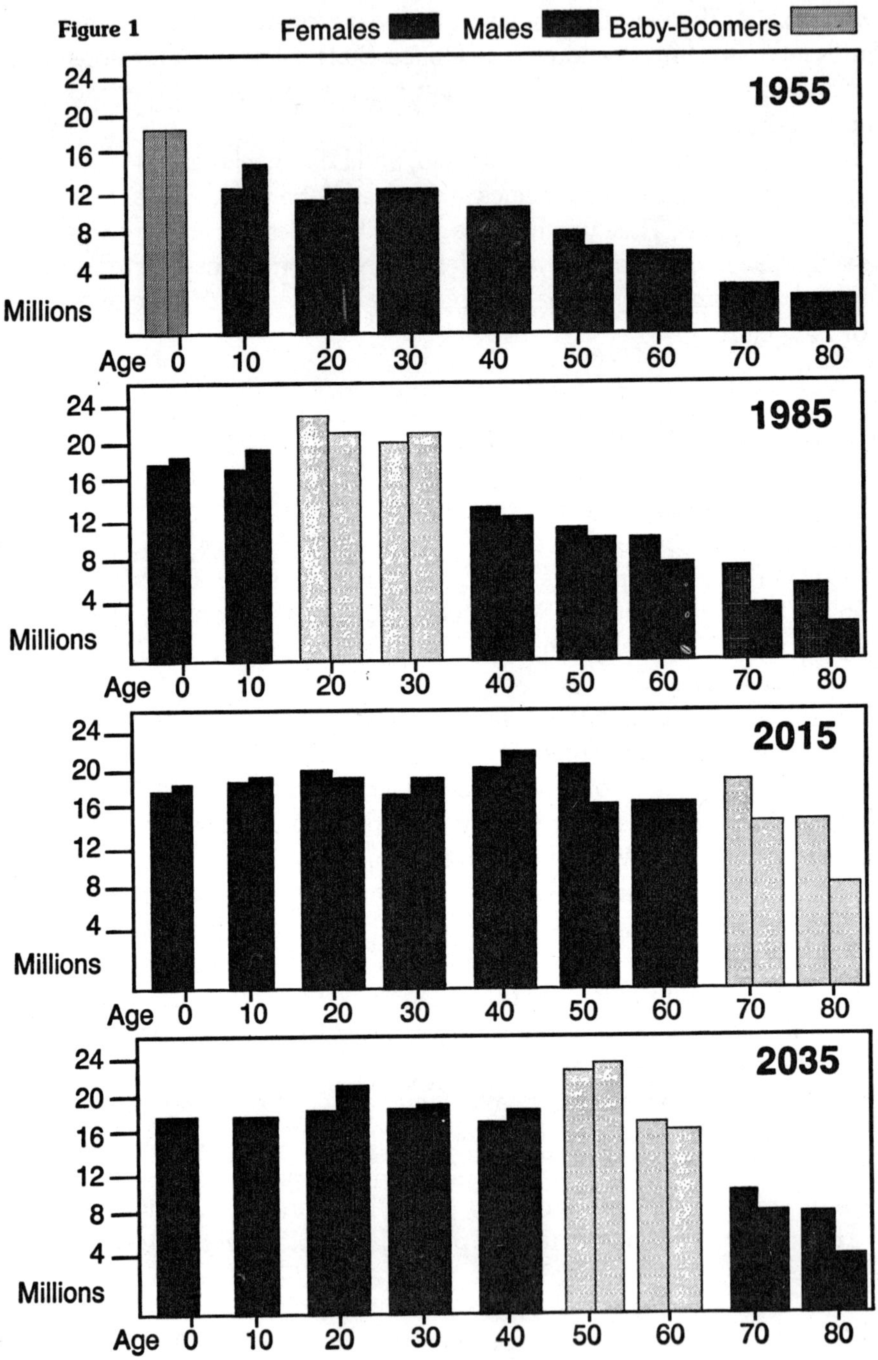
Females
Males
Baby-Boomers
1955
1985
2015
2035
24
20
16
12
8
4
Millions
Age 0 10 20 30 40 50 60 70 80

State Activity

In 1983, the rental business became the third largest industry in California, ranking behind only tourism and agriculture. Of total households, 44% were renter households. Over one-half million Californians were employed in the rental housing business, valued at over $130 billion, with rental units averaging $300 per month statewide.

One year later, California had a population of over 25.5 million persons, with over nine million households. Homeowners made up 55% of that number; renter households made up 45%. The rental housing market was valued at over $171 billion, with the average unit worth $40,500. There were 2.36 persons per rental household, and the average rental rate had risen to $380 per month.

By 1989, demand for California housing exceeded 100%, causing rents to skyrocket. One-bedroom apartments cost over $400 per month; two-bedroom units over $700 per month; three-bedroom houses over $1000 per month. Resort areas, beach cities, and high-rent areas far exceed these numbers. Average move-in costs for tenants rose from under $500 to over $1000 for a one-bedroom, over $1500 for a two-bedroom, and over $2500 for a three-bedroom house.

By 1995, California is projected to have an additional half a million residents and over 200,000 new households. Total California population is projected to reach 31.6 million, an increase of 17.2% over 1986.

Generally, an increase in population means higher rents, which increase property values. Let's take a brief look at how this works. New employment opportunities generate increased immigration (both foreign and domestic) and with an increased population there is increased demand. Increased demand causes a rise in the rental rates. In turn, as the building's income increases, so does the value of the building. The higher the rental income, the higher the net operating income, the higher the value of the building. The higher the building value, the more opportunity investors have to make profits. Builders can more easily attract investors. Then as rents and building values increase, more housing units are constructed. As more units enter the market, there is more competition for tenants. Competition makes the market price decrease, and the cycle continues. Figure 2 shows the enormous variation in the number of units started over a period of several years.

Figure 2

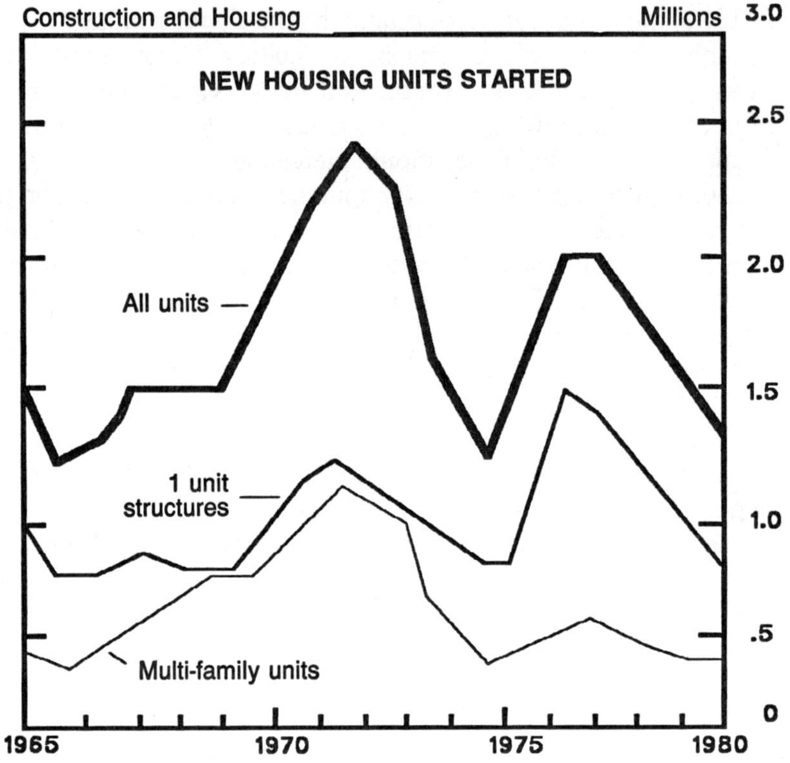

Regional Activity

The Sacramento and San Diego regions are projected to be the fastest growing large economic regions in California, with each growing by more than 20% by 1995. The Greater Los Angeles economic region, however, holds the dominant status on the basis of solid job growth. Additional jobs create greater demand for housing in these areas, stripping existing supply, and driving existing prices even higher.

There are, however, many regional factors to counterbalance an assumption of automatic rent increases. Within each region are pockets of less desirable areas, necessitating rent adjustments. For example, many multi-family properties are located in areas predominantly under some kind of public assistance programs, which limits the maximum rents (discussed in Chapter 15). Also, commercial properties located near an airport or railway command higher rents than properties within the same region without close proximity to these means of transportation.

Understanding regional demographics is vital to successfully managing property. A person's age group and total income bears a direct relationship to the amount of rent he or she can afford. For instance, people pay more for housing between the time they leave home and the age of 35 than at any other time in their life. Then, between age 35 and 45, housing drops behind the cost of eating food away from home, and again drops into third place by age 45, when health care costs move into first place.

Figure 3

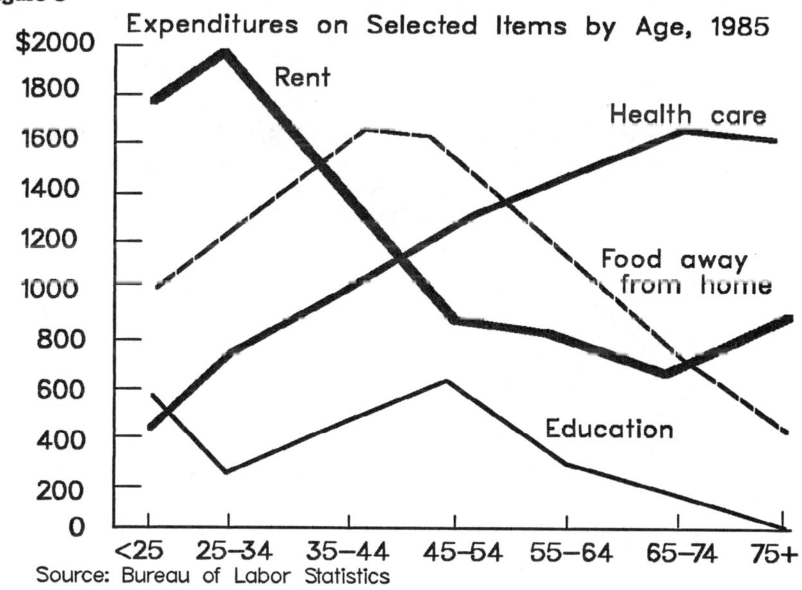

Also, by determining the area's population composition, developers and planners can better forecast the demand for different sizes of units. For example, in California's auto-oriented society, there is a healthy market for units having two bedrooms, two bathrooms, and a four-car garage. On the other hand, the demographics in many regions indicate a need for several smaller-sized bedrooms to accommodate larger family sizes.

Figure 4

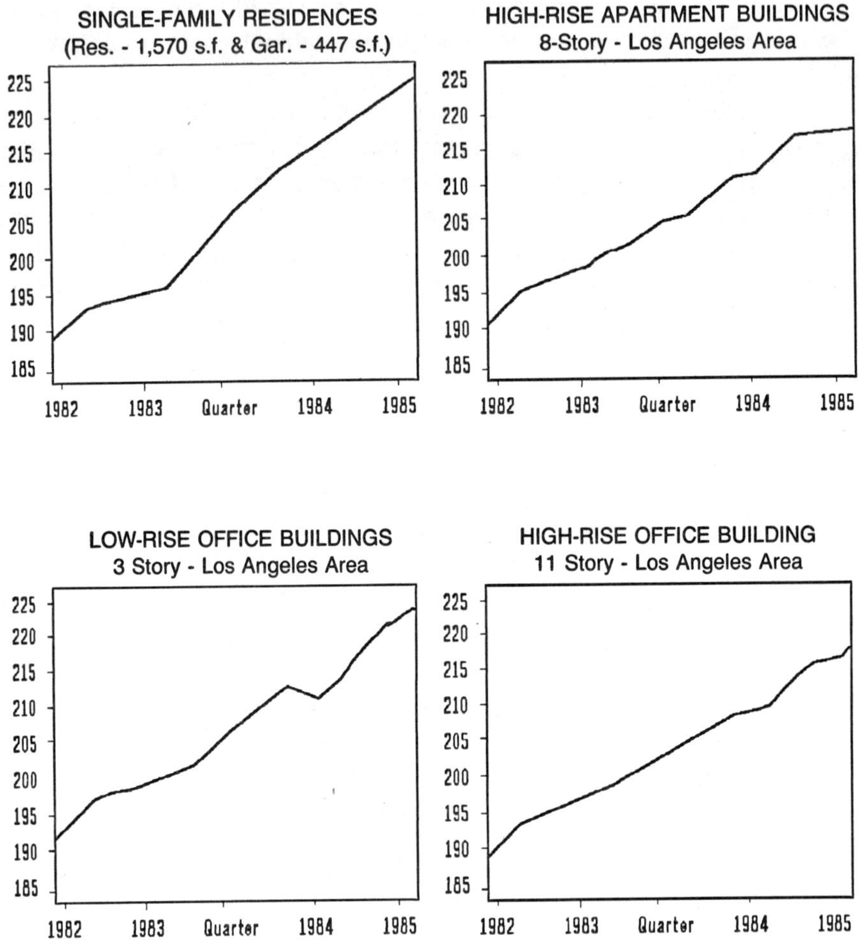

Overbuilt high-rise office buildings level off, while construction dollars are used to build single-family residences and low-rise office buildings, instead of much needed high-rise apartment buildings.

The federally-assisted housing units declined from over 200,000 in 1980 to about 25,000 in 1987 for new construction. There has been a sharp drop by the U.S. Department of Housing and Urban Development from 1980 to 1987 by about 75%.

In reviewing regional activity, the property manager must also look at local construction. If there is little or no building activity, or an area has strong no-growth or slow-growth proponents, rent levels will rise as the demand for existing space increases. Conversely, if overbuilding occurs, the result is **technical oversupply** and rents will be lower. During the mid-1980's, a good portion of high rise office space and many small, strip shopping centers were vacant because too many of these projects were built. Overbuilding causes lower occupancy rates until the demand can catch up with the supply.

Technical Oversupply
Where there are less consumers in a given area than units available.

Regional population growth varies greatly across the country. Northeastern cities of the United States are growing very modestly. From 1980 to 1987, New York City grew 3% and Chicago grew 2.7%. Due to weather, lifestyle, and more-affordable housing, Texas grew at the fastest pace between 1980 and 1987, with Houston increasing by 18.3% and the Dallas/Fort Worth region increasing by 30.4%. (Current growth in Texas is the result of recovery from the earlier oil-crunch layoffs.)

In California, regional growth has been consistently healthy due mainly to the diversified employment base. San Francisco population grew 10.6% between 1980 and 1987, a phenomenal rate. But even this growth rate is dwarfed in comparison to the southern California rate. Long Beach/Los Angeles grew 14.1%; Anaheim/Santa Ana grew 14.6%; and Oxnard/Ventura increased by 18.9%. The Riverside/San Bernardino region grew the most, at 35.2%, making southern California's overall total growth 17.3% from 1980 to 1987.

Most of these 13.5 million additional people rent when they first come to California (paying high southern California prices) until they locate the neighborhood they want to live in. This pattern is reflected in California's homeownership statistics, which are lower than the national average. However, as these new residents accumulate wealth, many more potential buyers will be entering the housing market. In the meantime, these regions lack affordable rental units. To ease the burden of high rents and utilities, many families double-up, increasing the ratio of number of people per unit.

The Local Government Practices

As the California market adjusts to the increase in population and demand for housing, so does the government. Harsh conditions, such as dramatically increasing rents, poor sanitation, and uninhabitable premises all encourage government involvement.

Because of the high demand, landlords often establish **nuisance rent raises** without fear of vacancy. Some landlords even evict existing tenants to make units available for new occupants at higher rents. Rents are sometimes charged on a per-person basis to achieve a maximum price.

Nuisance Rent Raises
The amount of money a Property Manager who is familiar with local conditions can raise current rents without causing a vacancy, based upon the theory that the tenant will stay and pay the increase rather than bother with the trouble and expense of moving.

Those under age 25 and over 64 suffer the greatest, as the level of rent increases the percent of total income they have to spend on rent. Overcrowding is often the last resort for those who cannot afford the high rental rates.

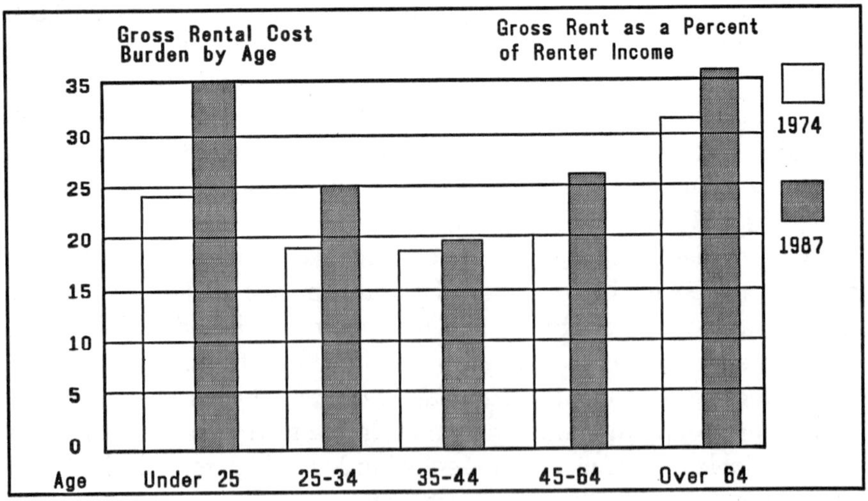

Local Legislation

To help ease the effects of these conditions, local health and safety officers, planning and zoning departments, fire departments and local officials have assumed the role of enforcing the National Housing Goal.

National Housing Goal
To provide decent, safe and sanitary housing for Americans.

For example, overcrowding is addressed in the *Space and Occupancy Standards of the Uniform Housing Code (Health & Safety Code* §17922). These *Occupancy Standards* are enforced by ten Commissioners appointed by the Governor (with the approval of the Senate). The Commission uses the *Uniform Housing Code* as a guide. A portion of the *Housing Code states:*

> "Every dwelling unit shall have at least one room which shall have not less than 150 square feet of floor area. Where more than two persons occupy a room used for sleeping purposes the required floor area shall be increased at the rate of 50 square feet for each occupant in excess of two."

The general rule-of-thumb is that the limitation should be at least as liberal as two-per-bedroom-plus-one. Those managers trying to use occupancy limitations to discriminate against families with children, however, are investigated by the California Department of Fair Employment & Housing, authorized by *Civil Code Section 51* of the *Unruh Civil Rights Act.*

Even with the shortage of available units, some areas have many vacancies. This is due to **economic oversupply.** Economic oversupply is the inability of tenants to afford current rents. Affordable housing is still well beyond the means of many renters. Between 1974 and 1983, the total number of residential units priced at under $300 per month declined by nearly one million units. Builders have little or no incentives to construct lower-rental rate units. Thus, the building you want to manage may be in an area where there is a high demand for housing but little ability to pay for it.

Economic Oversupply
The lack of ability of tenants to pay currents rents.

Public assistance programs limit the rental rate based upon number of bedrooms, unit size, and family size. Schedules determine the amount of rent the tenant can be expected to pay. The tenant must pay his or her share of the rent separately and the Housing Authority pays its portion separately. In the event of default, a landlord must proceed with the eviction process in the same manner as non-public assistance tenants.

Rent Controls

Rent controls affect the projected performance of any project. Critics claim rent controls place the government's burden of supporting the poor on the shoulders of private property owners. Rent controls decrease incentives to purchase and keep up private property. In addition, critics feel they have lost another constitutional right when the ability to charge fair market rents is taken away from them by the government.

Properties Affected. Single-family residences are usually exempt from rent controls. On the other hand, almost all mobile home communities in California fall under rent control ordinances. Individual cities, such as Santa Barbara and West Los Angeles, often have some form of rent control or a rent review board covering apartments. Some hotel units are subject to control. 1988 real estate legislation prohibits public entities from enacting or enforcing rent controls on specific commercial property. The prudent property manager must check not only present rent control conditions, but anticipated conditions as well.

RENT CONTROL ORDINANCES (as of February 1988)

LOCATION	VACANCY DECONTROL PROVISIONS	PROVISIONS FOR RENT INCREASES	OTHER EXEMPTIONS
BERKELEY	No	Rent board establishes allowable increases	•Owner-occupied duplexes if unit was owner-occupied 12/31/79 •Accessory units
BEVERLY HILLS	Yes Decontrol/recontrol	Formula based on CPI; additional increase allowed in some cases; for luxury units, flat 10% increase	•Single-family •Condos (including new conversions)
COTATI	No	Formula based on CPI annually; as of 10/87, 3.3% annual	•Owner-occupied duplexes, triplexes
EAST PALO ALTO	No	Formula based on CPI; individual increases allowed upon rent control board approval	•Four units or less
HAYWARD	Yes-permanent decontrol is allowed if unit voluntarily vacates & rehabilited. Otherwise recontrol	5% annual	•Four units or less
LOS GATOS	Yes Decontrol/recontrol	70% of CPI or 5%, whichever is more	•Two units or less •Single-family condominium or planned unit development
L.A. CITY	Yes Decontrol/recontrol	Tied to CPI with 8% maximum 3% minimum; Allowable 1988 increase: 4%	•Luxury units •Single-family detached homes •Second units
OAKLAND	Yes Decontrol/recontrol	Rent board establishes allowable increases each year; currently 6%. Tenant can initiate hearing in front of rent control board when increase exceeds 8½%	•None
PALM SPRINGS	No	Formula based on 75% of CPI	•Apt/mobile home complexes of four or fewer units if one unit is owner-occupied
SAN FRANCISCO	Yes Decontrol/recontrol	Formula based on CPI. Cannot be less that 4% nor exceed 7%	•Owner-occupied four units or less (six months after owner moves in)
SAN JOSE	Yes Decontrol/recontrol	8% annual for apartments; 5% for mobile homes	•Single-family •Duplexes
SANTA MONICA	No	Established by rent control board; as of 9/87, 4% annual	•Owner-occupied three units or less •Single-family
THOUSAND OAKS	Yes. Upon voluntary vacancy unit is permanently decontrolled	Annual minimum allowed: 3% Annual maximum allowed: 7%	•Four units or less •Luxury units •Single-family •Units where tenants offered 3-5 year leases with 7% rent caps and 3% caps for seniors
WEST HOLLYWOOD	Yes, but limited	75% of increase in CPI with certain limitations	•Units owner-occupied since Jan. 1984

Limited Growth

Proponents of limiting growth in California communities use different methods to accomplish the same ends. Under the provisions of the Williamson Act, agricultural preserves are established and property tax incentives make it beneficial to keep the property undeveloped. Some local governments use zoning to prohibit growth. Ordinances require minimum lot sizes of one acre, five acres, or up to 60 acres per single-family home. Utility moratoriums are used when communities reach their limits on water supply or sewage disposal capacity. Some areas charge very large developer fees, or require the donation of large public lands as part of their approval process. Also, any resident can file suit against a developer to halt the construction on the grounds that the environmental review was inadequate.

> **Example:** Petaluma, about 40 miles north of San Francisco, is California's most famous example of limited growth restrictions. A 25% increase in population occurred in a two-year period. Anticipating increased property values, many investors and property managers purchased additional property to develop income-producing properties. However, to slow the unprecedented growth, the city established explicit quotas on the number of new building permits that could be issued each year (not to exceed 500 dwelling units per year). Eight to twelve percent of these units were to be low- and moderate-income units. Each dwelling unit was thought to represent about three people. Many of the investors/developers were stopped in their tracks and their capital tied up for years because of these restrictions.

CHAPTER 2–BIBLIOGRAHPY

McClellan, Grant S., ed. *Land Use in the United States: Exploration or Conservation.* New York: H. W. Wilson Co., 1971.

"Southland Ranked 3rd Fastest Growth Area in the Nation." *Press-Telegram [Long Beach, CA],* 10 June 1988, E5.

"Growth in California." *CREEA Newsletter,* Oct. 1987.

Rental Industry Facts. California Apartment Association and California Department of Housing and Community Development.

"Rent Control." *Los Angeles Times,* 6 March 1988, VIII, 1.

"Petaluma." *New Republic,* 21 Sept. 1974, p. 10.

"Highlights of New Real Estate Legislation." *Tax & Real Estate Law Update,* March 1988.

"Harvard Housing Study Paints Grim Future for Poor." *CPM Aspects.* Institute of Real Estate Management, May/June 1988.

Construction and Housing. p. 748

CHAPTER 2–QUIZ

1. Local property management in California interacts with markets:

   a. internationally
   b. nationally
   c. statewide
   d. All of the above

2. Property managers study population trends to determine building rents in relation to:

   a. supply
   b. demand
   c. cause and effect
   d. liquidity

3. When population decreases, which oversupply results?

   a. Technical
   b. Economic
   c. Legislative
   d. Projected

4. The main reason for property management needs in urban areas is due to population increases caused by California's climate, lifestyle and:

   a. investment capital
   b. rent rates
   c. home prices
   d. job opportunities

5. Persons spending the most of their total income for housing are aged:

   a. under 30
   b. 30—45
   c. 45—55
   d. 55—65

6. When tenants cannot afford the current rental rates, it is a case of:
   a. technical oversupply
   b. economic oversupply
   c. economic phenomena
   d. economic enterprise

7. According to critics, rent controls discourage:
   a. construction
   b. remodeling
   c. tenant mobility
   d. All of the above

8. An economic rent raise is:
   a. when a landlord tests the market
   b. usually a very small rent increase
   c. based on fair market rents when a few units are available
   d. where it costs the tenant more to move than to stay and pay the increased rent.

9. Which of the following is NOT a common method to limit growth?
   a. Restricting building permits on multi-family units
   b. Imposing utility moratoriums
   c. Setting minimum acreage requirements for single-family residences
   d. Subsidizing property managers to prevent rent increases

10. The National Housing Goal is to provide for all Americans housing that is decent:
   a. and that complies with the Uniform Housing Code
   b. under public assistance programs
   c. and safe and sanitary
   d. and affordable

CHAPTER 2–QUIZ ANSWERS

1. d
2. b
3. a
4. d
5. a
6. b
7. d
8. c
9. d
10. c

3

Money and Property Management

References

Anderson, Lowell, and Dennis McKenzie. *California Real Estate Principles.* 3rd ed. New York: John Wiley & Sons, Inc., 1987.

Betts, Richard, and Dennis McKenzie. *The Essentials of Real Estate Economics.* 2nd ed. New York: John Wiley & Sons, Inc., 1980.

DeCarlo, J., CPM. *California Real Property Management. Study Guide.* Sacramento: California Community Colleges, 1986.

Last Chapter Review

The second chapter related property management operations to international, national, state and local markets. You saw how supply and demand (as well as government involvement) affect property values. And, of course, both of these have a direct bearing on a property's performance. You also learned the importance of demographics, rent levels, and construction as they interact with the National Housing Goal.

Chapter Overview

In this chapter you will learn the definition of money. You will see how it is used to purchase other goods and services and how it is treated as a commodity. You will also see how its availability affects real estate financing and the sources of that financing.

INTRODUCTION

Even in the earliest days of civilization, there was a need to exchange one item for another. Ancient peoples developed the barter system, which varied depending on the needs of the people and the era. For example, food might be exchanged for a crude weapon. Later on, furs were traded for sugar and ammunition. Later still, grandparents traded child care for food and shelter. Today, tenants exchange money for housing accommodations. Investors exchange their capital for an expectation of a future return. Property managers exchange their services for a fee or commission.

In our society, money is the major medium of exchange. It goes by many names, from the colloquial to the formal: gravy, wampum, dough, wad, bucks, bread; or, funds, capital, interest, return, yield; or, payment, salary, wages, profits; or, gold, silver, cash, currency, checks, bills, notes, legal tender. In other countries, it may be called: *dinar, peso, franc, rupee, lira,* or *pound.* Whatever its name, money is the commodity that is easily exchanged.

Money
Something of value accepted as a medium of exchange

MONEY AS A COMMODITY

In the United States, the medium of exchange is the dollar. Its value is in its use: the ability to exchange it for goods and service, both domestically and in the international market.

The Free Market

Since 1973, the exchange value of the dollar and most other currencies has been determined in the free market. If demand for a currency rises, so does its price in relation to the currency of other countries. The value of the dollar affects the number of people who are willing to invest in it. Volatile exchange rates fuel speculation, which in turn affects international investments (both positively and negatively).

As with stocks, bonds, and futures, the dollar vies for investor attention. Up until the mid-1980's, the dollar's value was on the increase. Between 1980 and November, 1985, the dollar's value rose more than 40% against other major currencies. This strength hurt United States manufacturers, as consumers began to buy less expensive foreign-made goods. As the United States continued to import more goods to meet consumer demand, it exported fewer. (U.S. goods were too expensive on foreign markets.) A trade deficit developed. Industrial output fell, meaning lower tax revenues, and a higher federal deficit, which can fuel a tax increase.

More recently, the value of the dollar has declined significantly. Although a devalued dollar sounds dangerous, it has had advantageous consequences for the general economy. A lower dollar has made American-made products more competitive; consumers (both foreign and domestic) are buying more U.S. products than before. This means fewer imports and more exports. The trade deficit decreases, and industrial output rises. More tax dollars are collected, which lowers the federal deficit. As both the federal deficit and trade deficit decrease, economists become more optimistic, encouraging even more economic growth. As economic growth increases, investors have more faith in the dollar and, as they begin to invest in it, the dollar's value begins to rise. (Figure 1)

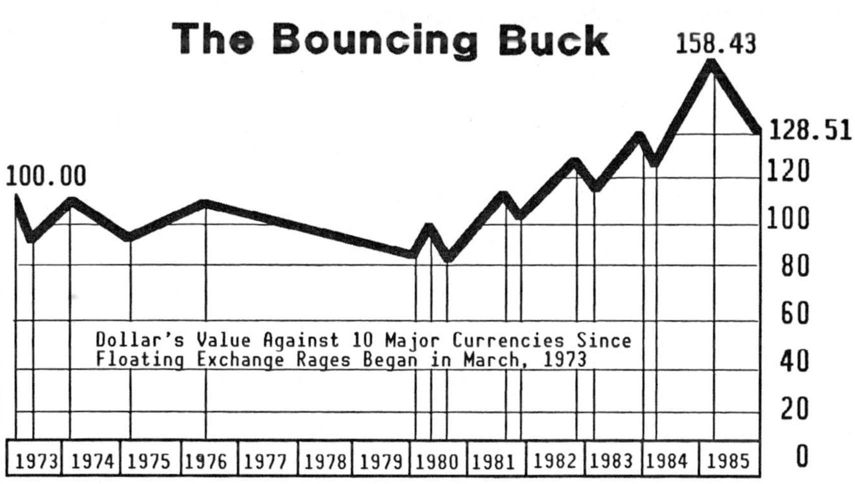

U.S. NEWS & WORLD REPORT, Nov. 25, 1985

Government Influences

Aside from the free market system, various government agencies affect the value of the dollar. The Federal Reserve has a great deal of influence on the value of the dollar. To lower the dollar's value, the Fed can expand the money supply. This action brings down interest rates, and makes the dollar less attractive for foreigners to own. Domestic goods become more competitive. Exports and sales at home make the economy busier, which produces more revenues for tax collectors and reduces the size of the budget deficit. On the other hand, to increase the value of the dollar, the Fed can raise discount rates and reserve requirements and decrease the supply of the money. (The Federal Reserve is discussed in more detail later in this chapter.)

Foreign Investment Affects Real Estate

The value of the dollar, and its effect on investment, have a significant impact on real estate management. In 1986 alone, a record $146 billion dollars from foreign investors poured into the United States. About 75% went to portfolio investments (such as stocks, bonds, and mortgage-related securities) and about 25% went into direct ownership of United States real estate or business enterprises. Investor confidence in U.S. markets by foreigners is due to:

- higher yields in the U.S. than abroad,
- fewer profitable enterprises available in investors' home countries, and
- the safety of U.S. investments due to political stability.

This influx of money was in part the result of U.S. financial instruments providing higher yields than those abroad. (Figure 2.)

Figure 2 June/July 1987

Estimating the Impact of Foreign Finance on U.S. Housing	
Estimated foreign portfolio investment in the U.S. during 1987 (foreign investment net of equity investments and direct investments)	$105 billion
Share of domestic credit allocated to net new mortgages on 1—4 family structures	x 22.5 percent
Net new 1—4 family mortgage credit from inflows of foreign funds	= $23.6 billion
Weighted average mortgage	÷ $37,000
Additional 1—4 family home purchases made possible by inflows of foreign funds	= 650,000
Weighted average home price	x $84,000
Estimated value of homes sold because of foreign fund inflows	= $55 billion

The effect of foreign investment on the U.S. real estate market can be seen in the following examples. In the 1980's, Middle Eastern investors surged into the real estate market, followed by Europeans purchasing huge sections of midwest farmland. The Far East, especially Hong Kong, invested heavily in U.S. real estate from 1980 to 1982, followed by a return flight of investor money in 1982 back to the Far East, forcing major sales.

MONEY IN NON-REAL ESTATE INVESTMENTS

The real estate market must compete against other types of investments funds: stocks, bonds, futures, gold, etc. One primary advantage of some types of competing investments is their liquidity. For instance, stocks are generally considered to be more liquid than real estate because the investor can sell them quickly for cash.

Liquidity
Assets are capable of being quickly and easily converted to cash.

Economic activity tends to fluctuate to different degrees in various segments of the market. Some are more stable while others are more volatile. Non-real estate markets are more international, using U.S. currency as its foundation. Funds flow into and out of Euro-dollar deposits, time deposits, savings depostis, checking accounts, and T-bills or CDs. These funds move through the U.S. markets as investments in stocks, bonds, and in the commodities.

Stocks and bonds offer an array of investment amenities. Typically, the stock market has two types of investors: those seeking short-term profits and desiring easy access to their funds, and those seeking stable yields to add to a well diversified portfolio of investments.

Bonds, however, attract investors seeking good interest rates with fixed returns, little or no management, and less risk. Conservative, long-term returns are expected from the bond market. (Figure 3)

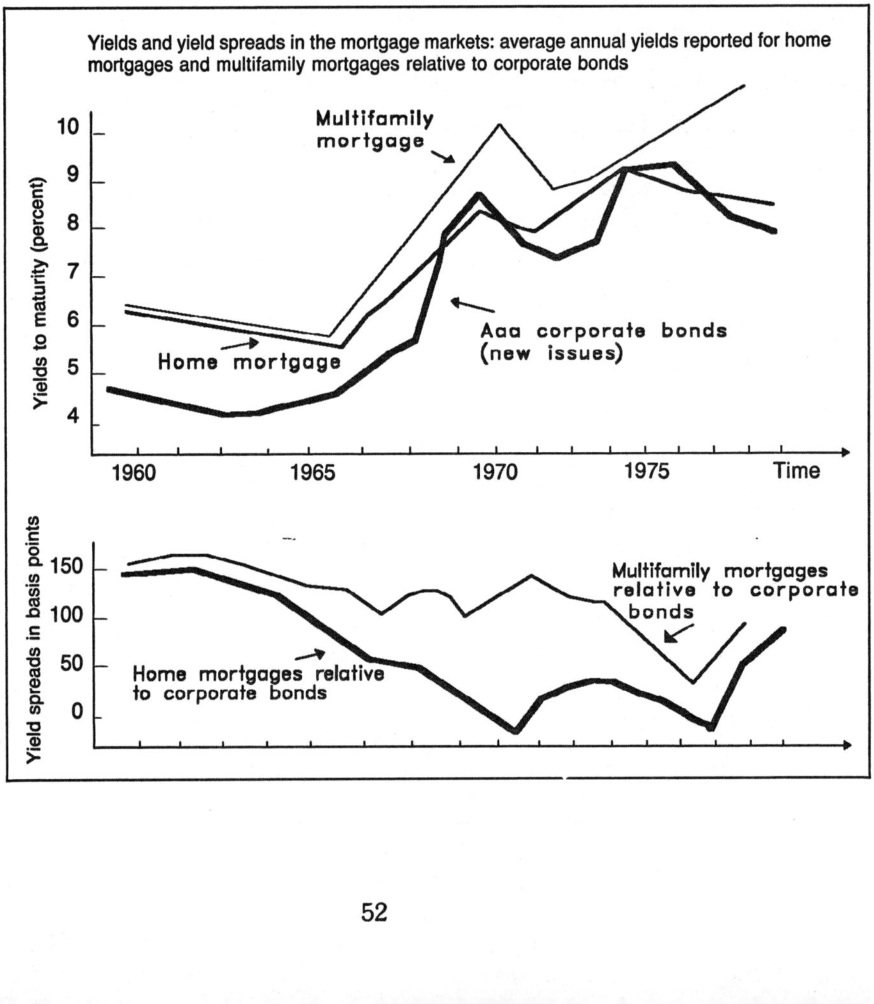

The gold, silver, and precious metals markets have quick, dramatic fluctuations in returns. This is also true of the futures markets.

During periods of inflation or unsure politics (e.g., the period immediately after a presidential election), investors often move their holdings out of banks and savings and loans and into precious metals, art, antiques, and real estate. Money becomes a bad investment as its value is likely to decline due to temporary instability. On the other hand, precious metals, real estate and other more limited resources skyrocket in price. When public confidence returns, their prices level off or decline and money becomes a good investment again (e.g., savings deposits, CDs, bonds). If inflation continues unchecked, however, and the prices of tangible goods continue to rise, these goods become more desirable as long-term hedges against inflation. This was the case with real estate in the late 70's, when real estate values escalated rapidly.

SOURCES OF MONEY FOR REAL ESTATE

Real estate requires the consistent availability of long-term money. When funds are scarce and interest rates rise, the real estate market slows. But when long-term, moderate-rate financing is available, activity picks up.

The importance of finance to the real estate market is due to the fact that most real estate activity is based upon leverage. Leverage is the use of borrowed money to increase the investors return on a property. The investor pays only a small portion of the purchase price, but gets a return on the whole property, not just the portion actually paid for by the investor.

Leverage
Using a small amount of your own money to make a major real estate purchase, but getting the returns on the whole property, not just the portion paid for. Leverage requires the use of financing.

Example: a $75,000 gain on a $5,000 investment using $95,000 leverage.

1985:		**1990:**	
$5,000	cash downpayment	$175,000	sales price
$95,000	new loan	93,000	loan balance
$100,000	purchase price	82,000	equity
		- 5,000	original cash investment
		- 2,000	principle reduction payment
		$75,000	gain

Property managers often become responsible for managing property with financial problems. The property manager must be able to analyze the underlying loan obligations in the hopes of restructuring the financing so as to turn around the building's performance. This may involve evaluating overall interest rates or payment schedules, and examining the possibility of using acquired equity. The property manager must know where to obtain funds in the marketplace when they're needed, at the best rates and under the best terms. By knowing which institutions offer the best program for a particular property, the property manager can enhance the performance of that property.

Types Of Lenders

California real estate markets are dependent on the ready supply of available money. Money, or loan funds, can be obtained from institutional or non-institutional lenders. Institutional lenders include savings and loans, commercial banks, and life insurance companies. Non-institutional lenders include mortgage companies, private parties, REITs, credit unions, and syndications and partnerships. Each has its own characteristics, which will be discussed below.

Institutional Lenders
• Savings and Loans • Commercial Banks • Life Insurance Companies

Non-Institutional Lenders
• Mortgage Companies • Private Parties • Real Estate Investment Trusts (REITs) • Credit Unions • Syndications and Partnerships

The distribution of mortgage funds for housing has changed over the years. Pooled funds now dominate over any other source. While savings and loans held far more individual mortgages than commercial banks prior to federal deregulation of the banking industry, the newly competitive market of the 1990's should see a redistribution of the business to all sectors of the mortgage loan field.

Institutional Lenders

Savings and Loans. Savings and loans get their funds primarily from depositors. Since the deposits are generally long-term savings deposits, S&Ls can make long-term real estate loans without having to worry unduly about liquidity. They make long-term real estate loans at rates higher than they pay their depositors, thus operating at a profit. These institutions are either state- or federally-chartered. The majority of their loans are used for residential real estate, mostly in single-family units, but also in multi-family properties and mobile homes.

Commercial Banks. Commercial banks remain one of the largest sources of investment funds in the country today. As their name implies, they are oriented towards commercial lending activities.

Commercial banks are also state- or federally-chartered and their main source of funds is also customer deposits. Commercial banks serve a vital role in the real estate market because of their ability to make short-term real estate loans. Their short-term financing sustains the construction industry. They also are a major source of long-term, large commercial property loans, as well as medium range business loans. In addition, they are a widely used source of junior liens and homeowner equity loans.

Life Insurance Companies. A life insurance company's funds come from life insurance premiums paid by customers. These funds are mostly long-term and thus life insurance companies are mainly interested in large, long-term loans. They often lend money for the development of new housing subdivisions and very large commercial shopping centers, office buildings, and industrial complexes. Their funds are usually channeled through intermediaries (loan correspondents), such as mortgage companies. The projects financed by life insurance companies are almost always under the watchful eye of a professional property manager, who may be a direct employee of the borrower, or an outside consultant.

Noninstitutional Lenders

Mortgage Companies. Mortgage companies work on a fee basis and are paid according to the amount of work they perform. The services they offer include loan origination and processing, closing, and servicing the loan after closing. Servicing a loan includes collecting the payments and forwarding them to the lender.

Mortgage companies get their loan funds from life insurance companies, banks, savings and loans, or other companies. Pooled funds and pension funds often enter the California real estate market through mortgage companies.

Some mortgage companies loan their own funds. A mortgage company may loan its own funds for an attractive but risky project that an institutional lender would turn down, thus filling a gap in the market.

Private Lenders. Private lenders make direct loans, or loans placed through an intermediary. Although private lenders are not limited to any type of loan, they seem to concentrate on making junior loans.

> **Example:** A seller carrying back a portion of the purchase price is making a second (junior) loan.

Many private investors turn around and sell these loans to other investors (at a discount). The loan amounts are typically small and for a relatively short period of time. Often, property managers use a second loan to fund building rehabilitation or to recast loans on projects with existing second, third, or fourth loans. More flexible payment plans, interest rates, prepayment penalties, late fees, and due dates are typical of this type of loan.

Real Estate Investment Trust. A real estate investment trust (REIT) is an organization of small investors who pool their funds together to raise venture capital for real estate transactions. The popularity of REITs depends largely upon current tax laws and public favor, but they have become more common in recent years. Some REITs have stabilized their offerings to the extent that their shares are now traded on some stock exchanges. Their portfolios tend to be more diversified in loan types and investment projects.

Credit Unions. Credit unions are also made up of the pooled funds of small investors and are like a specialized REIT in that they usually make loans only in their local real estate markets. Associations, employee groups, or organizations deposit and use their funds as a checking account. The credit union invests the deposits, often in real estate, to make a higher yield on the funds than it pays its depositors.

Syndications and Partnerships. Syndications and partnerships are special types of real estate investors. Their funds come directly from the members or partners. They often handle a project from its inception to completion—including funding the construction loan, long-term funding, and on-going management of the property. Their popularity is tied to the current tax laws. Often, their performance falls short of expectations because the participants may lack the necessary expertise in property development and management. However, they remain viable sources of funds and many syndications or partnerships now include a CPM or other professional property manager.

MONEY AND GOVERNMENT

Earlier we discussed how the value of the dollar fluctuates, depending on general economic conditions. Another prime factor in the value of money and its availability for real estate lending is government influences in monitoring, reacting to, and handling economic trends.

The government has been involved in the economic affairs of the nation for a long time. At various times in history, the government has implemented different economic policies, each with its own effect on the economy, and in turn, on the real estate market.

At the time of the American Revolution, Adam Smith described a laissez-faire economy—the economy was run by individuals motivated by profit. This freely competitive market would force the most efficient allocation of available resources and would work most effectively without government interference. However, the United States faced successive periods of recession, suffered unemployment, and had to face the issues of the homeless, poor, and elderly.

Towards the end of The Great Depression, John Keynes challenged the traditional economic theory by advocating that some government interference was necessary to balance the economy, to offset the peaks and valleys of the natural economic cycles. In recent years, Milton Friedman has stressed that if the money supply increased at a rate equal to the real growth in the gross national product (GNP), inflation could be kept under control.

Government Policies

Over the years, the public has come to expect, even to rely on, some government control to help prevent economic disaster (even though this contradicts the free enterprise system). The government uses two policy tools to this end: monetary policy and fiscal policy. Monetary policy refers to the government's control of the money supply: increasing or decreasing the supply of money can help counteract recession, unemployment, and inflation. Fiscal policy refers to the government's ability to collect taxes, spend money, and borrow money to counteract recession, unemployment and inflation. The effect of these policies will stimulate or slow economic activity.

The Federal Reserve. The Federal Reserve is the primary government regulator in monetary policy activities. The Fed's role is to regulate the supply of money and credit so the nation can have economic growth with acceptable levels of unemployment and inflation.

The Fed controls the supply of money and credit in three ways:

- setting reserve requirements,
- setting federal discount rates, and
- engaging in open market operations.

Not all banks are members of the Federal Reserve Board, even though the majority are. Those institutions who are part of the Federal Reserve System are called member banks.

When the Fed changes the reserve requirements it greatly influences the economy because the reserve requirement is the percentage of deposits that commercial banks are required to maintain on deposit. The original purpose of the reserve requirement was to help avert financial panic by giving depositors some confidence that their deposits were safe and accessible. The reserve requirement protects depositors by ensuring that enough funds are available to meet unusual customer demand.

The reserve requirement also enables the Fed to exercise some control over the growth of credit. By increasing the reserve requirement, the Fed can reduce the amount of money that banks have available to lend. On the other hand, a reduction in reserve requirements frees more money for investment or lending by banks. An increase in the reserve requirement, then, tends to decrease available loan funds and increase interest rates. Conversely, a decrease in the reserve requirement tends to increase funds available for lending and to decrease interest rates.

Federal discount rates are the interest rates charged by Federal Reserve Banks on loans to its member banks. Increasing the discount rate usually results in the banks charging higher interest rates to their customers, since they have to charge more interest on the money they lend if they have to pay more interest on the money they borrow.

The Fed also buys and sells government securities. These sales are called open market operations. They are the primary method relied upon by the Fed to control the money supply, and with the money supply, inflation and interest rates. When the Fed purchases government securities from the public, the money supply is increased (there is more money in circulation). When the Fed sells government securities, the money supply is decreased (the investors who buy the securities have less money to invest in other areas).

United States Treasury. The United States Treasury is the primary actor in fiscal policy operations. As the nation's fiscal manager, the Treasury is responsible for managing the government's finances, including the national debt. Treasury funds come from a number of sources, but the largest source is personal and business income tax.

When federal income is less than federal expenditures, a shortfall called a federal deficit occurs. When there is a deficit, the Treasury covers the shortfall by issuing interest-bearing securities to investors. By doing so, the government is actually borrowing money from the private sector. The more money the government borrows, the less there is for investment in real estate or other areas.

Taxation is another important tool of fiscal policy. Lower tax rates mean that taxpayers have more funds for lending and investing. High tax rates mean that taxpayers not only have fewer funds to invest, but that they will be more likely to invest in tax-exempt securities instead of real estate.

The Treasury Department also oversees the U.S. Printing Office, which has the power to increase the amount of the nation's money. This act typically decreases the value of the dollar and can spur inflation. This affects real estate investments by altering the cost and availability of loan funds.

Current Problems

The balancing of economic growth and inflation is not an easy task for government. As market conditions change, the government must quickly act or react to the fluctuations. While on the one hand, the government relies on economic growth to help lessen the looming federal deficit, continued economic growth also fuels inflation. But fighting inflation often requires higher interest rates, which in turn increases the value of the dollar, adding to the problem of the trade deficit. (Figure 4)

Inflation
An abnormal increase in the volume of money and credit resulting in a substantial and continuing rise in the general price level.

Figure 4

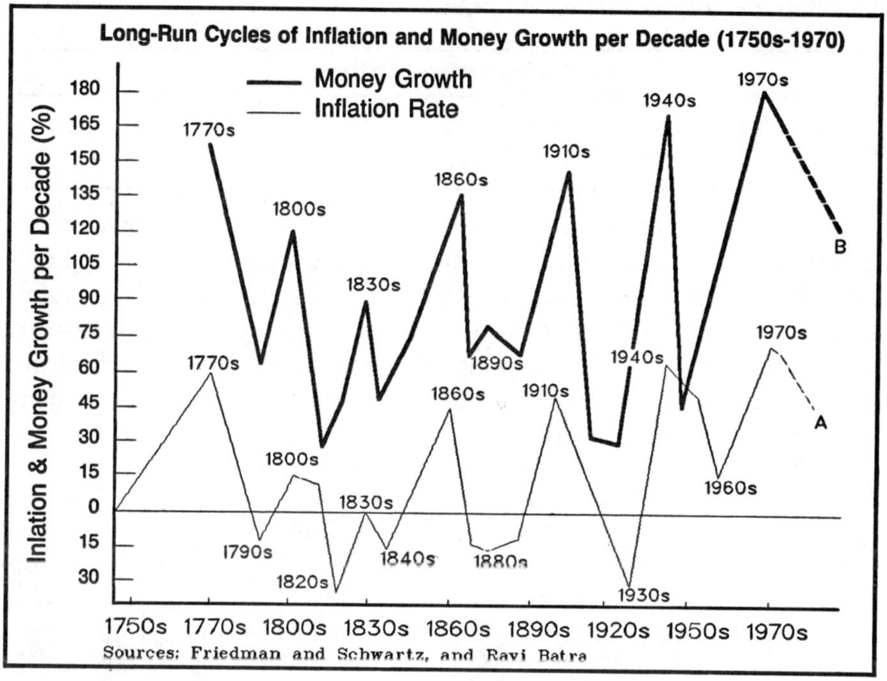

At the time of this writing (early 1989), inflation is one of the biggest fears. Inflation affects real estate in many ways. It makes loan repayment worth less, so lenders raise interest rates as a hedge against future revenues. Increased interest rates make it more difficult for buyers to qualify for loans, reducing housing demand. A decrease in homebuyers means increased demand for rentals, forcing rental rates higher. Increased rents causes more vacancies on the top-end rental units, and overcrowding on lower-end rental units. If vacancies continue, foreclosures increase on the more expensive units. The poor especially suffer because lower-income units become more difficult to find.

Inflation also has a harsh effect on lending institutions. Customers, fearing a decrease in the value of the money, take their money out of savings accounts and invest it in other markets offering higher returns. This is referred to as *disintermediation,* and decreases the amount of money available for mortgage loans, further increasing interest rates. Inflation also causes the cost of construction materials to increase, making new construction even more expensive for investors and driving smaller investors out of the real estate market.

Disintermediation
The withdrawal of funds from banks for investment in other instruments at higher yields, e.g., government securities.

As you can see, the real estate market is closely interrelated to the general business economy of the nation. For example, the general collapse in the real estate market in 1928 spurred on the Great Depression (which began in 1929). A recession or depression, called **deflation,** is prevalent where there is a shortage of available money. A look at the general business cycle shows periods of inflation, deflation, and a general equilibrium, called **unflation.**

Figure 5

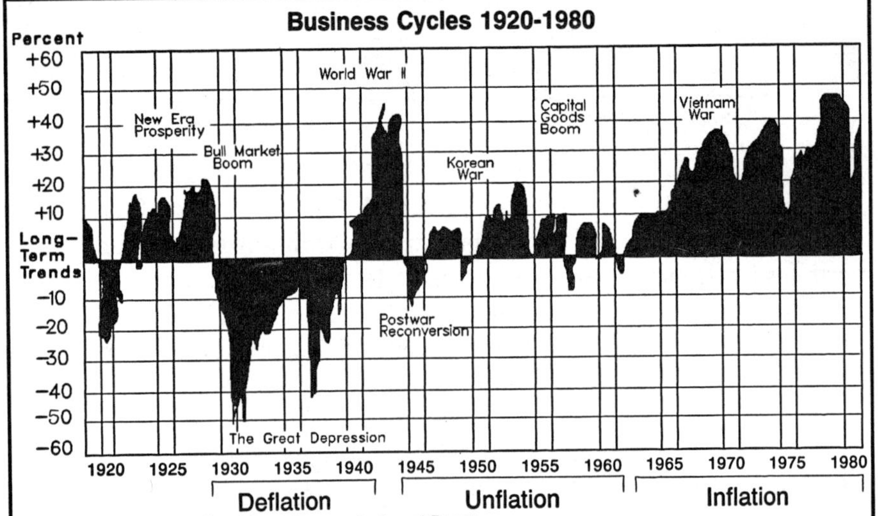

Sources: Adapted from Ameri Trust Company's Annual Report.

While fears of inflation creep over the U.S. economy, California is already experiencing inflation in the real estate market. The national inflation rate is expected to remain moderate for a time (under 6%), but California construction and sales prices are increasing far above the national average. Four of the top ten most costly housing areas in the nation for homes are in California: Orange County (3rd), San Francisco (4th), Los Angeles (7th) and San Diego (8th).

Some economists are predicting a sharp decline in home values on the East Coast by 1990, similar to what happened in the Mid-West in 1985-1987. But, California's diversified employment base, immigration investment expansion, and the existing capital of those already in the Golden State, should prevent any marked decline. A nation-wide recession, however, could decrease the number of jobs available, weed out the more marginal investors, and use up capital reserves of Californians. Obviously, this would weaken some California markets. Those particularly vulnerable would be outlying, highly speculative areas where high leverage was used and appreciation has not yet had time to fully develop. Also, poorer neighborhoods are most affected during a recession, as the property owners tend to have less reserves to meet mortgage payments should they lose their job. The owners also tend to have less residual funds to maintain the property. Therefore, poorer areas usually suffer more blight during tough economic times.

CHAPTER 3–BIBLIOGRAPHY

"The Dollar-Deficit Connection." *Nation's Business,* Feb. 1985, p. 13.

"The Hunt for Ways to Tame the Dollar." *U.S. News & World Report,* 25 Nov. 1985, p. 29.

"The Ebb & Flow of Foreign Capital" *Real Estate Today,* July/Aug. 1985, p. 10.

"Economic Outlook 1986." *Real Estate Today,* Jan 1986, p. 16.

"An International Role for U.S. Real Estate." *Real Estate Today,* June/July 1987, p. 20.

"1988 Outlook: The Challenges of a New Economic Order." *Real Estate Today,* Jan/Feb 1988, p. 16.

"Fuller, Doris. Builders Preparing for a Boom in Rental Units." *Los Angeles Times,* 27 February 1983, V. 3.

Betts, Richard, Dennis, McKenzie. *The Essentials of Real Estate Economy.* 2nd ed. New York: John Wiley & Sons., Inc., 1980.

Anderson, Lowell; McKenzie, Dennis. *California Real Estate Principles.* 3rd ed. New York: John Wiley & Sons, Inc.; 1987.

CHAPTER 3–QUIZ

1. An asset capable of being easily converted to cash is called:

   a. money
   b. liquid
   c. leveraged
   d. disintermediated

2. Since floating exchange rates began in 1973, the dollar has:

   a. sharply increased, nearly doubling
   b. bounced with many fluctuations
   c. remained as a constant stable
   d. drastically declined

3. The impact of foreign finance on U.S. housing is due to their portfolio investment. In 1987, alone, they invested an estimated:

   a. $105 billion
   b. $100 million
   c. $200 thousand
   d. $20 billion

4. Relative to AAA corporate bonds, annual yields from mortgages have been best in:

   a. mobile home parks
   b. multi-family residences
   c. single-family residences
   d. mini-warehouses

5. Which is a non-institutional lender:

   a. savings and loan
   b. commercial bank
   c. mortgage company
   d. life insurance company

6. The government affects the California real estate market by:

   a. Housing Authority programs
   b. Redevelopment Agency loans
   c. Federal Reserve Board actions
   d. All of the above

7. Inflation affects California real estate by increasing:

   a. demand for rentals
   b. rental rates
   c. vacancies
   d. All of the above

CHAPTER 3–QUIZ ANSWERS

1.	b
2.	b
3.	a
4.	b
5.	c
6.	d
7	d

4
The Real Estate Investor

References

DeCarlo, J., CPM. *California Real Property Management. Study Guide.* Sacramento: California Community Colleges, 1986.

Downs, J., CPM. *Principles of Real Estate Management.* 12th ed. Chicago: Institute of Real Estate Management of National Association of Realtors, 1980

McKenzie, Dennis, L. Anderson, F. Battino, and C. Hopkins. *California Real Estate Principles.* 3rd ed. New York: Wiley & Sons, 1987.

Last Chapter Review

The last chapter covered the definition of money, its value, and its uses. We also reviewed where real estate money comes from, and the government's methods of controlling money supply.

Chapter Overview

The professional property manager needs to know his or her client: the property owner. To achieve this, the property manager must be familiar with the forms of ownership and the various goals each owner may have. By knowing the form of ownership and the ownership goals, the property manager can help match the right property owner to the right kind of property.

TYPES OF OWNERSHIP

Before someone purchases property, he or she must make a series of decisions. First, the prospective owner must decide that alternative forms of investment are not more appealing. Then the investor must decide on the type of property he or she wishes to invest in. Another decision is how long to own the property and how to take title to it. The method of ownership can have an enormous impact on the income, tax, and liability consequences of property ownership.

Types of Ownership
The Individual
Partnerships
Syndicates
REITs
Corporations
Cooperatives
Condominiums

The Individual

Individuals own more income-producing properties than either partnerships or corporations. For instance, one person may own an apartment building "in severalty" (by herself), or a married couple may own property jointly as community property, or two business associates may own property jointly as tenants-in-common. An individually owned concern is called a sole proprietorship, in contrast to a partnership or corporation.

For the most part, these people own small-scale residential income properties (with an average of 12 units). Individual property owners share the common goals of wanting to accumulate long-term assets while taking advantage of short-term tax benefits.

In the past, the small property owner almost always managed his or her own property. He or she had enough time and experience to handle the building, the tenants, and the financial aspects of the property. Today, however, many of these people hire outside help — to do their taxes, handle the evictions, and perform overall management functions.

The change was caused, in part, by the increasing complexity of the laws and regulations that govern property management. For instance, as discrimination, health and safety, and eviction laws become increasingly complicated, the private individual may want the security of having a knowledgeable property manager handle some or all of these issues. Business operations in general are also more sophisticated. The individual property owner may not want to spend the time and money buying and learning to operate the computer equipment that makes property management more efficient.

As property management gets more complicated, greater opportunities become available in this segment of the market. Many owners view their income-property investment as ancillary to another, full-time job. These owners may not want to devote their leisure hours to managing the property, and willingly delegate the burden to a property manager. Other owners are retired and are, like the part-time investor, unwilling to spend their hard-earned leisure days tied down to the daily management chores of an income property.

Some of the advantages of individual property ownership include low organizational costs, direct taxation, fewer legal restrictions (on the business itself), and maximum control. Some of the disadvantages include unlimited liability for financial obligations, difficulty in raising additional funds to meet unforeseen needs, and the success of the project is more dependent on the competence and mental health of the individual.

Partnerships

Partnerships are another popular way of taking title to real estate.

Partnership
An association of two or more persons, to carry on, as co-owners, a business for profit.

There are two different kinds of partnerships: general partnerships and limited partnerships. Each has distinct advantages and disadvantages.

General Partnerships. The partners in a general partnership all share in the profits, debts, and management of the partnership. Each has an equal right to possess the partnership property. The partners' interests in the partnership profits, losses, and property are proportionate to their capital investment, unless otherwise agreed. Each partner is a fiduciary of the other and each partner is individually liable for all partnership expenses and debts.

Each partner has the power and authority to act on behalf of the partnership. Typically, one partner handles the management—by hiring an outside property manager to handle operations, or by doing it him or herself, while the other handles all the maintenance and repairs. One or more of the partners may be a tenant in the apartment, office space, or commercial center.

General partnerships have several advantages: they are relatively easy to form, capital contributions are easier to obtain, management duties are spread over more people, and the risk of loss is shared. Their disadvantages include: less individual control, unlimited liability, and the partnership must be dissolved on the death of one of the partners, unless there is a provision in the partnership agreement to the contrary.

Limited Partnerships. In a limited partnership, there must be at least one general partner who has the right to manage the partnership and who is liable for the debts of the partnership. There is also one or more limited partners. A limited partner has no voice in management and no authority to act on behalf of the partnership. The limited partner is liable for partnership debts only to the extent of the amount of the original capital contribution into the partnership.

This ownership form is widely used to restrict financial liability, and to obtain the tax advantage of being able to pass the tax deductions and losses generated by the property through to the individual partners. If profits are distributed to the partners, they only pay income tax on it once (they escape the double taxation problem of corporations).

Limited partnerships are excellent ways to finance the construction of large projects, when many investors are needed to raise the necessary capital. A property manager may have the opportunity to become a member of a partnership, acting as the general partner and managing the property.

Limited partnership agreements are recorded at the county recorder's office in the county where the partnership operates its business, so the property manager does have access to the agreement. The agreement will contain the name of the authorized signator and the property manager should be sure that this person is the same one who signed the property management agreement.

Limited partners find the limited liability and lack of personal involvement significant benefits to limited partnerships. For the general partner, the advantages and disadvantages are the same as for a general partnership. The disadvantage to the limited partner is the inability to contribute to any phase of the management of the project. If a limited partner becomes involved in management, he or she would lose the limited liability.

Syndicates

A syndicate is a group of investors who pool their financial resources to engage in real estate ventures. The syndicate, as such, is not a recognized legal entity. The underlying ownership is usually in the form of a limited partnership, although it could also be a corporation, general partnership, or trust.

Syndicates are usually interested in large, expensive pieces of property to be used for development, investment, or speculation. The participants range from individuals to other legal entities such as corporations. The interest of each member is usually limited to a fixed share or a percentage. The Corporations Commissioner regulates the formation and sale of syndicates in California. The advantages and disadvantages of syndicate ownership depend on the type of underlying ownership entity.

Real Estate Investment Trusts

A Real Estate Investment Trust (REIT) is an ownership entity authorized by the Internal Revenue Code of 1960. REITs invest in real estate and real estate mortgages—at least 75% of the gross income must be generated from real estate investment. There must be 100 or more investors to form the trust.

The trust is unincorporated, so it avoids corporate taxation. The REIT is only taxed on its retained earnings, provided that 90% or more of its income is distributed to the shareholders; thus, large distributions of income to the shareholders avoid taxation to the trust, and shareholders receive the tax/depreciation benefits directly.

The popularity of REIT ownership frequently waxes and wanes according to specific tax provisions and general economic conditions. For example, REITs were very popular in the early '70's, but lack of management, excessive debt, and a poor real estate market led to widespread failures in the late '70's-early '80's. REITs have enjoyed more popularity in California, where property values have steadily appreciated.

The REIT is advantageous because small investors can take advantage of big investment opportunities by pooling resources and because it provides potentially higher returns from diversified, more risky investments. Disadvantages include the inability to gather enough investors for smaller projects, loss of capital, and lack of participation in project management.

Corporations

Corporations are artificial legal persons composed of individuals empowered to conduct business as one entity, the corporation. The corporation is a separate entity from its stockholders; it is capable of perpetual existence and the death of a stockholder (even a major one) does not affect its "life". The corporation, not the individual stockholders, owns the corporate property. The daily management functions are carried out by the elected officers of the corporation. The stockholder's liability is limited, and they have only the right to share in the profits of the corporation.

A corporation that invests in real estate is subject to the same rules and regulations of all other corporations. Real estate investor corporations raise money for their operations by selling stock, just like other corporations. The stockholders elect a Board of Directors, which elects a Chairman of the Board, to manage the corporation's business. The property manager may be the chairman, or may report to the chairman.

Because the corporation owns and operates the property rather than the stockholders, the property manager has no contact with the stockholders. The property manager deals directly with the corporation through its authorized representative. The property manager must also be sure to obtain the proper corporate authority. The property manager should always require a "corporate resolution", which authorizes approval of the management contract, before beginning to manage the property.

A corporation has several advantages over other forms of ownership: its existence is perpetual and does not depend on the life of any stockholders, funds are easily raised by selling stock, and stockholders enjoy limited liability—they are not liable for any corporate debts or losses (they only risk losing the amount they paid to purchase the stock). There are several disadvantages as well. The time and money necessary to form the corporation is higher than for other ownership forms. Strict regulation of corporate activities make ongoing operations expensive, e.g., regular board meetings and stockholder meetings must be held. Stockholders have no direct control of corporate activities, other than voting for the officer. Double taxation is a serious detriment—the corporation pays taxes on its income, and what is distributed to the stockholders is taxed again at the individual stockholder's rate.

Cooperatives

A property manager may be hired by a cooperative. In this form of ownership, the property is owned by a corporation. The individual unit occupant purchases shares of stock and the corporation gives him or her a proprietary lease for the unit. Cooperatives are popular as commercial or special use properties, such as jewelry marts on the west coast, as well as residential properties.

The property manager is hired to manage the common areas, and prepare tentative budgets to be reviewed by the board of directors and voted on by the stockholders. Again, proper written authorization is important. The property manager often pays the utilities, gardener, and maintenance crews.

One major disadvantage to cooperative ownership is that if one individual owner defaults, the total costs must be spread between the remaining owners. For example, if there are 100 units and one owner defaults, the remaining 99 owners must make the total building payments.

If ten owners default, the financial burden is split between the remaining 90 owners, and so on. Also, the owner never actually gets a deed to the individual unit, only a long-term lease. The advantages of cooperative ownership are shared common facilities and shared liability.

Condominiums

Condominium ownership is very popular in California. The number of available units is likely to increase even more because they are less expensive than detached homes, offering the benefits of homeownership for less money.

With the condominium method of ownership, the unit owner owns the individual unit as separate property, and the common areas are owned jointly with all the other unit owners. The owner of the condominium unit receives a deed giving him or her absolute ownership of the unit. The owner secures his or her own financing, receives an individual tax bill, and may acquire a title insurance policy on the property. The condominium unit consists of the airspace within the surface of the walls, floor and ceiling, plus anything that projects into the space, such as light fixtures. The walls themselves are part of the common area.

A governing board of directors, elected by the condominium owners' association, performs the management function. The association often hires a property manager to handle the billing, expenses, maintenance and repairs for the association and to report to the board of directors. The association owns the common areas: the land under the unit, the surrounding property (e.g., parking area, grass area, tennis courts, pools, ponds, lakes), exterior walls, duct work, roof, lobbies, elevators, etc. Many developers maintain control of the homeowners, association after the units are sold, and only lease the common areas to the unit association. But in California, by and large, the individual unit owners own the homeowners, association.

The advantages of condominium ownership include individual ownership of the unit, use of the common area facilities, and limited liability of the unit owners. The disadvantages include the lack of participation in the management, inability to separate the unit from the association, and the additional cost of association dues.

Banks or Other Lenders

Lending institutions often acquire properties through their foreclosure process. They also may acquire property through wholesale liquidation, merger or joint venture operations of their banking or savings and loan operations. These financial institutions also maintain trust departments that administer holdings for others. Property management opportunities are vast and vary from one institution to another. Each has different policies and procedures on income-producing properties. The property manager who handles "real estate owned" (REO) properties for lenders must obtain specific instructions on whether they prefer the unit vacant, ready to resell, or occupied with rent-paying tenants. Lender policies vary on these issues.

Advantages to owning these properties include a quick response time for management decisions and the complete authority to act. Disadvantages include the inability to make improvements to the property to enhance total value.

Insurance Companies

Insurance companies and other larger investors, such as mutual funds and pension funds, develop and manage many properties. They often hire employees to manage the property rather than outside property managers. These investors tend to concentrate on long-term holdings in the non-residential markets. They are considered the most conservative income-property owners and they seek top-quality, first-class commercial property.

Advantages to managing these properties include security, professionalism, and management control. Disadvantages are conservatism, detailed paperwork, and office politics.

The Government

The government is the largest single landlord in the United States. State, federal, and county governments all have significant property holdings. They directly own and operate, or indirectly contribute to more rental programs than any other single residential owner. They often hire private property managers to handle the daily operations of the building management. They use their own government-approved management agreements and rules of operations.

Most government involvement in the rental market, however, is not through direct property ownership. The government's biggest role is through their approved programs:

- The National Housing Act of 1934: created the Federal Housing Administration (FHA), which was given the authority to insure mortgage loans for housing and home improvements.
- The United States Housing Act of 1937: established the Public Housing Authority, and set up loan programs and annual contributions to local public housing agencies for low-rent housing and slum clearance.
- The Housing Act of 1949: provided federal assistance to local agencies for slum clearance, urban redevelopment and construction of low-rent public housing; and new rural housing programs.
- The Housing and Urban Development Act of 1965: created the U.S. Department of Housing and Urban Development (HUD) to stimulate housing development.
- The Housing and Community Development Act of 1974: authorized Section 8 housing assistance program through block grant programs.

OWNERSHIP GOALS

Matching the right investor with the right property is too often accomplished by accident, rather than by design. An owner should predetermine the best type of property, thoroughly check the building prior to ownership, select the most advantageous method of ownership, and then reap the financial rewards of this careful planning. In reality, investors often make uninformed investment decisions governed by tax considerations, financial constraints, or time limitations.

However the property was initially acquired, to properly manage it, the property manager must discover the goals of the owner. Knowing the owner's goals will help the manager make a variety of decisions. Should rents be raised? Long-neglected repairs made? Operating expenses lowered? The present financing altered? Certain tenants evicted? The present on-site manager fired? Only by knowing and striving to fulfill the owner's goals can the property manager make the best decisions.

Type of Goals

The benefits of ownership fall into three major categories:

- present monetary benefits,
- future monetary benefits, and
- non-monetary benefits.

These goals vary between buildings held by the same owner, and between different owners of the same building.

Present Monetary Benefits. Some owners want a substantial income now. The cash flow must be positive to offset other income losses; they depend on the cash flow for their retirement income; or the funds may be needed to build up reserves for future improvements.

Some owners want properties that are at a break-even point for the present time—they don't have to pay additional income tax, and there are enough funds coming in to meet current building expenses.

Alternatively, the owner's current financial situation may be helped the most by a negative cash flow. Losses are often desired for their tax advantages. Tax laws change over time and these benefits diminish or gain in value depending on Congressional attitudes.

Another vital tax benefit to income-property ownership is depreciation.

Depreciation
A loss of value of an asset from any cause — age; physical deterioration; or functional, economic, or social obsolescence.

Depreciation (called cost recovery deductions) can be deducted from the owner's income. The deductions reduce the owner's taxable income and allows the owner to recover the cost of an asset used for the production of income or used in a trade or business.

The entire expense of acquiring the asset cannot be deducted in the year the expense is incurred, as is permitted with many business expenses. However, the acquisition expense can be deducted over a number of years (from 15 to 31½, depending on the type of real estate and when it was purchased). The number of years is a reflection of legislative policy and has little relationship to the property's economic life.

The depreciation deduction is a certain portion of the original cost of the asset, which is theoretically put away, or invested for the future (called a "depreciation expense"). This is referred to as "book depreciation." When the value of the asset has been depreciated down to zero, or zero book value, the owner should have saved enough money to acquire a replacement asset.

The tax preparer uses Internal Revenue Service guidelines to determine what amount can be deducted from taxable income. The 1986 Tax Reform Act changed the depreciation schedule significantly. Property is now depreciated over a period of 31½ years for commercial property, and 27½ years for residential property. The state of the current depreciation schedules assures investors of one thing: constant change. Under current law, an investor purchasing a rental property for $315,000 would be able to take $10,000 per year depreciation if it were a commercial rental, and $11,454 a year if it were a residential property. This method of depreciation has altered the investment activities of many real estate investors.

Before any depreciation can be determined, a property's **cost basis** must be established. The cost basis is the amount of the owner's investment in the property. The cost basis must be allocated between the value of the land and the value of the improvements because land cannot be depreciated—only the improvements are depreciable. Each owner begins depreciating the property anew; the buyer does not continue on the same depreciation schedule as the seller.

Cost Basis
any cash downpayment + all loans and carrybacks + other property value traded

Depreciation expenses begin with the month of closing. An acceptable alternative, especially for construction projects, is to begin depreciation when improvements are completed and the property is ready for occupancy.

When depreciated property is sold, the amount of the deductions taken increases the owner's gain from the sale. This is called "depreciation recapture". Because the amount of depreciation taken increases gain, income taxes on the sale also increase. One alternative to this increase (referred to as "paying back depreciation") is to exchange the property for another. While the exchange of property is not tax free, the taxes are deferred. The cost basis from the original property, which is reduced by the amount of depreciation deducted from that property, transfers to the new property. Then the owner may begin depreciating the new property (using the amount of the transferred cost basis to determine the depreciable amount). The depreciation schedules from the year the basis originated with the old property is used for the basis that is carried forward.

Any exchange should be reviewed and approved by a tax expert. To avoid potential tax liability, the statutory requirements for an exchange transaction must be met exactly. Otherwise, the transaction will be declared a sale.

Note that depreciation works differently for tenants. For example, business trade fixtures are depreciated as personal property, not real property. However, a tenant's entire cost of acquiring and improving a leasehold interest, including a ground lease, is depreciable as real property.

Installment sales are another way to enjoy tax deferrals. Taxes are paid on the gain only as the installment payments are received. Again, when involved in an installment sale, the parties should seek expert tax advice to make sure the transaction will qualify.

One additional tax consideration is of major importance. Whether income is made from a "passive" or an "active" investment has important tax consequences. For example, losses (including depreciation deductions) from passive investments cannot be deducted from active income—wages, salaries, or interest. However, just what constitutes "passive" income has not yet been clearly defined. Some advisors believe that a property owner can turn income from rental properties into active income by merely approving the forms used in the operation of the rental business. They take the position that if the investor sets the guidelines for the business operation by approving rental terms and conditions, this will make the investment active for purposes of an IRS audit.

However, it is this author's recommendation that for rental income to qualify as "active" income, the property owner must be involved in more than setting a minimum rent and approving some forms. The owner should also engage in such activities as giving the final approval for each prospective tenant, signing the rental agreement and other forms, approving all capital improvements. The owner should actively participate in the management of the building on a continuous basis. By setting up regular procedures for owner involvement, property managers can easily comply with the legal requirements and protect all the parties. (Forms are shown in Chapter 12 on Maintenance.)

Future Monetary Benefits. Most real estate is owned for the long-term benefits, including investment diversification and leverage. Appreciation, however, is the most attractive benefit to most owners. Over the long run, property tends to increase in value at a rate that is higher than the inflation rate. This allows the owner, who purchased the property at a lower price, to use the appreciation (or equity) for other purposes. This equity build-up can equal hundreds of thousands of dollars.

Equity
The difference between the value of a piece of property and the charges (or debts) against it.

When there is inflation, real estate ownership becomes more popular as people use it as a hedge against the declining value of money. Future-minded ownership goals include keeping in tune to market indexes and the business cycle to take full advantage of assets during inflationary times.

Non-monetary Benefits. Owners also hold property for non-monetary reasons. Some investors build a property for their retirement, and although other opportunities may be more financially rewarding, they prefer this particular site. Some property has been in the family or occupied by a family for a long time, and the owners want to keep it that way. Some owners are afraid of complicated exchanges and tax considerations and are comfortable with the present situation. Others want to come back home to a property after they travel. Many investors feel more secure owning real estate than owning other types of investments such as stocks or bonds.

The objectives of the property owner can have a major impact on the policies of the property manager. Clear communication of these goals and objectives paves the way to a smooth team effort. It is the responsibility of the property manager to use these goals as his or her guide when making decisions affecting property.

Matching The Owner To The Property

Each property is unique and each kind of property has a different practical impact on ownership and ownership goals. A brief review of the major benefits of different types of residential property ownership is warranted.

Single-Family Residential. A single-family residential unit has many advantages. For investment purposes, homes tend to be the most flexible. If the investment market is weak, they can usually be sold more readily to an owner-occupant. This property usually appreciates well, allowing the owner to borrow against the equity to purchase additional property. (Figure 1)

Home Prices in Early '88

During the first three months of the current year, according to the National Association of Realtors, the metropolitan areas in the United States with the most costly and least costly housing (in terms of median prices for existing single-family homes) were:

Most costly housing areas:		Least costly housing areas:	
Honolulu, Hawaii	$198,400	Louisville, Ky.	$51,100
New York, N.Y.	186,600	Lansing, Mich.	53,400
Orange County, Calif.	183,800	Des Moines, Iowa	54,500
San Francisco, Calif.	178,800	Grand Rapids, Mich.	55,400
Boston, Mass.	176,900	Oklahoma City, Okla.	56,500
Hartford, Conn.	166,400	Toledo, Ohio	56,500
Los Angeles, Calif.	159,900	Akron, Ohio	57,100
San Diego, Calif.	134,000	El Paso, Tex.	57,800
Washington, D.C.	132,400	Omaha, Neb.	58,300
Providence, R.I.	123,300	Tampa, Fla.	60,200

SUNDAY, JULY 24, 1988/PRESS-TELEGRAM

Location is often a factor, determining both desirability of the property and ease of management (proximity to the owner's home is beneficial for daily management operations).

Vacancy rates tend to be low because tenants tend to stay longer. However, when there is a vacancy, there is no income at all. Tenant selection needs to be more rigid because of the high cost of eviction. Potential physical damage is also greater. Routine maintenance is usually less because the tenant is often responsible for at least part of it, and often voluntarily performs additional services.

In terms of cash flow, a larger downpayment is often required for non-owner-occupant financing. A smaller loan often ensures the loan payments can be paid from the rental proceeds.

Condominiums. Condominium units have many of the same advantages as single-family residences. With the association dues added to the loan payment, a larger downpayment may be required for a break-even cash flow. However, the dues are a good investment, since they include the cost of the gardener, pool maintenance, and other exterior maintenance (such as roof, driveways, and paint). The investor needs fewer funds for reserves and replacements.

Tenants like the features of the units and the amenities of common areas, which often include tennis and golf facilities, pools, spas, or other items. As rental households become dominated by younger singles and the elderly, a maintenance-free condominium lifestyle will become even more desirable.

Multi-Family Properties–One to Four Units. Small multi-family properties are very popular because they are affordable for the small investor. Many investors can only afford to start with a duplex. Even using the rental income to help qualify for the financing, these smaller properties are within the reach of so many more investors than a 20-unit building.

One-to four-unit properties may be detached units, such as three-on-a-lot, or a duplex behind a house. They tend to appreciate at a moderate rate, providing a fair hedge against inflation. They also provide a steady income over the long term. Smaller properties are less likely to be subject to rent control. (But some areas of California are trying to include these under rent control ordinances.)

These units are excellent buys for the person receiving funds from the sale of his or her home who needs to transfer the funds into another property to avoid taxable gain. The purchaser can live in one unit and reap the tax advantages of owning income-property from the other units.

When reviewing the performance of these smaller properties, the real expense of operating the property tends to be understated. The cost to manage and maintain the property in terms of time and money can be overwhelming to the new, inexperienced owner.

Four to Sixteen Units. These properties have good flexibility in terms of potential resale and for exchange purposes. They are good tax shelters for income earned from other sources.

Due to financing, however, new purchasers can expect the largest negative cash flow from this type of investment. Larger properties can spread vacancy costs over more units. Plus, these properties are often financed with variable-rate loans and as loan payments rise, owners pass the increase along to the tenants in the form of rent increases. With smaller properties, there are less units to spread the cost between, and the rent increases can cause vacancies if market conditions are not evaluated carefully. Less sophisticated owners tend to pay less attention to rental levels than the professional property manager.

Maintenance costs may be higher, on a per unit basis, than for other properties. Smaller properties usually have less wear and tear, and the tenants tend to do more of the maintenance. Larger properties need regular maintenance crews or an on-site handyman. Turnover costs on medium-sized properties can be higher because frequently there is no one readily available to show the vacant unit.

Owners of mid-sized properties are unaware of how heavily their business operation is regulated. It is not unusual for an owner to have a tenant do some maintenance and yard work, plus show vacancies and collect rents. In other words, the tenant acts as an on-site manager in return for a reduction of that tenant's rent or some other benefit. This subjects the owner to the responsibility of having that person treated as an employee, subject to workmens' compensation claims, unemployment contributions, minimum wage and tax laws, filing quarterly payroll returns, etc.

Sixteen to Fifty Units. Owners of larger properties, 16 to 50 units, are typically more educated on the employer-employee relationship. Full maintenance work crews and on-site managers have training classes and off-site supervision.

These properties require an on-site manager by law, and are often subject to rent controls. The tenant selection is done by guidelines set by credit standards, and business techniques are employed. The ownership purpose is appreciation and tax benefits.

Fifty or More Units. These properties are usually developed as a long-term holding. As inflation increases, these properties appreciate at a faster rate than smaller properties. They are often owned and operated by larger investors who directly manage the building themselves.

These larger buildings are professionally run, and maintenance is part of a regular budget item. They are usually subject to rent control. The typical owner seeks tax sheltered profits. Typical expenses include the cost of tax preparation and government forms preparation, as opposed to the duplex owner's time (contributed free of charge) which is not a tax deductible expense of running the property.

PURCHASING THE PROPERTY

Many investment property purchasers are entering the investment property market for the first time. Although they have heard of the many advantages of ownership, they have not personally experienced any of the disadvantages and they often do not know what to look for or ask about. They often use the real estate agent who helped them purchase their personal residence, and who may have no experience in property management or investment properties. Both real estate agents and prospective purchasers will benefit from including as part of their purchase agreement "Addendum A" for residential properties, or a similar addendum for non-residential properties. (Figure 2).

ADDENDUM A

1. Seller to furnish to Buyer a written Personal Property Inventory list, through escrow, listing approximate date of purchase, model or serial no., and size/color. This is to include drapes, carpets, fixtures, appliances, etc., and shall specifically list what is included and what is excluded from the sales price.
2. Seller to transfer all security and other tenant deposits to Buyer through escrow.
3. Seller to furnish Buyer name, address, & phone number, at home and work, of all occupants over age 18. Seller to have each tenant fill out attached credit application, to be signed by tenant and delivered to Buyer through escrow. Until escrow is cancelled or closed, Seller shall not re-rent any apartment on other than a written month-to-month basis. Buyer must approve such rental agreement in writing and shall approve all new tenants.
4. Seller to furnish to buyer through escrow tenant rent record from the date of occupancy, or since January 1, 19____, showing date of payment, amount paid, type of payment (money order, cash, check, etc.), and concessions, gifts, or other offsets or incentives.
5. Seller to furnish buyer a copy of the past 12 months' utility expenses, including water, trash, insurance, tax, sewer, electric, and gas bills, within 15 days of opening of escrow.
6. Buyer to have walk-thru prior to close of escrow, including laundry area, carport/garage, storage, and individual unit interiors, plus an interior inspection within five days of acceptance of this offer.
7. Seller to furnish buyer current signed rental agreement that is in effect and any modifications, alterations, or additions that have been made. As a part of this agreement, tenant(s) to sign new rental agreement of buyer's choice, prior to close of escrow, or seller to have unit vacant.
8. Seller to furnish key(s) to all lock areas, including apartment unit doorknobs and deadbolts, mailbox locks, storage, laundry rooms, garages, fire extinguishers, timer boxes, security doors, etc.
9. Buyer to obtain roof, magnasite and driveway surface, pool, air condition, plumbing or electrical or general contractor or inspection service company inspection/certification, AT BUYER'S EXPENSE and buyer's choice of inspector; and, seller to furnish access to crawl space, decks, and areas for inspection purposes with such workmen, at no cost to the seller.
10. Seller to furnish buyer a skematic of all underground lines, including (but not limited to) water lines, sprinkler lines, sewer lines, gas/electric lines, septic/sewer/leech lines (if any), location of fire extinguishers; and
11. All yards to be trimmed, edged, mowed at close of escrow. All yard areas to be free of debris/trash/rubbish. All screens to fit properly with no holes in them. Fence to have no broken slats and stand correctly upright. Bushes/trees to be trimmed back. All window glass to be unbroken. All screen doors to be free of holes and to be hung correctly. All light globes to be unbroken. No plumbing leaks/drips to be present.
12. Seller to furnish buyer a copy of all trust deeds, trust notes, mortgages or underlying loans or contracts affecting subject property, including laundry machine, solar, pool maintenance, gardening or other agreements which are approved within 15 days from receipt.
13. Seller warrants that any and all work, materials and labor carried out which affects subject property at the close of escrow is paid in full by seller; and, seller specifically indemnifies buyer from any and all claims that may arise about said property by any person in this regard.
14. Seller shall comply with Californina Civil Code Section 1134.5 by disclosing to buyer, in writing through escrow, any known structural additions or alterations, or the installation, alteration, repair or replacement of any significant components of the structures upon the property and to disclose whether made with or without appropriate permits.
15. Seller to furnish buyer with a copy of all permits available, and a list of any prior claim affecting the property, such as any fire upon the premises, the death of any person, or any earthquake damage or repair.
16. Seller to furnish buyer with known government involvement with this private property transaction, including pending or actual rent control; units under any Housing Authority, Section 8 or other subsidised rental program; or, zone changes within a one-mile radius of the property; or, any other item which may affect subject property at close of escrow.

Paragraph 1

A personal property inventory is necessary for insurance coverage information. Should a loss occur through tenant theft or building fire, the carrier wants detailed data to calculate depreciation and replacement cost. For income tax purposes, the IRS has depreciation schedules for appliances, drapes, carpets, hot water tanks, and other features considered personal property, as opposed to the scheduled real property guidelines. Your replacement cost schedule would be based upon the age of appliances and other items in your management operations.

Paragraph 2

All tenant funds, held on behalf of the tenant until lease termination must be carefully accounted for. The property manager should hold these in a separate fund until they become rental income, or until paid to a workman for repair of damages, or until refunded to the tenant. (Tenant funds received by the owner are not taxable income if held by the property manager in a trust account, but are taxable in the year received if deposited into the owner's account.)

Sometimes purchasers use the tenant deposits as part of the purchase price. They reduce the amount of the downpayment by the amount of the transferred deposits. However, this is not a recommended practice. The escrow agent should be instructed to make out a separate check to the property manager or the owner's deposit fund.

All deposits transferred should be verified, in writing, with the tenants. Clearly define what the deposit was collected for: last month's rent, deposits, etc.

Paragraph 3

If the ownership of the building transfers several times, the new owner often has no way to contact the tenants, except by physically coming to their door unannounced. This can immediately lead to confrontations. Calling first for an appointment to introduce the new management and review the rental policies is more professional and courteous, and saves wasted trips to the property when no one is at home. When each tenant completes a rental application, his or her phone number should be included for just this kind of situation.

This information should be kept current. The tenant's workplace when he or she moved in several years ago may not be correct today. If any tenant refuses to fill out the current information, the quality of that tenant is suspect. Many times the bank bases its loan approval on the quality of the building tenants, and the bank may ask for this information.

Some sellers mistakenly believe that it is better to have anyone in the unit than a vacancy at the close of escrow. In fact, it is better to have a vacant, rent-ready unit than a poor-quality tenant in possession with the prospect of immediate eviction.

However, a vacant unit that is not rent-ready may mean an additional cost to the seller—deposits collected from the prior tenant may be inadequate to cover the costs of repair. It is therefore recommended that during the last 30 days prior to the close of escrow, the buyer or designated property manager review prospective tenants to avert future problems.

Paragraph 4

Tenants should be evaluated for the previous six or more months. A review of the rent roll determines the amount of turnover, how recent, and by whom. The buyer needs to determine why turnover occured to prevent future problems. Did everyone just move in to get a free microwave, even though rents were too high? Did all rents just get raised the month before the building went on the market? If the buyer is planning on increasing rents to meet the new loan payments, this can cause hostile tenants and additional vacancies.

What are the rental payment policies? The past operations may have called for collecting the rent from 25 units at $500 per month, with tenants paying in cash. The over $12,000 cash held by the on-site manager is not insurable in the event of loss. As crime in the cities increases, the opportunity for the manager to be physically injured is greater. Money orders cost tenants a little extra, but they give greater protection to both the manager and your rental payments. You must determine your policy for each property, as different types of units warrant varying considerations.

Paragraph 5

A review of expenses is important. It may even show why the property is for sale. For instance, perhaps there is a series of major repairs needed that the seller could not afford. All buildings incur replacement costs over time. If the seller just replaced the plumbing, the buyer will want to know this to estimate future reserve and replacement funds.

Good sources of information about the building's expenses are utility companies. They are helpful in giving amounts of past usage, future expectations of costs, and cost-saving recommendations. California's buyer/seller disclosure statement for income-producing property should include a seller's declaration on maintenance and expenses.

Paragraph 6

Too often, areas are inaccessible because keys are missing, no one knows who uses the storage areas, or someone doesn't want the present owner to sell. Finding a large hole in a wall between a storage or garage area with access from behind the couch in a unit, converted into an extra bedroom, is not surprising in today's overcrowded areas. Inspect areas for hazardous materials or highly flammable materials, like lawn mowers with gasoline cans. Check to see if the insurance is invalidated due to tenants having dangerous items on the premises.

Paragraph 7

With rental agreements, the form is not as important as the substance. Any written rental agreement is better than an oral one. Written contracts establish the names of the parties, amount of rent, due date, move-in date, and deposits. It often contains data on sub-leasing, overcrowding provisions, and other important matters. If there is no written agreement, get one.

The rental agreement should include provisions for sending notices for "Change in Terms of Tenancy," such as the rental due date, rental raises, and changes in who, where, or how to pay rent, etc.

With a written rental agreement, the landlord is awarded court costs and attorney fees in addition to rent and damages in an eviction action.

Paragraph 8

It is not unusual to drive by a building and see the outside lights on during daylight hours because the timer box keys were not transferred. No one has gotten around to sawing off the old locks and buying new locks and keys. Or, the prior gardener has the sprinkler control box key, and the new owner doesn't know how to reach the gardener. All of this process is unnecessary with just a little forethought. Asking for all keys saves the unnecessary expense of rekeying many areas. Include the fire extinguisher box lock.

It is not unusual for tenants to change the doorknob or dead bolt lock, or both, after they move in, and never let the manager know it, nor furnish anyone a key. This is especially true in areas of higher crime where new tenants believe old tenants, or their friends and relatives, or workmen may have keys to their apartment. Also, this is common in areas of very high rents, where tenants want privacy. Key access for repairs is discussed in the chapter on maintenance.

Paragraph 9

The buyer may wish to inspect the physical building for themselves, or hire a professional. An outside contractor, who may get the job if work is needed, is NOT a disinterested third party. Inspection services have become popular to assist in this area. Property managers are often consulted to give opinions on deferred maintenance.

Typically, crawl spaces are located in halls or closet ceilings of units. This allows the prospective buyer to see not only water stains on the inside rafters, but also the entire rental unit interior, which may otherwise not have been offered for viewing.

Paragraph 10

Many California areas are not connected to a city sewer and leech lines may be in place. Or an unsuspecting new duplex owner, digging trenches to install a sprinkler system may accidentally sever the gas line. It is best to get all permits from the city, and layout the lines, plus easement information from the title company. Many investors buy newly rezoned lots where only one structure previously existed. When they attempt to build a second unit, they discover it is over an irrigation well, a sewer line, or some other easement or right-of-way problem.

Paragraph 11

On-going minor maintenance and upkeep should be well maintained until the actual transfer is made to the purchaser. Sellers should keep the property extra sharp, not only to increase the appraised value (for loan purposes), but also to encourage tenants to stay pending possible rent increases. This also helps assure a quick resale should this transaction not close. It is good insurance for the seller.

Paragraph 12

Who collects the laundry room income? Who is the gardener or who takes care of the pool? Review the costs of all service contracts. When does it renew? What maintenance and services are excluded? Do the vendors have liability insurance? What is included in their fees? A prudent property manager wants this data for an analysis of which vendors should be replaced, retained, or renegotiated.

Paragraph 13

Ensuring all bills are paid in full averts the possibility of litigation in conjunction with mechanics' or vendors' liens.

Paragraph 14

It is standard today for California's disclosure agreement to include data on permits, etc. The buyer may not want the gardening/pool equipment shed that doesn't have a permit. The key here is that the disclosure is made.

Paragraph 15

The disclosures in this section deal with the items that property managers must disclose to prospective tenants, or that this buyer will need to disclose when a future sale occurs.

Paragraph 16

Any buyer of large city property should check with the local police for the crime index, and the drug- and gang-related activity around the subject property. Although the parties cannot warrant future activities, even based on past events, they should disclose the current situation.

Different investors may have additional items they want included in their purchase contract. But, by making "Addendum A" part of the transaction, the parties have used due diligence to comply with California real estate laws. By reviewing the items closely, you will find that there is little or no cost to complying with the items. Most of the items involve only time on someone's part to get the information or permits or keys. The Addendum helps protect all parties from future liability.

CHAPTER 4–QUIZ

1. The main reason for pre-purchase property management data is to:

   a. get the property back into shape for the price they are asking
   b. blow the deal because the agents won't disclose the information
   c. comply with California disclosure laws, and aid in the operations after the close of escrow
   d. show the present management what they lack, to obtain a better price for the property

2. The most costly United States Metropolitan housing areas are:

   a. Los Angeles to San Francisco and Washington, D.C., to New York
   b. Dallas/Fort Worth to Oklahoma City and the Tennessee Valley
   c. Tampa to Miami and Seattle to Portland
   d. Lansing to Grand Rapids and Akron to Toledo

3. Rent control usually does not affect:

   a. single-family residences
   b. 4 to 16 units
   c. 16 to 50 units
   d. over 50 units

4. The most off-site property management opportunities are in residential properties of:

   a. single-family residences
   b. duplexes
   c. triplexes
   d. 4 to 16 units

5. A major difference between a general partner and the limited partners is:

   a. insurance requirements
   b. liability
   c. tax considerations
   d. inflation

6. The property manager must check to see if the contract signer has property authority under all the following except:

   a. corporation
   b. partnership
   c. REIT
   d. individual owner

7. The largest landlord in the United States is:

   a. partnerships
   b. REITs
   c. the government
   d. corporations

8. Ownership goals for the present time would NOT include:

   a. cash flow
   b. diversification
   c. appreciation
   d. leverage

9. Non-monetary goals include:

   a. inflation
   b. amenities/aesthetics
   c. equity
   d. depreciation

10. The property manager must always manage property:

   a. to maximize profits
   b. according to the owner's objectives
   c. under the policies and procedures of the office
   d. as time and resources permit

CHAPTER 4–QUIZ ANSWERS

1. c
2. a
3. a
4. d
5. b
6. d
7. c
8. c
9. b
10. b

5

Income Property Valuation and Financial Analysis

References

Goldinger, Jay. "Standing on Solid Ground." *U.S. Air,* June 1988

Glickman, Les. "Estimating Real Estate Values with Capitalization Rates." *Real Estate Today,* Nov./Dec. 1987

Kaske, R.I. "Financial Planner, Rosemead, California." *Tax Service Newsletter,* Issue No. 6

Little, James. "Is IRR Overrated?" *Real Estate Today,* June 1985

McKenzie, Dennis, et al. *California Real Estate Principles.* 3rd ed. New York: Wiley & Sons, 1987

"Instructor Quarterly." *First Tuesday.* Winter 1988

Van Horne, James. *Fundamentals of Financial Management.* 4th ed. New Jersey: Prentice-Hall, 1980

Last Chapter Review

Before the property manager can effectively manage property, he or she must understand the property owner and his or her goals. Thus, the methods of property ownership and types of ownership goals were discussed. The basic benefits of owning different types of properties were also presented, to help property managers better match the owner with the appropriate type of property.

Chapter Overview

It is important for property managers to be familiar with the methods of valuing property. Owners, lenders, appraisers, and prospective purchasers vary in their manner and approach to value. Accounting and financial statements provide the basis for the analysis, which are reviewed in this chapter, along with the particular techniques for valuing property.

APPRAISAL DEFINED

An appraisal is an estimate or an opinion of value. An appraisal usually takes the form of a written statement, called an appraisal report, setting forth the appraiser's opinion of the value of a piece of property as of a given date.

The real value of the appraiser's estimate is that it is an expert, independent opinion of value. This objective value should be the basis for the actions of all parties to the transaction.

Appraisal
An estimate or opinion of value for a property as of a specific date and time made by a qualified appraiser.

VALUE DEFINED

The most common definition of value is "the present worth of future benefits." But value is in the eye of the beholder. Value has a different meaning according to the objectives of the individual or institution considering the property.

One method of classifying value is by considering the user value. Value in use is the value of a property to the existing owner. This **utility value** may include tax deductions, cash flows, or just having a roof over one's head. **Exchange value** is the value a property offers to an owner because of what this particular property can be traded for. This benefit may be the owner avoiding a capital gains tax by purchasing the property using the proceeds from the sale/exchange of a previously owned property. The **savings value** is the expectation of future appreciation in price, instead of the value of the current cash flow. It works like a forced savings account in that the owner will not receive the cash today, but can take advantage of the huge "savings balance" at the time of sale.

Subjective value is the emotional value the owner associates with the neighborhood, schools, proximity to work, and the status of the area.

The prospective purchaser bases a decision to buy on two other values. The value of the particular property is determined after looking at other properties in the place that are available within the same range or size, price, usage, neighborhood, and the like. This is referred to as **market value.** For example, if a great number of homes are for sale in an area featured on the ten o'clock news as having gang shootings and drug-related activities, a prospective purchaser could make a lower offer on several properties in the neighborhood, until one seller accepted.

The **investment value** is part of a prospective purchaser's decision to buy. This analysis is based upon the return of the real estate investment compared to non-real estate investments.

> **Example:** A couple gets a job transfer from a small mid western town to California. They would sell their acreage to purchase a relatively small California home. Conversely, the same family moving from California to the Midwest would rent out their California home, even at a loss, and would rent in the Midwest. This is because the California house valued at $200,000 and renting for $200 a month less than the loan payment loses $200 per month, and $2400 a year; but, the home increases in value by 10% a year, increasing its value by $20,000 that year. This investment value is the $20,000—$2,400 = $17,600 profit potential for the first year alone. Today's real estate buyers are acutely aware of real estate's hedge against inflation.

Lenders value a property according to their own guidelines. Their primary guideline is the **default value** of the real estate loan. They must be reasonably certain they can recover the loan amount on a particular property should the borrower default on the loan. **Liquidity value** is the amount the loan can be sold for in the secondary market. If the loan was made under the approved guidelines, the loan can be sold and the funds returned to the lender. Properties that do not have a liquidity value must be maintained and serviced in the lender's own portfolio.

The appraiser is assigned the task of placing a specific value on a property. It is based upon the highest and best use of the property, irrelevant to any other party's interest at the time. The appraiser values the property according to many factors.

VALUE FACTORS FOR SPECIFIC PROPERTY TYPE

There are specific characteristics that affect the value of certain types of property. For example, the neighborhood surroundings may be far more important in estimating the value of a luxury apartment project than in estimating the value of a heavy industrial manufacturing plant, such as a steel mill.

Industrial Property
• Special Use Design • Location • Market Activity • Current Trends

Industrial Property

Special Use Design. A lot of industrial property, particularly manufacturing property, is special-use property, which may be costly to convert to any other use. This results in a higher rate of functional obsolescence (defined and discussed later in this chapter) than for other types of property, and also results in a greater reliance on the cost approach in appraising industrial property.

Location. Industrial property requires a location close to: raw materials, or transportation facilities for the finished products; public transportation; housing; recreation areas; schools and other amenities for employees; and affordable fuel and utilities.

Market Activity. Historically, less market speculation existed in industrial property because of its special use nature. Buildings were constructed to fit a specific tenant's needs. Greater emphasis was placed on the cost approach of appraisal because of its special use design. Fewer market comparables existed, so the market data approach was not very practical. Much industrial property was owner-occupied, which resulted in little comparable rental data to use for an income approach to value. For the lender involved in a transaction, this resulted in greater reliance on the financial position of the borrower and less on the value of the property than is true with other income property loans.

Current Trends. Many large industrial parks have been built in California. These are often built to house types of industries, rather than a specific tenant. They are built to accommodate the linear pattern of materials handling, with large storage areas for finished products. Commonly found in the outlying suburban growth pattern California communities, proximity to airport and trucking-freeway patterns is particularly valuable.

Examples of these industrial parks include the Ontario Airport and Silicon Valley facilities. The Ontario Airport area in Southern California encompasses three major railroad lines, half a dozen freeways, and an international airport that can accommodate the largest planes made. Hundreds of thousands of square feet of speculative industrial and warehouse space was built to accommodate unknown tenants. Silicon Valley, likewise, was constructed to house high-tech users without specific owner user or previously agreed upon, built-to-suit tenants. With this kind of development, rental rates and even sales data should become more readily available.

Retail Store
• Economy • Lease

Retail Store

Economy. National, regional, and local economies affect the value of retail store property. Information regarding the buying power of potential customers is extremely important. This buying potential must be measured against the number of existing and proposed retail outlets to see if the customers expansion ability has been reached.

The value in retail property is based on the expected number of customers who can be attracted to the property and how much they will buy.

Lease. The appraisal must include a thorough analysis of the existing lease(s) for pass-through expenses, in addition to base rents.

Shopping Center
• Entirety

Shopping Center

Entirety. A shopping center is valued as a whole. Parking is common to the entire center. The anchor positions are usually the tenants for the magnet department store(s) around which the shopping center is designed. They are expected to act as the main draw to attract shoppers, which benefits all other retail stores in the center.

Strip Shopping Centers are retail stores clustered without a major tenant. They vary widely in mix, but theme centers tend to fare better than incompatible mixed-use stores. For example, a center dominated by several clothes, shoe, and jewelry stores, plus health food, hair salon and barber shops that exist in a center makes it inappropriate for a vacancy to be filled with an automotive store, rather than a cleaners.

A **market survey** is required of the area from which the center is likely to draw customers to find the number of families in each income bracket.

Office Buildings
• Location • Negative Elements

Office Buildings

Location. Convenience to transportation, stores, banks, restaurants, and the prestige of the location rate high.

Negative Elements. With population growth rates in California at high rates, many speculative office buildings were constructed. The primary locations, such as downtowns and airport centers have remained in demand. Secondary locations, however, have suffered extensive problems attributed to high vacancy factors.

Motels, Hotels, Lodges
• Location • Appearance • Amenities • Income

Motels, Hotels, Lodges

Location. Access from freeways or highways and prominence (easily observed or marked for visibility) are of utmost importance to motel-type facilities.

Appearance. The initial appearance of physical facilities is extremely important in attracting and keeping patronage. Therefore, there is more emphasis on clean, modern appearances and on good maintenance programs.

Amenities. The elements that instill customer loyalty include the many features available on or near the facility. These can include a pool, spa, jacuzzi, lounge, and room services. Airport pick-up, laundry/valet, and a barber shop also add value. Many motel-type facilities have exchange agreements for patron usage to near-by health clubs, recreation center discounts, or the like, which are part of the valuation.

Income. A motel is more likely to have significant income from sources other than rent, such as food and beverage sales, cable television, vending machines, and the like. These are included in estimating value through the income approach.

Apartment Building
• Location and Neighborhood • Nuisances • Maintenance and Management

Apartment Building

Location and Neighborhood. Proximity of public transportation, reputation of schools, convenience to shopping, types of churches, variety of recreational facilities, and the general tone of the area are important.

Nuisances. Excessive noise, busy streets, crime rates, and smoke or odors from manufacturing plants are detrimental.

Maintenance and Management. The curb appeal (the exterior appearance) affects the ability to attract the high quality tenants. The long-term value of the physical structure is affected by the maintenance of the property. Deferred maintenance would have a large impact on the property value.

METHODS OF APPRAISAL

Property is appraised in an orderly and systematic manner. While there is no official standardized procedure, appraisers generally carry out the appraisal process in a series of steps.

First, they identify the property, namely that of clarifying the value of the property for a particular purpose. Then they determine the kinds of data needed and where it can be found. For example, the appraiser may need to track down information on the population trend and economic circumstances for a particular area. The appraiser then seeks out the necessary information.

The next step is to take the information gathered and use it to apply one or more of the three valuation approaches: the cost approach, the income approach, and the market data approach. After arriving at estimates of value using the various appraisal approaches, the appraiser correlates these values into one final estimate of value and presents that value in the form of an appraisal report.

Cost Approach to Value

The cost approach to value is one of the three methods of appraisal. The cost approach involves estimating the cost to reproduce or replace existing buildings, deducting accrued depreciation, then adding the estimated value of the site (**land value**). The land value may be based on comparable sales of lots. The current replacement cost for new construction is fairly easy to obtain, but actually computing the accrued depreciation is difficult.

Because the cost approach involves estimating the value of the land and buildings separately, then adding them together, it is sometimes called the **summation method.**

It is generally assumed that the cost method identifies the ceiling of the market value because buyers will not pay more for property than it would cost them to replace it, provided there would be no costly delay in finding the replacement. This method is primarily used for newly constructed buildings, public buildings (schools, libraries), special purpose property, and unique property (historic landmarks).

Replacement Cost Methods. There are three ways to estimate the replacement cost of a building:

- the square foot method,
- the unit-in-place method, and
- the quantity survey method.

Square Foot. The square foot method involves multiplying the cost per square foot of a recently built comparable structure by the number of square feet in the subject property. Because it involves comparing costs, it is sometimes called the **comparative cost method.** It is the method most often used by appraisers.

The comparable building is not likely to be exactly the same as the building being appraised because there will be variations in design, shape, and grade of construction that will moderately or substantially affect the square foot costs. The appraiser must make refinements in his estimates to reflect the cost variations. When a comparable new building is not available, the appraiser relies on current manuals for basic construction costs.

Unit-in-Place. This method involves a series of estimates of the cost to replace specific component parts of the building. The estimates use cost measurements, such as square or cubic feet, when defining the replacement costs of the various components.

For example, one of the estimates might be "X" dollars for each 100 square feet of roofing. Another might be "X" dollars per cubic feet of concrete. By using this method, the appraiser estimates separately the cost to replace all of the structure's component parts, adding them together in the end, thus finding the replacement cost of the structure itself.

Quantity Survey. Sometimes called **price take-off method,** a quantity survey involves a detailed estimate of the quantities and prices of construction materials, as well as the costs of installation (labor). These are added together, then the indirect costs (building permit, survey, builder's overhead and profit) are summed together for the replacement cost estimate.

Depreciation. Depreciation is the difference between the value of the existing improvements and the cost of replacing them. It represents a loss in value due to age, neglect, undesirable features within the property, or negative influences from outside the property.

When appraising a used property, the value is determined by estimating the replacement cost, deducting the depreciation, then adding the value of the land. In the absence of extraordinary circumstances, a used building is not worth as much as a new one. The difference is the depreciation.

Estimating depreciation accurately is the most difficult phase of the replacement cost valuation technique. In many cases, the depreciation estimates are highly subjective. They are, of course, only as reliable as the judgment and skills of the appraiser making the estimates.

Depreciation takes three forms: physical deterioration, functional obsolescence, and economic obsolescence.

Physical Deterioration. This depreciation is also called **deferred maintenance** because the loss of value is evident by wear and tear, decay, cracks, and structural defects. It is usually the most obvious form of depreciation. The extent of physical deterioration is measured by the cost to correct it. Accordingly, it is the simplest kind of depreciation to spot and estimate. Physical deterioration may be **curable** or **incurable.**

When looking at a building that is in overall good condition, but has badly peeling facial boards and wood surfaces, it is fairly easy to get estimates on the cost to quickly scrape, fill cracks, repaint and seal all exterior wood surfaces—these are curable. If, when looking at the foundation boards, rafters and beams, it is clearly visible that dryrot and termites have eaten so much of the wood that the building is about to fall down—these may be incurable.

Functional Obsolescence. This is a loss in value due to functional inadequacies, such as poor floor plan, unappealing design, or outdated fixtures. For example, an office building in a warm climate without air conditioning, or a two-story retail store without an elevator or escalator would suffer from functional obsolescence.

The appraiser will classify functional obsolescence as either **curable** or **incurable.** The determination is usually based on the economic feasibility of correcting the problem. For example, old wooden windows that do not slide open due to layers of paint and swelling of the wood may be replaced with modern metal casement windows at a reasonable cost according to today's standards. Large, central columns found in the center of old five-and-ten-cent stores may cost too much to remove, as they give the ceiling support, and a change would involve removing the roof and resupporting the structure.

Economic Obsolescence. This represents value losses from causes outside the property. It is a kind of depreciation resulting from the action of forces beyond a property owner's control. As a result, it is virtually always incurable. Examples include: zoning changes; neighborhood deterioration; adverse changes in traffic patterns, where a new freeway reroutes traffic away from a motel; exposure to nuisances, such as noise from airport proximity for an apartment complex.

Comparative Market Value Approach

The market data approach to value involves comparing market information of properties of a certain kind and class against the features of the property being appraised.

Appraisers use this method whenever possible, because it reveals the actions of buyers and sellers in the marketplace. Where there is an adequate number of recent sales of similar properties, the value indicated by the market data technique can be very reliable.

In the application of this technique, it is the appraiser's task to gather pertinent information about comparable sales, making feature-by-feature comparison against the subject property, then translating these findings into the appraiser's opinion of the value.

Elements. Usable comparable properties are sometimes in short supply because they often have many dissimilar characteristics which makes it more difficult for the appraiser. Market data is the method most often used when appraising single-family residences because there is more often ample comparable sales data to assist the appraiser in his quest for value. Overwhelmingly, single-family residential sales account for the majority of real estate sales nationwide. Ideally, an appraiser wants at least three to five reliable comparables before there is enough data to form and support an opinion of value.

Value. This approach is based upon the concept that the value of similar properties are determined by the supply and demand in the open market place. The property should be on the market a reasonable length of time, and sold in an arm's length transaction between a willing buyer and willing seller, neither of which are under undue pressure to act, and both of which have agreed upon a price and the terms of sale.

For example, if there are five fourplexes on each side of a street, and there were three recent sales by three different sellers, and three different buyers who did not know each other, the sales price of those properties would indicate a valid comparable value of fourplexes on that street.

Elements of Comparison
• Time • Location • Physical Condition • Financing Terms • Terms of Sale

Elements of Comparison. When using the market data approach for income property, the primary elements of comparison are time, location, physical characteristics, and financing terms.

Time. Recent sales will be a more reliable indication of market values than sales from the distant past. Economic conditions change so that in just a few months significant changes can occur. If the change is a steady, measurable increase or decrease in property values in the area, the appraiser makes adjustments to compensate for the affected value.

Location. Finding identical structures in the same neighborhood is not always easy. But, the closer in location to the subject property, the more likely it will be that the price will provide a meaningful guide to the value.

Physical Condition. This includes both the site and the structures. Important site comparisons are frontage, depth, area, landscaping, and contour. Building characteristics include the number of units, square footage, quality of construction, age, and functional utilities.

Financing Terms. In markets where interest rates are higher, financing terms have a greater impact on the sales price. Typically, buyers are willing to pay more for a property where the seller will give an extension of credit to the buyer (a loan) at a low interest rate or with low initial payments, as part of the financing.

Terms of Sale. The price paid for a comparable property can only be used if the sale of that comparable was an "arm's length transaction." This means that the sale must have been:

- a transaction between a willing buyer and willing seller,
- when neither party was under any undue pressure to act,
- when both were aware of material facts affecting the value of the property, and
- the property was exposed to the market for a reasonable period of time.

Once the appraiser has found a sufficient number of comparable properties, he or she can compare them to the subject property and thus estimate the value of the subject property.

Income Approach To Value

The income approach to value is based on today's value of projected future income. It is the method most often used to value income-producing property.

The value is derived by taking the total possible gross income (GI), subtracting an estimated vacancy factor and uncollectible rents (a percentage of GI) to arrive at the effective gross income (EGI).

total gross income − vacancy/bad debt factor = effective gross income

The annual operating expenses (OE) are then subtracted to obtain the net operating income (NOI). This figure represents the building's income after the building's expenses, but does not include the property owner's loan/debt service (DS) nor personal income taxes.

effective gross income − operating expenses = net operating income

The appraiser then uses an overall rate of return common to the type of property for the particular area. This percentage is called the **capitalization rate** (cap rate). The value of the property is derived by dividing the NOI by the cap rate.

net operating income ÷ capitalization cap = value

Often, the appraiser uses a cap rate that is different from an actual purchaser's expectation of returns. The seller's motivation, existing and projected returns, and individual circumstances influence and vary actual rates.

Several problems are associated with the use of the income approach to value. For example, vacancies and bad debts may vary widely due to turnover, evictions, management changes, and similar factors. Thus effective gross income figures may change a great deal from month to month. Another common problem is accurately estimating operation expenses, which vary widely between building owners.

Contract Rent vs. Economic Rent. To use the income approach to value, you must first determine the property's net income by estimating the potential rents and other income of the property. If the space were vacant, rent-ready, and presently available for rent on the open market, the amount of rent the unit could earn is called **economic rent.** This amount is often different from what the actual unit rents are currently earning, which is called **contract rent.**

The income approach is based upon the theory that an investment property's value is the price an informed investor will pay today for the net income produced over the balance of the property's economic life.

Figure 1

Income Approach

If the property is appraised using a capitalization rate of 11%, what will the estimated value be?

POTENTIAL GROSS INCOME	
Rents:	
10 × $900/mo. x 12 =	*$108,000.00*
10 × $960/mo. x 12 =	*115,200.00*
15 × $1,035/mo. x 12 =	*186,300.00*
15 × $1,080/mo. x 12 =	*+ 194,400.00*
	603,900.00
Bad debts/vacancies	*− 30,195.00*
Total potential gross income	*$573,705.00*
Coin machines	*+ 4,950.00*
EFFECTIVE GROSS INCOME	*$578,655.00*
EXPENSES	
Fixed Expenses:	
Property taxes	*$76,500.00*
Insurance premiums	*+ 8,875.00*
	$85,375.00
Variable expenses:	
Management *($573,705.00 × 6%)*	*$34,422.30*
Janitorial services	*24,300.00*
Electricity	*9,000.00*
Water & sewer	*4,050.00*
Repairs, maintenance	*+ 35,500.00*
	$107,272.30
Reserves for replacement:	
Appliances	*9,500.00*
Carpet	*24,000.00*
Roof	*+ 1,750.00*
	$35,250.00

Fixed expenses	$85,375.00
Variable expenses	107,272.30
Reserves	+ 35,250.00
TOTAL EXPENSES	$227,897.30

Effective gross income	578,655.00
Total expenses	– 227,897.30
NET INCOME	$350,757.70

Value = Net Income ÷ Capitalization Rate
Value = $350,757.70 ÷ .11
Value = $3,188,706.40

According to the income approach, the building is worth approximately $3,188,706.40.

So, the investor is more concerned with the property's **earnings potential** (economic rent) than it is with today's actual earnings (contract rent). Of course, to estimate earnings potential you must take into account rent control ordinances, if any.

Contract rent that has already been paid is called **historic rent.** Historic rent is often a reliable indication of the property's earnings potential, and can indicate the present owner's motivation for selling.

Both investors and property managers should be wary of purchasing /managing a property when the current owner/manager advocates an immediate rental increase to justify a purchase price/value. Buildings are often sold with the idea that the rents can be immediately raised to pay for an inflated purchase price. Many times, sellers raise their rents just before the property went on the market, so additional rent increases after the close of escrow create additional vacancies and loss of income. Often, market conditions make it difficult to get tenants to pay the rents necessary to generate enough income to carry the building.

Figure 2

Unit#	Current Rent	Increases	Comparable Rent
		2-Bachelor Units	
31	340	0	340
32	340	0	340
		12 - 1 Bedroom, 1 Bath	
5	375		395
10	370	5	395
11	365	10	395
12	375		395
13	365	10	395
14	365	10	395
19	370	5	395
24	375		395
25	375		395
26	375		395
27	355	20	395
28	375		395
		Increase $60/Month	
		16 - 2 Bedroom, 1 Bath	
1	490	35	525
2	490	35	525
3	500	25	525
6	500	25	525
7	491	34	525
8	525		525
15	490	35	525
16	485	40	525
17	495	30	525
20	458	67	525
21	500	25	525
22	491	34	525
29	500	25	525
30	485	40	525
33	525		525
34	515	10	525
		Increase $460/Month	
		4 - 3 Bedroom, 1½ Bath	
4	595	30	625
9	569	56	625
18	600	25	625
23	625		625
		Increase $111/Month	

	Historic Rents	Proj. Contract Rent	Economic Rent
	$15,449	$16,080	$16,320
	× 12	× 12	× 12
Annual Gross	$185,388	$192,960	$195,840

† Value of building (assuming value is 8 times gross income)

	† = $1,483,104	† = $1,543,680	† = $1,566,720

Evaluating Rentals. A property may be offered for sale by a local broker using the California Association of Realtors form. Some information is given about the existing loans, acceptable new loans, property features, income, expenses, and investment information on these forms. Many listings show only the annual income, and do not show the monthly rent per unit.

By evaluating the rentals on a per unit basis, along with unit size, the prospective purchaser can determine whether the total rental income can be increased. For example, income data could be analyzed as shown in Figure 2. In this example, the highest current rent for a one-bedroom is \$375 per month, yet some units are only paying \$355, \$365, or \$370. By increasing the amount of rent for the various units, all units of the same size will be generating the same amount of rent. This would increase rental income by \$60 per month for the one-bedrooms. The same would be done for the two-bedroom units, so all 16 would be at \$525 per month. Three of the four-bedroom units would be raised to \$625 per month. The bachelor unit rents would remain the same, at \$340 per month.

The historical rent is indicated in the "Current Rents" column on Figure 2: \$15,449 per month. The contract rent could be the "increase" column—\$16,080 per month, by using the subject property comparable rent for comparable units. The economic rent may show that the neighboring buildings are getting \$340 per month for bachelor units, \$395 per month for one bedrooms, \$525 per month for the two bedrooms,and \$625 per month for three bedrooms. Thus the economic rental income would be:

$$[\{\$340 \times 2\} + \{\$395 \times 12\} + \{\$525 \times 16\} + \{\$625 \times 4\}] = \$16{,}320$$

Other Income. Other income is too often overlooked when evaluating a property's value. A prime example is the money generated by laundry rooms and vending machines. This is one area where the operating income can often be substantially increased with improved management.

Ways To Increase Income. In the larger metropolitan areas of the city, storage space is at a premium. Garages and storage areas can be rented separately from the units. Of course, the tenant must agree not to use the space for human or animal habitation or for the storage of flammable or hazardous materials.

The property manager must remember not to sell garage or parking spaces to other persons until the city requirements for tenant parking are met. However, this source of additional income is very popular in densely populated areas.

In the example given in Figure 2, the rental income was shown to currently be $15,449 per month, for an annual rental income of $185,388, not including any laundry room income for the 34 units. If the laundry room income was $300 per month, the annual income would be $3600. At a gross rent multiplier of eight, the increased value of the building would be $28,800, or about $850 per unit increased value, using the income approach.

Laundry rooms are an important, often overlooked, source of income. They can be handled in one of three ways. The building owner can own the machines and service, insure, depreciate washer(s), dryer(s), and the room itself. The staff empties the coin boxes, and sorts, counts, and deposits the funds. Regular inspections of equipment should be scheduled.

Another popular method is to have an outside vendor handle all phases of the operation, and just send the owner a check for the owner's portion of the total income. This is the simplest and quickest method. The vendor owns the machines, pays the appropriate city tax to operate at your building, has its own workman's compensation insurance, and pays its own employee taxes. For smaller buildings where on-site personnel are not required, this relieves the owner from having to maintain the insurance and taxes, and the burden of liability of having a tenant handling the laundry room funds. The vendor keeps the machines clean and operable. It has the key to the coin box, collects the money, deposits it, and writes the owner a check for a percentage of the total income. This method increases the net income of the building, because it is an amount that is received after expenses are deducted.

The third method is a new system, one that is still not available in many smaller California communities. If available, however, it has many advantages, especially in the larger cities. The machines are operated by a card instead of coins. The property manager sells the cards to the tenant. If the rate is raised or lowered, the card is sold for more or for less. No physical alteration to the equipment is necessary. As there is no money in a coin box, there is no money available on the premises. This can be a major advantage in some areas where theft and burglary rates are high.

This eliminates a major reason for breaking into the room and destroying the equipment. The cost of repairs are significantly reduced.

When evaluating laundry room income, include determining if the machines are set at too low a rate, thus generating an inadequate income to offset the cost to maintain the system. By selling the cards at a fixed price, the income is generated whether the machine is used or not. The card may have ten or twenty-five usages per card. If the card is lost, stolen, or unused, it still was originally purchased by the tenant for all the allowable usages. And it's more convenient for the tenant because he or she doesn't have to keep change on hand to do laundry.

Another source of overlooked income is vending machines and video games. The laundry room can also dispense soap, bleach, and fabric softener in machines. Central pool and recreation area sites can have video machines. These can bring in extra hundreds of dollars of total income per year. Some managers discourage these because of the extra clean-up required around these high use areas. But if properly trained personnel know how to manage these areas with enforced, posted hours and locked, secure doors, this can mean additional revenue, and greatly increased total building value.

Bad Debt Vacancy Factor. It is unrealistic to expect a rental property to be fully occupied throughout its productive life. Vacancies must be expected. Also, there will inevitably be tenants who do not pay their rent. An allowance is made for these vacancies and unpaid rents. Called the **bad debt vacancy factor,** this expense is usually calculated as a percentage of the gross income. It is deducted from potential gross income (PGI) to determine the **effective gross income** (EGI).

The vacancy and collection loss factor can vary widely depending upon economic conditions, the local market, the type of property and the management. For apartment houses and office buildings, vacancy factors may range from 5% to 10%. For some types of property, such as motels and hotels, the vacancy factor may be as high as 30% to 40%. Due to available construction funds, overbuilding of smaller neighborhood strip shopping centers in secondary locations in California has lead to vacancy rates exceeding 50% in many areas.

Expenses Analysis. From the effective gross income, expenses are deducted that are connected with operating the building. These are called

operating expenses. They fall into three classifications, and may be fixed or variable expenses:

- fixed expenses,
- maintenance expenses, and
- reserves for replacement.

Fixed expenses. These include real estate taxes, hazard insurance, permits, license fees, and administrative costs.

Variable expenses. These include the **maintenance expenses** such as utilities, supplies, cleaning, painting and decorating, grounds and pool services, building employee wages, and repairs.

Reserves for Replacement. These are budgeted allowances set aside to replace building and equipment items expected to wear out before the transfer in ownership of the building. They are variable, in that a prudent property manager will need to increase these at some cost-of-living ratio to offset the future increased cost of labor and materials. Included are items such as roof, heating equipment, air conditioners, and major appliances.

Reducing Expenses. The best way to increase the income of a property, and thus the building's value, is to decrease the expenses. A careful analysis of all expenses helps the property manager focus on areas that are out of line. There are many ways to accomplish this task.

Many expenses can be decreased through tenant-awareness programs. For example, utility companies offer various water saving devises. A brochure to review with the tenant can be obtained from many local water districts. Utility companies have an energy study program, where if the property manager requests them to go through the property, they will assist the tenant and landlord. They will indicate all the high use and non-energy efficient areas. Such programs help everyone.

An experienced property manager watches for increases in expenses when rents are raised. Increased vandalism may be the result of tenant hostility, and may include such things as broken exterior lighting, water lines, and sprinkler heads; graffiti; trash and glass in parking areas; and damage to the grounds.

The property manager should analyze the expense figures for non-essentials. If the laundry room utility expenses for gas, water, and lights amounts to $110 per month, and the total income generated is only $100 per month, there is a problem. Considering the added costs to keep the area clean, it may be advisable to shut down the laundry room facility. The room could be rented as a storage room to generate income with a corresponding decrease in expenses.

Many property management firms handle such a large number of units within a given area that their in-house computer analysis can calculate data on price per square foot, average income per unit, total income, and average expenses. The more units in the data base, the greater the degree of accuracy and the better the comparison for specific buildings.

The Institute of Real Estate Management (IREM) publishes an annual report that shows major categories of expenses. (The report can be purchased. However, if you contribute your building's data to IREM, you may be able to receive a credit towards the price.) The property manager can compare the performance of his or her building with the regional report, and then better analyze the maintenance and operating expense ratios. A sample portion of the report, covering 1983 through 1987 is shown in Figure 3.

For example, most property in California has had a large increase in insurance costs over the past few years. But, how does our building compare to the average in our area? Category 4 of Figure 3 indicates the following guidelines:

1983—9.2%
1984—9.2%
1985—8.4%
1986—9.4%
1987—10.4%

If our building has had about a 1% increase in taxes and insurance over the past five years, it is operating in line with similar properties and other owners within our area. If the building expenses far exceed these amounts, the property manager would check to see if a tax revaluation could lower the costs. The property manager would obtain competitive bids for similar coverage to see if insurance costs could be decreased. A thorough analysis of the present coverage could be made to see if noncritical coverage could be dropped. Insurance coverage is discussed more thoroughly in Chapter 14.

Figure 3

GRAPHIC ILLUSTRATION

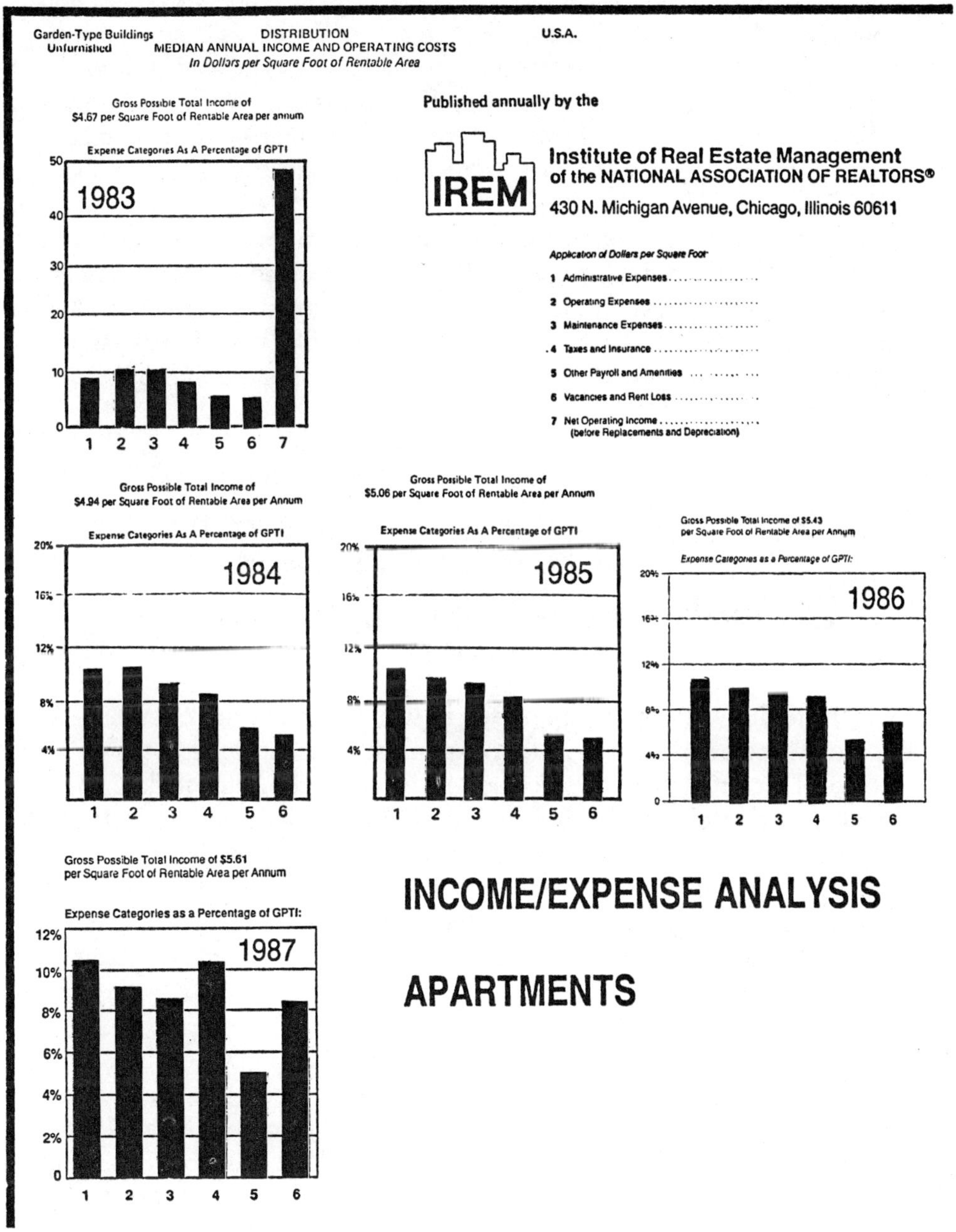

The Institute of Real Estate Management publishes in its Annual Income and Expenses Analysis the average costs of expenses by the type of building. Sections of the report cover elevator buildings, high-rise, and low-rise units. For example, the average cost of expenses in some northern California areas have exceeded the national average of 9.32% for the past five years, and are far higher than the Western regional average of 7.3% for the same time. Most of the cities are below the regional average. This comparison indicates total operating expenses average about 36.75% in California.

Suppose for the property shown in Figure 2, taxes and insurance run about 14.5% of present income, or 13.7% of projected income for a new buyer. This is higher than the national, state, regional, and metropolitan area averages. A decrease in expenses by only 5% would increase the value of the building by $23,400, assuming expenses are $58,650, with eight times gross.

$185,388 × 8 = $1,483,104 value

$185,388 (income) + $2,932.50 (expenses $58,650 × 5%)
= $188,320.50 × 8 = $1,506,564

$1,506,564 (new value) – (less) $1,483,104 (old value)
= $23,460 increased value

Note that the income approach to value uses the net operating income. There are, however, other expenses. These include the owner's personal income taxes, depreciation reserves, and mortgage/loan payments, called **debt service.** These items are not deducted from the effective gross income and are not considered operating expenses from an appraisal standpoint. However, they are a major consideration from the lender's point of view and for both the prospective purchaser and property manager in valuing the building with regards to financing terms.

SHORT-TERM INVESTORS

In the example given in Figure 2, the rental income is $15,449 per month, for an annual $185,388 income, and a value of $1,483,104. (The calculations are shown at the bottom of Figure 2.) Projected contract rent increases increased the building's value to $1,543,680. And the projected economic rent of $16,320 increased the annual rental income to $195,840. The economic rent increased the value to $1,566,720.

An appraiser would use the actual rental income data, and an appraised value of $1,483,104 would be justified. The seller would value the building by using the projected contract rents, for a building value of $1,543,680 (Note: the seller is asking $1,500,000, rounding down). Notwithstanding rent control areas, the property manager would project the value according to economic rent, with a value of $1,566,720. The difference amounts to $66,720 and represents 4.45% of the $1,500,000 asking price, which is a normal market difference between a seller's asking price and a buyer's offering price—but is a substantial variation in dollar amount.

Further, when the appraiser uses existing rents and gets an appraised value of $1,483,104 when market rents could be at $1,566,720, the $83,616 difference is too often an incentive for the short-term money investor to buy the building. This type of investor buys the building, raises the rents to market rates without doing any maintenance or long-term planning, then immediately puts the property back on the market, merely to reap a quick profit of about $80,000 in a relatively short period of time.

Capitalization. The process of converting income produced by an investment property into a meaningful value is called **capitalization.** The mathematical procedure is expressed as follows:

Annual Net Operating Income ÷ Capitalization Rate = Value

If Net Operating income were $118,500, the cap rate would be figured:

$$\$118{,}500 \div \text{cap rate} = \$1{,}500{,}000$$
$$\$118{,}500 \div \$1{,}500{,}000 = \text{cap rate}$$
$$\text{cap rate} = 7.9\%$$

The **capitalization rate** is the rate of return an investor receives or seeks to receive on a particular investment according to the amount of risk involved and the amount of management required for the investment.

Ordinarily, income-producing property is purchased for investment purposes. The investor seeks a certain rate of return on the capital invested in the property, including both the initial downpayment and the outgoing cash flows during the holding period. When the desired return is selected, the equation shown above indicates the maximum price the investor is willing to pay.

Capitalization Rate Selection. The appraiser determines the overall capitalization rate by comparing several similar income properties. To be reliable, the properties must be comparable (land, building, and income flow) to the subject property. This is called the **direct comparison** or **direct capitalization rate.**

In May 1989, Long Beach Savings and Loan Associations' Real Estate Loan Division for apartment building capitalization rates guidelines indicated 8½% as a common cap rate, and a range of 8% to 10% for Southern California—except in rent control areas, where West Los Angeles and Beverly Hills used 7½% cap rates.

The cap rate chosen has a great effect on the value of the property. In the previous example, the building had a 7.9% cap rate—the seller is offering the purchaser the opportunity to earn this amount on his or her investment. If, however, an investor insisted on a return of at least 10% (a 10% cap rate), the purchaser would only offer to pay $1,185,630 for the building. An investor who wanted only a 6% return would be willing to offer as much as $1,975,000 for the building.

Regardless of how the capitalization rate is selected, two very important considerations are the quality and durability of the investment property's income. Quality and durability influence the risk factor. The greater the risk, the higher the capitalization rate and the lower the value. Quality refers to the likelihood that the income will be received (do the tenants pay?) and durability refers to the length of time the income may be expected to continue (leases or month-to-month tenancies?).

INVESTMENT ANALYSIS

Various methods of analyzing a real estate investment are used by the different persons involved in a transaction. The "return" an investor wants has distinct meanings when discussed by a buyer or seller or attorney, accountant, real estate agent, or financial planner. The property manager must be familiar with not only the numerous methods, but also their advantages and weaknesses in order to help advise the owner.

Gross Rent Multiplier (GRM). As the name indicates, this method uses the annual gross income. The higher the GRM, the better the area and higher the property price. A low GRM indicates a poor area, long-term rent control, or deferred maintenance. Used primarily because it is fairly easy to master in a short time, GRM disregards all expenses—operational, past performance, and projected building requirements. Investors who use this method use a flat percentage figure for their prediction of expenses, like 35% of income.

Capitalization Rate. This method converts the annual net operating income into a capital sum, so an investor can compare the real estate return to alternative investment option rates. Investors who use this method for income property analysis expect two types of return:

- return **of** the investment (**recapture**), and
- return **on** the investment (**interest**)

The recapture and interest rate together comprise the capitalization rate. The recapture rate takes into consideration risk premium, meaning the amount of potential risk, or the amount of safety, for this type of investment as opposed to other ventures. The interest rate is the return that the owner receives on all cash invested into the property, including the original downpayment, and all cash outlays during the holding period. The two elements may be considered separately or together. An overall capitalization rate includes both.

For example, if the conservative rate of return (the rate for T-bills, bonds, etc.) were 7%, and the investor needed a 1% non-liquidity factor (because of the time, effort, and money to sell), and a 1½% risk premium (because of poor neighborhood, deferred maintenance, or poor quality tenants), the investor would require a cap rate of 9½% before purchasing the building.

Internal Rate of Return (IRR). This method takes the discounted cash flow that is the basis of the valuation and takes into account both the magnitude (amount of dollars received) and the timing (when the money will be received) of the expected cash flows.

Internal Rate of Return
The IRR for an investment proposal is the discounted rate that equates the present value of the expected cash outflows with the present value of the expected inflows.

When the property manager uses an IRR to value a building, several features of this method must be noted. One problem is that when investment cash flows alternate between positive (future cash flow incomes) and negative (initial investment outlay/downpayment), it is possible to have multiple rates of return, which confuses investors. Because future negative cash flows (capital improvement expenditures) are often required, these future cash outflows should be considered part of the cost of the investment.

An alternative would be to use a modified IRR that could handle the reinvestment rate and multiple rates of return in the analysis of the investor's cash flows. In the final analysis, if the IRR exceeds the rate required by the investor for his or her return yield, the project is acceptable to the purchaser. If the IRR is less than the minimum required rate of return, the building is rejected.

This method requires the property manager to look carefully at the operating expenses and projected maintenance and rehabilitation costs. Expert opinions, such as contractor bids, are advised in addition to obtaining inspection certificates by professionals at the onset of the analysis. But, if done correctly, this method is an excellent way to evaluate a building's worth.

Net Present Value (NPV). Similar in many respects to IRR, the present value method is a discounted cash flow approach to capital budgeting. All of the cash flows are discounted back to the present using the required rate of return as prescribed by the investor. In other words, why purchase this investment if it cannot yield at least as much as other investments?

In the present value method, if the discounted cash flows are equal to or greater than zero "0," the proposed building is acceptable. If the sum of the discounted cash flows is less than "0," the project is rejected. In other words, the acceptable criteria is that the present value of cash inflows exceed the present value of cash outflows. In the end, the building was a cash break-even—so that the investor yielded the tax deduction items during the holding period, and received the appreciation value at time of resale.

Investor's Valuation. Each investment evaluation method has strengths and weaknesses. The basic differences are based on how each investor perceives the data. Some look at the present income, others at the future income. Some take expenses into consideration, others do not. Some want to value a dollar received today higher than a dollar received a year from today. The property manager needs to understand each method so they can competently talk to individual investors, appraisers, and lenders.

FINANCING ANALYSIS

As a property manager, you may be involved in analyzing the property's financing. Income property financing is a complex subject, and this section is by no means meant to make you an expert on it. However, there are some very basic principles of income property financing that you should be familiar with.

Most income-producing properties managed by property managers are nonowner-occupied. Lenders feel that nonowner-occupied property is more of a risk than owner-occupied property. This is because lenders feel that if there are not adequate funds to make both the payment on the owner's personal residence and the property held for investment, then the owner's home loan will be paid first. This premise is an important concept in the analysis of the financing aspects of investment property. Many prospective purchasers don't know there are far different loan criteria for investor loans. Lenders typically require all investor borrowers to fill out a different set of forms, often using some type of quasi-government forms, such as the Fannie Mae Form 216. (Figure 4)

Residential Lending

One- To Four-Unit Properties. Single-family homes as an investment have seen healthy activity during the past few years. Lenders have developed guidelines for analyzing the value of these properties, with the

FannieMae

Figure 4

Operating Income Statement

One- to Four-Family Investment Property and Two- to Four-Family Owner-Occupied Property

Property Address

Street ______ City ______ State ______ Zip Code ______

General Instructions: This form is to be prepared jointly by the loan applicant, the appraiser, and the lender's underwriter. The applicant must complete the following schedule indicating each unit's rental status, lease expiration date, current rent, market rent, and the responsibility for utility expenses. Rental figures must be based on the rent for an "unfurnished" unit.

	Currently Rented	Expiration Date	Current Rent Per Month	Market Rent Per Month	Utility Expense	Paid By Owner	Paid By Tenant
Unit No. 1	Yes ___ No ___	______	$______	$______	Electricity	☐	☐
Unit No. 2	Yes ___ No ___	______	$______	$______	Gas	☐	☐
Unit No. 3	Yes ___ No ___	______	$______	$______	Fuel Oil	☐	☐
Unit No. 4	Yes ___ No ___	______	$______	$______	Fuel (Other)	☐	☐
Total			$______	$______	Water/Sewer	☐	☐
					Trash Removal	☐	☐

The applicant should complete all of the income and expense projections and for existing properties provide actual year-end operating statements for the past two years *(for new properties the applicant's projected income and expenses must be provided)*. This Operating Income Statement and any previous operating statements the applicant provides must then be sent to the appraiser for review, comment, and/or adjustments next to the applicant's figures *(e.g., Applicant/Appraiser 288/300)*. If the appraiser is retained to complete the form instead of the applicant, the lender must provide to the appraiser the aforementioned operating statements, mortgage insurance premium, HOA dues, leasehold payments, subordinate financing, and/or any other relevant information as to the income and expenses of the subject property received from the applicant to substantiate the projections. The underwriter should carefully review the applicant's/appraiser's projections and the appraiser's comments concerning those projections. The underwriter should make any final adjustments that are necessary to more accurately reflect any income or expense items that appear unreasonable for the market. *(Real estate taxes and insurance on these types of properties are included in PITI and not calculated as an annual expense item.)* Income should be based on current rents, but should not exceed market rents. When there are no current rents because the property is proposed, new, or currently vacant, market rents should be used.

Annual Income and Expense Projection for Next 12 months

Income *(Do not include income for owner-occupied units)*	By Applicant/Appraiser	Adjustments by Lender's Underwriter
Gross Annual Rental *(from unit(s) to be rented)*	$______	$______
Other Income *(include sources)*	+______	+______
Total	$______	$______
Less Vacancy/Rent Loss	−______(%)	−______(%)
Effective Gross Income	$______	$______

Expenses *(Do not include expenses for owner-occupied units)*		
Electricity	______	______
Gas	______	______
Fuel Oil	______	______
Fuel (Type - ______)	______	______
Water/Sewer	______	______
Trash Removal	______	______
Pest Control	______	______
Other Taxes or Licenses	______	______
Casual Labor This includes the costs for public area cleaning, snow removal, etc., even though the applicant may not elect to contract for such services.	______	______
Interior Paint/Decorating This includes the costs of contract labor and materials that are required to maintain the interiors of the living units.	______	______
General Repairs/Maintenance This includes the costs of contract labor and materials that are required to maintain the public corridors, stairways, roofs, mechanical systems, grounds, etc.	______	______
Management Expenses These are the customary expenses that a professional management company would charge to manage the property.	______	______
Supplies This includes the costs of items like light bulbs, janitorial supplies, etc.	______	______
Total Replacement Reserves - See Schedule on Pg. 2	______	______
Miscellaneous	______	______
......	______	______
......	______	______
......	______	______
......	______	______
......	______	______
......	______	______
......	______	______
......	______	______
Total Operating Expenses	$______	$______

Income Property Valuation & Financial Analysis

Replacement Reserve Schedule

Adequate replacement reserves must be calculated regardless of whether actual reserves are provided for on the owner's operating statements or are customary in the local market. This represents the total average yearly reserves. Generally, all equipment and components that have a remaining life of more than one year—such as refrigerators, stoves, clothes washers/dryers, trash compactors, furnaces, roofs, and carpeting, etc.—should be expensed on a replacement cost basis.

Equipment	Replacement Cost		Remaining Life			By Applicant/ Appraiser	Lender Adjustments
Stoves/Ranges	@ $ ______	ea. ÷	______	Yrs. x	______ Units =	$ ______	$ ______
Refrigerators	@ $ ______	ea. ÷	______	Yrs. x	______ Units =	$ ______	$ ______
Dishwashers	@ $ ______	ea. ÷	______	Yrs. x	______ Units =	$ ______	$ ______
A/C Units	@ $ ______	ea. ÷	______	Yrs. x	______ Units =	$ ______	$ ______
C. Washer/Dryers	@ $ ______	ea. ÷	______	Yrs. x	______ Units =	$ ______	$ ______
HW Heaters	@ $ ______	ea. ÷	______	Yrs. x	______ Units =	$ ______	$ ______
Furnace(s)	@ $ ______	ea. ÷	______	Yrs. x	______ Units =	$ ______	$ ______
(Other)	@ $ ______	ea. ÷	______	Yrs. x	______ Units =	$ ______	$ ______
Roof	@ $ ______	÷	______	Yrs. x	One Bldg. =	$ ______	$ ______

Carpeting (Wall to Wall) Remaining Life

(Units) ______ Total Sq. Yds. @ $______ Per Sq. Yd. ÷ ______Yrs. = $ ______ $ ______

(Public Areas) ______ Total Sq. Yds. @ $______ Per Sq. Yd. ÷ ______Yrs. = $ ______ $ ______

Total Replacement Reserves. (Enter on Pg. 1) $ ______ $ ______

Operating Income Reconciliation

$ ______ Effective Gross Income − $ ______ Total Operating Expenses = $ ______ Operating Income ÷ 12 = $ ______ Monthly Operating Income

$ ______ Monthly Operating Income − $ ______ Monthly Housing Expense = $ ______ Net Cash Flow

(Note: Monthly Housing Expense includes principal and interest on the mortgage, hazard insurance premiums, real estate taxes, mortgage insurance premiums, HOA dues, leasehold payments, and subordinate financing payments.)

Underwriter's instructions for 2-4 Family Owner-Occupied Properties

- If Monthly Operating Income is a positive number, enter as "Net Rental Income" in the "Gross Monthly Income" section of Freddie Mac Form 65/Fannie Mae Form 1003. If Monthly Operating Income is a negative number, it must be included as a liability for qualification purposes.
- The borrower's monthly housing expense-to-income ratio must be calculated by comparing the total Monthly Housing Expense for the subject property to the borrower's stable monthly income.

Underwriter's instructions for 1-4 Family Investment Properties

- If Net Cash Flow is a positive number, enter as "Net Rental Income" in the "Gross Monthly Income" section of Freddie Mac Form 65/Fannie Mae Form 1003. If Net Cash Flow is a negative number, it must be included as a liability for qualification purposes.
- The borrower's monthly housing expense-to-income ratio must be calculated by comparing the total monthly housing expense for the borrower's **primary residence** to the borrower's stable monthly income.

Appraiser's Comments *(Including sources for data and rationale for the projections)*

Appraiser Name ______ Appraiser Signature ______ Date ______

Underwriter's Comments and Rationale for Adjustments

Underwriter Name ______ Underwriter Signature ______ Date ______ help of government secondary agencies, such as the Federal National Mortgage Association. The value of the property is often based on the amount of rental income it can produce. A rent grid, such as is shown in Figure 4, Chapter 6, is used to determine comparable rents (for the market data approach to value) if enough closely related rental homes can be found. If the income, or capitalization method is used, only 80% of gross rental income is considered in valuing the property. The maximum loan amount is usually between 70% and 75% of the lender's appraised value (compared to 90%-95% for owner-occupied homes).

Present leases or other sources of income verification are used so that the property's income can be added to gross income of the borrower, especially if he or she is planning to occupy one of the units. Owner-occupied income property has become more common.

If the property's net cash flow is positive, it is added to the borrower's income. If the net cash flow is negative, it is treated as a long-term debt, even though the purchaser/investor plans to increase rents immediately to bring the property back to a break-even point.

Investors do not always understand the lender's point of view when analyzing the net income of a property. For example, a buyer wants to purchase three houses on a lot. The seller has receipts, financial statements, and rental agreements showing the following data:

- each tenant has paid a 5% per year increase in rents for the past five years,
- one tenant has resided on the premises for 17 years, another for 12 years, and the newest for five years, and
- the income has been very stable, and turnover virtually nil.

Yet, the lender will still insist on using a 3% to 5% vacancy factor. Borrowers often do not understand why any vacancy rate is used, when there has not been a vacancy for over five years. However, the borrower has to remember that under a residential month-to-month lease, the tenant can merely give notice and be out within 30 days. Also, these very old move-in dates indicate that little or no deposits were collected at the original move-in time, so the owner bears all the risk of short-term losses in income.

Five or More Units. The financing of larger nonowner-occupied properties will vary from lender to lender. Neither FNMA nor FHLMC will allow cash-out refinances. If a refinance is used to consolidate loans or meet a balloon payoff requirement, the maximum loan to value is 70% of the current appraised value.

Vacancy factors are usually calculated at 3% to 5%. With the current overbuilding in some areas of California, some lenders have begun applying higher vacancy factors—ranging from 4% to 8%. Expenses are calculated to be 28% to 35%, with higher rates used for furnished units, units 40 years or older, or if the tenant composition is predominantly singles.

Condominiums/PUD. Individual condominium units are treated as single-family residential units in terms of the property being used as an income-producing investment. The additional homeowners' association assessment fees are, however, included as another expense of the property in the qualifying analysis. Loans are placed on a case-by-case basis, as many lenders restrict the number of loans they make in any one complex, usually limiting themselves to no more than 35% of the total number of units. In the case of condo conversion units, lenders will require a licensed engineer's report and the income/expenses statements for the past two years.

Non-Residential Loans

Commercial/Retail. A vacancy factor of 5% is often used, with expenses estimated at 25%. With triple-net leases, expenses are projected at only 5%. Capitalization rates range from 9½% to 11%.

Office Buildings. Vacancy factors begin at 5% and are increased in many areas. The rate increases as it moves from primary locations to secondary centers. Expenses are calculated either as a percent or a price per foot. Thirty-two percent to 35% or $4 to $5.50 per square foot are commonly used amounts. Capitalization rates are 9½% to 10%.

Industrial Buildings. Flat amounts are used for industrial buildings, with the vacancy factor 5%, expenses 20% (with triple-net leases, use 5%), and capitalization rates of about 10%.

Mobile Home Parks. A common vacancy factor is 5%, with expenses projected as 30% to 35%, and a capitalization rate of around 10%.

Mini-Warehouses. The vacancy and bad debt factor is broken into two separate components for mini-warehouses. A 10% total is usually used, but a 7% vacancy rate is common, and the remaining 3% balance reflects the collection problems. Adjustments in the rate are usually a result of an analysis of the collections. Expenses are estimated at a straight 25%, and a capitalization rate of 10% is commonly used.

New Construction. Lender guidelines for new construction include requiring a statement of all hard costs, a closing statement on the purchase of the land, copies of construction notes and trust deeds, and copy of the building and loan agreement and signed contract with the building contractor, and a certificate of occupancy. A pro-forma statement is required on all new properties projecting the income and expenses of operating the building.

Loan Analysis

Every property is considered on an individual basis, and each lender will carefully examine all the facts about a particular property before deciding whether to make a loan and how much the loan amount should be.

The amount of funds necessary to make the monthly loan payment is called the **debt service.** This amount may be interest only, or a combination of principal and interest. The monthly obligation is determined by the terms of the note. The payment may be impounded and include payments to the lender for reserves for taxes and insurance.

A prudent lender will underwrite the loan so that there is sufficient income, after expenses, to pay the debt service. The amount of available funds required by the lender will be based on the lender's analysis of the risk. At a minimum, lenders are presently requiring that there be at least $1.10 of net income for every $1.00 of debt service.

Loan Package Requirements

When submitting a loan for approval, the following items must be included:

Borrower Information. If a corporation is the borrower, a management plan for subject property, including information on resident manager and off-site management, must be submitted. The corporation's current financial statement, a signed profit and loss statement, the past two years of tax returns, and personal financial statements of the senior corporate offices must also be submitted. Additional paperwork needed would include a corporate resolution authorizing the corporation to borrow the loan funds, a copy of the recorded Certificate of Incorporation, Articles of Incorporation, by-laws, and a Certificate of Good Standing from the California Department of Corporations.

If the borrower is a partnership, a management plan for the property and information on the resident manager and off-site management is required. Current financial statements on the partnership and all general partners, including their personal financial statement and personal income tax returns, must also be submitted. In addition, a copy of the partnership agreements, recorded certificate of partnership, fictitious business name statement (if any), and a credit report will be required.

If the borrower is an individual, a multi-family loan application and management plan needs to be included, along with a personal financial statement, credit report, and two years of personal tax returns, including supporting schedules. If self-employed, year-to-date profit and loss statements are required.

Other Requirements. All borrowers must submit employment verifications for the past two years. Verifications of deposits must show the source of the downpayment and closing costs. If other real property is owned, the lender will require a verification of the borrower's payment history.

The operating statement for the subject property must show the past two years and the present year-to-date figures. A current rent schedule, certified by the borrower showing each occupant's name, unit number, unit type, rent, rental agreement type, expiration date, and utilities furnished by the borrower is also required. If it is a leasehold property, a recorded copy of the ground lease is requested. Of course, an appraisal by an approved appraiser is also necessary.

CHAPTER 5–QUIZ

1. Which is a reasonably curable form of depreciation when considering cost:

   a. equity build-up
   b. book depreciation
   c. social obsolescense
   d. functional obsolescence

2. The monthly loan payment is referred to as:

   a. underwriting expense
   b. debt service
   c. mortgage loan servicing
   d. loan value

3. Lenders do not use 100% of residental rental income because:

   a. tenants can move fairly quickly
   b. operating expenses increase
   c. variable rate loans change payments
   d. borrowers can always raise rents to increase income

4. Appreciation most nearly describes:

   a. market value
   b. utility value
   c. default value
   d. savings value

5. A building's income can be greatly improved by careful detail to all of the following except:

   a. valuing similar units to make rents the same for each
   b. increasing administrative expenses to monitor income
   c. increasing laundry room and vending machine income
   d. converting a laundry room to storage rental areas

6. Which of the following is not a good source to compare expenses for a building to similar building's expenses:

   a. insurance reports
   b. IREM Income and Expense Analysis
   c. owners of other buildings
   d. local apartment association directors and members

7. Which is not a method an owner usually would use to value a 12-year old four-unit apartment building:

   a. gross rent multiplier
   b. internal rate of return
   c. cost approach
   d. present value

8. The income approach to value is based on:

   a. present value of the future income
   b. comparable sales of similar properties
   c. averaging the sales of similar properties
   d. replacement cost of the improvements plus land value

9. The income approach to valuation is arrived at by:

   a. GI - Vac & Bad debt = EGI − OE = NOI ÷ Cap Rate = Value
   b. Gross monthly rental income × GRM = Value
   c. EGI − EO = NOI − DS ÷ Cap rate = Value
   d. GE + Appreciation = Net value × PV ÷ Time = IRR Value

10. Special use design is an important factor in valuing which type of property?

    a. residential
    b. retail
    c. motel/hotel
    d. industrial

CHAPTER 5–ANSWER KEY

1. d
2. b
3. a
4. d
5. b
6. a
7. c
8. a
9. a
10. d

6

The Owner's Objectives For Project Management

References

Hanford, Lloyd D., CPM. *The Property Management Process.* 2nd Printing. Institute of Real Estate Management of National Association of Realtors, 1972.

Downs, James C., Jr., CPM. *Principles of Real Estate Management.* 12th ed. Institute of Real Estate Management of National Association of Realtors, 1980.

DeCarlo, J., CPM. *California Real Property Management. Study Guide.* Sacramento: California Community Colleges, 1986.

McKenzie, Dennis, and Richard, Betts. *The Essentials of Real Estate Economics.* 2nd ed. New York: John Wiley & Sons, Inc., 1980.

Last Chapter Review

The mathematics of property management determines the financial analysis of the property. Different investors prefer valuing a building by net present value (NPV), capitalization Rate (Cap Rate), gross rent multiplier (GRM), or internal rate of return (IRR), so the property manager must know each. These valuations are based upon income and expenses, which vary between buildings and owners.

Chapter Overview

The most significant goal of the property manager is to fulfill the objectives of the property owner. Thus the management strategy of each property must be tailored to satisfy the desires of each individual property owner. This chapter outlines the process of developing a marketing strategy, or management plan, and breaks down the components of analysis.

THE MANAGEMENT PLAN

Many facts must be gathered, compiled and analyzed to put together a management plan for a particular income-producing property. These facts range from the physical characteristics of the property to government regulations governing the property's operation.

It is important that the management plan be written out so that all parties have a clear understanding of what is to be done. The specific powers, responsibilities and obligations of the property manager should be clearly stated to avoid later confusion.

For a very small property, a letter of management confirmation may be all that is needed (Figure 1). For medium-sized properties, a more in-depth analysis will probably be required by the owner. A thorough, detailed management plan necessary for a large property should include all of the elements shown below (Figure 2). The format of the formal plan is not vital, but the contents should be accurate and complete. Often, institutional lenders, insurance companies, and government agencies require a particular format for their own projects.

Preparing for the Management Plan

Expertise. A successful management plan requires an experienced property manager. The formal management plan is a comprehensive study that combines expertise in many areas, including finance, economics, appraisal, land descriptions, title and escrow. Areas of study that are especially helpful to those preparing a management proposal are accounting, business, finance, structural engineering and business law/contracts.

Figure 1 **Management Confirmation Letter (Sample)**

Date

Dear ___________:

Thank you for the opportunity to handle the property management of your real estate investment. This letter is to confirm our understanding of your goals for this specific property.

Although you bought this single-family residence for your home, you have now moved (pick one from list below):

- close to town to decrease your commuter drive
- to another city due to a change in job location
- out of your home so you can travel in your motorhome
- to your second/retirement home

and selling your home was not in your best interest at this time because there is (pick one from list below):

- so little sales activity
- so little equity now, after the costs of sale
- hope that you will move back into the home in the future.

Over a long holding time, this property should benefit from future values. At present, however, you desire to rent the property so that it (pick one from list below):

- has no more than $200 a month negative cash flow
- carries itself over the year, with no additional taxable income to you, but also no cash outlay to support the property
- earns at least $500 a month positive cash flow for you to live on
- generates enough income to offset the negative cash flow on your other property

We look forward to serving you. We hope the above outline is correct, and invite you to comment or correct any misunderstanding that we may have gotten. Our goal is to achieve your goals for the ownership of this property.

Sincerely,

Property Manager

Figure 2 **The Formal Management Project**

Table of Contents

- Cover Page
  - Title
  - Author
  - Property Description
  - Date
- Synopsis Page
  - Owner's Goal
  - Brief Summary
- Past Data
  - History of Area
  - Property
  - Economy
  - Growth Pattern
  - Resources
  - Topography
- Present Data
  - Analysis of Region, Neighborhood, Market & Property Use
  - Operations
    - Policies and Procedures
  - Economy
  - Demographics
  - Lifestyles
- Future Data
  - Alternative Uses
  - Conversion
  - Rehabilitation
  - Upgrades/Change
- Monetary Assessment
  - Finance
  - Value
- Findings and Suggestions
- Bibliography
- References

Real estate markets and property performance vary considerably from region to region. Many out-of-state dollars have been unwisely invested into projects that lacked local expertise. If an investor is not familiar with the area where the property is located, he or she should consult a local certified property manager. In this way, the investor obtains the local market information that can mean the difference between success and failure. Local Boards of Realtors usually maintain a list of local CPM's or experts specializing in the area who would know the particulars of a building. Consulting fees are relatively low, and should be included in the initial development costs, along with the architect's and engineer's fees.

Research. An effective management plan also depends on a considerable amount of research. Documenting factual information is usually a prerequisite to obtaining funds to improve the property, whether it be remodeling or new construction. The property owner will also benefit from the same information. There are many sources for obtaining accurate up-to-date data. (Figure 3)

INFORMATION SOURCES

Federal Sources
Department of Commerce
U.S. Bureau of the Census
Regional Federal Reserve Bank
Department of Labor
National Assn. of Realtors/IREM
Deparment of HUD

Local Government
City Hall
Building Department
Planning Department
Regional Planning Commission
Redevelopment Agencies

State Sources
Employment Office
Department of Labor
Housing Authority
California Assn. of Realtors
Department of Real Estate
Department of Transporation

Business Sources
Trade Associations
  Board of Realtors
  Apartment Association
  Chamber of Commerce
Utility Companies
Banks and Savings & Loans
Library
Insurance Companies
College & University (research)

Methodology. The introductory portion of the plan should include the property manager's methodology. Often, a property owner may have inflated expectations about the property. He or she may be expecting more income, a rosier economic picture, or more favorable financing. By discussing in an orderly fashion the information sources and the methods of analysis used, the management plan takes on more credibility.

Flexibility. Lastly, flexibility is a necessity. The property manager must allow for all the unforeseen market conditions that may occur. The property manager who has several alternatives ready eases the discomfort of change when adverse circumstances arise.

It is important for the alert property manager to be able to advise the owner to abandon an area hit by economic disaster, to pull out of an inflationary hot spot, or to invest in another type of property. To be able to do this successfully, the property manager must have a good relationship with the owner, one where loyalty and trust are not an issue.

REGIONAL ANALYSIS

The property's location has an important impact on its performance. An apartment complex situated in a bustling metropolis will certainly outperform an identical building found in a small farming town. Thus, the first step to take in developing the management plan is to analyze the area where the property is located. The material gathered should include general economic conditions, physical attributes, population growth and distribution, growth rate of business and industry, public facilities, public transportation, and educational opportunities.

Regional History

It enhances the credibility of the management report to include the historical development of the area. For instance, the origins of most towns or cities developed near some kind of transportation artery (e.g., river, stockyard center, or railroad depot). Many early California communities began as loading centers for citrus crops, agricultural produce, or timber.

Discovering the origins of the original town site often brings other factors to light, for example, why the town survived and grew, and whether these reasons for growth still exist. Historical origins can also help explain community norms—what is or is not an acceptable development for the area. A community that allows a six-story saw mill may rally up in arms at the prospect of a three-story glass and chrome structure.

Some California communities are set up to increase greatly in size during the influx of migrant farm workers, then shrink back to a far smaller permanent population. Other communities were developed for retirement or recreation, and permanent, high-growth activity is discouraged; e.g., a ski-lift installed in a quiet mountain community. The region may have had its development based on the topography. Valley communities and hillside towns have historically opposed any construction that would hinder the mountain views. These early growth patterns are often carried into the present, as people radiate out from the original growth arteries, up streams, through valleys, and along foothill ridges.

Present Data

The general growth pattern of the community is one of the most vital considerations in the management plan. Is the population increasing, stable, or declining? Since the demand for the property (i.e., number of potential tenants) affects its value, a trend of healthy population growth is usually desirable.

Population growth typically radiates out from the original town site. Generally, a property's potential value is best when it is located in the natural growth pattern, although sometimes areas are bypassed when growth follows a "leapfrog" pattern. Inverse growth patterns have also become more common—where older, intercommunity areas are redeveloped into commercial, residential or other productive and profitable uses.

Good access is vital to any California development. Substantial marketing costs can be averted if the property manager does not have to direct the public to the property.

The property manager must also incorporate political factors into the management plan. The community land-use controls will, of course, have a major effect on the property's final use. For example, if the property manager knows that a zoning variance will never be approved by the local planning commission, time and money spent on trying to obtain the variance would be wasted. One community may require the "donation" of a park, school, crosswalk, stop light or freeway offramp by the property owner in return for project approval.

The availability of police and fire protection is another important consideration. The cost and availability of water and sewer services should also be examined—water and sewage treatment limitations are a factor in over one-third of California's land use restraints. Moratoriums on development because of these problems are not textbook theories of urban planners, but realities that must be dealt with.

NEIGHBORHOOD ANALYSIS

After thoroughly studying the region, the property manager examines the specific neighborhood where the property is located. Is the neighborhood more desirable than the region as a whole? What is it that would attract potential tenants to the neighborhood? Is the neighborhood economically sound? Is is geographically desirable?

What constitutes a neighborhood is likely to vary from region to region. In rural areas, a neighborhood may consist of many square miles, while in an urban area it may be only a few square blocks. Important neighborhood information includes level of maintenance, growth or decline in population, and economic level.

Information about the social composition of the neighborhood where the property is found is critical in terms of the use and acceptance of the project. For example, Sacramento's "Old Town" has been a success because of its proximity to downtown, and the specialized shops with old store fronts have been welcomed by both tourists and locals. On the other hand, the downtown Pomona Mall is not successful because it is located near too many newer freeway offramps and larger malls. The community simply cannot afford to support the shops.

Demographics

Demographic composition of the neighborhood is important. The average age of the neighborhood population would determine the consumers' pattern of spending. In today's world, age statistics vary widely depending on the time of day the data is gathered. There will be significant differences between data gathered at 11 a.m. and that gathered at 11 p.m. Different age groups may work in a particular place during the day, seek entertainment there during the evening, and sleep there at night. Much of California's population is highly transitory, living, working and playing in different cities.

However, in neighborhoods with a more local flavor, public transportation, parks and proximity to shopping, day care centers and medical facilities become important aspects to the success of the property.

Another social influence affecting the property in residential neighborhoods is average household size. For example, if the average household size in the neighborhood is two adults and two children, five-bedroom apartments will probably not be very successful. Likewise, if the average household size is two adults and three children, lavish one-bedroom apartments will not fare very well either.

Economics

Economic factors influence the property more than any other single item. The property manager should determine the median and average income in the neighborhood. There are often several levels of income within each community.

The property manager should list two or three major employers and other local employment centers. It is important to know how broad the base of employment is. If one particular plant closes down or lays off substantial numbers of workers, does the area have a divergent enough employment base to quickly absorb the unemployed back into the labor force?

The decision to go ahead with a property should be based upon the economic ability of the area to produce rent-paying tenants, whether they are renting store fronts or apartments. The employment base should be checked against future expectations of general and local economic growth. Job stability and diversity will support the continued income to the property,

PROPERTY ANALYSIS

The next area to analyze is the physical structure of the property and the quality of its occupants.

Physical Condition

The current physical condition of the building is based on a normal structural analysis. This may be done by a paid inspection service, by the property manager with the property's maintenance supervisor, or handled with a report from a contractor. An informal "eyeball" appraisal is not acceptable.

The types of information the property manager will be searching for include:

- number and size of the living units or number of rentable square feet,
- the visual impression of the property and rent space (age, layout, style, view, etc.),
- the physical condition of the building,
- the physical condition of the rentable space,
- the kinds of amenities provided (e.g., laundries, janitorial services),
- the current occupancy rate and tenant composition, and
- the current staff size and efficiency.

California, a state known for its mild climates, does not have the more extreme cold or rainy seasons. Instead, California's seasons are measured by fire, flood, mud, smog and earthquake. This means that the property must be checked for conditions that might have been caused by these elements. Prior patching, slipping hillsides, shifting foundations, etc., all affect its present condition and give an indication of future danger.

A complete analysis of the physical condition of the property requires studying various documentation, including lot plans, floor plans, and photographs.

Lot Plan. The property analysis should include a detailed lot plan. The complete layout of the land should be inspected, including all easements and right-of-ways. A specific lot plan should show the exact location of the building on the site, plus fences, dimensions, all detached structures, and trees.

Floor Plan. The floor plan, also vital, should show halls, corridors, elevators, lobbies, balconies, and stairwells, in addition to the units. All appliances, vending machines, pools, etc., should be shown in place. Present uses of all space should be described, including storage, garage and closet areas.

Photographs. Photographs, although not mandatory, do enhance the management plan. They show existing signs, curb appeal and overall aesthetics. They are also an excellent way to illustrate items that are in especially poor condition, such as faded parking striping, rusted equipment, poor drainage conditions, roof patches, graffiti, laundry and trash handling, and present decorating, carpets, window coverings and paint.

Current Management

If the property is an existing building, the present management should be examined. A comparison with several other building managers should help reveal the strengths and weaknesses of on-site personnel. Current policies and procedures should be listed (Figure 4) and compared to similar projects.

Tenant quality must also be examined. Their financial qualifications determine the stability and economic value of the rents received. Rent rolls should be checked to determine present vacancy, expenses, and cash flow.

Current financing arrangements also affect the property's performance. The property manager should investigate existing loan terms and determine if they are adequate or need revision. Too high a debt service (mortgage payment) has a drastic effect on the profitability of the property.

MARKET ANALYSIS

To accurately predict the profitability of a project, the property manager must become familiar with the competition by performing a market analysis. This projects the building's performance.

First, the manager determines what the relevant market is. The major subcategories of real estate include commercial, retail, industrial, and residential. Each of these can be further broken down. For instance, the residential market can be divided into single-family residences, the duplex, the garden apartment, the walk-up apartment and the multi-story apartment building.

Figure 5

Property Management at Present For Subject Property

Curb Appeal:

– Trees & shrubs overgrown
– Wood trim needs paint
– Parking strips need new paint
+ Grass green, cool & lush
+ Pool area clean, fenced with good sign
+ Safety & laundry signs good

On-Site Appearance:

– Mgr. upstairs around corner, hard to find
– Manager sign needs paint
– No door drop or Mgr. message mail box
– No message board or Mgr. posted hours
+ Sharp appearance, professional attitude
+ Manager unit spotless

Accounting:

– Quarterly financial statement
+ Very detailed computer analysis
+ Bank reconciliation monthly

Off-Site Management:

– Tenants do not have access information
– Company sign not posted
+ Good on – site training program
+ Good forms

Policies:

– Late fee of $1 per day
+ Automatic eviction on 5th day
+ Posted signage
+ Written rental agreement & forms

Procedures:

– Accept cash for rent
– No safe, pick up can be 5 days later
+ Forms excellent
+ Advertising smooth
+ Maintenance good

Other:

The property manager must determine what kind of properties in what geographical region compete directly with the subject property. Is the competitive market all multi-story apartment buildings in the community, or only all multi-story apartment buildings within a three-mile radius?

Once the market is determined, market data must be gathered. For example, how many units are there for rent in the area? What is the average condition of these units? How many prospective tenants for these

Figure 4

Income Comparison and Estimation Valuation

Subject Property Name/Address: *Bandera Arms — 123 Elm St., Montclair*
Type of Unit: *2-bedroom, 1-bath apartment in 12 units*

	Subject	Comp #1	Comp #2	Comp #3	Comp #4	Comp #5
1. Grid Map	21C2	21C2	21B2	21C2	21B1	21C1
2. Building Age	15	20	20	15	12	25
3. Appearance	Good	Sharp	Good	Poor	Sharp	Good
4. Recreation	Pool	—	Pool	—	Pool	—
5. Appliances	Disposal D/W-Stove	—	Dishwasher Stove	D/W-Refrig. Stove-Disp.	D/W Disposal	Disposal
6. Heat/Cool	F/A CA/C	Wall Wall	Wall —	Wall —	F/A CA/C	Wall —
7. Parking	1 Car	2 Carport	1 Garage 1 Carport	Street	1 Garage	2 Garage
8. Other	—	Extra 1/2 Bath	—	—	—	View
9. Rent/Month	600	650	600	625	675	615
10. Square Feet	750	850	700	800	750	725
11. $/sq. ft./mo	.80	.764	.857	.781	.900	.848

Adjustments to Make Comparable Equal to Subject Property

1.		0	−5	0	−5	+ 5
2.		+ 5	+ 5	0	−5	+ 10
3.		−10	0	+ 10	−10	0
4.		+ 10	0	+ 10	0	+ 10
5.		+ 15	+ 10	−5	+ 10	+ 5
6.		+ 10	+ 15	−10	0	+ 15
7.		+ 5	−5	+ 5	0	− 10
8.		−20	0	0	0	−10
Adjustments		+ 10	+ 20	+ 10	−10	+ 25
9. Adj'd Rent	635	660	620	635	665	640
11.	.846	.776	.886	.794	.887	.883

units are there in the area? What is the occupancy rate for these units? What is the average rental price of these units?

A rent survey is developed to determine maximum market rents. (Figure 5). The property manager lists addresses, rents and amenities for similar rental units (commercial, industrial, residential, etc.). Adjustments are made to the comparable properties to make them similar to the subject property. With several comparables, the property manager should have a good idea of the potential income of the property, including rents, laundry room, parking, vending machines and other income.

The operating expenses of similar building operations should also be compared with the subject property. The astute property manager knows what to look for, where costs are too high or out-of-line, and when actual costs are not figured correctly. For example, many individual property owners in California operate small units. When the property is sold to an off-site investor who prefers to have outside management, the costs of management must be added.

> **Example:** The prior owner who does his or her own maintenance and rent collection cannot bill any hourly rate for his or her time (according to the IRS). The operating statement reflects that this time is worth nothing. But the new owner, the off-site investor, hires someone to do the maintenance and rent collecting. These fees are now shown as tax deductible operating expenses.

ALTERNATIVES TO PRESENT USE

After analyzing the region, neighborhood, property and market, the property manager may decide that the present use is not the most valuable. The property manager may end up recommending that an entirely different use would be the most beneficial to the owner. Sometimes there are alternative uses, but no one use is clearly superior to the others. This portion of the management plan discusses the possible alternatives and sketches out the benefits and drawbacks of each.

Formulating Alternatives

This portion of the formal management project allows for the most creativity. Let yourself go, and imagine "What if..." Initially, no idea is unacceptable; money is no object; anything can be done.

First list all your ideas, then add the projected costs and income. This process filters all the alternatives into a few viable possibilities. Even some of these may not be acceptable to the property owner, nor allowed by the local community or government. But a complete management plan should cover many options. Properties may be managed for one owner's objectives, and then sold later to another owner who has different goals. Also, these alternatives might become more attractive later if social or economic conditions change.

Gather Projected Data

Pay particular attention to future data: project the future growth pattern for the area and its effects on the property. Overbuilding, rehabilitation, no-growth, and rent control issues need to be addressed, along with future zoning, density, land use and development moratoriums.

The future data should include a five-year stabilized income and expense and valuation projection. This should include expected vacancies, management costs, and inflation. A final value and rate of return on the finished project, both as is and as modified, must be given.

Projected demographic characteristics of age, family size, lifestyle, ethnic composition, education level, and income levels should be outlined in relation to the property's performance.

State Alternatives

Include the future economic forecasts into the formalized management project. Then include the projected costs and incomes of the alternatives, illustrating the connection between the two. The projected income and expenses will help determine the final choice:

- maintain the property as is,
- modernize or rehabilitate the property, or
- tear down the existing buildings and begin again.

The plan will often include suggestions from tenants, on-site personnel, government agencies or neighbors. Tax considerations also play a role: tax laws change so frequently that the original tax intent of a project is often defeated.

SUMMARY

The final property management report is the compilation of the past, present and future analysis of the property, including its relationship to the region and neighborhood. Different owners have different objectives for the same physical property. The management plan attempts to lay out a course of property management that will meet these objectives, taking into consideration the property's economic and physical characteristics. The conclusion of the management plan must gather together all the various data into a manageable whole for the property owner.

CHAPTER 6–QUIZ

1. Which of the following are true?

   a. Smaller properties may use only a management confirmation letter
   b. Medium properties may use a less formalized property management report
   c. Larger properties tend to use a formalized management project
   d. All are correct

2. A good source of national data would NOT include:

   a. Department of Commerce
   b. Department of Labor
   c. local trade association
   d. National Association of Realtors/Institute of Real Estate Management

3. Transportation arteries determine:

   a. cultural needs
   b. original site and growth patterns
   c. social issues
   d. None of the above

4. The character and composition of California communities has recently:

   a. changed quite a bit
   b. stayed the same
   c. decreased
   d. None of the above

5. Political factors of a community that affect property do NOT include:

   a. zoning
   b. moratoriums
   c. rent control
   d. floor plans

6. Demographic information includes:

   a. building valuation
   b. average income
   c. topography
   d. taxes

7. Operating statements often omit the true cost of:

   a. management
   b. utility expense
   c. maintenance
   d. insurance

8. The economic analysis includes:

   a. climate
   b. utility expense
   c. consumer sentiment
   d. rate of return

9. Future data looks at:

   a. past
   b. present
   c. future
   d. All of the above

10. The main management goal is to meet:

    a. ethnic groups
    b. owner's objective
    c. income levels
    d. cash flow analysis

CHAPTER 6–QUIZ ANSWERS

1. d
2. c
3. b
4. a
5. d
6. b
7. a
8. d
9. d
10. b

7

Residential Marketing and Management

References

Downs, James C., Jr., CPM. *Principles of Real Estate Management.* 12th ed. Institute of Real Estate Management of National Association of Realtors, 1980.

DeCarlo, J., CPM. *California Real Property Management. Study Guide.* Sacramento: California Community Colleges, 1986.

Last Chapter Review

A management proposal is only feasible when it takes into account both the objectives of the owner and the property's attributes. The proposal contains data on the past, present, and projected future performance of the property, including an analysis of the historical influences of the region, neighborhood, and property on that performance. Flexibility is a must, and alternatives must be included in a good long-term plan. The finished project is used by the property owner, lender, and prospective purchaser.

Chapter Overview

Marketing a property is an on-going process for the property manager, who seeks both new management clients and new tenants for those properties being managed. In California, residential tenants have become more mobile than the national average. This means marketing and tenant selection and retention is more vital than ever for better building performance.

The techniques of marketing residential property will vary with the building and unit size, as well as the geographical area and the client. But the property manager must remember that all marketing actions radiate a building image and, therefore, they should be clearly defined, carefully planned, and efficiently executed.

ADVERTISING

In General

Information on marketing techniques is available from many sources. The different types of media (radios, newspapers, telephone companies, etc.) often provide helpful brochures on effective layouts, ad language, and other advertising tips. Of course, advertising agencies are available to help create new ads, logos, and slogans in your effort to increase market share. College courses and books from the library or bookstore also offer many helpful marketing tips.

Marketing
All business activity involved with moving goods and services from producers to consumers.

The Purpose of Advertising

The purpose of advertising is to obtain prospects. It takes several inquiries to get qualified prospects to show up; then the property manager can pick the best applicant.

Property managers advertise to market specific properties. This may include trying to lease space in a newly constructed project, upgrading the image of an already existing property, or changing the composition of current tenant mix. Another reason to advertise is to create goodwill among existing tenants so they will stay in the building longer. This reduces the turnover costs of cleaning, painting, and making minor repairs.

The property manager must ensure that all aspects of building operations are a part of a coordinated marketing campaign. Marketing efforts do not begin when there is a vacancy. Marketing is an on-going process that creates a positive building image even when there are no vacancies. "Marketing" takes place each time the telephone is answered, each time a prospect drives by the building, each time a pamphlet or brochure is sent to an interested party, and each time an ad is placed. The building's appearance and landscaping, the on-site manager, and unit itself are all a part of the marketing process. So are the renting techniques, rental application forms, rental agreements, and walk-thru and property management policies and procedures.

The purpose of this on-going process is to create a waiting list that can be used when a vacancy does occur. Constant merchandising makes the difference between a prolonged vacancy and having a prospective tenant who is ready to move in as soon as the old tenant moves out.

Merchandising
All aspects of marketing that create a desire for a particular product (over other choices) that appeals to ready, willing and able buyers in the marketplace.

Before placing the advertisement, the property manager should analyze how much money should be spent, how long the ad should run, where the ad should run, and which type of media should be used.

How much money to be spent is part of the projected budget expenses. Advertising costs should be a budgeted item, based upon projected vacancies, turnover, and market conditions. Less experienced property managers tend to use the advertiser's cost breaks, instead of following an historical building average.

> **Example:** A newspaper gives a special seven-day rate, so many people place an "on-going" ad which they cancel if the unit is rented. This approach spends needless dollars. The building may have a history of finding a tenant with one day of advertising.

To the question of "How much?" some believe that "more is better." However, this view violates the theory of diminishing returns. To be effective, ads should look clean and fresh. Tenants usually look carefully at weekend ads and then think that Monday's ads are the "leftovers"—units no one wanted. An ad running Wednesday through Sunday, with a new heading each week appears fresh, as if it just came onto the market. As a "new" ad with a different lead in, it catches the reader's eye, even if the body of the ad is substantially the same.

The length of time an ad campaign should run depends on the advertising goal. Many high-rent commercial properties maintain on-going billboards, even when there are no vacancies. These become status symbols for the tenants, and often carry the name of one or more important tenants. Industrial parks use placement of the tenant's name on the park entrance signs as part of the property merchandising. Senior citizen complexes have on-going marketing campaigns to create waiting lists in popular California retirement areas.

Types Of Media

Where to advertise depends on what market you want to reach. If you are trying to reach new rental property owners as clients, an ad in a local legal or medical association journal may attract the audience you are seeking. If you are trying to attract local residents, 3" x 5" ad cards, placed on the laundromat or supermarket bulletin board can be very effective. The target market would also determine which heading to put a newspaper ad under.

Television. There are many differences between the various types of media. The most expensive method of advertising is television, especially the major networks. Obviously, television would not be used for renting a single apartment. However, local cable station rates are not as expensive as one might think and could be appropriate when a large development is being introduced. A "Leisure World" development or large resort community might benefit from this method of marketing.

Radio. Radio can be very effective because stations specifically target a particular market. Many colleges have on-campus stations with a small broadcasting range, and if college dormitories are expensive and full, this may be a good market to tap. These small stations are always looking for donation-sponsors.

Print. Print is the most often used advertising method for marketing rental property. This includes billboards, benches, bus backs, or taxi signs, as well as building signs. The telephone book yellow pages, magazine ads, directories, and newspaper ads are all types of print advertising.

Billboards are predominately used for large, new projects. Commercial and industrial site leasing is aided by this media. Located along major thoroughfares, billboards offer high visibility to large numbers of people. While intended for a long-term advertising campaign (due to the length of the contract for the billboard space), it is sometimes possible to have short-term space in between major advertisers. Check with local advertising firms for possibilities.

In areas where high commuter traffic depends upon public transportation, bus benches can be very effective. Most of California is automobile oriented, but the Bay area BART, the L.A. Metro Rail, and San Diego-to-points-north Amtrak system provide excellent apartment unit exposure to those using rapid transit systems. Persons waiting at a train stop have idle time to read the signs. Taxi cab signs and bus signs also reach a high reader volume.

An ad in the telephone book is the most important source of reaching property owners to obtain new clients. These inquiries usually come in first thing Monday morning, after the owner has had a problem-filled weekend. The Monday morning after the first weekend of the month (when rents are due) is a critical time to have top notch personnel answering these inquiry calls.

Some tenants will make inquiries from a yellow pages ad. This is not an efficient use of funds for firms who do not accept outside fee management and who only own and operate their own buildings.

Display advertising in apartment locator directories, magazines, and the like are good sources for attracting prospective tenants, especially for large residential complexes. California has many such projects that feature a wide array of luxury amenities. Since the projects are vying for the same tenants, they spend the most on printing costs for advertising, investing in high gloss, color layouts and brochures. The ads typically feature the most attractive amenities of the project, such as pictures of the golf course, tennis courts, pools, etc.

The newspaper classifieds are the most often used type of advertising. The professional property manager knows that many owners read these ads to help determine who they will use to manage their property.

If the ads are appealing, they know the property manager can make their property look good as well. Prospective tenants also look at classified ads in their search for housing. The paper's classified advertising department will usually guide the novice through placing an ad.

Agencies. Various agencies can be excellent places to advertise for tenants. Relocation firms, college housing offices, and military personnel offices should be on your mailing list. A prepared list of vacancies can be sent to several places to increase ongoing inquiries (Figure 1). Local, major companies will often post a vacancy list if you mail it to them. Some agencies charge tenants a fee for available rental lists that show features, price, and the contact person.

Personnel. Lastly, the property's on-site personnel are walking advertisements. On-site personnel are discussed in detail in Chapter 8. Office staff must remember that all contacts are potential prospects. Wrong numbers, vendors, and maintenance personnel all rent or have acquaintances who do. It is important to project a professional on-going image with these contacts to generate potential leads.

The Advertisement

The ad should catch the readers eye. The heading may be in bold print. Tell the newspaper (or other advertiser) that you insist on full words, with no abbreviations.

Example: Read outloud the following poor ad as it is written:

MDTN. 2Bd. 1Ba. Apt. CAC. 1st & Dep. No Pets. Yd. 555-1212

This ad has only one readable sentence, and that is a negative image — "No Pets." The rest is jargon, slang, or trade terms. It conveys the idea that the advertiser is too frugal to place a decent ad. It is hard to read and gives the reader no incentive to call. Often, when a prospect calls on this type of ad, he or she gets an answering machine.

A much more appealing way to word the ad might be:

MIDTOWN apartment. 2-bedroom with air and yard. 555-1212

Figure 1

RENTALS
AVAILABLE THIS WEEK
(714) 983-7775

Professional Property Management
P.O. Box 227
Ontario, CA 91761
983-7775

Equal Housing Opportunities

COMMISSION	$200.00	$100.00	$100.00	$100.00
ADDRESS	1121 Philadelphia	714 E. Monterey	716 E. Monterey	5820 Buckthorn
CITY	Ontario	Pomona	Pomona	Alta Loma
DIRECTION	West of Grove	S/Holt-E/San Antonio	S/Holt-E/San Antonio	N/19th-W/Beryl
TYPE	Home	Apartment	Apartment	Home
BEDROOM	4	1	2	4
BATH	2	1	1	2
DEN	X			D/R
FAMILY	X	D/R	D/R	X
AIR-COND			X	X
DISPOSAL	X			X
DISHW	X			X
FRIG				
FIREPLACE	X			X
CARPETS	X	X	X	X
DRAPES	X	X	X	X
STOVE		X	X	X
GARAGE	2 Car			2 Car
PATIO	Covered			Covered
POOL				
FENCED	X			X
YARD	X	X	X	X
AGE	20	25	25	7
UNFURN	X	X	X	X
RENT	$1,500.00	$300.00	$340.00	$800.00

The prospective tenant is interested in certain vital pieces of information. This essential data should be included in the ad: where the unit is located and the rental amount. A good ad tells the street address, total move-in costs, size of the unit, and amenities.

A good ad heading is one or two bold print words that describe something of interest to the reader. Good headings include town or section location, unit size, or amenities. A poor heading would be the apartment complex name, or a misrepresentation. Be careful when you word your ads—you could be liable for any misrepresentation relied on by the reader. Be especially wary of claiming an attribute you cannot guarantee, such as "security building," because it depends on conditions outside the property that could change.

> **Example:** If someone moves into the unit because the ad read "Quiet and Safe," and he or she suffers a gang-related incident, the advertiser could be open for a misrepresentation suit.

Similarly, the property manager must carefully choose the colors, lettering style, and words of the banners, flags and complex name signs. Different types of signs create distinctly different images. The logos of the building and property management firm give specific messages to the public and should be carefully considered.

RENTING THE UNITS

Once the advertising has created a desire on the prospect's part to inquire about the property, a whole new marketing phase begins. It is now up to the management team to sell the prospect on the unit.

A systematic, thorough rental system is necessary for a successful rental program. Not every method will work in every area of California, but a specific program is necessary. As a particular method is used and experience with the market gained, changes can be implemented and refinements put into place.

Handling Inquiries

The skills needed to handle inquiries are easily learned, but often neglected. Also, many of the office staff may have the wrong idea about the objective of this phase. For example, in real estate sales, the purpose of an ad is to make the phone ring, so you can make an appointment with the prospect. You have to meet with the prospect before you can sell him or her anything, even if it isn't the property he or she originally called to see. However, the goal in property rental is to get one or two specific units rented—bait and switch techniques are the wrong methods to meet this goal. Even large complexes usually only have one or two different models. Therefore, the telephone technique for rental property is not to convince the caller to come see you, but to give the caller as much information about the unit as possible. If the unit is not what the caller really wants, it is a waste of the property manager's time to set up an appointment with him or her.

Property managers should have specific training in telephone techniques. Local phone companies often provide some help, and many training tapes are available.

Phone Lines. Property management offices should have at least two distinctly separate, non-sequential telephone numbers. They may have a number of rotary lines, depending on the size of the firm and number of units managed. Some firms have a third number for incoming ad calls only.

Figure 2

Incoming Telephone Log

<table>
<tr><th>Hour</th><th>Owner</th><th>Ad Call</th><th>Tenant</th><th>Maintenance</th></tr>
<tr><td>8:00 a.m.</td><td>||</td><td>|</td><td></td><td>||</td></tr>
<tr><td>8:30 a.m.</td><td>|</td><td>|</td><td></td><td>|||</td></tr>
<tr><td>9:00 a.m.</td><td>|||</td><td>|||</td><td></td><td>|</td></tr>
<tr><td>9:30 a.m.</td><td></td><td></td><td>|</td><td></td></tr>
<tr><td>10:00 a.m.</td><td>||||</td><td></td><td></td><td></td></tr>
<tr><td>10:30 a.m.</td><td></td><td>|</td><td>|</td><td></td></tr>
<tr><td>11:00 a.m.</td><td></td><td>|||</td><td></td><td></td></tr>
<tr><td>11:30 a.m.</td><td></td><td>|||||</td><td></td><td></td></tr>
<tr><td>12 noon</td><td></td><td>||||| ||||| ||</td><td></td><td></td></tr>
<tr><td>12:30 p.m.</td><td></td><td>||||| ||||| |||||</td><td></td><td>|</td></tr>
<tr><td>1:00 p.m.</td><td></td><td>||||| |||</td><td></td><td></td></tr>
<tr><td>1:30 p.m.</td><td></td><td>||||| |</td><td></td><td></td></tr>
<tr><td>2:00 p.m.</td><td>|||</td><td>|</td><td></td><td></td></tr>
<tr><td>2:30 p.m.</td><td></td><td>|</td><td></td><td></td></tr>
<tr><td>3:00 p.m.</td><td></td><td>||</td><td>|</td><td></td></tr>
<tr><td>3:30 p.m.</td><td></td><td></td><td></td><td></td></tr>
<tr><td>4:00 p.m.</td><td></td><td>|</td><td></td><td></td></tr>
<tr><td>4:30 p.m.</td><td>|</td><td>|||</td><td></td><td></td></tr>
<tr><td>5:00 p.m.</td><td></td><td>||||</td><td>|</td><td></td></tr>
<tr><td>5:30 p.m.</td><td></td><td>||||| ||</td><td></td><td>|</td></tr>
<tr><td>6:00 p.m.</td><td>|</td><td>||||| ||||| ||</td><td></td><td>|</td></tr>
<tr><td>Answering Service Message</td><td>|</td><td>||||| ||||| |||||</td><td>||</td><td>|</td></tr>
</table>

One line is used for tenants, the other for owners and business operations. The tenant line handles incoming ad calls, tenant maintenance requests, and other tenant business. The business line is the telephone number printed on the business cards, stationary, and checks. Vendors, suppliers and staff personnel call this line. The accounting, administration, and maintenance departments all have access to this number, so owners can reach all these departments with one phone call. As the business grows, a separate number is often given for the maintenance department. If another split is needed because of the number of incoming calls, accounting and computer operations can be separated.

An incoming call log should always be maintained to keep track of all inquiries. A small tally mark is made for each call, each hour, to register the time of day that most calls come in. This helps the property manager schedule personnel working hours and breaks. For example, many prospective tenants make inquiries on their lunch hour, which means office personnel need to be available at this time.

Dealing With Prospects. Prospects calling about ads should need only a little additional information. All the essential information should have been included in the advertisement. If you wrote a successful ad, the only thing the prospect will really need is interior access to the unit.

A good phone system for handling inquiries could include a recorded message describing the showing hours, open-house hours, and any additional features. Important information about the unit should not be hidden. Otherwise the prospect simply discovers that he or she isn't interested or that it costs too much money.

Some owners may want to hide data for discriminatory purposes—so they can discriminate when they screen the phone calls. This is unacceptable behavior and can lead to legal action. A property management business must never participate in unfair practices. Not only will uniform and consistently fair policies avoid legal liability, they also breed referrals.

Showing the Unit

The rental process includes several merchandising techniques. One is to schedule open houses at the property during peak traffic hours so commuters can stop in to see the unit. Advertised open houses for lunch hours can also be effective in some areas. Bonus programs—e.g., resi dents get free laundry tokens for referring prospects who end up renting a unit—can also get great results. Discount incentives—e.g., tenants get reduced parking fees for prospects—are also helpful. For larger buildings where there are maintenance crews, offering a free apartment cleaning for referring a future tenant can get excellent results. (You should always check with the local apartment association and/or Department of Real Estate to see what incentive programs are legal in your area.)

Another good merchandising technique is to print a specific time when phone inquiries or on-site inspections can take place. This is especially effective for those buildings where there is no on-site manager. Obviously, the manager can't be on the premises at all times, but the vacancy still needs to be filled. When you can tell three to five people that you'll be showing the unit at 5 P.M. today, you have a good chance of getting one or two to show up.

To save needless trips to the building to show the property, you should always ask the prospect if he or she has driven by the property and seen the building. Tell the prospect the window coverings are open so he or she can see in, and that you only schedule interior appointments after the prospect has driven by. If people drive by and don't like the area, street, neighbors or property, they won't want to see the inside either. On the other hand, if prospects see other people looking at the same property, they may be spurred into taking immediate action.

Be sure the property has excellent curb appeal. See to it that prospects like what they see when they drive by. Paint the front door, eaves, and trim to give a crisp, clean image. (A new paint job is less expensive than a weekend ad, and may attract more tenants.) What really sharpens a place up in many California areas is landscaping. So much of the state is semi-arid, desert-like land. Rye grass can be added to the lawn as a topper, and is often green in two weeks. Sulfate of ammonia feeds the lawn for a quick green effect. Feeding the lawn takes lots of water and needs to be done often, especially while the unit is vacant. Trim the shrubs and trees. Put out a free standing pot or two of bright flowers. Attract the prospect's eye, and he or she is much more likely to enter the front door.

Be sure to explain any credit report fee or other charge to prospects before they go to the property. Many California property managers charge the local apartment association credit and unlawful detainer check fee plus $5 for processing. If there is a fee, remind prospects it must be paid in cash. People without acceptable credit may think nothing of writing a bad check. A prospect may also stop payment on the check if he or she is not accepted for the unit.

Once you have spent all the time, money and effort to get prospects to the property, have a plan for merchandising the unit itself. The value of the first impression can never be overstated. This means that you never show a dirty unit. If the unit is not rent-ready, don't show it, apologizing and explaining what will be done. People who say it looks fine are unlikely to care about the unit's appearance, and it will only look worse when they move out. People who would take care of the unit will be wary of moving in. Worse yet, many will try to negotiate for reduced rent or less deposit in return for finishing the work themselves. Unfortunately, they often never finish the work, or use poor materials and non-professional workmanship. You eventually have to redo what you've already paid for.

When showing the unit, describe benefits, don't list features. There is not much appeal in saying, "Here is an air conditioner. There is the fireplace." They can see the physical features. Instead, point out the benefits of the features. Point out the ease of keeping up the unit. It is much more effective to say something like: "Even though our area usually has mild temperatures, you'll still enjoy this air conditioner when we get those weeks of 90° days. And a cozy fire takes the chill off those nippy winter nights." A humorous approach can also be effective: "I heard a rumor that this walk-in closet is so big a family lost their kid in there for days, and thoroughly enjoyed the peace and quiet."

When showing the unit the property manager must ask questions. Do they want monthly maid service? Do they have pets? Waterbeds? Regularly visiting relatives? Child custody periods? How many cars will they need parking spaces for? Are they night or morning people? (A difference in neighbor's habits will affect their satisfaction with the building, and the property manager will have to unravel any complaints about noise.)

Rental policies (laundry room hours, pool rules, maintenance expectations, and use of common area facilities) can be best explained at this point. Rent collection policies should also be discussed during this time. Need for renting appliances or other furniture can be discussed.

Figure 3

APPLICATION TO RENT

(all sections must be completed)

Individual applications required from each adult occupant.

SAMPLE
California Only
Current Copy

LAST NAME	FIRST NAME	MIDDLE NAME	SOCIAL SECURITY NUMBER

DATE OF BIRTH	DRIVER'S LICENSE NO.	STATE	HOME PHONE NUMBER

1 PRESENT ADDRESS		CITY	STATE	ZIP CODE
DATE IN	DATE OUT	OWNER MGR NAME		OWNER/MGR PHONE NO
REASON FOR MOVING:				

COMPLETE SECTIONS 2 & 3 ONLY IF YOU HAVE LIVED AT ADDRESS #1 FOR LESS THAN 5 YEARS

2 PREVIOUS ADDRESS		CITY	STATE	ZIP CODE
DATE IN	DATE OUT	OWNER MGR NAME		OWNER MGR PHONE NO
REASON FOR MOVING:				
3 NEXT PREVIOUS ADDRESS		CITY	STATE	ZIP CODE
DATE IN	DATE OUT	OWNER MGR NAME		OWNER/MGR PHONE NO
REASON FOR MOVING				

PROPOSED OCCUPANTS	NAME	AGE	NAME	AGE
LIST ALL IN ADDITION TO YOURSELF				

WILL YOU HAVE PETS?	DESCRIBE	WILL YOU HAVE LIQUID FILLED FURNITURE?	DESCRIBE

A PRESENT OCCUPATION	EMPLOYER NAME
HOW LONG WITH THIS EMPLOYER?	EMPLOYER ADDRESS
NAME OF YOUR SUPERVISOR	EMPLOYER PHONE NO.

COMPLETE SECTION B ONLY IF YOU HAVE BEEN WITH PRESENT EMPLOYER FOR LESS THAN 5 YEARS

B PRIOR OCCUPATION	EMPLOYER NAME
HOW LONG WITH THIS EMPLOYER?	EMPLOYER ADDRESS
NAME OF YOUR SUPERVISOR	EMPLOYER PHONE NO

CURRENT GROSS INCOME	CHECK ONE		
	WEEK	MON	YR.
$ PER			

PLEASE LIST ALL OF YOUR FINANCIAL OBLIGATIONS BELOW

NAME OF YOUR BANK	BRANCH OR ADDRESS	ACCOUNT NUMBER
		CHECKING
		SAVINGS

NAME OF CREDITOR	ADDRESS	PHONE NO	MO PYMT AMT

CAA APPROVED FORM
CALIFORNIA APARTMENT ASSOCIATION
3.0 REVISED 6/84 COPYRIGHT 1980

(continued)

IN CASE OF EMERGENCY, NOTIFY:	ADDRESS	PHONE	CITY	RELATIONSHIP
1.				
2.				
IN CASE OF EMERGENCY, NOTIFY:	ADDRESS	PHONE	CITY	RELATIONSHIP
1.				
2.				

Mother's maiden name ____________________

Automobile — Make__________Model__________Year__________License Number__________

Automobile — Make__________Model__________Year__________License Number__________

Motorcycles (other vehicles)____________________

Have you ever filed for bankruptcy? ____________________

Have you ever been evicted or asked to move?____________________

Applicant represents that all the above statements are true and correct and hereby authorizes verification of the above items including but not limited to the obtaining of a credit report and agrees to furnish additional credit references on request.

The undersigned makes application to rent housing accommodations designated as:

Apt. No. __________located at____________________

the rental for which is $__________ per __________ and upon approval of this application agrees to sign a rental or lease agreement and to pay all sums due, including required deposits, before occupancy.

Dated: ____________________ 19________ ____________________

APPLICANT

CALIFORNIA APARTMENT ASSOCIATION CODE FOR EQUAL OPPORTUNITY

The California Apartment Association reaffirms its policy that equal opportunity in the rental industry can best be accomplished through leadership, example, education, and the mutual cooperation of the owners, managers, and the public. In the spirit of this endeavor, this association proclaims the following provision of its Code for Equal Opportunity to which each member is obligated to adhere.

I. In the rental, lease, sale, purchase, or exchange of real property, owners and their manager have the responsibility to offer housing accommodations to all prospects without regard to color, race, religion, sex, marital status, physical handicaps, national origin, or any unlawful discrimination, and including all other statutes applicable to equal opportunities.
II. Members shall stand ready to enter into owner/resident realtionships and to show housing accommodations to all equally.
III. Members, individually and collectively, in performing these functions have no right or responsibility to volunteer information regarding the racial, creedal, or ethnic composition of any neighborhood or any part thereof unless required by law.
IV. Members shall not print, display, or circulate any statement or advertisement with respect to the rental or sale of a dwelling that indicates any preference, limitations, or discrimination.
V. Members who violate the spirit or any provisions of this Code for Equal Opportunity shall be subject to appropriate action.

The Application

The next step is to have the tenants complete a rental application (Figure 3). Number the applications in the order received, and keep the credit check fee attached to each individual application. Then arrange to have the applicants' credit checked. It usually takes about four hours to run a credit check. Many apartment associations have Saturday credit report hours.

If approved, have the tenant furnish a copy of his or her California driver's license and last pay stub. The driver's license verifies the information on the application (e.g., their age), and serves as picture ID. It is wise to verify that the tenant is 18 years old and has the legal capacity to enter into a contract. This is also an excellent way to verify prior addresses (which are usually printed on the front or listed on the back of the license).

The pay stub should verify the data given on the rental application. It also verifies a tenant's financial ability to afford the rent, showing tax deductions for dependents, garnishments, insurance withholding, and investment contributions. With today's economy so unstable, it is important to get the most current employment information. Not only do you want to be sure the tenant can pay the rent, but your attorney will need the data to garnish wages should a rent default judgment be obtained in the future.

Handling the Paperwork

After everything is approved, it is time for the tenant to move in. Advise the tenant as soon as possible and make an appointment for the move-in paperwork, "walk-thru", and collection of any unpaid fees. Each adult should be present to sign the lease and other papers. Personal checks for initial move-in fees should never be accepted. However, the property manager should also refuse to accept cash, as cash is non-insurable and the liability to the property manager is too high. A money order is the best alternative.

Have the maintenance person present when the tenant moves in. While you discuss the rental agreement terms and conditions (example shown in Chapter 8) and get all the papers signed, the maintenance person should be removing all temporary window security clamps and devices, and removing the "For Rent" sign, and any flags, banners, and lock box that might have been used during the vacancy. He or she should also be changing all the door locks. (One key is made for the office, one for the maintenance department, and one for the tenant.) When new tenants see you rekeying when they move in, they are more confident of their security and the property's professional management. At this time, any overlooked repairs should also be made.

The tenant then completes, dates, and signs a walk-thru form (example shown in Chapter 8). While completing the rental agreement and walk-thru form, explain the policies and procedures with the tenant. Remind them to call 911 in an emergency, and then the office as soon as possible. Go over office business hours and what to do when the office is closed. Show him or her where the water main and other important utility shut-off lines are. Have the tenant turn on the faucets, sprinklers, disposals, dishwashers, etc. (This may save a maintenance call later.)

Give the tenant a copy of the paperwork when they sign it. Bring all duplicate copies necessary to complete the transaction. (Other paperwork, besides the lease agreement, may include a Pet Deposit, Waterbed Deposit, House Rules, Garage Rental Agreement, etc.)

PUBLIC RELATIONS

Maintaining good public relations is an excellent method of advertising your property management firm. The benefits of projecting a positive overall image are innumerable. You will receive resumes from people seeking employment with you, receive ongoing inquiries from prospective tenants, and build up a solid client base.

Many small local newspapers welcome weekly or monthly articles written by members of your staff to help them fill up their space. They allow you to write about items of general interest in your specialty field, and include your name and your company's name. As these papers grow, they may require you to pay for advertising space to keep your column running in the paper, but you are probably already advertising vacancies in the local paper. Large circulation newspapers have columns in the real estate or business sections about people on the move—new tract openings, new apartment complexes, promotions, and awards. The property manager should always have "3 x 5", black and white newspaper print photographs on hand for press releases. Forming good working relations with the local media is an on-going job that benefits the property manager, the firm, and all the units managed.

Tenants are customers. Good public relations with them mean a good working relationship as well as good referrals. Always treat tenants with courtesy and respect. While the owner of the property may be from the other side of the country, tenants are ongoing members of the local community.

Property managers can sometimes use the aid of a good public relations firm. A brief glance at typical newspaper coverage should tell you why. Newspapers are in the business of selling papers. "Successful" news is often that which arouses the reader's emotions. For instance, lately the hottest word in the California rental market has been SLUMLORD (Figure 7). To meet deadlines, reporters sometimes fail to research all the facts and often information is taken out of context. Many times, both sides of an issue are not covered.

A public relations firm may be able to get more balanced news printed—how the property owner put in thousands of dollars of improvements, only to have the tenants immediately tear them up. Well placed letters in the opinion section by a well-known person can also help a firm's or client's image. Public relations firms are very reasonably priced for these kinds of services.

THE REAL ESTATE LICENSEE

Real estate agents handle thousands of single-family rentals in California. No special license other than the salesperson's or broker's license is issued by the California Department of Real Estate. However, the REALTOR® Code of Ethics requires an agent to have some expertise in what he or she does. Training and property management classes are available through the California Community College system, where classes fulfill the state requirement for continuing licensee education.

Most property managers use the broker emblem or Certified Property Manager (CPM) designation logo in their merchandising. Property owners look for marketing images that emit professionalism when seeking out someone to handle their property.

According to California Real Estate License Law, an agent must make sure the property management contract gives him or her specific written consent to display signs on the property, use a lockbox, or place the property into the Multiple Listing Service (MLS) of the Board of Realtors.

Many licensees purchase income-producing properties and have to deal with their own tenants, as well as those of their clients. A few basic advertising rules must be complied with by a real estate licensee that a non-licensee owner can ignore. The Department of Real Estate may refuse to renew or may revoke a real estate license if an agent has placed false advertisements (e.g., when a property is advertised that is not available, but is being used to obtain leads). It is also a violation of the Real Estate Law to fail to disclose in the ad that there is an agent involved in the transaction by specifying "Agent' or "Agt." or the company name. Both owners and real estate licensees may not participate in any act of discrimination (under both state and federal law).

CHAPTER 7–BIBLIOGRAPHY

McMillan, Penelope. "Tackling the slumlords." *Los Angeles Times* 20 December 1987, II: 1

Spencer, Terry. "City attorney cited for rent violations." *Los Angeles Times.* 27 March 1988, X: 1

Currie, Don. "Long beach developer sued over 'Slum' Rentals." *Long Beach Press Telegram* 26 March 1988, E: 1

Woodyard, Chris. "Former residents sue long beach landlords." *Los Angeles Times* 27 March 1988, X: 1

CHAPTER 7–QUIZ

1. The marketing of rental property happens:

   a. when the phone is answered
   b. by all building landscaping and on-site personnel, except maintenance
   c. in weekend classified and display advertising
   d. All of the above

2. Which is the most expensive form of advertising?

   a. Radio and television
   b. Billboards and bus benches
   c. Public relations campaign articles
   d. Print media

3. A good rental technique to attract prospective tenants would be:

   a. lowering the rents
   b. requiring no deposits
   c. holding open houses
   d. buying tenants appliances

4. A copy of the driver's license and pay stub helps verify rental application data on:

   a. bank accounts
   b. address
   c. creditors
   d. autos

5. A vacant unit should never be shown:

   a. dirty
   b. occupied
   c. while prior tenants are out
   d. before the ad is placed

6. A list of available vacancies:

    a. creates an ostensible agency
    b. lists only the best property
    c. always reaches the advertising public
    d. should be posted on the inside window of vacant units so it can be read from the outside

7. An incoming telephone log is used to:

    a. assure accuracy of messages
    b. check on personnel
    c. schedule personnel for peak workload times
    d. prevent unfair practices

8. Which of the following would not be part of the move-in contract?

    a. Waterbed deposit
    b. Management agreement
    c. Pet deposit
    d. Walk-thru agreement

9. If a picture of the building you manage appears in the newspaper with the heading SLUMLORD, the professional property manager should:

    a. burn the building and collect the fire insurance
    b. cry, then get his or her sign off the building
    c. write his or her congressman
    d. hire a public relations firm to publicize the other side of the story

10. The real estate licensee, as a property manager:

    a. may discriminate if specifically instructed to do so in writing by the owner
    b. may use an ad on an already rented unit to attract prospects to another unit
    c. must disclose she is an agent in the ad, even if she is the owner
    d. can place a sign and lockbox on any property without written permission

CHAPTER 7–QUIZ ANSWERS

1. d
2. a
3. c
4. b
5. a
6. d
7. c
8. b
9. d
10. c

8
On-Site Personnel and Operations

References

DeCarlo, J., CPM. *California Real Property Management Study Guide.* Sacramento: California Community Colleges, 1986.

Downs, J., CPM. *Principles of Real Estate Management.* 12th ed. Chicago: Institute of Real Estate Management of National Association of Realtors: 1980.

CPM Aspects. Chicago: Institute of Real Estate Management, May/June 1987.

Official California Apartment Journal. Long Beach: Apartment Association California Southern Cities, July 1988.

Last Chapter Review

Marketing, merchandising, advertising, and public relations are important aspects of property management. The purpose of marketing was reviewed and methods of advertising were discussed. Renting the residential unit—from initial telephone inquiry to applying for the unit—was outlined. The importance of public relations was reviewed and, finally, the responsibilities of real estate licensees and property owners as to advertising and discrimination laws were examined.

Chapter Overview

This chapter reviews the types of personnel involved in property management operations. Giving these people clearly defined job descriptions, specific duties and responsibilities, and properly reporting their tax status are essential to effective property management. Fulfilling the legal responsibilities towards employees as to wages, benefits, and other obligations is imperative to avoiding liability. In addition, the duties of the property manager include training personnel to properly complete the many legal forms used in the daily operations of the business.

JOB DESCRIPTIONS FOR ON-SITE PERSONNEL

Many people are involved in the business of property management. Each person plays a vital role; each has unique opportunities to contribute to the successful management of the property. Each person should know their job description and have clearly defined responsibilities. This facilitates the smooth line of authority and chain of command necessary for the success of the building operations.

On-Site Manager

The on-site manager is the most important element in the successful operation of a building for residential, commercial and industrial sites. The residential manager usually works out of his or her apartment. However, very large buildings have separate office facilities in the common area. Many office building, industrial, and commercial on-site managers have a leasing/business office on the premises.

The on-site managers set the pace for the image of the building and the conduct of tenants. Their basic function is to assist the off-site property manager, whether it be the building owner or an authorized agent. The manager is responsible for maintaining the physical asset (the building and grounds), performing administrative tasks, and ensuring staff compliance with company policies and procedures in accordance with the owner's objectives.

Resident managers supervise all on-site staff and contract workers. Their primary job is to maintain good working relations with these people. They also interact with the management firm's personnel regarding accounting, data processing, maintenance, and other real estate-related activities.

On-site managerial duties may include approving maintenance, performing inspections, recommending replacements or repairs, supervising vacancies, reviewing all rental applications, preparing rental agreements and move-in contracts, completing move-out and refund forms, rent collection, serving legal notices, maintaining tenant files, inventorying supplies, and handling emergencies.

On-site managers must be able to understand finance issues, accounting procedures, and budgets. Good communications skills, a neat appearance, and attention to detail are a must. Resident managers also need legible handwriting for contract completion, receipt writing, and office forms.

A good way to find a qualified resident manager is to place a classified ad. Ask that applicants submit a written resume, screen all applicants, then follow up with a phone call and personal interview. Another method would be to get referrals from the local apartment association, IREM-ARM Chapter, community college property management class, or property management employment agencies.

Leasing Agent

Larger complexes, property management companies, and new buildings often have a separate position of "leasing agent." The primary function of leasing agents is to fill vacancies with qualified tenants. They also help maintain management policies and procedures in accordance with the owner's objectives. They help with marketing programs and sometimes fill in for an absent on-site manager.

A leasing agent is responsible for advertising and promotional activities, conducting market surveys, and keeping traffic reports. They assist with lease renewals and often handle the move-in and walk-thru inspections. They collect deposits and other move-in fees. They complete turnover reports, inspect vacancies, and report maintenance requests.

The appearance and manner of the leasing agent affects the image of the whole building. The entire character and tenant composition of a building can be determined by this key position. The ability to choose only the most qualified businesses and individuals as tenants, the ability to assume the on-site manager's responsibilities when he or she is unavailable, and a professional appearance and attitude are required qualifications for this position.

A leasing agent can be located through classified ads, associations or school contacts, or via real estate brokers. Many licensed real estate agents are excellent salespersons with the talents and qualities required of a good leasing agent. Arrangements can often be made for real estate agents to have open houses for residential vacancies. The broker gets the inquiries for those wanting to purchase the property, and the prospective tenants complete applications which are given to the property manager to review and approve.

Maintenance Personnel

Maintenance personnel have the responsibility for maintaining the physical condition of the entire property. They assist all other personnel in emitting a quality building image to facilitate leasing, tenant retention, and fulfilling the owner's objectives. They are responsible for prioritizing work orders, handling emergencies, inventorying and evaluating equipment, scheduling work, recommending contract services, preparing vacant units, and developing good tenant and staff relations to alleviate and dispel hostilities. Specific duties would encompass not only corrective maintenance, but preventative measures. Regular custodial and grounds work is as important as emergency repairs.

Maintenance personnel need extensive knowledge and expertise in the areas of power and utilities, plumbing, lighting, fire extinguishers and smoke detectors, gutters and downspouts, paint, trash disposal, appliances, landscaping, floor covering maintenance, locks and keys, windows and their coverings, and pesticides. They also often report the number of persons and pets in a residential unit. They report extension cord use and flammable product storage in non-residential facilities.

Maintenance personnel must be able to complete work order paperwork and personnel time sheets legibly. They must be able to describe not only the work performed, but also the nature or cause of the problem.

They must dress neatly and be well groomed. They need dependable transportation and their own tools. Their employment forms should include a discussion of past and present safety habits.

Although classified advertising will generate many applicants, qualified maintenance personnel are often hard to locate. If the operation is large enough to provide regular work, dependable personnel are easier to retain. However, most maintenance is handled on a contract basis with outside firms.

One way to find good maintenance personnel is to combine your building's maintenance jobs with those of another building. Between several buildings there may be enough work to keep one talented maintenance person busy on a full-time basis. Check to see who does the work in other buildings being managed, especially those in the same area. Another source is the local apartment association advertisers, sponsors and commercial vendors. Other off-site property management firms can make recommendations. Also, check with local union halls for referrals of good non-residential tradesmen.

Other Positions

Whether there are other positions depends on the size and make-up of the operation. Additional positions could include assistant property manager, assistant on-site manager, groundskeeper, pool keeper, janitor, custodian, recreation coordinator, and security staff.

Employee Policies

All personnel should have written, signed employment applications and contracts. These documents should include each person's job description, duties, responsibilities, insurance coverage, and compensation. All compensation, including percs, vacation, education reimbursement, training, holidays, mileage and travel reimbursement should be clearly defined. Dress codes, general employment, and termination policies are best handled with a written policy and procedure manual for the company—all policies and procedures should be uniform and consistent for all employees.

A packet of necessary government forms should be available for each new employee (W-2, W-4, INS, insurance, etc.). References should be thoroughly checked.

For personnel that live off the premises, a credit check is run to determine the financial stability of the person handling company money and supplies.

If personnel reside on the premises (such as in residential management and mini-warehouse storage businesses), a signed authorization for a credit check, similar to that run on any prospective tenant, should be processed to determine credit worthiness. Spell out the amount of rent with and without employment. Specific contract clauses should cover the required notice for termination. Termination and eviction policies need to be made clear to all parties. The amount, type of, and handling of deposits should be treated separately from the amount of rent that is offset by the cost of the tenant's labor and materials.

It is not required that all personnel live on the premises, but it is helpful. It also helps if personnel are able to readily reach one another to handle operations (for instance, with the use of pagers). Good policies and procedures make for a smoother operation of the building.

LEGAL REQUIREMENTS FOR ON-SITE PERSONNEL

License Law

A California real estate license is not required when an owner rents or manages his or her own property *(Business and Profession's Code 10133(a))*. Also exempt is the officer-manager who works for a corporation, handling corporate-owned property and compensated on a salary basis. Neither are partners subject to being licensed for managing and leasing office buildings, shopping centers, or business properties, provided all partners receive the same compensation. Under these circumstances, no fee, extra compensation, bonus, or additional benefits can be received when filling a vacancy, negotiating with tenants, or completing leases.

However, any person who locates tenants, handles rental properties, or collects rents on someone else's property and receives a fee or extra compensation for the performance of these services, must have or work under a California broker's license (except an on-site resident manager).

According to *Business and Profession's Codes 10131, 10133 and 10139,* a corporation can be fined up to $10,000 and an individual up to $1,000 and/or six months' imprisonment for violating this law.

A resident manager must be available on the premises of all residential apartment buildings with 16 or more units. This on-site manager does not need to be licensed and may be the owner, a janitor, or an agent. On the other hand, a license is required if the same person manages another building, even if that building is on the adjoining lot, because that person would then be a nonresident manager of the second building. Nonresident managers must have a license. A good rule of thumb is that a property manager who solicits tenants, negotiates rental agreements, and collects rents for someone else needs to be licensed, for both residential and nonresidential property.

Employee Status/Tax Liability

As of July 1, 1988, the government imposed new regulations for on-site managers regarding employment status and subsequent tax liability. While the off-site property manager may be an independent contractor, the resident manager is an employee. Further, the California Employment Development Department makes the on-site manager the employee of the property management firm rather than an employee of the property owner, even though the property manager and the property owner have specific written contracts to the contrary. The EDD contention is that the property manager hires, trains, oversees, compensates, and terminates the resident manager. The property owner has no direct control over the resident manager.

The property manager must report the resident manager as his or her employee on quarterly tax reports and handle tax liability and workman's compensation insurance coverage for the resident manager. This is so whether the expense is paid by the owner or is part of the management fee arrangement. The resident manager is subject to all normal employee deductions, e.g., for workman's compensation (premiums and claims) unemployment, FICA, FUTA, etc.

When an employee resides on the employer's premises as a condition of employment, the maximum monthly rent is two-thirds the amount that any other tenant would pay for the same unit. California law further limits the rent to $240 if only one employee occupies the apartment, and $335 if there are two employees in the same apartment. For example, an apartment that could rent for $535 per month to the general public would be treated as follows:

> As a credit against wages, the maximum monthly rent that could be charged for two employees sharing one apartment is $355. One employee pays $240 in rent, the other pays $115. This $355 is exempt from FICA and FUTA tax deductions, since it was a rent credit against wages.
>
> Another way to calculate this using the same circumstances would be: The employees pay the $535 per month for rent, like any other tenant in the building. The employer pays regular wages, without offsets for lodging credit, to meet minimum wage criteria, and FICA and FUTA taxes are required on all these wages. $535 x ⅔ = $356.67 in wages.

The state and federal law places resident managers in a category called "exempt employees." This does not mean they are exempt from coverage under the law, nor exempt from taxes, nor exempt from having to make the proper government reports. It means they are put into a special group, with different rules, than other regular, non-exempt employees. Other exempt employee groups include minors, the handicapped, and those receiving tips. Under federal law, the salary for exempt employees cannot include the rent on an apartment. Rent must be charged separately.

Minimum Wage/Hour Laws

Both state and federal law require a minimum salary of $900 per month for exempt employees. In addition, the minimum wage law for all employees applies to issues of regular rate, straight time, overtime and double-time pay.

A regular work week can include weekends, Sundays and holidays. Employment laws do not require vacation pay or severance pay. On-site employees can vary their work weeks to stagger the building's coverage. For instance, the full-time, on-site manager could be on a monthly schedule of working the 1st through the 5th, the 8th through the 17th, the

21st through the 24th, and the 26th through the 30th. The maintenance supervisor or leasing agent could work the alternate days.

Back-to-back work weeks, ten consecutive eight-hour days, are also permissible. One effective work schedule is having the resident manager begin work on the 26th of the month and work for ten days (26, 27, 28, 29, 30, 1, 2, 3, 4, 5) until the fifth of the month. This permits the manager to be working from the time most prospective move-ins are making inquiries up until the time when all rents should have been collected. The manager would have a day off before the 25th, before the cycle began, and on the sixth, after the cycle ends. No overtime would be due on this schedule and a back-up employee, like a janitor, could work the days that the resident manager has off.

Each employee should be provided a time card for reporting hours worked (Figure 1). In this manner, a clear record can be established as to regular hours or overtime worked. To help on-site personnel maintain their privacy, post specific hours during which they will be available to tenants. (Figure 2). Emergencies always alter posted hours, but stated office hours makes for happier employees and aids the effort to comply with labor laws. If office hours are not specified, enforcement officers may assume that all hours not spent sleeping and eating are hours worked.

It is always wise to have all real estate-related contracts in writing, and this includes employment agreements. (Figure 3). (Employment contracts are not required to be written, nor is a notice of discharge or severance.) It is good management to spell out the compensation of the employees as well as their duties. This clearly defines job expectations for everyone, and eliminates the problem of one employee "passing the buck" for a specific task to someone else. (Figure 4).

Immigration Law

The terms of the Immigration Reform and Control Act of 1986 affect all American employers. Under this Act, the employer must employ only U.S. citizens or aliens who are authorized to work in the United States. However, do not discharge present employees or refuse to hire new ones

Figure 1

Exhibit B — Report of Hours Worked

(Not required of exempt employees)

Name ______________________________ Position ______________________________

Your workweek for payroll purposes begins at ________________ on ________________

and ends at ________________ on ________________

Days of Month		Worked Assigned Hours		Hours Worked (if other than assigned)		**Reason for absence or failure to work assigned hours. If** none worked due to illness or absence enter 0 in Total for Day column. Were excess hours authorized? Result of emergency? Explain in detail.
Day	**Date**	**Yes**	**No**	**Extra Hours (If any)**	**Total For Day**	

Payroll period from __________ to __________

______________________________ ______________________________

Signature of Employee Approved

CAA APPROVED FORM
CALIFORNIA APARTMENT ASSOCIATION
1.5 Revised 7/78 COPYRIGHT 1980

Figure 2

OFFICE HOURS

In order to provide reasonable freedom from the duties of management and to comply with existing employment laws, the Manager will be on duty only during the following hours.

Day of Week	Hours	A.M.-P.M.
MONDAY	_______ to _______	_______
TUESDAY	_______ to _______	_______
WEDNESDAY	_______ to _______	_______
THURSDAY	_______ to _______	_______
FRIDAY	_______ to _______	_______
SATURDAY	_______ to _______	_______
SUNDAY	_______ to _______	_______

Your cooperation in this respect will be appreciated.

THE MANAGEMENT

Figure 3

RESIDENT APARTMENT MANAGER-EMPLOYER AGREEMENT

This agreement, between ______________________, hereinafter referred to as "manager" and ______________________, hereinafter referred to as "employer" for the resident management of the property known as ______________________, located at ______________________, California, shall be subject to the following conditions:

1. Compensation: Full compensation shall be $______ per hour, plus overtime as required by law, for time spent carrying out assigned duties. If hours required to carry out assigned duties should exceed ___ hours in any workday or _____ hours in any workweek, manager shall notify employer prior to performing such services and obtain consent therefore except in an emergency, when manager shall notify employer of additional hours worked within 48 hours.

2. Duties: Duties assigned to the manager are those shown on Exhibit A, Assignment of Duties, which forms a part of this agreement, and which shall be subject to review within 90 days of signing this agreement and annually thereafter.

3. Apartment: Since the apartment is provided as a condition of employment and at a reduced rate the manager agrees to vacate the apartment immediately upon termination of employment. The rent on the apartment shall be $ __________ per month payable either:

   _____ (a) By a credit against the agreed compensation.

   _____ (b) By the _____ day of each month in cash or check.

(Initial appropriate response)

NOTE: Employers subject to Federal laws may use only alternative (b) for all employees.

4. Days Off: Shall be one day in seven.

5. Excess Hours: Manager shall record excess hours worked carrying out assigned duties on Exhibit B, Report of Hours Worked, and shall so arrange his time as to carry out assigned duties and to provide the opportunity for not less than six hours uninterrupted sleep each 24 hours except for emergencies affecting health or safety.

6. The undersigned have read and understand the CAA Code of Ethics and the CAA Code of Equal Opportunity which are set forth on the reverse side of this agreement and are made a part hereof. The parties agree to abide by all the provisions thereto.

7. Termination: This contract may be terminated by either party (insert termination conditions):

____

____

____

Dated at ______________________, California this ________ day of ______________, 19________

Signed ______________________
Manager

____
Employer

Figure 4

Exhibit A — Assignment of Duties

Place a ✓ in the box under the title of the one individual who is *primarily* responsible for each duty.

Duty	Manager	Co-Manager	Owner or Agent	Outside Contractor
1. Renting Activities				
Advertising preparation	☐	☐	☐	☐
Inserting ads in newspapers	☐	☐	☐	☐
Sign ordering and placement	☐	☐	☐	☐
Showing vacancies	☐	☐	☐	☐
Completing resident application, rental agreements, and accepting deposits	☐	☐	☐	☐
Keeping vacant units cleaned	☐	☐	☐	☐
Phone answering	☐	☐	☐	☐
2. Rent Collections				
Distributing rental collection cards	☐	☐	☐	☐
Collecting rents when due	☐	☐	☐	☐
Executing receipts for money collected	☐	☐	☐	☐
Serving late rent notices	☐	☐	☐	☐
Collecting late rents and late charges	☐	☐	☐	☐
Serving 3-day notices to move or pay	☐	☐	☐	☐
3. Administration				
Depositing collections in bank	☐	☐	☐	☐
Writing checks for accounts payable	☐	☐	☐	☐
Reconciling bank accounts	☐	☐	☐	☐
Preparing federal and state payroll forms	☐	☐	☐	☐
Preparing employee's bond applications	☐	☐	☐	☐
Keeping reports on rents in competitive units	☐	☐	☐	☐
Compiling rent change notices	☐	☐	☐	☐
Maintaining rent collection records	☐	☐	☐	☐
Preparing late charge or delinquent notices	☐	☐	☐	☐
Preparing 3-day notices to move or pay	☐	☐	☐	☐
Preparing and filing unlawful detainer actions	☐	☐	☐	☐
Enforcement of apartment rules	☐	☐	☐	☐
Filing small claims court actions	☐	☐	☐	☐
4. Record Keeping				
Income receipts	☐	☐	☐	☐
Expenses	☐	☐	☐	☐
Resident name register	☐	☐	☐	☐
Manager's weekly time report	☐	☐	☐	☐
Unit maintenance card	☐	☐	☐	☐
Monthly income statement	☐	☐	☐	☐
Monthly expense statement	☐	☐	☐	☐
Manager's weekly apartment report	☐	☐	☐	☐
Record of location by unit of all furniture and equipment owned by apartment	☐	☐	☐	☐
5. Cleaning Apartments				
Vacuuming carpets	☐	☐	☐	☐
Shampooing carpets	☐	☐	☐	☐
Refrigerator cleaning	☐	☐	☐	☐
Plumbing fixture cleaning	☐	☐	☐	☐
Drape cleaning	☐	☐	☐	☐
Window washing	☐	☐	☐	☐
Screen cleaning	☐	☐	☐	☐
Stove and oven cleaning	☐	☐	☐	☐
Wall washing	☐	☐	☐	☐
Cabinet and closet cleaning	☐	☐	☐	☐
Heater cleaning	☐	☐	☐	☐

CAA APPROVED FORM
CALIFORNIA APARTMENT ASSOCIATION
1.4 Revised 7/78 COPYRIGHT 1980

(continued)

Duty	Manager	Co-Manager	Owner or Agent	Outside Contractor
Cleaning Apartments (continued)				
Sink, shower, and lavatory cleaning	☐	☐	☐	☐
Floor washing and/or polishing	☐	☐	☐	☐
Ceramic tile grout cleaning	☐	☐	☐	☐
Light fixtures	☐	☐	☐	☐
Tops of doorway and window trim	☐	☐	☐	☐
6. Property Policing				
Facade cleaning	☐	☐	☐	☐
Entry cleaning	☐	☐	☐	☐
Garage oils on floors and pavements	☐	☐	☐	☐
Nite light setting (time clock)	☐	☐	☐	☐
Sign cleaning	☐	☐	☐	☐
Driveway cleaning	☐	☐	☐	☐
Walkway and lawn policing	☐	☐	☐	☐
Garbage area cleanup	☐	☐	☐	☐
7. Maintenance				
Carpet cleaning	☐	☐	☐	☐
Air conditioner cleaning	☐	☐	☐	☐
Recreation, sauna, and bathroom cleaning	☐	☐	☐	☐
Fishpond or fountain cleaning	☐	☐	☐	☐
Laundry room cleaning	☐	☐	☐	☐
Hallway cleaning	☐	☐	☐	☐
Lightbulb replacement	☐	☐	☐	☐
Carport cleaning	☐	☐	☐	☐
Hallway vacuuming	☐	☐	☐	☐
Warm air heat filter cleaning	☐	☐	☐	☐
Warm air heat filter replacement	☐	☐	☐	☐
Water heater draining	☐	☐	☐	☐
Stair and deck cleaning	☐	☐	☐	☐
Stair and deck sealing or painting	☐	☐	☐	☐
Plumbing stoppage	☐	☐	☐	☐
8. Repairs				
Door or window screen repair	☐	☐	☐	☐
Door or window screen replacement	☐	☐	☐	☐
Window pane replacement	☐	☐	☐	☐
Window crank repair	☐	☐	☐	☐
Window crank replacement	☐	☐	☐	☐
Air conditioner repair	☐	☐	☐	☐
Stove burners	☐	☐	☐	☐
Stove and oven handles or knobs	☐	☐	☐	☐
Refrigerators	☐	☐	☐	☐
Dishwasher repair	☐	☐	☐	☐
Door knobs and cabinet catch replacement	☐	☐	☐	☐
Door and cabinet hinge replacement	☐	☐	☐	☐
Carpet repairs	☐	☐	☐	☐
Painting	☐	☐	☐	☐
Plumbing faucet washer replacement	☐	☐	☐	☐
Plumbing replacements	☐	☐	☐	☐
Electric switch replacement	☐	☐	☐	☐
Electric fixture replacement	☐	☐	☐	☐
Stucco patching	☐	☐	☐	☐
Stucco painting	☐	☐	☐	☐
Front door painting	☐	☐	☐	☐
Fence repairs	☐	☐	☐	☐

Duty	Manager	Co-Manager	Owner or Agent	Outside Contractor
Repairs (continued)				
Fence painting	☐	☐	☐	☐
Disposal stoppage	☐	☐	☐	☐
Disposal repair	☐	☐	☐	☐
Disposal replacement	☐	☐	☐	☐
Toilet seat replacement	☐	☐	☐	☐
Toilet seal replacement	☐	☐	☐	☐
Toilet tank repairs	☐	☐	☐	☐
Removal of door locks	☐	☐	☐	☐
Replacement of keys	☐	☐	☐	☐
Water faucet replacement	☐	☐	☐	☐
Wall painting	☐	☐	☐	☐
Woodwork painting	☐	☐	☐	☐
Mahogany door cleaning	☐	☐	☐	☐
Mahogany door varnishing	☐	☐	☐	☐
Warm air heater thermostat repair	☐	☐	☐	☐
Warm air heater thermostat replacement	☐	☐	☐	☐
Warm air heater repair	☐	☐	☐	☐
Warm air heater replacement	☐	☐	☐	☐
9. Landscape Care				
Watering lawns, shrubs, and trees	☐	☐	☐	☐
Watering planters and flower boxes	☐	☐	☐	☐
Mowing grass	☐	☐	☐	☐
Trimming grass	☐	☐	☐	☐
Trimming shrubs	☐	☐	☐	☐
Spraying shrubs	☐	☐	☐	☐
Fertilizing grass and shrubs	☐	☐	☐	☐
Repairing sprinklers	☐	☐	☐	☐
Replacing shrubs	☐	☐	☐	☐
Weeding lawns and planting areas	☐	☐	☐	☐
10. Swimming Pools				
Cleaning and sweeping	☐	☐	☐	☐
Chemical replacement	☐	☐	☐	☐
Repair of equipment	☐	☐	☐	☐
Replacement of equipment	☐	☐	☐	☐
Testing and logging pH readings	☐	☐	☐	☐
Servicing filter	☐	☐	☐	☐
Water temperature regulation	☐	☐	☐	☐
11. Miscellaneous				
Elevator cleaning	☐	☐	☐	☐
Roofing repairs	☐	☐	☐	☐
Master TV antenna and transformer	☐	☐	☐	☐
Snow removal and slippery walk protection	☐	☐	☐	☐
Personal property inventory	☐	☐	☐	☐
Furniture cleaning	☐	☐	☐	☐
Furniture repair	☐	☐	☐	☐
Furniture replacement	☐	☐	☐	☐
Vending machine repair	☐	☐	☐	☐
Vending machine collection	☐	☐	☐	☐
Vending machine stock	☐	☐	☐	☐
12. Employee Relations				
Pre-employment and termination interviews	☐	☐	☐	☐
Hiring and discharging employees	☐	☐	☐	☐
Performance evaluation and counseling	☐	☐	☐	☐
13. Other				
______________________	☐	☐	☐	☐
______________________	☐	☐	☐	☐
______________________	☐	☐	☐	☐

______________________ Manager Date ______________________ Owner or Agent Date

______________________ Co-Manager Date

Reviewed: Date ______________

Manager ______________ Co-Manager ______________ Owner or Agent ______________

Remarks ____

Reviewed: Date ______________

Manager ______________ Co-Manager ______________ Owner or Agent ______________

Remarks ____

CAA APPROVED FORM
CALIFORNIA APARTMENT ASSOCIATION
1.4 Revised 7/78 COPYRIGHT 1980

Figure 5 **EMPLOYMENT ELIGIBILITY VERIFICATION (Form I-9)**

1 EMPLOYEE INFORMATION AND VERIFICATION: (To be completed and signed by employee.)

Name: (Print or Type) Last	First	Middle	Birth Name
Address: Street Name and Number	City	State	ZIP Code
Date of Birth (Month/Day/Year)		Social Security Number	

I attest, under penalty of perjury, that I am (check a box):

- ☐ 1. A citizen or national of the United States.
- ☐ 2. An alien lawfully admitted for permanent residence (Alien Number A ________).
- ☐ 3. An alien authorized by the Immigration and Naturalization Service to work in the United States (Alien Number A ________, or Admission Number ________, expiration of employment authorization, if any ________).

I attest, under penalty of perjury, the documents that I have presented as evidence of identity and employment eligibility are genuine and relate to me. I am aware that federal law provides for imprisonment and/or fine for any false statements or use of false documents in connection with this certificate.

Signature	Date (Month/Day/Year)

PREPARER/TRANSLATOR CERTIFICATION (To be completed if prepared by person other than the employee). I attest, under penalty of perjury, that the above was prepared by me at the request of the named individual and is based on all information of which I have any knowledge.

Signature		Name (Print or Type)	
Address (Street Name and Number)	City	State	Zip Code

2 EMPLOYER REVIEW AND VERIFICATION: (To be completed and signed by employer.)

Instructions:
Examine one document from List A and check the appropriate box, *OR* examine one document from List B *and* one from List C and check the appropriate boxes. Provide the ***Document Identification Number*** and ***Expiration Date*** for the document checked.

List A Documents that Establish Identity and Employment Eligibility	List B Documents that Establish Identity		List C Documents that Establish Employment Eligibility
☐ 1. United States Passport ☐ 2. Certificate of United States Citizenship ☐ 3. Certificate of Naturalization ☐ 4. Unexpired foreign passport with attached Employment Authorization ☐ 5. Alien Registration Card with photograph	☐ 1. A State-issued driver's license or a State-issued I.D. card with a photograph, or information, including name, sex, date of birth, height, weight, and color of eyes. (Specify State) ________) ☐ 2. U.S. Military Card ☐ 3. Other (Specify document and issuing authority) ________	and	☐ 1. Original Social Security Number Card (other than a card stating it is not valid for employment) ☐ 2. A birth certificate issued by State, county, or municipal authority bearing a seal or other certification ☐ 3. Unexpired INS Employment Authorization Specify form # ________
Document Identification # ________	*Document Identification* # ________		*Document Identification* # ________
Expiration Date (if any) ________	*Expiration Date (if any)* ________		*Expiration Date (if any)* ________

CERTIFICATION: **I attest, under penalty of perjury, that I have examined the documents presented by the above individual, that they appear to be genuine and to relate to the individual named, and that the individual, to the best of my knowledge, is eligible to work in the United States.**

Signature	Name (Print or Type)	Title
Employer Name	Address	Date

Form I-9 (05/07/87)
OMB No. 1115-0136

U.S. Department of Justice
Immigration and Naturalization Service

based on foreign appearance or language (this could lead to a discrimination suit). Advise those hired after June 1, 1987, of the law and require them to complete and sign the verification form designated by the Immigration and Naturalization Service (INS) to certify eligibility for employment (Figure 5). The form should be kept for three years (or one year past the severance date). The employer should carefully examine the documents presented, record the information on the verification form, then sign the form. For additional data, write Immigration and Naturalization Service, 425 Eye Street, N.W., Washington, D.C. 20536, "Attention: Employer Facts."

RESIDENTIAL MANAGEMENT RENTAL FORMS

One of the most important functions of the on-site manager is making sure the rental forms are properly filled out, signed, and served upon the tenant. Many forms are crucial to the proper management of residential property, including the rental agreement, a move-in inspection form, and the deposit agreement. The following discussion will emphasize the use of these forms in the management of residential properties.

Rental Agreement

The rental agreement is the single most important contract in the management operation. As soon as the resident manager receives the signed rental application from the tenant (see Chapter 7, Figure 3) and the credit report is acceptable, the rental agreement is prepared (using the information found on the application). The rental agreement may be prepared at the off-site management office and signed on the premises; or the tenant may go to the off-site office, sign all the necessary papers, pay the move-in fees at the office, and bring the paid receipt to the on-site manager. The on-site manager then gives the tenant the keys and finishes the move-in paperwork. Of course, the resident manager may prepare, complete, and execute all documents on the premises.

Figure 6 **RENTAL AGREEMENT AND DEPOSIT RECEIPT**

RECEIVED FROM *John and Mary Jones* hereinafter referred to as Tenant the sum of ($*200.00*) *Two-Hundred and 00/100* DOLLARS, evidenced by *Cash* as a deposit which, upon acceptance of this rental agreement by the Owner of the premises, hereinafter referred to as Owner, shall apply said deposit as follows:

	RECEIVED	PAYABLE PRIOR TO OCCUPANCY
Rent for the period from *3/12/88* to *3/31/88*	$ *0*	$ *400.00*
Last month's rent	$ *0*	$ *0*
Security deposit	$ *200.00*	$ *800.00*
Key deposit	$ *0*	$ *50.00*
Cleaning charge	$ *0*	$ *0*
Other *Pet Dep. $100 + Waterbed Dep. $100*	$ *0*	$ *200.00*
TOTAL	$ *200.00*	$ *1450.00*

In the event that this agreement is not accepted by the Owner or his authorized agent, within *3* days, the total deposit received shall be refunded.

Tenant hereby offers to rent from the Owner the premises situated in the City of *Downey*, County of *Los Angeles*, State of *Calif.*, described as *461 #B Maple Leaf Rd.*, upon the following **TERMS** and **CONDITIONS:**

TERMS: The term hereof shall commence on *March 12,* , 19*88* and continue on a month-to-month basis thereafter, until either party shall terminate the same by giving the other party *(Sixty) 60* days written notice delivered by certified mail.

RENT: Rent shall be $*600.00* per month, payable in advance by cash, money order, or cashier's check only, upon the *1st* day of each calendar month to Owner, or his authorized agent, at the following address: *1000 Florence Blvd., #102, Downey, 90240* or at such other place as may be designated by Owner from the time to time. In the event rent is not paid within five (5) days after due date, Tenant agrees to pay a late charge of $5.00 plus $1.00 per day until rent is paid. *JJ & MJ*

MULTIPLE OCCUPANCY: It is expressly understood that this agreement is between the Owner and each signatory of Tenant(s) individually and severally. In the event of default by any one signatory, each and every remaining signatory shall be responsible for timely payment of rent and all other provisions of this agreement.

UTILITIES: Tenant shall be responsible for the payment of all utilities and services, except: *water & gardener*, which shall be paid by Owner.

USE: The premises are intended for use as a single-family residence and for no other purpose. Occupancy by guests or invitees staying over 15 days will be considered to be in violation of this provision. Only the following persons shall be allowed to occupy said premises:

Name *John* (Age *47*) Name *Fred* (Age *9*) Name *Grandma* (Age *60*)

Name *Mary* (Age *42*) Name *Jane* (Age *2*) Name *Collie dog-Lassie* (Age *4*)

PETS: No pets shall be brought on the premises without the prior written consent of the Owner.

HOUSE RULES: Tenant agrees to abide by any and all house rules, including, but not limited to, rules with respect to noise, odors, disposal of refuse, pets, parking, and use of common areas. Tenant shall not have a waterbed or other liquid-filled furniture on the premises without prior written consent of the landlord. Tenant must obtain written approval before placing additional locks on the premises and must furnish Owner or his agent with a duplicate key immediately. Attached Exhibit ☒ yes ☐ no

ORDINANCES AND STATUTES: Tenant shall comply with all statutes, ordinances and requirements of all municipal, state, and federal authorities now in force, or which may hereafter be in force, pertaining to the use of the premises.

ASSIGNMENT AND SUBLETTING: Tenant shall not assign this agreement or sublet any portion of the premises without prior written consent of the Owner which may not be unreasonably withheld.

MAINTENANCE, REPAIRS, OR ALTERATIONS: Tenant acknowledges that the premises are in good order and repair, unless otherwise indicated herein. Tenant shall be deemed to have possession of all said furniture and furnishings in good condition and repair, list provided herein, unless he objects thereto in writing within five days after receipt of such inventory. Tenant shall, at his own expense, and at all times, maintain the premises in a clean and sanitary manner including all equipment, appliances, furniture and furnishings therein and shall surrender the same, at termination hereof, in as good condition as received, normal wear and tear excepted. Tenant shall be responsible for damages caused by his negligence and that of his family or invitees and guests. Tenant shall not paint, paper or otherwise redecorate or make alterations to the premises without the prior written consent of the Owner. Tenant shall irrigate and maintain the surrounding grounds, including lawns and shrubbery, and keep the same clear of rubbish or weeds. A description of what constitutes the grounds of the premises is attached hereto. In the event the grounds are not maintained in satisfactory condition and Owner, or his agent, gives Tenant 30 days written notice of this fact, Owner, or his agent, may retain a gardening service and Tenant shall be responsible for the payment of this service. This payment is not to exceed $ *100.00* per month and is to be paid in addition to rent at the time the monthly rental payment is due. Owner, or his agent, shall be the sole judge of whether the Tenant has maintained the premises in satisfactory condition.

ENTRY AND INPECTION: Tenant agrees that Owner may at any reasonable time inspect the premises and/or make required and/or necessary repairs to same. Tenant further grees that Owner, or his agent, may show the premises to prospective tenants at anytime during the thirty- (30) day period immediately preceding the end of the existing term or to prospective purchasers of the property at anytime. It is expressly understood that Owner need make no appointment with the Tenant to arrange such showing; however, no showing without appointment will be conducted before the hours of 10:00 a.m. or after the hours of 6:00 p.m.

INDEMNIFICATION: Owner shall not be liable for any damage or injury to Tenant, or any other person, or to any property, occuring on the premises, or any part thereof, or in common areas thereof, unless such damage is the proximate result of the negligence or unlawful act of Owner, his agents, or his employees. Tenant agrees to hold Owner harmless from any claims for damages no matter how caused, except for injury or damages for which Owner is legally responsible. Tenant shall be responsible for all theft, fire or any claim to or on Tenant's personal property and possessions. Tenant expressly absolves Owner, and his agent, of any and all liability for damages caused by leakage from breaking pipes or other causes.

POSSESSION: If Owner is unable to deliver possessions of the premises at the commencement hereof, Owner shall not be liable for any damage caused thereby, nor shall this agreement be void or voidable. Tenant shall not be liable for any rent until possession is delivered. Tenant may terminate this agreement if possession is not delivered within *One* day(s) of the commencement of the term hereof.

DEFAULT: If Tenant shall fail to pay rent when due, or to perform any term hereof, after not less than three (3) days written notice of such default given in the manner required by law, the Owner, at his option, may terminate all rights of Tenant hereunder, unless Tenant, with said time, shall cure such default. If Tenant abandons or vacates the property, while in default of the payment of rent, Owner may consider any property left on the premises to be abandoned and may dispose of the same in any manner allowed by law. In the event the Owner reasonably believes that such abandoned property has no value, it may be discarded. All property on the premises is hereby subject to a lien in favor of Owner for the payment of all sums due hereunder, to the maximum extent allowed by law.

In the event of a default by Tenant, Owner may elect to (a) continue the agreement in effect and enforce all his rights and remedies hereunder, including the right to recover the rent as it becomes due, or (b) at anytime, terminate all of Tenant's rights hereunder and recover from Tenant all damages he may incur by reason of the breach of the agreement, including the cost of recovering the premises, and including the worth at the time of such termination, or at the time of an award, if suit be instituted to enforce the provision, of the amount by which the unpaid rent for the balance of the term exceeds the amount of such rental loss which the tenant proves could be reasonably avoided.

SECURITY: The security deposit, set forth above, if any, shall secure the performance of Tenant's obligations hereunder. Owner may, but shall not be obligated to, apply all or portions of said deposit on account of Tenant's obligations hereunder. Any balance remaining upon termination shall be returned to Tenant. Tenant shall not have the right to apply the Security Deposit in payment of the last month's rent.

DEPOSIT REFUNDS: The balance of all deposits shall be refunded within two weeks from date possession is delivered to Owner, or his authorized agent, together with a statement showing any charges made against such deposits.

ATTORNEYS FEES: In any legal action brought by either party to enforce the terms hereof or relating to the demised premises, the preveiling party shall be entitled to all costs incurred in connection with such action, including a reasonable attorney's fee.

WAIVER: No failure of Owner to enforce any term hereof shall be deemed a waiver, nor shall any acceptance of a partial payment of rent be deemed a waiver of Owner's right to the full amount thereof.

NOTICES: Any notice which either party may, or is required to give, may be given by mailing the same, postage prepaid, to Tenant at the premises or to Owner at the address shown below or at such other places as may be designated by the parties from time to time.

HOLDING OVER: Any holding over after expiration hereof, with the consent of Owner, shall be construed as a month-to-month tenancy in accordance with the terms hereof, as applicable.

TIME: Time is of the essence of this agreement.

ABANDONMENT: If Tenant abandons or vacates the premises, Owner, or his agent, may terminate this agreement. Any absence by Tenant from the premises for any period of five (5) days, or more without the prior written notice thereof to Owner shall constitute an abandoment of said premises by Tenant. Therefore, Tenant shall give written notice to Owner, together with Tenant's whereabouts for any proposed absence from premises in excess of five (5) days. In the event of any abandonment by Tenant, as herein described, Owner, or his agent, may remove all of Tenant's property from said premises; and Owner may store Tenant's personal property at Tenant's expense for a period not to exceed thirty (30) days, and notice thereof shall be given to Tenant at Tenant's known address, at Tenant's forwarding address, or last known employment address.

ENTIRE AGREEMENT: The foregoing constitutes the entire agreement between the parties and may be modified only by a writing signed by both parties. The following exhibits, if any, have been made a part of this agreement before the parties' execution hereof: ________
Waterbed Agreement and Pet Agreement

The undersigned Tenant hereby acknowledges receipt of a copy hereof. DATED: *3-11-88*

Sunbelt Investments Agent *John Jones* Tenant
P.O. Box 1659, Downey, CA Address/Phone *Mary Jones* Tenant
By *Donna Grogan* *1347 Elm St. 9213745* Address/Phone

The undersigned Owner accepts this offer and hereby acknowleges a receipt of a copy hereof.

________________ Owner ________________ Owner

Dated:____________

Rental Agreement
A written contract between a tenant and an owner, or the owner's agent, stating the terms of occupancy and the conditions of the use of the property.

Valid Contract. All of the elements of a valid contract should be contained in the completed rental agreement.

- This means the rental agreement should contain a set of mutual promises to exchange rent for the use of the property. This kind of contract is called a *bilateral, executory contract*—both parties are obligated to perform and part of the contract remains to be completed.
- All parties must be legally capable of contracting, so resident managers need to verify the age of all prospective tenants (to be sure they have reached the age of legal majority).
- There must also be "mutual consent," a requirement fulfilled by the process of offer and acceptance. When all parties sign and date the contract, this requirement is generally met.
- The purpose of the contract must be lawful. Under most circumstances, renting is a lawful purpose.
- A valid contract also requires consideration: paying the rent and move-in fees are considered sufficient consideration for the contract.
- According to the California Statute of Frauds, an agreement to lease for more than one year must be in writing. As a precautionary measure, all real estate agreements should be in writing, even if it is for less than a year.

Included Items. Many elements should be contained in the rental agreement. It should contain the full legal name of all parties, along with their address and telephone number, including area code and zip code. A description of the building and the unit being rented should be clearly stated. A clause should be included to indicate whether or not the tenant can sublet or assign the unit, and the conditions and penalties for such actions. The beginning and ending dates of the rental term need to be included, along with the requirements for termination. Renewal terms should be clearly stated: how, when, and for how long; or that it cannot be renewed.

Note: rental termination can be voluntary or involuntary. Voluntary termination occurs at the end of a periodic tenancy, or when both parties mutually agree to terminate a lease before the term is up. Involuntary termination can be caused by failure to pay rent, or by breach of another contractual promise (e.g., that the premises are habitable).

A good rental agreement includes the name and age of all occupants and defines additional occupant requirements. The rent amount, due date, and where it is paid to need to be clearly indicated, along with how it is to be paid (cash, check, money order). All moneys received at move-in should be duly noted, along with any amounts still due and owing. Late fees and additional fees and discounts need to be stated, as well as how and when rents can be raised.

Maintenance and care of the grounds need to be spelled out. Who pays what utilities should also be included in the rental agreement. Local laws may state that the apartment house must be responsible for the disposal of garbage, elevator service, and some utilities, such as water and trash. Most units in California, however, have individual meters for gas, electricity, and telephone service. Trash cans on the property, instead of a dumpster, can be a problem because of questions about who is responsible for setting them out to the curb for pick up. The location of the garbage cans, how many each apartment is entitled to, and who maintains the area around where they are stored must be explained. An example of the problems that could arise in this area is that if one tenant takes the cans to the curb for all the units, the property owner could become liable for workman's compensation insurance or other employee coverages to cover the possibility of an injury to that person.

Entry into and inspection of the unit should be reasonable for all parties and included as part of the rental agreement. Abandonment and holding over are both items needing clarification in the written agreement. A place for additional agreements and addendums also needs to be included. (Figure 6).

The rental agreement wording must be clear and in reasonably understandable language. All changes to the printed form must be agreed to and initialed by all parties. Each party gets a copy at the time they sign it.

Inspection Form

In addition to the rental agreement, a statement of condition, often called a walk-thru form, needs to be signed and dated by all tenants. The purpose of the walk-thru should be made clear to the tenant. It is not a work order to repair items—there is no guarantee that any item will be replaced or even fixed. Its purpose is to protect the tenant's security deposit so that, in the future, the tenant will not be blamed for any items that were already damaged when he or she took possession. (To be entitled to a refund of the security deposit, the premises must be left in the same condition as when he or she moved in, less normal wear and tear.) (Figure 7)

Theoretically, there will be no items noted on the walk-thru that need repairs, as all maintenance should already have been completed. And, with the maintenance person present at the move-in time, minor items can be completed on the spot. This gives the tenant a good idea of the quality of service given on the upkeep of the building. If something cannot be completed at that time, an appointment can be made for the specific repair.

New tenants typically do not have their phone connected for a while, and the property manager, who has to coordinate the work appointments from the office, often wastes much time traveling back and forth if there is no maintenance person on the premises. Many service companies charge a trip fee for trips to a unit when no one is home—someone will be stuck with the bill while the tenant is stuck with the problem of not having the item fixed.

A good walk-thru helps all parties in the long run. A quick-print camera also is helpful—attach a photograph of items to the file and have everyone sign and date the picture to verify the present condition of the premises. This can be specially helpful on the move-out inspection if charges are made from tenant funds to repair holes in the wall, take excessive garbage to the dump, or to take care of other visible damage.

Figure 7

STATEMENT OF CONDITION
CALIFORNIA ASSOCIATION OF REALTORS® STANDARD FORM

PROPERTY 3642 ELM VISTA UNIT #3

Type of Unit 8 UNIT APT Occupant ROSE GARCIA Move in Date 9-1-88

This move-in, move-out form is for your protection. When completing this form, be specific and check carefully. Among things you should look for are dust, dirt, grease, stains, burns, damages and wear. Use additional paper if necessary. California Civil Code 1950.5 stipulates that your security deposit is refundable to the extent not used for unpaid rent, damage and reasonable cleaning charges, normal wear and tear excepted.

ITEMS	CONDITION MOVE-IN	CONDITION MOVE-OUT
Living Room & Dining Room		
Doors and Locks	NEW	
Carpeting	NEW	
Floors and Baseboards	CLEAN	
Walls and Ceiling	NEW PAINT:	
Draperies	NONE	
Electrical Fixtures	OK	
Electrical Switches, Outlets	OK	
Windows, Screens	OK	
Misc		

ITEMS	CONDITION MOVE-IN	CONDITION MOVE-OUT
Kitchen		
Floors and Baseboards	CLEAN	
Walls and Ceiling	OK	
Electrical Fixtures	OK	
Electrical Switches, Outlets	OK	
Range, Fan, Hood	CLEAN	
Oven	CLEAN	
Refrigerator	NONE	
Plumbing	OK	
Sink & Disposer	OK	
Cabinets, Counter Surfaces	CLEAN	
Windows, Screens	OK	
Draperies/Curtains	NONE	
Misc		

To order, contact—California Association of Realtors®
525 S. Virgil Avenue, Los Angeles, California 90020

FORM MIMO-11

SEPARATE RECORD FOR EACH PROPERTY MANAGED
CALIFORNIA ASSOCIATION OF REALTORS® STANDARD FORM

Owner ______	Deposit ______
Address ______	Monthly Rent ______
Property ______	Commission:
Tenant's Name ______	Leases ______
Units ______	Collection ______
Remarks ______	Management ______

Date	Received From or Paid To	Description	Receipt or Check No.	Amount Received	Date Deposited	Amount Disbursed	Balance
3/12	SMITH - APT #A	ZELLER- MARCH RENT	R1679	500 00	3/12		500 00
3/12	SMITH - APT #C	HEFNER- MARCH RENT	R1680	500 00	3/12		1000 00
3/15	JONES - APT #12	HOFFMAN- MARCH RENT	R1681	600 00	3/16		1600 00
3/20	SMITH - APT #B	BABCOCK- MARCH RENT	R1682	500 00	3/20		2100 00
3/25	JONES - APT #10	CANTWELL- MARCH RENT	R1683	600 00	3/26		2700 00
3/28	ABC MORTGAGE	SMITH LOAN DUE 4/1	C3642			1000 00	1700 00
3/28	XYZ MORTGAGE	JONES LOAN DUE 4/1	C3643			1000 00	700 00
3/29	BANK RETURNED CHECK	JONES APT 10				600 00	100 00

To order, contact—California Association of Realtors®—525 S. Virgil Avenue, Los Angeles, California 90020

TF-11-3

EQUAL HOUSING OPPORTUNITY TT-L5-FG

DECLARATION OF SERVICE/NOTICE TO PAY OR QUIT/ CHANGE IN TERMS OF TENANCY

Three of the most frequently used forms in residential property management are the Declaration of Service or Proof of Service (Figure 8), and the Notice to Pay or Quit (Figure 9) and the Change in Terms of Tenancy (Figure 10). Each form is completed by filling in the blanks, and signing and dating it in the appropriate place. Exact, precise information is necessary. All personnel should be trained so that each form is completed as if a judge in a court of law is looking at it, as this may be the case in the long run.

The "service" form is used in California when any legal document is served upon any person, whether it be to appear in court, to pay child support, to increase rent, or to pay rent that is due. It must be served (delivered) by someone over age 18 and served upon or to someone over age 18. All parties 18 years and over who may reside on the premises must be treated as separate adults and each served separately in most California court jurisdictions. The form does not have a specific place for the time of day of service, but you should add this item at the top date line to indicate when you were with the person. It helps your memory if service is later denied in court.

Your business practices may require only personal service, instead of service by posting it on the door and mailing it. If this is so, train your personnel. Some California courts frown on not personally serving the tenant. Facing the tenant also gives the manager and tenant a chance to discuss why the rent is late, if the tenant is planning to move, or if there is a maintenance problem, etc. It is important to note that the tenant may be served at their place of employment. Many courts require proof that the manager tried to serve the tenant at work before allowing service by mail.

Every attempt should be made to make contact with the tenant. To properly serve the tenant, there cannot be any additional burden placed upon the tenant. Therefore, do not send the notice by certified mail, when the tenant has to go to the post office, sign for it, or do anything else to receive the letter. First class, pre-paid mail is sufficient.

The Notice to Pay Rent or Quit should never be used when there is an existing lease, residential or commercial. The form clearly states that

Figure 8

SUNBELT INVESTMENTS
P.O. Box 1659, Downey, CA 90240
(213) 861-3835

DECLARATION OF SERVICE OF NOTICE TO RESIDENT (Tenant)

I, the undersigned, declare that at the time of service of the papers herein referred to, I was at least EIGHTEEN (18) years of age, and that I served the following checked notice:

☐ Notice to Pay Rent or Quit
☐ Thirty (30) Day Notice of Termination of Tenancy
☒ Other *Change in terms of tenancy*

on the following resident(s) *Arthur James McNeil*

on the *Second (2nd)* day of *December at 5:50 p.m.*, 198*8*.

☒ BY DELIVERING a copy of the Notice to each of the above-named resident(s) PERSONALLY.

OR

☐ BY LEAVING a copy for each of the above-named resident(s) with a person of suitable discretion at the residence or usual place of business of the resident(s), said resident(s) being absent thereof;

AND MAILING by first class mail on said date a copy to each resident by depositing said copies in the United States Mail, in a sealed envelope with postage fully prepaid, addressed to the above-named resident(s) at their place of residence.

OR

☐ BY POSTING a copy for each of the above-named resident(s) in a conspicuous place on the property therein described there being no person of suitable age or discretion to be found at any known place of residence or business of said resident(s);

AND MAILING by first class mail on the same day as posted, a copy to each said resident by depositing said copies in the United States Mail, in a sealed envelope with postage fully prepaid, addressed to the resident(s) at the place where the property is situated.

I declare under penalty of perjury that the foregoing is true and correct and if called as a witness to testify thereto, I could do so competently.

Executed this *Second (2)* day of *December*, 198*8*, at *Downey*, California.

by Millie Emil
Signature of Declarant

Figure 9

SUNBELT INVESTMENTS
P.O. Box 1659, Downey, CA 90240
(213) 861-3835

NOTICE TO PAY OR QUIT

TO: *Susan Fernandez and Beverly Campos*
All residents (tenants and subtenants) in possession (full name) and all others in possession

WITHIN THREE DAYS after the service on you of this notice, you are hereby required to pay to the undersigned or *Sunbelt Services*, his authorized agent, the rent of the premises hereinafter described, of which you now hold possession amounting to the sum of *Five-Hundred and °°/100* ------- dollars ($*500.00*) enumerated as follows:

$*100.00* Due From *October 1* 19*88* To *November 1* 19 *88*
$*400.00* Due From *November 1* 19*88* To *December 1* 19 *88*
$______ Due From ______ 19___ To ______ 19 ___

OR QUIT AND DELIVER UP THE POSSESSION OF THE PREMISES.

The premises herein referred to are situated in the city of *Downey* County of *Los Angeles*, State of California, designated by the number and street as *6432 Rio Vesta Drive*, apt. *23*.

YOU ARE FURTHER NOTIFIED THAT, the undersigned does hereby elect to declare the forfeiture of your lease or rental agreement under which you hold possession of the above-described premises and lessor will institute legal proceedings to recover rent and possession of said premises which could result in a judgment against you including cost and necessary disbursements together with treble damages as allowed by law for such unlawful detention.

Date *November 2, 1988* *by Millie Emil*
OWNER/AGENT

Figure 10

SUNBELT INVESTMENT
P.O. Box 1659, Downey, CA 90240
(213) 861-3835

NOTICE OF CHANGE OF TERMS OF TENANCY

To: *Mark Edwards and Phillip Woods* and to all others in possession of the premises commonly know as *3* (Apt. No.)

4698 Elm Street (Street Address), *Downey* (City),
California 90240 (State).

You are hereby notified, in accordance with Civil Code Section 827, that 30 days after service upon you of this notice, or *12-1-88* (Date), whichever is later, your tenancy of the above designated premises will be changed as follows:

1. The monthly rent which is payable in advance on or before the *First (1st)* day of each month will be the sum of $ *625.00*, instead of $ *595.00*, the current monthly rent.
2. OTHER CHANGES:

Except as herein provided, all other terms of your tenancy shall remain in full force and effect.

DATE: *10-15-88* *by Millie Emil*
OWNER/AGENT

the tenant has a choice of paying the rent or vacating the premises. A tenant who wants out of a lease may stop paying rent, hoping to be able to choose the "vacate the premises" option. This would be an easy way for him or her to avoid liability under the lease.

The form requires the full name of all the occupants. If you fail to name one party, you cannot evict them as they were not officially served with the notice and given the opportunity to pay. The full amount due for each separate rental period should be listed clearly and separately so that a judge may easily figure the amounts. Do not include any moneys due other than the rental amount on this form. You may not collect late fees, security or other deposits, maintenance costs, etc., with this form. It is intended to be used for rent only.

The Notice of Change of Terms of Tenancy is used most often for rent increases, but it has many other uses as well. Under item #2 of the form, "Other Changes," any other changes can be listed. For instance, the form may be used to notify the tenant of the name, address, and telephone number of the new property manager. It may be used to indicate that rent is to be payable in money order or cashier's check, instead of personal check. It may be used to change the date rent is due, or specify that the tenant is to begin paying for certain utilities. All other lease terms remain the same, except what is specifically listed in the form.

Security Deposit Form

The area of greatest dispute in landlord/tenant relations is in the area of security deposits. A copy of *Civil Code Sections 1950.5* (for residential property) and *1950.7* (for non-residential property) should be kept on file. Whenever there is a disagreement, give everyone a copy of the actual law, so that each can interpret its meaning. Do not give legal advise. Again, act as if you are standing in front of a judge explaining your actions, because this often turns out to be the case. Tenants may take landlords to small claims court to recover their deposits.

The main items to remember regarding deposits are that all moneys, other than rent, are refundable deposits, and that an exact accounting must be given to the tenants in writing if you spend their money. (Figure 11).

Figure 11

§1950.5 [Security for performance of rental agreement for residential property]

(a) The provisions of this section shall apply to security for a rental agreement for residential property, that is, property used as the dwelling of the tenant.

(b) As used in this section, "security" means any payment, fee, deposit or charge, including, but not limited to, an advance payment of rent, used or to be used for any purpose, including, but not limited to, any of the following:

(1) The compensation of a landlord for a tenant's default in the payment of rent.

(2) The repair of damages to the premises caused by the tenant.

(3) The cleaning of the premises upon termination of the tenancy.

(c) A landlord may not demand or receive security, however denominated, in an amount or value in excess of an amount equal to two months' rent, in the case of unfurnished residential property, and an amount equal to three months' rent in the case of furnished residential property, in addition to any rent for the first month paid on or before initial occupancy. This subdivision shall not be construed to prohibit an advance payment of not less that six months' rent where the term of the lease is six months or longer.

This subdivision shall not be construed to preclude a landlord and a tenant from entering into a mutual agreement for the landlord, at the request of the tenant and for a specified fee or charge, to make structural, decorative, furnishing, or other similar alterations, such alterations being other than that cleaning or repairing for which the landlord may charge the previous tenant as provided by subdivision (e).

(d) Any security shall be held by the landlord for the tenant who is party to such lease or agreement. The claim of a tenant to such security shall be prior to the claim of any creditor of the landlord.

(e) The landlord may claim of the security only such amounts as are reasonably necessary to remedy tenant defaults in the payment of rent, to repair damages to the premises caused by the tenant, exclusive of ordinary wear and tear, or to clean such premises, if necessary, upon termination of the tenancy. No later than two weeks after the tenant has vacated the premises, the landlord shall furnish the tenant with an itemized written statement of the basis for, and the amount of, any security received and the disposition of such security and shall return any remaining portion of such security to the tenant.

(f) Upon termination of the landlord's interest in the dwelling unit in question, whether by sale, assignment, death, appointment of receiver or otherwise, the landlord or his agent shall, within a reasonable time, do one of the following acts, either of which shall relieve him of further liability with respect to such security held:

(1) Transfer the portion of such security remaining after any lawful deductions made under subdivision (e) to the landlord's successor in interest, and thereafter notify the tenant by personal delivery or certified mail of such transfer, of any claims made against the security, and of the transferee's name, address, and telephone number. If the notice to the tenant is made by personal delivery, the tenant shall acknowledge receipt of such notice and sign his name on the landlord's copy of such notice.

(2) Return the portion of such security remaining after any lawful deductions made under subdivision (e) to the tenant, together with an accounting as provided in subdivision (e).

(g) Upon receipt of any portion of such security under paragraph (1) of subdivision (f), the transferee shall have all of the rights and obligations of a landlord holding such security with respect to such security.

(h) The bad faith claim or retention by a landlord or transferee of a security or any portion thereof, in violation of this section, may subject the landlord or his transferee to damages not to exceed two hundred dollars ($200), in addition to any actual damages. In any action under this section, the landlord shall have the burden of proof as to the reasonableness of the amounts claimed.

(i) No lease or rental agreement shall contain any provision characterizing any security as "nonrefundable."

(j) Any action under this section may be maintained in small claims court if the damages claimed, whether actual or punitive or both, are within the jurisdictional amount allowed by Section 116.2 or the Code of Civil Procedure.

(k) To the extent that this section is a recodification of the provisions of Chapter 1317 of the Statues of 1970, as amended by Chapter 618 of Statutes of 1972, this section became operative on January 1, 1971, and shall apply only to payments or deposits made on or after such date.

The amendments made to the law, as effective on January 1, 1977, by the enactment of this section in the 1977-78 Legislative Session, exclusive of subdivision (e), shall be applicable to all tenancies, leases, or rental agreements for residential property created or renewed on or after January 1, 1978.

Subdivision (e) of this section shall be applicable to all tenancies, leases, or rental agreements for residential property terminated on or after January 1, 1978.

Figure 12

ITEMIZED DISPOSITION OF SECURITY DEPOSIT

Pursuant to Civil Code Section 1950.5, Owner, on the *5th* day of *December*, 198*9*, hereby furnished the following statement of disposition of security deposit monies to former resident(s):

Michael Johnson and Mary Knowles
(Name(s))

for the premises located at: *885 North San Antonio "D", Downey* (Address) California *90240* (Zip)

SAMPLE California Only Current Copy

Itemized Damages: *Replace 14 x 18 Window* *$97.00*

Replace Garbage Disposal *$99.00*

Replace 3 Broken Sprinkler Heads @ $10.00 ea *$30.00*

Repair Shower Curtain Rod *$24.00*

TOTAL DAMAGES $*250.00*

Necessary cleaning of premises upon termination:

Clean Interior *$250.00 - paint and rug shampoo*

Haul 3 loads to dump from garage and side yard $100.00

TOTAL CLEANING COSTS $*350.00*

Default in rent (explain):

December 1 to and including December 9, 1989

$600/mo ÷ 30 days = $20/day x 9 =

TOTAL RENT DUE $*180.00*

USE BACK OF FORM IF MORE SPACE IS NEEDED

SEND BALANCE DUE OWNER TO:

NAME *c/o Sunbelt Investments*

ADDRESS *P.O. Box 1659*

CITY, STATE, ZIP *Downey, CA 90240*

TOTAL CHARGES	$*780.00*
TOTAL SECURITY DEPOSITS RECEIVED	$*900.00*
BALANCE DUE OWNER PLEASE REMIT IMMEDIATELY	$ *-0-*
BALANCE DUE RESIDENT PAID BY CHECK NO.	$*120.00*

FORMER RESIDENT'S NEW ADDRESS

Unknown

Mailed to property address 12/6/89

OWNER/AGENT

CAA APPROVED FORM
CALIFORNIA APARTMENT ASSOCIATION
FORM 18.0 REVISED 7/82 COPYRIGHT 1982

UNAUTHORIZED REPRODUCTION OF THIS FORM IS ILLEGAL

It does not matter if you label the money a key deposit, pet deposit, cleaning deposit, security deposit, waterbed deposit, or anything else. All funds are fully refundable, except for legally deductible expenses. Deductible expenses include paying for any damage caused by the tenant that is not normal wear and tear. Use a clear-cut itemization of any legitimate deductions so that both the tenant and a judge would have no trouble understanding how you reached your calculations (Figure 12).

The landlord has only two weeks to make the refund, including Sundays or holidays. If the landlord fails to refund the deposit within the two-week period, the penalty is the amount of the original refund, plus $200 damages, plus any punitive fees the court may decide to award.

When a building is sold, landlords or their agents often overlook their legal obligation to notify the tenants of the name, address, and telephone number of the place their deposits have been transferred to. An itemization of the funds, and any deductions made, must be made for the new owner, even if the property is transferred by foreclosure, death of the owner, or otherwise. If the parties fail to do this, the new owner could be held liable if a future owner fails to properly transfer the funds at a much later date.

CHAPTER 8–QUIZ

1. Posted hours for the On-Site Resident Manager insures:

   a. regular hours and scheduled time off
   b. peace and quiet for the manager
   c. reasonable cooperation between tenants, management and state agencies enforcing labor laws
   d. five days on the job, two days off, and no overtime

2. A written Resident Apartment Manager-Employer Agreement:

   a. should be used instead of a rental agreement
   b. includes emergency and overtime pay
   c. spells out five days work and two days off
   d. includes duties assigned as a separate form

3. An assignment of duties:

   a. states who is primarily responsible for each, even though others may sometimes perform them
   b. includes work requirements for emergency, crisis, and evacuation procedures
   c. defines janitorial, custodian, and groundskeeper job descriptions, duties, and responsibilities
   d. lists allowable on-site expenditures, forms to be used and on-site duties are performed

4. A written rental agreement:

   a. is the same as a lease
   b. should be signed and dated by all parties
   c. takes the place of a walk thru
   d. guarantees prompt rent collection

5. A walk-thru is a statement of the condition of the premises:

   a. as of the date of the move-in
   b. indicating what repairs will be done
   c. listing items to be replaced
   d. which dissolves all future conflict

6. Service should always be:

   a. by certified or registered mail
   b. personal, if at all possible
   c. to the tenant's child who answers the door
   d. done at court

7. A notice served for nonpayment of rent:

   a. includes all money due and owning
   b. may include the monthly payment of deposits
   c. will list separately all late fees
   d. allows the tenant to move

8. The notice you would serve to notify the tenant that they will be responsible for payment of the water bill, instead of the landlord is:

   a. a three-day notice
   b. a five-day notice
   c. a Change of Terms of Tenancy
   d. a Disposition of Deposit

9. The provisions of the security deposit law include allowable deductions for all but which of the following:

   a. tenant-caused damage
   b. cleaning, upon termination
   c. nonrefundable move-in fee
   d. a default in rent

10. A good Itemized Disposition of Security Deposit would include:

    a. brand, color, and name of paint used
    b. date, number, and amount of refund check
    c. owner's name, address, and telephone number
    d. copies of receipts for all labor and materials

Chapter 8–Answer Key

1. c
2. d
3. a
4. b
5. a
6. b
7. d
8. c
9. c
10. b

9
Non-Residential Property Management

References

Mahoney, Kevin, et al. "The Real Estate Markets in 1988." *Journal of Property Management,* Mar./Apr. 1988.

Collins, Doug F. "Collins Opposes U.S. Plan to Cut Leased Office Space." *CPM Aspects,* Apr. 1988.

Downs, James. *Principles of Real Estate Management.* 12th ed. Chicago: Institute of Real Estate Management, National Association of Realtors.

Carpenter, Horace. *Shopping Center Management, Principles and Practices.* New York: International Council of Shopping Centers, 1978.

DeCarlo, James. *Property Management in California.* 3rd ed. Costa Mesa: 1988.

DeCarlo, James. *California Property Management Study Guide.* Sacramento: California Community Colleges, 1986.

Vincent, Roger. "Southern California Market Overview." *Guide to Commercial Real Estate.* Los Angeles. Fall, 1987.

"California Indicators." *California Business,* Oct. 1988.

McKenzie, Dennis, and Richard Betts. *The Essentials of Real Estate Economics.* New York: Wiley & Sons, Inc., 1980.

"California Indicators." *California Business,* Oct. 1988.

Westcott, Ray D. *The Real Estate Primer.* Compton: Real Estate Primer Publications, 1988.

Last Chapter Review

The last chapter dealt with on-site management operations and the people who carry out those operations. We discussed how each of these employees require training, job descriptions, and a clear understanding of policies and procedures. Well-qualified employees are essential for good on-site operations; and good on-site operations mean a well-run building. Property managers must remember that labor laws apply to their employees and must make sure to comply with them. Lastly, on-site residential management forms were discussed, to encourage accurate completion and ensure enforceability.

Chapter Overview

This chapter investigates the process of managing non-residential properties. Office buildings, commercial centers, and industrial complexes all have similar lease provisions, deposit handling, accounting reports, landlord/tenant relations, tenant criteria, and operations procedures. Non-residential management is distinctly different from residential management and should be treated as a separate discipline.

To manage non-residential property, a person needs a high level of knowledge and expertise to negotiate leases, understand tax implications and legal consequences, and decipher the economic aspects of the non-residential landlord/tenant relationship. Financing tenant improvement requirements, the lease itself, and disclosure of the property manager's agency relationship with the landlord are all part of the property management job. The property manager must monitor present and future needs for growth and contraction of the tenant's business, core utility requirements, floor space needs, and long-term services.

OFFICE BUILDINGS

Proper management of an office building is very important not only to the landlord and tenant, but also to the occupants—the employees and customers of the businesses who use the building. The property manager must look at an office building through these users' eyes. Excluding time spent in the bedroom/bathroom complex at home for rest and personal preparation, more waking hours are spent in the workplace than in any other environment.

It is a truism that businesses gain or lose business because of their employees' actions and attitudes. The business environment, the stuff of ergonomics, has a direct effect on these actions and attitudes. If personnel are uncomfortable because a locked thermostat makes the room too hot or too cold, that irritability can be directed towards the customers. People also react to such simple things as the color of the walls, halls, lobby, and restrooms. Business equipment placed in inconvenient locations because of electrical outlet locations, dangerous extension cords, and eye strain from poor lighting all influence people's state of being.

Property managers must learn to deal effectively with these human elements of the business. They must also be able to understand and handle a number of other elements that impact a building's performance.

Market Conditions

Office buildings have had a national vacancy of about 11%, with approximately 16% vacancy for downtown buildings. Regional submarkets, however, vary considerably, with Dallas at 20% and Boston's Back Bay area at only 2%. California has the same divergent range of office building vacancies within the state for much the same reasons—economic conditions.

Vacancy rates are attributed to two major factors. One is the demand for office space. Of course, the business economic cycle (both as to the economy as a whole and the economy of a particular industry) affects the demand for office space. When the economy is strong, there is a healthy demand for office space as new businesses are created and existing businesses expand. The second factor is the supply of office space. The rate of new building construction has a dramatic effect on vacancy rates. Considerable office space was built in the late 1970s and early 1980s. In fact, most markets were severely overbuilt and vacancy rates rose.

In the short run, lessees have tremendous opportunities to obtain attractive tenant improvements, rent concessions, and favorable lease terms when vacancy rates are high. As the absorption rate increases, vacancies are filled, and the market is stabilized. In the long run, office buildings provide relatively good yields to investors, with reasonable annual growth. For example, in the short run, rents have gone down since 1980 in many areas. In the long run, investors can expect office buildings to provide a rate of return ranging from the inflation rate to at least an 8% increase. In large part, this is due to the Pacific-Rim activity and overall population growth in California.

Development Restraints

In many California markets, the restraints on development are so prohibitive that it can take years to get the approvals needed to construct a major building. The EPA, the Coastal Commission, environmentalists, and local residents can either increase or decrease the pace of development. Where development is encouraged and relatively easy, overbuilding problems have occurred. Cities can have very high permit fees and long plan-check approval times, or vice versa, depending on whether it is a pro-growth or anti-growth region.

Physical Elements

The physical elements of a particular building will vary considerably, depending on the type of structure. The garden-type office building is usually a one-story facility with individual, outside door access, rather than a door opening onto a common hallway. Many of these buildings have central gardens, walkways, ponds (often with koi), and other features that require special maintenance agreements, contractors, or personnel to keep up the appearances.

Typical California office buildings are classified as low-rise buildings with stairways, halls, and possibly some central vending machine or lunch facility. They are popular in suburbs and in areas of lower-density population, or where local ordinances limit height. The high-rise office building in California is often found in business complexes or other areas of concentrated business activity. These are often adjacent to downtown centers and around airport facilities. Common area lobbies, elevators, underground and valet parking, and maintenance personnel are required for these large structures, as well as an on-site leasing and management office.

Office Building Criteria. The Building Owners and Managers Association (BOMA) is a trade association that supports and represents the needs and interests of the office building industry. Their standard method of measuring office space is frequently used by investors, owners and managers, tenants, architects, appraisers, and lenders.

Office buildings are also placed into four categories irrespective of the height of the building, the gross leasable area, or type of building. The category a building belongs to is determined by a series of criteria: location, neighborhood, transportation, prestige, appearance, lobby, elevators, corridors, office interior, tenant services, management, and tenant mix. These items are used to compare competing buildings and office space. The results of the comparison affect rental rates and sales prices.

The "Grade A" category includes buildings located in the very prestigious locations that have the most desirable tenants. Examples of "A" buildings include Century City, the TransAmerica Building, or the ARCO Towers. "Grade B" buildings are priced slightly below, and used to be Grade A buildings (such as the Atrium, or Bunker Hill). "Grade C" buildings are reasonably well maintained, but are older structures geared to a lower-income tenant. "Grade D" buildings are poorly maintained, usually located near downtown central business districts (CBD), and are older structures.

Maintenance. Like residential tenants, office building lessees expect the landlord to handle the maintenance, repairs, and general upkeep and image of the building.

Tenant Selection

A big difference between residential property and office buildings is the lease term. For residential properties, it is common to have a month-to-month tenancy, and the remedies for default can be sought in small claims court. Office space is rented under leases for periods of three to ten years or more. Options for longer periods are not uncommon. A breach of the lease terms causes a controversy over substantial amounts of money. This, understandably, causes the office property manager to have more rigid qualification criteria and investigate potential tenants more thoroughly.

The property manager must get a thorough and detailed financial history of the business owners, the business itself, and of the industry. If the prospective tenant is not within the acceptable range of existing tenants in the building, improper tenant mix may be a valid reason for not approving a prospect. Other reasons for rejecting a prospective tenant include a poor business reputation, an insufficient profit margin to maintain long-term rents, disruption of other tenants, the amount of physical alterations required, traffic and wear and tear that would be detrimental to the building, and expensive tenant expenses.

> **Examples:** A tenant that needs special electrical wiring, such as dental or medical offices; offices where furniture is constantly being moved into or out of the elevators; businesses with significant parking needs; jewelry businesses that require security systems; flower or food businesses that require refrigeration units; restaurants that require public restrooms and fire protection facilities.

Tenants that counsel or interact with criminals, the mentally-disturbed, or potentially dangerous people also require special consideration.

The Lease

Office building leases (Figure 1) include the names and addresses of all the parties, and describe the premises. The rental amount, due date, and place of payment are also included.

Some lease provisions need special attention. What use can the tenant make of the property? The parties often agree that the tenant can only operate a particular type of business on the premises. Usually a violation of this agreement affects another tenant in the building.

> **Example:** Tenant A operates a deli. Landlord agrees she will not allow any other tenant to run a deli or other business that would compete with Tenant A. One year later, Tenant B changes his business from a messenger service to a deli. Thus, Tenant B's actions have caused Landlord to violate her agreement with Tenant A.

The parties should also discuss who owns any improvements added by the tenant, the tax consequences of the improvements, the possibility of mechanics' liens, and the cost to remove the improvements. Parking, marquee, signboards, and business hours affect all building tenants and need to be specified in the lease.

> **Example:** A training school that meets from 6:00 to 8:00 a.m. means that the office space is inaccessible to morning cleaning crews. If students tie up all the parking places until 8:00 a.m., other tenants and their customers may be late for an 8 a.m. arrival time because they have to wait for an available parking space.

The rent is the most critical issue in the lease. If free rent is offered, the exact amount of free rent must be made very clear. The period of time that is rent-free should also be specified—the first, sixth, or twelfth month? Most office space is leased at a flat rate amount, payable monthly in advance. The rent amount, due date, and possible increases must be clearly spelled out in the lease. Add-on fees are payable with the rent for those costs tranferred to tenants based on their percentage of square feet or proportional usage.

Rent increases in office buildings are usually annual and tied to an index. A commonly used index is the Consumer Price Index (CPI). (Figure 2) The 12th District Cost of Funds is also commonly used for California leases. Other adjustments can be specific percentage increases each year, or an index tied to wage levels, financial rates, or similar.

Figure 1

COMMERCIAL LEASE AND DEPOSIT RECEIPT

RECEIVED FROM ____
____, hereinafter referred to as LESSEE,
the sum of $ ______________ (______________________________ DOLLARS),
evidenced by ______________________, as a deposit which, upon acceptance of this lease, shall belong to Lessor and shall be applied as follows:

	TOTAL	RECEIVED	BALANCE DUE PRIOR TO OCCUPANCY
Rent for the period from ________ to ________	$ ________	$ ________	$ ________
Security deposit	$ ________	$ ________	$ ________
Other	$ ________	$ ________	$ ________
TOTAL	$ ________	$ ________	$ ________

In the event that this lease is not accepted by the Lessor **within** ________ **days**, the total deposit received shall be refunded.

Lessee hereby offers to lease from Lessor the premises situated in the City of ______________________, County of ______________,
State of ______________, described as ____
____
____

upon the following TERMS and CONDITIONS:

1. TERM: The term hereof shall commence on ______________, 19____, and expire on ______________, 19____.

2. RENT: The total rent shall be $______________, payable as follows: ______________________
____
____

All rents shall be paid to Owner or his authorized agent, at the following address: ______________________
______________________, or at such other places as may be designated by Owner from time to time.

3. USE: The premises are to be used for the operation of ______________________
____

and for no other purpose, without prior written consent of Lessor.

4. USES PROHIBITED: Lessee shall not use any portion of the premises for purposes other than those specified hereinabove, and no use shall be made or permitted to be made upon the premises, nor acts done, which will increase the existing rate of insurance upon the property, or cause cancellation of insurance policies covering said property. Lessee shall not conduct or permit any sale by auction on the premises.

5. ASSIGNMENT AND SUBLETTING: Lessee shall not assign this lease or sublet any portion of the premises without prior written consent of the Lessor, which shall not be unreasonably withheld. Any such assignment or subletting without consent shall be void and, at the option of the Lessor, may terminate this lease.

6. ORDINANCES AND STATUTES: Lessee shall comply with all statutes, ordinances and requirements of all municipal, state and federal authorities now in force, or which may hereafter be in force, pertaining to the premises, occasioned by or affecting the use thereof by Lessee. The commencement or pendency of any state or federal court abatement proceeding affecting the use of the premises shall, at the option of the Lessor, be deemed a breach hereof.

7 MAINTENANCE, REPAIRS, ALTERATIONS: Lessee acknowledges that the premises are in good order and repair, unless otherwise indicated herein. Lessee shall, at his own expense and at all times, maintain the premises in good and safe condition, including plate glass, electrical wiring, plumbing and heating installations and any other system or equipment upon the premises and shall surrender the same, at termination hereof, in as good condition as received, normal wear and tear excepted. Lessee shall be responsible for all repairs required, excepting the roof, exterior walls, structural foundations, and: ______________
____

which shall be maintained by Lessor. Lessee shall also maintain in good condition such portions adjacent to the premises, such as sidewalks, driveways, lawns and shrubbery, which would otherwise be required to be maintained by Lessor.

No improvement or alteration of the premises shall be made without the prior written consent of the Lessor. Prior to the commencement of any substantial repair, improvement, or alteration, Lessee shall give Lessor at least **two (2) days written notice** in order that Lessor may post appropriate notices to avoid any liability for liens.

Lessee shall not commit any waste upon the premises, or any nuisance or act which may disturb the quiet enjoyment of any tenant in the building.

8. ENTRY AND INSPECTION: Lessee shall permit Lessor or Lessor's agents to enter upon the premises at reasonable times and upon reasonable notice, for the purpose of inspecting the same, and will permit Lessor at any time **within sixty (60) days** prior to the expiration of this lease, to place upon the premises any usual "To Let" or "For Lease" signs, and permit persons desiring to lease the same to inspect the premises thereafter.

9. INDEMNIFICATION OF LESSOR: Lessor shall not be liable for any damage or injury to Lessee, or any other person, or to any property, occurring on the demised premises or any part thereof, and Lessee agrees to hold Lessor harmless from any claims for damages, no matter how caused.

10. POSSESSION: If Lessor is unable to deliver possession of the premises at the commencement hereof, Lessor shall not be liable for any damage caused thereby, nor shall this lease be void or voidable, but Lessee shall not be liable for any rent until possession is delivered. Lessee may terminate this lease if possession is not delivered **within** ________ **days** of the commencement of the term hereof.

11. INSURANCE: Lessee, at his expense, shall maintain plate glass and public liability insurance including bodily injury and property damage insuring Lessee and Lessor with minimum coverage as follows: ______________________
____

Lessee shall provide Lessor with a Certificate of Insurance showing Lessor as additional insured. The Certificate shall provide for a ten-day written notice to Lessor in the event of cancellation or material change of coverage.

To the maximum extent permitted by insurance policies which may be owned by Lessor or Lessee, Lessee and Lessor, for the benefit of each other, waive any and all rights of subrogation which might otherwise exist.

12. UTILITIES: Lessee agrees that he shall be responsible for the payment of all utilities, including water, gas, electricity, heat and other services delivered to the premises.

13. SIGNS: Lessor reserves the exclusive right to the roof, side and rear walls of the Premises. Lessee shall not construct any projecting sign or awning without the prior written consent of Lessor which consent shall not be unreasonably withheld.

14. ABANDONMENT OF PREMISES: Lessee shall not vacate or abandon the premises at any time during the term hereof, and if Lessee shall abandon or vacate the premises, or be dispossessed by process of law, or otherwise, any personal property belonging to Lessee left upon the premises shall be deemed to be abandoned, at the option of Lessor.

15. CONDEMNATION: If any part of the premises shall be taken or condemned for public use, and a part thereof remains which is susceptible of occupation hereunder, this lease shall, as to the part taken, terminate as of the date the condemnor acquires possession, and thereafter Lessee shall be required to pay such proportion of the rent for the remaining term as the value of the premises remaining bears to the total value of the premises at the date of condemnation; provided however, that Lessor may at his option, terminate this lease as of the date the condemnor acquires possession. In the event that the demised premises are condemned in whole, or that such portion is condemned that the remainder is not susceptible for use hereunder, this lease shall terminate upon the date upon which the condemnor acquires possession. All sums which may be payable on account of any condemnation shall belong to the Lessor, and Lessee shall not be entitled to any part thereof, provided however, that Lessee shall be entitled to retain any amount awarded to him for his trade fixtures or moving expenses.

16. TRADE FIXTURES: Any and all improvements made to the premises during the term hereof shall belong to the Lessor, except trade fixtures of the Lessee. Lessee may, upon termination hereof, remove all his trade fixtures, but shall repair or pay for all repairs necessary for damages to the premises occasioned by removal.

17. DESTRUCTION OF PREMISES: In the event of a partial destruction of the premises during the term hereof, from any cause, Lessor shall forthwith repair the same, provided that such repairs can be made **within sixty (60) days** under existing governmental laws and regulations, but such partial destruction shall not terminate this lease, except that Lessee shall be entitled to a proportionate reduction of rent while such repairs are being made, based upon the extent to which the making of such repairs shall interfere with the business of Lessee on the premises. If such repairs cannot be made **within said sixty (60) days,** Lessor, at his option, may make the same within a reasonable time, this lease continuing in effect with the rent proportionately abated as aforesaid, and in the event that Lessor shall not elect to make such repairs which cannot be made **within sixty (60) days,** this lease may be terminated at the option of either party.

In the event that the building in which the demised premises may be situated is destroyed to an extent of not less than one-third of the replacement costs thereof, Lessor may elect to terminate this lease whether the demised premises be injured or not. A total destruction of the building in which the premises may be situated shall terminate this lease.

In the event of any dispute between Lessor and Lessee with respect to the provisions hereof, the matter shall be settled by arbitration in such a manner as the parties may agree upon, or if they cannot agree, in accordance with the rules of the American Arbitration Association.

18. HAZARDOUS MATERIALS: Lessee shall not use, store, or dispose of any hazardous substances upon the premises, except use and storage of such substances if they are customarily used in lessee's business, and such use and storage complies with all environmental laws. Hazardous substances means any hazardous waste, substance or toxic materials regulated under any environmental laws or regulations applicable to the property.

19. INSOLVENCY: In the event a receiver is appointed to take over the business of Lessee, or in the event Lessee makes a general assignment for the benefit of creditors, or Lessee takes or suffers any action under any insolvency or bankruptcy act, the same shall constitute breach of this lease by Lessee.

20. REMEDIES OF OWNER ON DEFAULT: In the event of any breach of this lease by Lessee, Lessor may, at his option, terminate the lease and recover from Lessee: (a) the worth at the time of award of the unpaid rent which was earned at the time of termination; (b) the worth at the time of award of the amount by which the unpaid rent which would have been earned after termination until the time of the award exceeds the amount of such rental loss that the Lessee proves could have been reasonably avoided; (c) the worth at the time of award of the amount by which the unpaid rent for the balance of the term after the time of award exceeds the amount of such rental loss that Lessee proves could be reasonably avoided; and (d) any other amount necessary to compensate Lessor for all detriment proximately caused by Lessee's failure to perform his obligations under the lease or which in the ordinary course of things would be likely to result therefrom.

Lessor may, in the alternative, continue this lease in effect, as long as Lessor does not terminate Lessee's right to possession, and Lessor may enforce all his rights and remedies under the lease, including the right to recover the rent as it becomes due under the lease. If said breach of lease continues, Lessor may, at any time thereafter, elect to terminate the lease.

Nothing contained herein shall be deemed to limit any other rights or remedies which Lessor may have.

21. SECURITY: The security deposit set forth above, if any, shall secure the performance of the Lessee's obligations hereunder. Lessor may, but shall not be obligated to apply all or portions of said deposit on account of Lessee's obligations hereunder. Any balance remaining upon termination shall be returned to Lessee. Lessee shall not have the right to apply the Security Deposit in payment of the last month's rent.

22. DEPOSIT REFUNDS: The balance of all deposits shall be refunded within two weeks from date possession is delivered to Owner or his authorized Agent, together with a statement showing any charges made against such deposits by Owner.

23. ATTORNEY'S FEES: In case suit should be brought for recovery of the premises, or for any sum due hereunder, or because of any act which may arise out of the possession of the premises, by either party, the prevailing party shall be entitled to all costs incurred in connection with such action, including a reasonable attorney's fee.

24. WAIVER: No failure of Lessor to enforce any term hereof shall be deemed to be a waiver.

25. NOTICES: Any notice which either party may or is required to give, shall be given by mailing the same, postage prepaid, to Lessee at the premises, or Lessor at the address shown below, or at such other places as may be designated by the parties from time to time.

26. HOLDING OVER: Any holding over after the expiration of this lease, with the consent of Lessor, shall be construed as a month-to-month tenancy at a rental of $______________ per month, otherwise in accordance with the terms hereof, as applicable.

27. TIME: Time is of the essence of this lease.

28. HEIRS, ASSIGNS, SUCCESSORS: This lease is binding upon and inures to the benefit of the heirs, assigns and successors in interest to the parties.

29. TAX INCREASE: In the event there is any increase during any year of the term of this lease in the City, County or State real estate taxes over and above the amount of such taxes assessed for the tax year during which the term of this lease commences, whether because of increased rate or valuation, Lessee shall pay to Lessor upon presentation of paid tax bills an amount equal to ______% of the increase in taxes upon the land and building in which the leased premises are situated. In the event that such taxes are assessed for a tax year extending beyond the term of the lease, the obligation of Lessee shall be proportionate to the portion of the lease term included in such year.

30. COST OF LIVING INCREASE: The rent provided for in paragraph 2 shall be adjusted effective upon the first day of the month immediately following the expiration of ______ months from date of commencement of the term and upon the expiration of each ______ months thereafter in accordance with changes in the U.S. Consumer Price Index for All Urban Consumers (1982-84 = 100) hereinafter called the "CPI." The monthly rent shall be increased to an amount equal to the monthly rent set forth in paragraph 2 multiplied by a fraction the numerator of which is the CPI for the second calendar month immediately preceding the adjustment date and the denominator of which is the CPI for the second calendar month preceding the commencement of the lease term. Provided, however, in no event shall the monthly rent be less than the amount set forth in paragraph 2.

31. OPTION TO RENEW: Provided that Lessee is not in default in the performance of this lease, Lessee shall have the option to renew the lease for an additional term of ________ months commencing at the expiration of the initial lease term. All of the terms and conditions of the lease shall apply during the renewal term except that the monthly rent shall be the sum of $________________ which shall be adjusted in accordance with the cost of living increase provision set forth in paragraph 30.

The option shall be exercised by written notice given to Lessor not less than ______ days prior to the expiration of the initial lease term. If notice is not given in the manner provided herein within the time specified, this option shall expire.

32. LESSOR'S LIABILITY: The term "Lessor," as used in this paragraph, shall mean only the owner of the real property or a Lessee's interest in a ground lease of the premises. In the event of any transfer of such title or interest, the Lessor named herein (or the grantor in case of any subsequent transfers) shall be relieved of all liability related to Lessor's obligations to be performed after such transfer. Provided, however, that any funds in the hands of Lessor or Grantor at the time of such transfer shall be delivered to Grantee. Lessor's aforesaid obligations shall be binding upon Lessor's successors and assigns only during their respective periods of ownership.

33. ESTOPPEL CERTIFICATE:

(a) Lessee shall at any time upon not less than **ten (10) days' prior written notice** from Lessor execute, acknowledge and deliver to Lessor a statement in writing [1] certifying that this Lease is unmodified and in full force and effect (or, if modified, stating the nature of such modification and certifying that this Lease, as so modified, is in full force and effect), the amount of any security deposit, and the date to which the rent and other charges are paid in advance, if any, and [2] acknowledging that there are not, to Lessee's knowledge, any uncured defaults on the part of Lessor hereunder, or specifying such defaults if any are claimed. Any such statement may be conclusively relied upon by any prospective purchaser or encumbrancer to the Premises.

(b) At Lessor' option, Lessee's failure to deliver such statement within such time shall be a material breach of this Lease or shall be conclusive upon Lessee [1] that this Lease is in full force and effect, without modification except as may be represented by Lessor, [2] that there are no uncured defaults in lessor's performance, and [3] that not more than one month's rent has been paid in advance or such failure may be considered by Lessor as a default by Lessee under this Lease.

(c) If Lessor desires to finance, refinance, or sell the Premises, or any part thereof, Lessee hereby agrees to deliver to any lender or purchaser designated by Lessor such financial statements of Lessee as may be reasonably required by such lender or purchaser. Such statements shall include the past three years' financial statements of Lessee. All such financial statements shall be received by Lessor and such lender or purchaser in confidence and shall be used only for the purposes herein set forth.

34. COMMON AREA EXPENSES: In the event the demised premises are situated in a shopping center or in a commercial building in which there are common areas, Lessee agrees to pay his pro-rata share of maintenance, taxes, and insurance for the common area.

35. ADDENDUM: An addendum, signed by the parties, ☐ is attached, ☐ is not attached hereto.

ENTIRE AGREEMENT: The foregoing constitutes the entire agreement between the parties and may be modified only by a writing signed by both parties. The following Exhibits, if any, have been made a part of this lease before the parties' execution hereof: ________________________________

The undersigned Lessee hereby acknowledges receipt of a copy hereof.

DATED: ____________________

____________________ Agent	____________________ Lessee
____________________ Address	____________________ Lessee
____________________ Phone	____________________ Address
By ____________________	____________________ Phone

ACCEPTANCE

The undersigned Lessor accepts the foregoing offer and agrees to lease the herein described premises on the terms and conditions herein specified. The Lessor agrees to pay to ________________________________, the Agent in this transaction the sum of $______________(________________________________ DOLLARS) for services rendered and authorizes Agent to deduct said sum from the deposit received from Tenant. This agreement shall not limit the rights of Agent provided for in any listing or other agreement which may be in effect between Owner and Agent. In the event Tenant shall purchase the property from Owner prior to the expiration of this lease, Owner agrees to pay the Agent a sales commission of ________% of the sale price.

The undersigned Lessor hereby acknowledges receipt of a copy hereof.

DATED: ____________________

____________________ Owner's Authorized Agent	____________________ Lessor
____________________ Address	____________________ Lessor
____________________ Phone	____________________ Address
By ____________________	____________________ Phone

FORM 107(a) (12-88)

PROFESSIONAL PUBLISHING

Figure 2

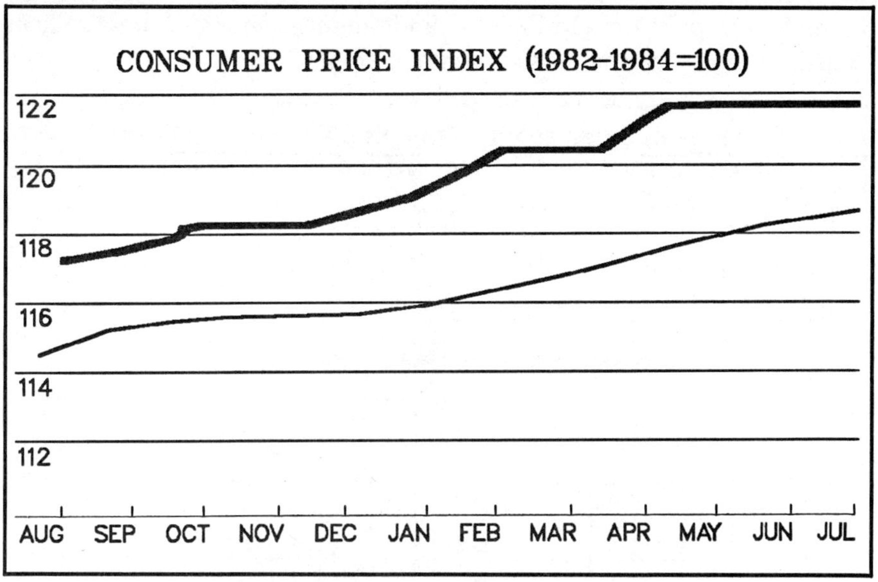

COMMERCIAL SHOPPING CENTERS

The two-income family and "shop 'til you drop" affluence on the West Coast has kept vacancies in California's regional malls below the national 4% rate. The national 8% vacancy rate in neighborhood centers and community centers is also lower than California's rate. However, in many California areas, overbuilding has occurred because neighborhood and strip shopping centers have been the preferred investment for many institutional investors.

Renovation, remodeling, and upgrading existing shopping centers has increased because many of these centers are in prime locations. Income is still generated from existing tenants during remodeling, even if rents are reduced during the construction period. An even bigger advantage is the financial benefits of using an existing facility instead of beginning new construction, with its associated zoning changes, environmental and energy impact studies, community and city approvals, etc.

In the late 1980s and early 1990s, investors may switch from shopping centers back to the more stabilized office buildings to increase the yield on their investment. But California's demographics are vastly different from those on a national scale. While national figures indicate bigger changes (for the worse) in malls and regional shopping centers, California's immigrant population and Pacific-Rim influences should dramatically increase business for the smaller centers. (Figure 3)

Changes in Sales at U.S. Shopping Centers: 1981-1987
(Percent Change from Preceding Third Year in Parentheses)

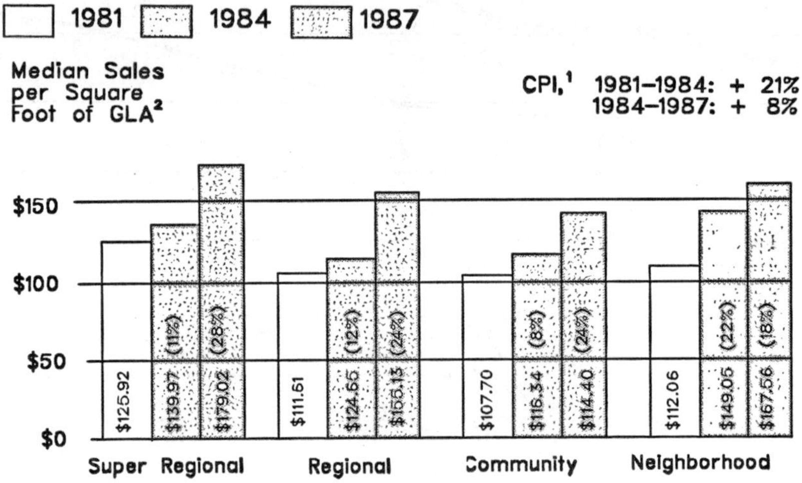

¹ Consumer Price Index ² Gross Leasable Area
Source: Urban Land Institute, *Dollars & Cents of Shopping Centers, 1981, 1984, 1987*

Categories Of Shopping Centers

Shopping centers are usually grouped into several categories. These categories include the regional mall, the community center, the neighborhood center, the strip center, and the specialty/theme center.

Regional Mall. The largest type of shopping center is the regional mall. These malls are found throughout California's suburban areas and usually consist of multi-story, multi-winged designs with over one million square feet of gross leasable area. Some regional malls have central recreational facilities, such as a skating arena. However, in California these costly amenities are rarely needed to attract customers. A major attraction to Californians living in the hotter inland valleys is the air-conditioned facilities.

These regional malls often contain theater complexes, financial centers, restaurants, and at least three or more major department stores directly in or surrounding the perimeter. They also require large expanses of land for parking. There is an overall lack of public transportation for these shoppers, and a prevalence of individual auto use. Parking areas often take up as much land as the shopping area structure. These parking areas mean additional costs in the form of security staff, lighting, paint stripping, sweeping service, and landscape.

To be successful, the California regional mall needs a surrounding population of over 150,000 people within a 15-mile radius. Most Californians measure distance in driving time, and regional malls must be within a 30- to 35- minute drive (including freeway time) of their customers.

Older California regional malls usually have between 500,000 to one million square feet of gross leasable area and need a population base of at least 100,000 within a ten-mile radius. They are rarely over two stories high and usually contain at least two major department stores. A California driver needs to be able to get to the mall within 15 to 30 minutes.

Community Centers. Community centers have 100,000 to 300,000 square feet of gross leasable area, and need a population base of at least 50,000 within a five-mile radius. In California, these typically contain at least two major tenants, such as a large home-improvement center store and a supermarket, or a large discount department store and a large discount supermarket.

Neighborhood Centers. Neighborhood centers contain one large store, either a supermarket, discount, or variety store. They have 25,000 to 100,000 gross leasable square feet, and meet the needs of the immediate area, serving about a two-mile radius, or those with no more than a ten-minute drive. Ethnic neighborhood centers are very popular in many of the rapidly growing ethnic neighborhoods. Customer loyalty to these smaller centers is being challenged head-on by the larger supermarkets and department stores that devote store space to specialized ethnic products. This battle between the larger and smaller shopping centers will continue as California communities grow.

Strip Centers. Neighborhood centers also compete with the smaller strip centers, which usually have a quick convenience store, independently or often with a gas station. The strip center has under 30,000 gross leasable square feet and serves a one-mile radius or a freeway off-ramp. Customers take less than five minutes driving time to get to the facility.

Specialty/Theme Centers. The smaller specialty or theme center has no minimum or maximum square footage nor immediately surrounding population. They range from downtown garment districts, jewelry marts, and motorhome/auto centers to "Old Town" boutiques. Usually located near California freeways or tourist attractions, they give shoppers a great deal of variety within a particular specialty. Examples include Fisherman's Wharf or Horseshoe Pier, handicraft and hobby centers, or a jewelry center where one store specializes in emeralds, another in turquoise or Black Hills gold, etc. People will drive up to an hour to visit a theme area, especially when coupled with a tourist attraction. Because of the cost of the products, they are usually situated in and about the more affluent neighborhoods.

Management Elements

The property manager needs to have expertise in handling many factors that are unique to shopping centers. The physical elements of parking lots, sky lights, and truck/delivery bays are as important as interior and exterior security patrols for unchaperoned minors and professional criminals. Insurance liability increases in direct proportion to the traffic count. A good tenant mix and complimentary establishments must be the goal of the selection process.

The common areas of shopping centers often carry the added responsibility of not only maintenance, repairs, and upkeep, but also publicity and promotions. Common areas are often devoted to a variety of themes throughout the year, from elderly care and health issues, to miniature train displays, to Christmas trees decorated by local school children. The property manager often meets with the merchants' association to approve and coordinate themes, insurance, and marketing. The marketing and advertising for such promotions should have the prior approval of the landlord, including all holiday, religious, and seasonal events.

The Tenant

Many problems are associated with qualifying the shopping center tenant. One main area of concern is determining who is the business owner.

Is the prospective tenant under a parent company overseas and out of California court jurisdiction, or an independent franchise that has a big name but is virtually on its own? Commercial leases typically allow the landlord to approve a change in ownership. Another problem is the issue of how subletting concessions are handled in regards to liability and responsibilities. For example, many antique dealers have independently rented booths. Import/export dealers have concessionaire subtenant displays. And some local supermarkets use independent contractors for the meat, produce, or dairy departments within their store.

The Lease

Shopping center leases contain the name and address of the tenant, a description of the premises, a rental due date, and standard non-residential clauses about intended use. The rent provisions must include not only the base rent, but also the method of calculating increases, and when these increases are effective.

Some leases call for increases in accordance with specific formulas. These increases can also be tied to any one of several indexes, similar to office building rents. It is not uncommon to have stepped-up leases where minimum guaranteed increases are pre-set within the lease. Rental increases are often based on the Cost of Living Index. Another alternative is to tie the rent to the sales figures of the business tenant. One common method is to charge a fixed, flat rate, or "minimum amount due." This is usually due on the first day of each month. Additional rent is based upon the tenant's sales volume (a percentage of gross or net sales). The accounting problems associated with clear definitions of what constitutes net sales takes time and paperwork; careful consideration should be given before agreeing to this method.

The rent almost always includes 100% pass-through provisions for most or all of the operating expenses. The utilities, insurance, taxes, assessments, parking area and building maintenance, management fee, and administration costs are assessed to each tenant. They may be billed on a monthly, quarterly, semi-annual, or annual basis.

The expenses for the common area must be allocated in easily understandable terms. The shopping center property manager often begins with the building pro forma statement (obtained from the original developer) to work out the costs of the stabilized operations. (Figure 4). Expenses are usually prorated according to the total square foot rented by each tenant.

Figure 4

XYZ SHOPPING CENTER

Pro Forma Income and Expense Statement

(First Full Year)

Income:		
Minimum Rent		$__________
Estimated Overage Rent		__________
Miscellaneous:		
Public Telephones	$__________	
Kiddie Rides	__________	
Other Concessions	__________	__________
Common Area Payments		__________
Total Income		$__________
Expense:		
Real Estate Taxes	$__________	
Insurance	__________	
Maintenance	__________	
Common Area	__________	
Promotion	__________	
Legal and Auditing	__________	
Management Fee	__________	
Vacancy	__________	
Miscellaneous	__________	
Total Expense		$__________
Cash Flow Before Debt Service		__________
Mortgage of $________ @______% for ______ years		
Constant annual payment @______%		__________
Net Cash Flow		$__________

PROPOSED OPERATING BUDGET *Fiscal Year Beginning January 1, 19..*				
		Current Year		
Income and Expense	*Last Year Actual*	*Budget*	*Est. Actual*	*Next Year Proposed*
Income:	$	$	$	$
Minimum Rent				
Overage Rent				
Other Charges to Tenants				
Other Income				
Total Income				
Expense				
Common Area Maintenance				
Other Maintenance & Repairs				
Advertising & Promotion				
Interest				
Depreciation				
Real Estate Taxes				
Insurance				
General & Administrative				
Miscellaneous				
Total Expense				
Net Income (Loss)				
Add: Depreciation				
Deduct: Amortization of Debt				
Other Capital Costs				
Net Cash Flow				

INDUSTRIAL PROPERTY

The industrial market is less overbuilt than most other types of non-residential properties, primarily because new investment capital is obtained from tax-motivated developers. In other words, the money was obtained to buy the land and build the structures because of the tax benefits being received, not because the investor wanted to use the building or thought it would increase in value. Only a building is depreciable, land is not. Coupled with the lack of tax write off, the cost of land in California is so high in many areas that the developer rarely wants to build a structure in advance, only to have it sit vacant. Many lots have signs advertising "build to suit" because industries vary so widely in their required use and layout of a structure.

As the nation continues to shift its emphasis from the manufacturing sector to the service sector, the demand for traditional manufacturing space has decreased. The 1987 national vacancy rate for industrial properties averaged about 11%, and decreased through 1988. (Figure 5.)

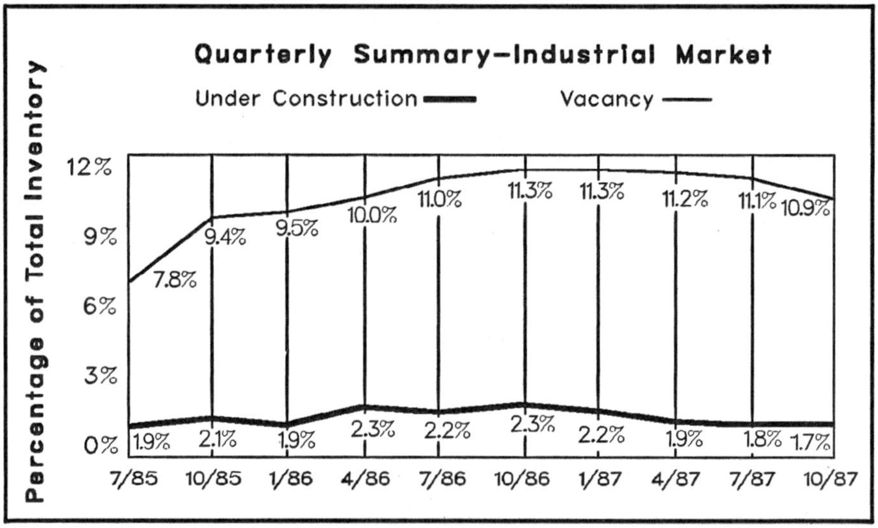

There has been a short supply of warehouse and distribution space in many California areas due to the population increases, transfer of out-of-state firms to California, and expansion of existing companies. Failing thrifts have made less money available for the construction of distribution space. With less new construction, rents are gradually increasing for warehouse space. Distribution centers, like Long Beach, Anaheim, Oakland, Sacramento, San Francisco, and San Diego have high growth in bulk distribution, called "hi-cube" warehouses. Because the costs of inland valley land is less, freight comes into the high rent port, then is trucked to storage and distribution centers in the more remote regions. Pre-lease tenants are the key to rehabbing existing structures closer to metropolitan areas where land costs are higher, to meet distribution center needs.

Market Characteristics

There are several unique characteristics to the industrial real estate market. For instance, the value of the dollar has a dramatic impact on this specialized market. When the value of the dollar declines, there is often an increase in demand for storage and manufacturing space as the foreign demand for U.S. goods increases. In California's coastal port cities, the decline also decreases the amount of warehouse space that foreign suppliers use. In order to maintain an equilibrium, the property manager must try to balance their space between domestic and foreign users.

The demand for warehouse space is usually about six to twelve months behind the rate of consumer buying. Industrial and warehouse space are adversely affected by declines in spending. The same is true of recessions, an increase in inflation, or a wholesale decline in employment. On the other hand, when the economy is strong, industrial rental rates increase.

The overall returns for industrial property are usually very good because there is little speculative construction. Most property is built for a specific pre-lease tenant. This creates a more stable return with less cyclical variations.

Professional Organizations

The property manager who wishes to stay atop the industrial market should be affiliated with professional organizations for this field. The Institute of Real Estate Management (IREM) of the National Association of

Realtors (NAR) in Chicago has special areas of study for office building and industrial property management. The American Industrial Real Estate Association in Los Angeles is another group that can be most helpful. The Society of Industrial and Office Realtors (SIOR) in Washington, D.C., is a network of office and industrial members (Figure 6). For more general data, the Commercial-Investment Real Estate Council (CCIM) of the National Association of Realtors in Chicago has books and courses for commercial income-producing properties. Their materials cover specifics in this area, from acquisition and development, to renting, to maintaining ongoing operations.

California Industrial Real Estate

In the past, and even today in much of the U.S., industrial real estate was owned by the company that occupied it. The building was considered part of the capital investment needed to operate the business and the company's staff managed the building. But in California, significant amounts of investment capital and large expanses of available land made industrial parks feasible. These areas are large tract developments of warehouse, manufacturing, and assembly structures designed for modern, linear movement of inventories. Entire communities, such as the City of Industry, or the City of Commerce, are made up of these buildings. Unlike any city in the U.S., these cities are virtually without residents. There is less than a 5% residential population in the City of Industry. When an existing home is resold, the property ceases to be residential property due to new zoning ordinances and laws. It is only a matter of time until this city will have no residents. The city is located by many railway lines, and sandwiched between many freeways. The surrounding cities are single-family residential neighborhoods where the workers/employees live.

These industrial parks and cities accommodate both office buildings and industrial warehouses, often in the same structure. Large expanses of employee/worker parking lots, air strips for commuting executives, perimeter hotels/restaurants for training or commuting executives are all part of the functional area complex. Airport, trucking, and railway access are important elements. Employee needs are met with chains of fast food restaurants, drive-thru banking, and similar lunch-hour conveniences.

Figure 6

SOCIETY OF INDUSTRIAL AND OFFICE REALTORS®

Society of Industrial and Office REALTORS®
777 14th Street, N.W.
Washington, D.C. 20005
(202) 383-1150

Designation

SIOR P.R.E., Professional Real Estate Executive

Purpose

The Society of Industrial and Office REALTORS® (SIOR) is a professional organization whose members specialize in marketing industrial and office properties and in meeting the real estate needs of corporate and industrial clients. The Society provides a unique network of brokers, consultants and appraisers internationally and serves as a forum for the exchange of information, listings and services.

Educational Programs and Publications

SIOR offers various courses on industrial real estate and commercial marketing topics. The Society also publishes industrial surveys and several periodicals, including the bi-monthly newsletter, *SIOR Reports.*

Membership Benefits

- Expanded contacts and market resources.
- Networking with over 1,100 industrial and office brokers.
- *SIOR Reports.*
- Annual membership directory and biennial photo roster.
- Access to SIOR library.
- Legislative tracking on federal legislation and regulations.
- National meetings.

Membership Requirements

- Passing of rigid entrance examinations.
- Reputation for integrity and ability in the field.
- Creditable record in industrial real estate transactions or in purchasing, selling and leasing office real estate.
- Hold REALTOR® or REALTOR® —Associate membership.
- Actively engaged as either industrial or office real estate salesperson or broker.

P.R.E. Designation Requirements

- Six years as SIOR Corporate Associate Designee.
- Fifteen years industrial or office-related experience in firms that qualify as Corporate Associate members.
- Passing SIOR examination or completion of SIOR course.
- Attendance at four of the most recent eight national or regional conventions.

Types Of Industrial Property

Industrial real estate typically falls into the following groups:

- The **market-oriented** industrial complex is often located close to the downtown garment district. Most major producers are located within just a few blocks of each other, usually in high density, multi-story structures.
- Industries that are **material oriented** are found near the raw material source, such as mineral smelting plants and California's large immigrant farm worker industry for the vast inland valley crop production.
- **Labor-oriented** industries are situated closest to available specialized personnel, such as California's Silicon Valley: highly-trained technical specialists, found in Palo Alto and similar areas.
- **Footloose** industries are those that are capable of locating almost anywhere. For instance, computer software programmers are working out of their home in Eureka and other smaller Northern California communities.
- **Transportation-oriented** industries are typically found near ports, railway junctures, large truck depot terminals, airports, and the like.

The property manager of industrial property must keep abreast of developments for these types of industries, including aspects of transportation, the cost of labor and materials, and industrial markets to be able to advise clients and to seek and keep tenants.

Government Involvement

The government is very involved in industrial property development. At the federal level, the Urban Renewal Administration provides much California funding for slum clearance and rehabilitation in the aftermath of earthquake damage in many older downtown areas. The Environmental Protection Agency (EPA) oversees compliance with federal pollution standards. The National Environmental Policy Act (NEPA) requires the preparation of an environmental impact study for approval for any industrial facility. These studies are often required by California cities as well. The

Federal Water Pollution Act, Clean Air Act, Noise Control Act, Flood Disaster Protection Act, and National Coastal Zone Management Act all put extensive requirements on industrial properties. Currently, there is a strong consumer push for enforcement of the national laws, and state laws on the same issues are equally strict.

The California Environmental Quality Act requires an Environmental Impact Report (EIR) before approval of any construction is granted. In addition, the California Coastal Commission has had strong effects on industry in California. Local level officials monitor the actions of industry to see that California maintains its image of having lower levels of pollution.

The Lease

The standard industrial lease lists the parties and their addresses, contains a description of the premises, states the rental due date, and specifies property uses. There are several particularly industrial issues that should be dealt with in industrial leases, such as: what happens if the industrial tenant violates pollution laws (it is usually considered a breach of the lease); and what are the landlord's obligations if picket lines block other tenants' access to their industrial site.

The property manager must include specific insurance protection clauses for the public, the property manager, and the owner. Storage, handling, and uses of hazardous waste material need to be defined within the terms of the lease. The pass-through expenses, how allocated, when payable, and the basis of determination, should also be part of the lease. Lease options, lease extensions, and the possibility of special assessments need to be outlined.

Rents

Just as with the office building lease, the industrial lease can call for rent at a fixed rate, minimum rent plus a cost-of-living or index increase, and pass-through expenses. Rent increases can be based on a specific percentage increase, an index, a guaranteed increase, or the like.

The Sale/Leaseback

Industrial property is commonly developed with a specific tenant in mind, on a "build-to-suit" basis. It is common for the user to build the structure to its own specifications, take the construction cost tax benefits, and then sell the property to a long-term investor. The seller then gets a guaranteed long-term lease of the property. This sale/leaseback arrangement gives the tenants an opportunity to free up their capital and put it back into their business—to developing, producing and marketing their product. It gives the investor a tax shelter, guaranteed occupancy, no rent-up costs, and a steady cash flow.

Special Purpose Properties

There are several other types of non-residential properties that provide management opportunities. These include the mini-warehouse, medical and dental buildings, and government agency property.

Mini-Warehouse

A popular type of non-residential property in California is the mini-warehouse. These storage units provide security for possessions when off-premises facilities are needed. Originally, these were located around large apartment complexes, where neighborhood tenants needed the use of additional space. It did not take long, however, for the business community to see the benefits of renting space for their growing records management and furniture/equipment storage requirements. Often the mini-warehouse rates are well below the office floor space rental rate. Volumes of records can be securely and privately stored with limited employee access. Government reports, tax returns, former employee files, and past operations data are all cumbersome and expensive to maintain within office space.

The mini-warehouse storage areas are usually constructed of primarily metal or block walls; they are more fire-retardent than many homes. The size of the storage area can range from the size of a large garage to units as small as post office boxes. These mini-postal boxes have become popular, especially in urban areas where government postal boxes are all rented, and a consistent waiting list is in use.

Income And Expenses. Rents are usually not established merely on a square foot basis. The property manager must survey similar spaces to determine market rents and project income figures against expenses. If U.S. postal boxes are $30 a year for the tiniest box, a fifty cents per square foot rent would be the wrong calculation methods for a 3 x 5 mail box rental. Likewise, a space equal to a one-car garage can easily be rented for over $100 per month in most California areas.

Many California mini-warehouse facilities also rent out space for vehicle storage. Motor homes, boats, antique cars, and extra vehicles are part of the California lifestyle. Many people do not have enough space to park these at home and many California cities charge permit fees for overnight parking on the public street. These parking facilities are popular and useful, and generate good revenues for the mini-warehouse operation. Separate fencing and guarded ingress and egress are important.

Expenses include elaborate security systems and lighting. A common expense is handling past due payments. Legally, the mini-warehouse manager must follow specific procedures for the eviction of non-paying tenants and the disposition of their personal property. The manager sends out an initial letter stating a request for payment, indicating the amount due, including any late fee, and the grace period within which the last payment will be accepted.

If the tenant fails to make the payment, an ad must be placed in a paper of local, general circulation where the mini-warehouse is located. The ad must be published at least three times within a 21-day period. The ad indicates the default, states the date of public sale, and usually lists the contents of the unit. The items in the unit are sold, and the proceeds pay the costs of the sale, then the sales tax owed to the government, and then what is due on the rental. Any balance is paid to the owner of the property. If the person cannot be located, the funds are sent to the state.

Security. Security is an important issue with the mini-warehouse. The typical new complex has individual door access to each unit, plus the main door access. The tenant often has to walk through the office and then through the door to a specific area. The tenant then enters a computer code number into a machine to get the door to open. The tenant would then be in the post office box or vault room, or in an outside walkway that provides access to the garage areas. The gate for car access to the garage units usually must be opened electronically by office personnel.

The property manager changes the master code numbers the first of each month. When the rent is paid, the tenant receives the new month's code number for those gates or areas he or she needs access to. The tenant provides his or her own lock for the individual storage unit, if locks are required. Postal box and small units have only code numbers or keys.

It is common for mini-warehouse facilities to have an apartment above the office for the on-site manager's living area. The expense of this unit and camera surveillance are on-going operational expenses. After the initial construction costs, the security locks are not expensive to maintain in comparison with the income they generate. Maintenance contracts for these security systems is common.

Property Management Functions. The property manager is often responsible for preparing a budget and projecting income, expenses, and cash flow. The property manager often establishes the policies and operating procedures for the establishment. Access hours, administration of payroll, and arranging for on-site personnel (for office operations, maintenance, repairs, and cleaning) all fall under the property management realm. The property manager must be familiar with the handling of this specialized field—the rental agreement provides for the sale of personal property on default, security and on-site administration are unique, and eviction proceedings and processing of tenants are distinctly different from other property management operations.

Medical-Dental and Legal Buildings

Physical Considerations. Medical and dental buildings are unique in that they are thought of as office buildings by many users, but can have core requirements that exceed complex industrial requirements from the property management point of view. For example, the infrastructures of these buildings require heavy electrical and clinical machines and equipment. Standard requirements include dark rooms for in-house x-ray processing, vaults for gold and other expensive or highly regulated materials, container handling for removing hazardous chemicals, and other highly specialized internal planning needs.

Just as residential property has restrictions on pets, so do medical and dental buildings. Offices often have very large fish tanks in their waiting rooms that can leak and damage floors or ceilings. These require outlets for filters, pumps, etc. Research facilities often use small rodents and other animals and organisms that the property manager must consider in initial tenant negotiations. Experiments could possibly endanger the building, surrounding tenants, and the neighborhood.

The physical layout of floor space is important for medical and legal tenants. A central law library, reprographic center, pharmacy, and records storage and retrieval areas are vital to their business operations. Security is of the utmost concern. Janitorial scheduling can be centralized for common areas, and available for individual tenants at their expense, or included in the total rent.

Secure parking areas are essential. Some people mistakenly believe that doctors and nurses carry drugs in their cars and try to break into them. An attorney's file in the wrong hands can injure many parties. Also, many tenants have luxury cars and expensive auto accessories (stereos and car phones).

Maintaining the common areas of these buildings requires special consideration. Because ill persons visit medical buildings, tenants prefer active disinfectant cleaning. In legal facilities, a clean and professional image is an absolute minimum requirement. In addition to common area libraries, many buildings have central cafeteria or lunch room facilities. Non-smoking has become so common that a smoking area needs to be provided within or near the inside of the entrance. If the smoking issue is not dealt with by the property manager, the area just outside the entry doors, hallways and restrooms will bear the results. One set of restrooms for clients and one for employees are common for legal buildings. For medical offices, patients often need access to restrooms in each doctor's office for giving medical samples.

Medical facilities need extra wide halls and doors to accommodate stretchers, wheelchairs, and large, special equipment. Both medical and legal buildings need to accommodate the handicapped, both inside the building and in the parking areas. Conference rooms, client meeting rooms, and case study areas are important to legal tenants.

The Lease. The lease terms are usually far longer for these types of buildings. This takes into account the sometimes extensive remodeling needs of tenants. Notice periods to terminate the lease are also longer than for other types of buildings. For example, even though the lease term is for only three years, the notice period may be six months or longer. This long notice period gives the property manager a better opportunity to find a new tenant for these specialized facilities.

Government Agency Property

Non-residential government or quasi-government property management has been an integral part of California property management growth. The majority of these property managers belong to joint regional associations, such as the league of cities. Many are Certified Property Managers, active in BOMA and similar groups. The majority are part of the International Right of Way Association, which has local California chapters. Members include California city and county governments, railroad companies, electric and gas companies, the department of highways, water districts, redevelopment agencies, appraisers and attorneys, engineers and title companies, rapid transit groups, regional park districts, colleges, and the United States government agencies of the Internal Revenue Service, Postal Service, Forest Service and the U.S. Navy and Coast Guard.

These property managers acquire, develop, and dispose of hundreds of thousands of dollars of California real estate on a daily basis, including the land under power lines, freeway on- and off-ramps, etc. The maintenance and landscaping, litter control, fencing, and facilities management are administered by these property managers. In areas of high density, where land is at a premium, parking facilities and storage yards are leased to non-government parties by real property agents.

The property manager needs special knowledge in contract law; government policies, practices, and procedures; documentation; administration; and negotiation to have the skills necessary for these positions. The growth in many California areas of rapid transit, harbor and waterways, and utilities means the property manager needs to keep very current on political issues that could affect his or her job. For instance, different agencies often work closely together towards a common goal. The regulations or other activities of one agency can have an important impact on the agency the property manager is working for. For example, nothing is more frustrating than to have the street in front of your building torn up for six months while resurfacing is done, and then, when it is completed, to learn they will tear up the street again to lay sewer lines.

NON-RESIDENTIAL LEASES

The leases for office buildings, shopping centers, industrial, and other non-residential properties contain many similar provisions. The more common and important provisions will be reviewed here.

Parties

The property manager must pay careful attention to the parties to the lease. Are they corporations, partnerships, or individuals? If individuals, are they married or single? The identity of the parties has important implications as to authority to act.

The property manager needs to have an original copy of a corporate resolution if leasing to a corporation. A corporate seal is beneficial, but not necessary, and it should be signed by the secretary and president of the firm. The resolution should specifically approve the lease, and indicate the name and address of the business operation in California and the address of the home office. If the party is a subsidiary of the corporation and acting under a different name than the parent company, this relationship must be clarified and all names included.

If the tenant is a partnership, the general partner(s) needs to sign the agreement. The lease should include a provision which specifies the requirement of a current fictitious business name (DBA) to be on file with the landlord. For individuals owning a business, the signature of both the husband and wife should be required (because of community property issues).

Addresses

The address called for in the lease may not be as simple as it may appear. The tenant's business address may not be merely a street address. If the location is industrial land or a parking facility, for example, it may not have a commonly known street number. In these cases, it would be necessary to include the legal description, a survey, or the plot plans. Include the post office box or other form of mailing address for all the parties to the agreement.

Possession

It is important to specify the date possession transfers to the tenant. Possession may be subject to completion of construction, which can be held up because of bad weather, labor problems, material shortages, delays by officials and inspectors, or a variety of other reasons. Occupancy may also be delayed if the prior tenant fails to vacate the premises, or if repairs are necessary. The lease should clearly state the consequence of such events.

Fixtures

Tenants often make interior improvements at their own expense. This allows them to take advantage of depreciation tax benefits. However, leases are often vague as to who owns these improvements at the termination of the lease. Lighting fixtures, plumbing, and non-trade fixtures are expensive to remove or cause considerable damage when they are removed. Whether the improvements become part of the real property or remain trade fixtures (and removable) should be clearly stated in the lease. If the fixtures can be removed, the lease should specify that the tenant will pay for removal and also indemnify the landlord for any mechanics' liens that may arise from the installation.

Before making alterations, the tenant should have the owner's written consent. The owner should require building permits, even if the tenant performs the work him or herself. The owner needs to post a notice of non-responsibility on the premises, in a conspicuous place, within ten days from the beginning of the work, to avoid liability for payment.

Use

The lease will usually specify what uses are permissible on the premises. There are often clauses in leases restricting the use of one tenant to protect the business of another tenant. For example, the landlord may promise a tenant that no competing business will move into the building. These provisions should be spelled out in the lease. A change of use should require prior written permission.

Common Area

Both the tenant's and the landlord's rights and responsibilities as to the common area must be clearly defined. These rules and regulations should provide for ingress and egress, costs to maintain, liability for harm to customers, and the like.

Signboards

The signs used by individual tenants can radically alter the appearance of a building. Uniform and consistent color and lettering styles, and restrictions on sign placement are commonly used in California, and often are included in the lease. Neon or blinking signs inside the rental unit, but visible from the street, should also be addressed in the lease. Banners, sale flags, and balloons for advertising should require the landlord's prior written approval.

Capital Improvements

The lease should limit the dollar amount of capital improvements that can be done without the landlord's approval. This will help protect the premises from alterations that reduce the value of the property. The lease should also require city approval and building permits for any structural modification. Responsibility for damage caused to other tenants and customers should be allocated in the lease.

Miscellaneous

Other issues to address in the lease include eminent domain, entry and inspection, and damage or destruction of the premises. Bankruptcy, holdover, reversion, and right of first refusal to buy, lease, or expand are also important and should be discussed. Any other covenant of promises between the parties should also be included in the lease.

HVAC

Heating, ventilating, and air conditioning are of major concern to California tenants. Monitoring peak demand, scheduling time of usage, and holidays and night set-backs are crucial to economic use of energy. Air circulation is also an issue. "Tired air" means lower staff productivity. Energy-saving devises can be used as incentives to attract new tenants and keep existing tenants. The cost of upgrading these improvements should be specified in the lease.

Audit

Audits are performed by the landlord to calculate the rent due when it is based upon the tenant's sales. For example, if the rent is to be 5% of gross sales, the property manager must determine the amount of the tenant's gross sales. Frequently, estimates are used to determine the rate initially, based upon prior records or industry averages. But the actual amount of sales is then determined by an audit of the books, and a balance due billing, or credit towards future rents is made when the actual figures are known.

The lease should specify the audit periods for assessments. When and where this is conducted varies with the business. The landlord may wish to send an auditor to the out-of-state corporate office, or receive an annual report of their California operations, or have the tenant furnish the audit data. Major tenants audit the landlord's pass-through costs and square foot figures to reduce minor errors in calculations and to question accounting procedures. Landlords and tenants have an equal interest in the outcome of audits, so it is vital to clarify who performs them and who covers the expense of the audit.

Insurance

The lease should specify what kinds of insurance both the tenant and landlord are required to carry. Liability, fire, extended coverage, workman's compensation, business interruption, lost rents, machine, boiler, and plate glass coverages are all unique and have different deductibles, coverage, and exclusions. Subrogation, disposition of proceeds, additional named and co-insurance clauses may be a part of the lease. The lease should clarify the results of a claim or cancellation to both parties. A thorough discussion of insurance is given in Chapter 14.

Taxes

The tenant's payment of taxes to state, federal, and local governments for personal property, business licenses, etc. are beyond the scope of most leases. Real property taxes are usually assessed on a pro rata share between the tenants, based upon square footage or usage. Many times local assessment sums or lump sum bond payments are passed directly through to the tenant. The method of payment must be in the lease—whether they are billed monthly, quarterly, or annually.

Security Deposit

The lease should define the security deposit—that it is not the last month's rent or any other form of prepaid rent. It should also clarify that it is not to be used during the term of the tenancy for taxes, insurance, or any other tenant costs.

Area

The leased area is the total square footage on which rent is actually being paid. The net square footage is the total gross square footage, less areas like halls, stairs, common restrooms, elevator areas, lobby/equipment/storage area, etc.

Rent

Non-residential rental rates vary considerably; they differ by geographic area and common use, by industry practice, by type of building, and by negotiation between the specific tenant and the landlord. There are several basic types of rent arrangements, which are often modified to meet individual circumstances.

Percentage Lease. The percentage lease is commonly used for supermarkets, restaurants, and many retail businesses where total volume of goods sold is significant. The rental amount is a percentage of the tenant's sales. This is usually based on gross sales volume, but may also be on net sales. As the final amount of rent due is not known until sales figures are in, and rents are due and payable in advance, a fixed minimum rent is paid monthly and applied against the actual amount when it becomes known.

Step-up Lease. A step-up lease calls for a set rental amount which is due until an increase is triggered. These increases, called "bumps," may be triggered by a phase of construction being completed (such as when the "certificate of occupancy" is issued), or when a certain dollar sales volume by the tenant is reached, or by a specific calendar date, usually annually. The rent increases each period based upon a flat fee amount, a percentage over the prior rent, or a similar method.

Rent increases are often tied to some index. The Consumer Price Index (CPI) is the most common. All lease provisions providing for rental increases are known as escalation clauses, and protect the owner's income from inflation by passing on increased costs to the tenants.

Gross Lease. Under a gross lease, the landlord pays all the specified expenses, such as utilities, insurance, management fee, repairs, taxes, janitorial services, interior and exterior building maintenance. The modified gross lease spells out which costs the tenant pays, and which the landlord pays. These are often referred to as a net-net lease.

Net Lease. Under a net lease, the tenant pays all the specified expenses. These are also called net-net-net leases, or triple net leases. Under a gross lease, the property owner receives a rental amount, but must pay expenses with it, so the owner never knows the net amount received because of fluctuations in utility and other expenses. Whereas under a net lease, the owner receives a constant amount because the owner has no other expenses.

For more general data on non-residential property management, the Commercial-Investment Real Estate Council of the National Association of Realtors (CCIM) in Chicago is a good source. It has books and courses on managing specific non-commercial, income-producing properties, from acquisition and development, to leasing practices, to maintaining ongoing operations.

CHAPTER 9–QUIZ

1. Important matters of non-residential property management include:

    a. ergonomics
    b. HVAC
    c. energy studies
    d. All of the above

2. California development has been hindered by all of the following except:

    a. the Coastal Commission
    b. the EPA
    c. environmentalists
    d. Pacific-Rim investors

3. Office building rent increases are often tied to the:

    a. T-bill rate
    b. ARM
    c. CPI
    d. IRS

4. The theme shopping center:

    a. has a 25,000 to 100,000 gross leasable area
    b. needs at least 50,000 people within a five-mile radius
    c. includes specialized shops for tourists
    d. is located within a 30-minute driving distance from shoppers

5. Overbuilding has occurred the least in:

    a. industrial property
    b. research & development markets (R & D)
    c. office buildings
    d. shopping malls

6. Which is incorrect?

   a. Hi-cube refers to high rise, glass-n-chrome offices
   b. Bumps refer to rent increases
   c. Absorption rate is how fast new, vacant units are filled
   d. DBA means an operation is doing business as...

7. The Urban Renewal Administration provides California funding for:

   a. development and expansion of industrial environs
   b. slum clearance and rehabilitation
   c. razing pollution-causing industries
   d. studing the impact of industrial hazardous waste

8. A standard lease clause should include:

   a. security deposit amounts used for business tax payment
   b. the name of both husband and wife for an individual business
   c. insurance and liability requirements of vendors
   d. entry and inspection by auditors

9. Standard lease payments include all but which of the following?

   a. Gross lease
   b. Increase lease
   c. Percentage lease
   d. Step-up lease

10. Property management expertise is commonly needed for:

   a. negotiating leases
   b. preparing tax forms
   c. litigating damages
   d. appealing reversal decisions

CHAPTER 9–QUIZ ANSWERS

1. d
2. d
3. c
4. c
5. a
6. a
7. b
8. b
9. b
10. a

10

Management Of Homeowners' Associations

References

Expense Analysis: Condominiums, Cooperatives and PUDs. IREM, 1988.

Downs, James C., Jr., CPM. *Principles of Real Estate Management.* 12th ed. Chicago: IREM, 1980.

McKenzie, Dennis, et al. *California Real Estate Principles.* 3rd ed. New York: Wiley & Sons, 1987.

Razzi, Elizabeth. "Condo 'Catch-22'." *Realtor News.* [Chicago] 10 Oct. 1988.

California Real Estate Trends Newsletter. Jan. 1988.

Shmishkiss, Kiss, CPM. "Why Condominium Developers Need Property Managers." *Journal of Property Management.* Chicago, Sept./Oct. 1988.

Last Chapter Review

The non-residential property is most likely to be an office building, commercial shopping center, or industrial property. The design, layout, lease requirements, site analysis, parking, and tenant qualification of specialized non-residential properties were reviewed to guide the property manager in these areas.

Chapter Overview

The management of any homeowners' association requires knowledge and skills in personal relations, finance, organization, auditing, and real estate. Managing homeowners' associations also requires the ability to communicate well, administrative and maintenance expertise, and above all, patience and tact. The nature and scope of the property manager's required talents, the structure of these associations, and some basic mechanics of their management will be reviewed in this chapter.

THE HOMEOWNERS' ASSOCIATION

Condominiums, planned unit developments (PUDs), and similar types of non-traditional housing are the fastest growing segment of the California housing market. A major factor in this growth is the fact that these housing units are relatively inexpensive when compared to detached, single-family units. Furthermore, many consumers prefer the virtually maintenance-free living this type of housing offers. Others consider the often plentiful added amenities, such as recreational facilities, to be their greatest feature.

California has many types of homeowners' associations that need the services of professional property management. Each will be discussed, along with the characteristics unique to the specific type of association. While all are called homeowners' associations, there may actually be few full-time owner-occupants. The lack of full-time residents means that the property manager must take a more active part in managing these associations. The property manager must maintain lines of communication with the absentee owner, tenant-occupant, leadership directors, local regulatory agencies, and regional association managements.

Before discussing the different types of homeowners' associations, we will first review some basic characteristics of this type of property ownership.

Common Physical Layouts

A typical type of building exterior is the California bungalow, with one- or two-story units, often vertically stacked. Although a few have elevators, most are "garden" types with exterior stairwell access. These low-rise units often have interior common areas, including the lobby, hallways, a balcony, or similar community facilities.

Another type of physical layout is the high-rise building, which features many interior common areas that require the property manager's attention. Usually four or more stories, these buildings are found only in highly developed regions of California that permit high-rise development. These buildings are not only used for residential purposes, but are also developed for office/business purposes. Typical features that must be managed include the elevator and lobby area, hallways and corridors, unit signboards, entry marquee, smoking areas, floor restrooms, shared lunch rooms, and exterior parking areas (often assigned). It is also common for the property manager to supervise plant/greenery contracts for the interior common areas, in addition to exterior landscape maintenance agreements. Maid service is often available to tenants on an individual basis. Valet parking attendants and security patrol personnel also require professional management.

The townhouse is another type of housing design. It may be a single-family home or part of a condominium or cooperative housing project. These two-story units avoid the inconvenience of having another owner/tenant unit overhead. Townhouse units typically have a ground floor living room, garage, and laundry area, and bedrooms upstairs. However, in units built on hillsides where there are desirable views, the bedrooms are downstairs (built into the hill where it is dark and quiet) while the living area and balconies or decks are on the top floor.

The Institute of Real Estate Management (IREM) has defined the various types of units and layout designs. These will be used throughout our discussion. (See Figure 1.)

Advantages To Shared Ownership

One advantage of shared ownership is the common areas. Individuals cannot afford the many amenities provided by common ownership

Figure 1

DEFINITIONS

CONDOMINIUM
A property in which the space within each unit is individually owned, while the common elements of the property are jointly owned, including the building structure and the land.

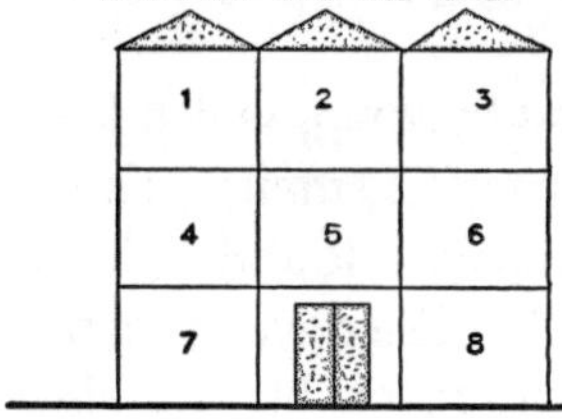

COOPERATIVE
A property wholly owned by a corporation in which the members holding shares are entitled to the proprietary lease of a specific unit located in the building.

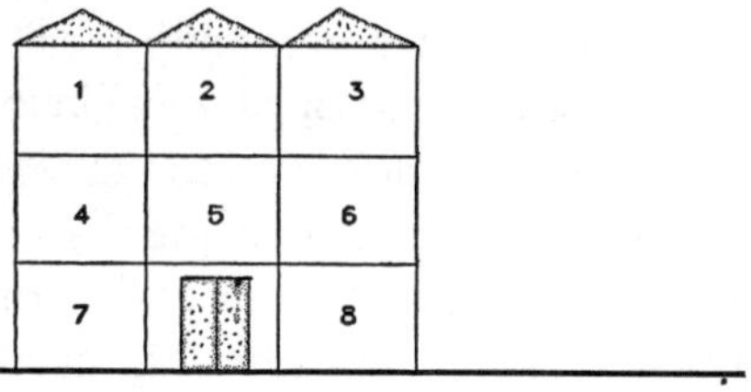

PLANNED UNIT DEVELOPMENT
A form of development generally containing a mixture of building types and land uses, with community facilities and open spaces owned and maintained in common, and with individual ownership of the land underlying and immediately adjacent to each residential structure.

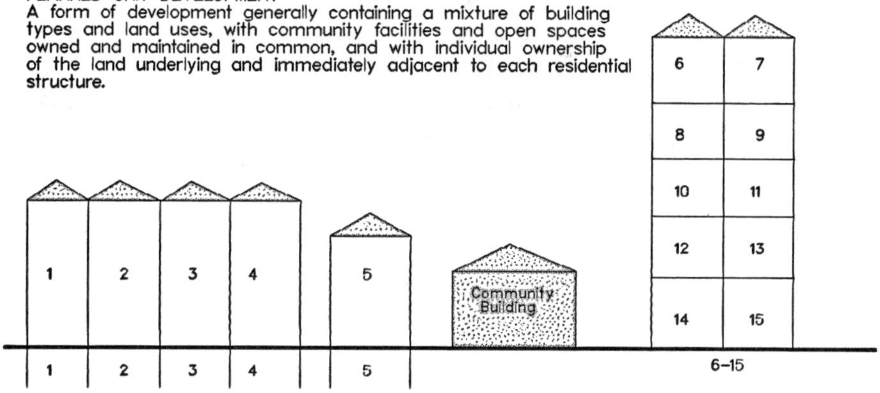

HIGH–RISE
4 or more stories–Units stacked vertically–Interior common areas

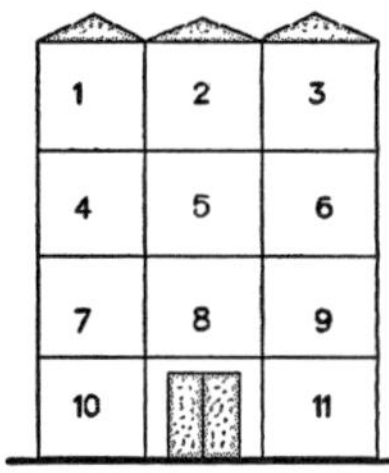

LOW–RISE
2 or 3 stories–Units stacked vertically–Interior common areas

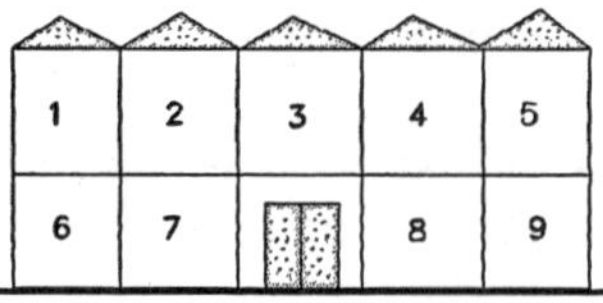

TOWNHOUSE
No stacking of units–No interior common areas–Attached or detached

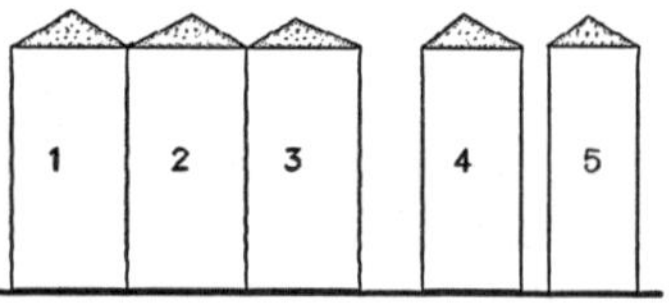

properties. These can include tennis courts, pools, spas, recreation/fitness centers, saunas, bike and hike trails, clubhouse party rooms, boat slips, golf courses, stable facilities, and/or security gate patrols. The price of these ownership benefits become affordable when they are shared by many.

In addition to affordability, the maintenance-free lifestyle appeals to many busy Californians. The association dues include the costs of exterior maintenance (e.g., roof repair, painting, landscape service, pool service, driveway and walkway maintenance, exterior lighting, and guard service/patrol). Furthermore, the individual owner need not be concerned with arranging or supervising that maintenance. No time is spent on getting maintenance bids, overseeing the work, arranging for insurance and liability bonds for workmen, or paying for the work. An individual owner would be hard pressed to get these monthly services for the $80 to $130 dues paid to the average California homeowners' association.

Other advantages include the benefits of homeownership over apartment living: the individual owner has control over the interior as to color, floor and wall coverings, window treatment, and appliances. Homeownership also gives the owner substantial tax benefits. In addition, the owner is building up equity in the property as it increases in value. The equity is often used as a way to move into the single-family residential market. Lastly, the monthly payments for the units are often not much more than rental payments. Yet the fear of eviction is eliminated, generating greater pride-of-ownership security for the occupant.

One benefit of shared ownership increases in value as the "graying of America" continues. This benefit is the social advantage to group living. Group activities are often coordinated by on-site management personnel and include local, regional and international functions. For instance, the association may arrange tours to foreign countries, and vacation and cruise packages. Residents often take local trips as well, shopping or attending sporting or entertainment events. By going as a group, the association members avoid driving on California freeways, alleviate parking problems, and take advantage of group discounts. The clubhouse often doubles as the bridgeclub room, monthly birthday/anniversary party place, and pool or dart tournament area.

Management Disadvantages

There are several disadvantages to managing homeowner association properties. For example, the property manager has no control over the unit occupant, only over the unit owner. A common complaint is that too many units are owned by absentee owners for their rental potential; many associations have found that 50% of the units are tenant-occupied. The association manager who tries to enforce the rules and regulations often hears, "I don't rent from you." The property manager must then get the association's approval to cite the unit owner for any violations. This process is obviously more time consuming and costly. Convincing the unit owner to evict a paying tenant because he or she parks in front of a neighbor's garage door is often difficult. Getting the board to take action against the unit owner is virtually impossible in some associations. Many associations have tried to require owner occupancy, but because it was not a restriction in the original *Covenants, Conditions, and Restrictions* (CC&Rs), the change must be voted in. Obviously, such a proposal would not get the votes of the absentee owners.

Property managers also have problems overseeing the common areas. Theft of clubhouse equipment is often a dilemma. Too much security means the equipment is rarely used, which defeats the purpose of providing it in the first place. Lax security means high replacement costs, or even eliminating the facility altogether, decreasing unit values and removing an amenity purchased by the owners.

Clubhouse facilities can create additional problems if they are used as the gathering place of undesirable non-residents or unchaperoned youths. These groups may discourage many residents from approaching the facilities they paid to use. Additional cleaning crews, posted hours, and a security patrol can help maintain the integrity of these areas.

Another problem created by clubhouse use is its administration: the waiting list, the permission process, and the high, refundable deposits often required to book the facility for private use. Cleaning deposits and liability insurance coverage (for damages and injury to guests) may also be required.

The property manager must deal with the common complaints about association dues. While owners like the low $60 to $100 range for monthly dues, usually these cover only the basic costs of daily management. When dues are too low, the property manager must educate owners about the true costs of running the association. In most California regions, dues should range from $100 to $150 per month to cover not only daily operations, but also reserves for replacements. If reserves for replacements are not accumulated, there will be no money to repave the parking lot, reroof the building, recarpet the clubhouse, resurface the pool, etc. Without reserves, a bill is presented to the owners for immediate payment, but the owners don't have the cash available to meet the expense.

Collections are another unpleasant task that must be handled by the property manager. If a tenant in an apartment does not pay the rent, the eviction process is relatively inexpensive and usually takes less than two months. Non-payment of association dues, however, means litigating a foreclosure proceeding. The costs are substantial and the process takes at least four months. And, of course, even if the association wins the lawsuit, it loses in the long run. The association is not in the business of owning real estate. A foreclosed unit means needed income is not collected, and if the unit is not properly maintained, it becomes an eyesore and/or a danger to the other owners. This in turn can lead to additional collection problems, more foreclosures, and increased maintenance costs.

TYPES OF ASSOCIATION DEVELOPMENTS

Several different types of developments may have homeowners' associations. These include cooperatives, condominiums, and planned unit developments.

Cooperatives

A cooperative is based on the corporate method of property ownership. The corporation sells shares of stock to individuals, and uses the funds collected to purchase a piece of property. The corporation may also purchase the personal property necessary to the operation of the real property, such as community room furnishings and recreation equipment. The corporation then gives the individual stockholder a **proprietary lease** to his or her unit. Thus, the owners own a share of stock in a corporation, not a deed to a specific piece of real estate.

Cooperatives are popular outside California where luxury units are hard to find. For example, when individuals are looking for specific features, such as boat slips at a marina, they may form a cooperative. In California, commercial and agribusiness ventures frequently use this method of real estate operation.

The difference between cooperative ownership and other types of ownership has mainly to do with the financing. The corporation, as the owner, has a *blanket mortgage* that encumbers the entire property. The corporation must pay for the mortgage, property taxes, and operational expenses. In return, the corporation receives all the lease income. The corporation files its own income tax return and the individual stockholder gets an annual financial statement on the corporate activity and possible dividend.

The property manager must be aware of this ownership structure and its disadvantages. For instance, the shareholders are tenants under a lease. They have no equity in the property and cannot obtain a second trust deed on their share of stock. They do not get the tax advantages of property ownership. They can only sell their stock to an interested party.

The property manager needs to monitor collections closely and watch for that critical bottom line of management. Should collections be running slow, the property manager must have adequate working capital to avoid foreclosures. With only one loan on the entire complex, a lack of funds can mean a redistribution of expenses among the rest of the shareholders. If one owner defaults on his or her payments, expenses increase for the remaining shareholders. As expenses increase, fewer can afford the increased costs, so less can afford to make their payments, thus causing additional foreclosures.

It is difficult for individuals to buy into cooperatives that increase in value and build up equity. The larger the equity, the larger the required cash downpayment. So as the value increases, owners find it more difficult to sell their stock and the property manager must be able to work with frustrated individuals who cannot find purchasers for their stock.

A year-end summary of 1987 cooperative operating data, published in 1988, shows a total median annual expense of $2634.74 per unit for the USA. (Figure 2). This amounts to $219.56 per unit per month for dues

Figure 2

COOPERATIVE ANALYSIS

All Types Combined | **Median Annual Expenses**

EXPENSES	**TOTAL USA**		**DOLLARS PER UNITS**		
Administrative Exp	**Projects**	**Units**	**Med**	**Low**	**High**
Office Salaries	58	24,642	126.29	99.73	201.34
Office Expense	97	28,564	32.57	16.55	54.74
Management Fee	99	28,248	178.79	124.82	209.95
Legal, Audit	97	28,505	52.91	26.30	79.12
Other	80	26,590	23.52	8.38	45.68
Subtotal Administ.	**100**	**28,638**	**383.51**	**263.42**	**494.28**
Operating Expenses					
Elevator	42	19,824	64.32	51.22	102.33
Heating Fuel	74	13,160	383.72	221.22	493.02
Electricity	98	28,474	93.88	44.26	182.31
Water/Sewer	97	28,033	140.64	106.35	188.86
Natural Gas	49	19,547	43.38	17.86	106.25
Exterminating	82	26,833	7.97	4.82	12.05
Rubbish Removal	65	23,883	41.28	17.44	54.79
Window Washing	5	704	16.28	12.33	16.89
Miscellaneous	52	20,658	12.80	4.08	54.52
Subtotal Operating	**100**	**28,638**	**712.57**	**405.69**	**864.02**
Repair and Maint.					
Security	33	18,744	84.00	11.00	183.37
Ground Maintenance	79	25,293	67.93	33.88	128.92
Custodial	72	25,330	259.34	29.48	494.37
General Maintenance	100	28,638	278.17	149.31	444.72
Heat/AC/Vent	68	11,970	34.44	13.01	75.95
Paint-Int CA Only	51	7,919	19.66	8.06	56.59
Paint-Exterior	25	17,853	22.02	9.82	75.68
Recreational	25	16,068	17.36	9.43	43.36
Garage & Parking	53	20,048	34.57	8.49	115.76
Subtotal Rep/Maint.	**100**	**28,638**	**735.12**	**485.60**	**1020.46**
Fix Expenses					
Real Estate Tax	85	25,204	480.95	312.61	1108.31
Other Tax	70	24,113	18.95	4.78	54.95
Insurance	100	28,638	198.19	138.90	281.02
Subtotal Fixed Exp.	**100**	**28,638**	**669.46**	**435.51**	**1401.08**
Total All Expenses	**98**	**28,285**	**2634.74**	**1845.07**	**3432.10**
Ground Rent	14	1,845	397.73	46.24	821.10
Replacement Reserve	75	25,097	125.89	70.74	233.93
Amenities					
Pool	13	14,486	21.84	13.30	36.24
Rec Building	2	13,014	115.37	3.60	115.37
Outdoor Rec. Facility	2	13,014	138.11	11.51	138.11
Garage & Parking	3	476	98.92	2.14	98.92

FOOTNOTE: For an explanation of the report layouts and method of data analysis, refer to the sections entitled *Guidelines for Use of this Data* and *Interpretation of a Page of Data*. For definitions of the expense categories, refer to the Appendix.

to cover expenses, plus $10.49 per month for replacement reserves, for a total of $230.05 per month median association dues for a cooperative. (This figure includes administrative and operating expenses, repairs and maintenance, and the fixed expenses of real estate property tax and insurance, plus reserves for replacement. The mortgage loan payments are not included in the calculation of association dues.)

Condominiums

The condominium method of ownership combines two separate forms of ownership. The first is the absolute fee simple title that the owner holds to the interior portion of the individual unit. The second form of ownership is the undivided interest that a unit owner has in the non-profit homeowners' association, which owns the common areas of the property.

The Unit Owner. All the benefits of fee simple ownership are afforded the condominium owner. Each owner has title to his or her own unit. The owner maintains his or her own separate financing for each unit. It is common for the developer to arrange for the original financing on any new construction. The units are pre-approved for a specific loan amount. As the developer sells off individual units, each owner qualifies for his or her own loan. Then, as these original owners resell their units, the selling price varies according to the market conditions at the time of sale.

Each owner receives an individual tax bill for his or her unit. Homeowner's insurance for personal items is paid for on an individual basis. The unit owner also enjoys the income tax benefits of property ownership. Each unit owner receives a monthly bill from the homeowners' association, which is not tax deductible unless the owner uses the unit for income-generating purposes. If the unit owner fails to pay the fee, it becomes a lien against the unit.

Owners can benefit from their equity buildup by obtaining secondary financing and cashing out their equity. Or they can sell the property at a higher price than they paid, getting an immediate benefit from the increase in value. The new purchaser would get a deed to the unit from the seller.

One disadvantage to condominium ownership is that the financing may be difficult under certain conditions. For example, if the owner-occupant/tenant-occupant ratio dips below 70/30, it may be difficult to get a loan. Also, lenders limit the number of loans they make in any one given project, as they prefer to spread their risk over several projects for a more diversified portfolio. Even the Mortgage Guarantee Insurance Corporation (MGIC) limits itself to insuring only one-third of the units in a single project. This can mean that as a project nears the 30% tenant-occupied status, it becomes virtually impossible to obtain financing from the most obvious sources of funds—already participating lenders.

A common problem within condominium ownership is the legal requirements that must be complied with when one owner accumulates many units within the same complex. The California real estate law requires every owner who has five or more lots or parcels to file for and obtain the Real Estate Commissioner's Department of Real Estate Amended Public Report, as provided for under the Subdivided Lands Act. This can be costly and time consuming, especially if an owner of five units is in escrow to sell one unit and has not already obtained the necessary approvals. The disclosures must be made and can hold up the close of escrow for months.

The Homeowners' Association. The homeowners' association pays for the costs of doing business. These include the ownership and upkeep of the common areas: swimming pools, spas, tennis courts, playgrounds, golf course, clubhouse, hallways, sidewalks, basements, elevators, lobbies, exterior and interior walls, roof, duct work, and piping. The association gets a separate property tax bill for all the common areas and for the land under the units, which are owned by the association.

Other expenses include the association utilities, maintenance, and insurance. As the unit walls are connected, a fire in one unit affects the adjoining units. The association gets one blanket insurance policy to cover the entire project and charges each unit owner their pro-rata share. The water and trash disposal costs are allocated in the same manner, but gas and electricity are usually billed separately. All these items are administered by the association property management.

The Property Manager. The property manager is instrumental in each phase of the condominium project. Most developers do not want to be involved in the daily management details, which interfere with the operations of the new sales office. It can be very expensive to forfeit a sale because a salesperson is handling an irate unit owner or their tenant.

The property manager prepares the 12-month cash flow spreadsheet, and forecasts projected monthly dues. Creating budgets, handling expenses, and setting up capital reserve accounts are all part of the property manager's duties. The property manager may be better able to negotiate contracts for maintenance services, insurance, and unit services, such as cable TV, appliance maintenance agreements, etc. The property manager is a valuable liaison for on-going business relationships.

Condominium property management is a rapidly growing part of the field. In the past, some unlicensed, unscrupulous, or untrained persons acting as the manager for a condominium association mismanaged the association or left with the association funds. However, the Federal Housing Authority (FHA) has set guidelines for the creation of federally insured loans on the units in these projects. State and federal laws have tightened. Using a Certified Property Manager (CPM) who is licensed, bonded, and insured is a good basic criteria to use to qualify for this specialty area.

The major reason for the rise in condominium associations in California is affordability. In the past, condominiums were overbuilt for the existing California market demand and little appreciation in value was seen. But the demand in the late 1980's has absorbed the supply, and sales prices are rising by over 6% per year. Experts project condominium ownership to grow in market strength in the future as well. (Figure 3)

A year-end summary of 1987 condominium operating data, published in 1988, shows a total median annual expense of $1203.18 per unit for the USA. (Figure 4). This amounts to $100.27 per unit per month for association dues to cover expenses, plus $14.80 per month for replacement reserves, for a total of $115.07 per month median association dues for a condominium.

Planned Unit Development

A planned unit development (PUD) combines two types of ownership. One is the fee simple ownership of an individual unit and on the land underneath that unit. The other is the undivided interest held in the common area.

The typical layout is where single-family residential units are placed on individual lots. The home may be one or more stories. They may be

Figure 3

JANUARY 1988
Statewide Market Trends

BOARDS REPORTING: 32 PERCENT OF SAMPLED SALES: 33.3%	Detached Single-Family Homes	Condominium Units
Median Time on the Market		
Current month	**55.0 days**	**68.0 days**
Previous month	49.0 days	61.0 days
Previous year	63.0 days	61.0 days
Time on the Market Before Sale		
Less than 30 days	31.1%	23.3%
31-60 days	22.4%	22.0%
61-90 days	18.7%	17.1%
91-120 days	10.9%	12.5%
Over 120 days	16.9%	25.1%
Unsold Inventory Index		
Current month	7.2 mos	12.1 mos
Previous month	5.3 mos	8.2 mos
Previous year	8.6 mos	16.1 mos
Type of Financing		
Cash to new loan	86.1%	81.6%
Cash to new loan plus 2nd	0.3%	0.0%
Assumptions	3.9%	4.8%
Owner carry	2.1%	2.0%
All cash	5.8%	9.6%
Other	1.9%	2.0%
Statewide Median Sales Price		
Current month	$147,281	$113,835
Change from previous month	1.4%	0.6%
Change from previous year	18.2%	6.4%
Market Share of Sample	**78.0%**	**22.0%**

Figure 4

CONDOMINIUM ANALYSIS

All Types Combined — **Median Annual Expenses**

EXPENSES	TOTAL USA		DOLLARS PER UNITS		
Administrative Exp	**Projects**	**Units**	**Med**	**Low**	**High**
Office Salaries	278	54,318	105.85	57.63	168.09
Office Expense	1063	129,128	14.61	8.17	29.07
Management Fee	1178	132,563	124.53	100.00	162.00
Legal, Audit	1142	134,846	19.15	9.65	38.18
Other	703	90,465	7.39	2.93	18.16
Subtotal Administ.	**1217**	**139,177**	**186.90**	**136.36**	**275.65**
Operating Expenses					
Elevator	323	47,293	59.69	37.04	101.33
Heating Fuel	284	40,016	262.20	67.37	405.26
Electricity	1151	134,253	73.89	40.00	136.71
Water/Sewer	1132	132,644	138.63	81.10	212.23
Natural Gas	444	63,386	61.72	16.79	113.47
Exterminating	841	105,348	11.10	5.27	19.56
Rubbish Removal	979	116,139	43.75	28.56	65.01
Window Washing	154	28,725	18.21	8.23	30.45
Miscellaneous	433	60,543	36.32	7.22	90.07
Subtotal Operating	**1207**	**138,507**	**372.59**	**214.63**	**598.56**
Repair and Maint.					
Security	477	77,253	45.20	15.63	173.20
Ground Maintenance	1185	137,137	146.68	71.25	251.85
Custodial	679	88,767	87.15	26.30	210.74
General Maintenance	1174	135,893	120.79	58.29	216.33
Heat/AC/Vent	285	44,327	29.41	7.32	79.05
Paint-Int CA Only	231	37,156	12.41	3.90	29.11
Paint-Exterior	338	45,591	21.32	3.96	80.56
Recreational	742	99,375	39.20	23.03	69.29
Garage & Parking	424	54,634	26.46	8.52	72.93
Subtotal Rep/Maint.	**1206**	**138,695**	**470.83**	**315.00**	**715.83**
Fix Expenses					
Real Estate Tax	22	3,735	158.44	9.15	343.62
Other Tax	701	85,150	8.44	2.96	22.35
Insurance	1201	138,066	141.07	94.33	218.07
Subtotal Fixed Exp.	**1208**	**138,450**	**150.94**	**100.00**	**236.62**
Total All Expenses	**1211**	**138,661**	**1203.18**	**885.32**	**1824.74**
Ground Rent	38	3,020	338.92	13.64	993.05
Replacement Reserve	971	115,202	117.65	103.72	293.28
Amenities					
Pool	648	87,369	33.89	20.33	60.33
Rec Building	163	26,833	8.89	2.75	22.10
Outdoor Rec. Facility	89	14,759	4.78	2.16	16.67
Garage & Parking	47	8,509	18.48	8.26	41.67

FOOTNOTE: For an explanation of the report layouts and method of data analysis, refer to the sections entitled *Guidelines for Use of this Data* and *Interpretation of a Page of Data*. For definitions of the expense categories, refer to the Appendix.

detached single units, or townhouse-style units with common walls. Each lot is substandard, as a small part of land has been taken from each lot to be donated to the common area, often called greenbelt, beachfront, marina, or the like.

There are several advantages to PUD ownership. All of the finance and tax benefits are afforded the property owner, just as with other separate forms of ownership; units have individual liens and encumbrances; individual deeds convey title; and each lot often has a separate front and back yard. PUD's usually have the look of a regular tract of homes, so pride-of-ownership and individual decorating styles prevail. Plus, owners can take advantage of the common area pools, tennis courts, playgrounds, and clubhouse. The equity in PUDs often increases at a faster pace than other association housing.

Disadvantages include the common problem of inadequate parking areas, narrow streets, and crowding due to the smaller lot sizes. High tenant occupancy can cause rundown neighborhoods because front yard landscape and maintenance are not included in the association dues and are the unit owner's responsibility. Individual units are some distance from the common areas, so owners tend to use them less frequently.

The management operations require less work than other association management as the property managers only manage the common area operations and not the land under the unit, utilities, or exterior maintenance. The property manager only oversees the park area, ponds and streams, jogging paths, playground, bridle trails, clubhouse operational expenses, and utilities and insurance on the common area. Owners get their own unit insurance policies and tax bills, and handle their maintenance.

A summary of operating data, published in 1988, shows total median expenses of $899.20 per unit for the USA. This amounts to $74.93 per month for association dues to cover expenses plus $14.66 per month for replacement reserves, for a total of $89.59 per month median association dues for a planned unit development.

GOVERNING STRUCTURE

California associations are often structured in a similar manner to that shown in Figure 5. The original declaration is made by the developer to

Figure 5

Declaration Of Covenants, Conditions And Restrictions Establishing A Development With An Association

I. Recitals
   A. Declaration
   B. Definitions
II. Property Rights, Rights of Enjoyment and Easements
   A. Owners Non-Exclusive Easements of Enjoyment
   B. Delegation of Use
   C. Easements Granted by Association
   D. Easements Reserved and Granted
   E. Conveyance of the Common Area
III. Use Restrictions
   A. Residential, Garage and Land Use
   B. Commercial Use
   C. Oil Drilling
   D. Offensive Conduct and Nuisances
   E. Parking Restrictions and Use of Garages
   F. Signs
   G. Antennae, External Fixtures, etc.
   H. Restricted Use of Recreation Vehicles, etc.
   I. Trash Disposal
   J. Clotheslines and Storage
   K. Exterior Alterations and Modifications
   L. Compliance with Laws
   M. Drainage
   N. Unkeep of Lot
   O. Party Walls
   P. Vending or Liquor or Other Alcoholic Beverages
   Q. Temporary Structure
   R. Storage of Materials, Junk, Trash and Manure, etc.
IV. The Association
   A. Formation
   B. Association Action. Board of Directors and Officers
   C. Powers and Duties of Association
      1. Powers
         a. Assessments
         b. Right of Enforcement
         c. Delegation of Powers
         d. Association Rules
      2. Duties of the Association
         a. Operation, Maintenance and Report of Common Area and Lot Maintenance and Repair
         b. Exterior Building Maintenance
         c. Taxes and Assessment
         d. Utilities for the Common Area
         e. Insurance
         f. Enforcement of Restrictions and Rules

- D. Personal Liability
- E. Annual Meeting and Notice
- F. Balance Sheet and Operating Statement
    - 1. First Accounting Date
    - 2. Subsequent (Annual) Accounting Dates
    - 3. First Operating (Income) Statement
- G. Limitations on Powers of the Board
    - 1. Voting Power Requirements
    - 2. Board Authority to Contract
        - a. Public Utilities
        - b. Insurance
        - c. Professional Association Management
        - d. Capital Improvements

V. Memembership and Voting Rights

- A. Membership
    - 1. Qualifications
    - 2. Members Rights and Duties
    - 3. Transfer of Membership
- B. Voting
    - 1. Number of Votes
    - 2. Cumulative Voting
- C. Removal of Board Members
- D. Terms of Board Members
- E. Specially Elected Director

VI. Assessments

- A. Agreement to Pay
- B. Personal Obligation
- C. Purpose of Assessments
- D. Assessments
    - 1. Initial Fiscal Year Assessment
    - 2. Regular Assessments
    - 3. Special Assessments
- E. Uniform Rate of Assessment
- F. Assessment Period
- G. Notice and Assessment Installment Due Date
- H. Increase in Assessment
- I. Estoppel Certificate
- J. Unsegregated Real Estate Taxes
- K. Use of Funds Collected by the Association
- L. Notification of Sale of Lot

VII. Collection of Assessments and Liens

- A. Right to Enforce
- B. Creation of Lien
- C. Notice of Default and Foreclosure
- D. Waiver of Exemptions

VIII. Insurance

- A. Liability Insurance

- B. Common Area Insurance
- C. Trustee
- D. Other Insurance

IX. Destruction of Common Area Improvements
- A. Destruction
- B. Procedures Respecting Rebuilding
- C. Contract regarding Rebuilding
- D. Priority of Mortgagee

X. Term of Declaration, Compliance with Rule Against Perpetuities

XI. Protection of Mortgagees
- A. Mortgage Permitted
- B. Subordination
- C. Voting Rights on Default
- D. Effect of Breach
- E. Foreclosure
- F. Non-Curable Breach
- G. Loan to Facilitate
- H. Notificiation
- I. Mortgagee Protection
    1. By Act or Omission
    2. Method of Determining Obligation
    3. By Change in Common Area
    4. Fire Coverage
    5. Hazard Insurance Proceeds for Losses
    6. Architectural Design Change
    7. Sell
- J. Appearance at Meetings
- K. Right to Furnish Information/Collection of Insurance Premiums
- L. Right to Advance Delinquencies
- M. Examination of Books
- N. Right of First Refusal
- O. Conflicting Provisions

XII. Amendment
- A. Amendment Prior to Close of First Sale
- B. Amendment Subsequent to Close of First Sale
- C. Conflict with Article XI
- D. Business and Professions Code
- E. Reliance on Amendments

XIII. Eminent Domain to Common Area

XIV. Miscellaneous Provisions
- A. Districts
- B. Waiver regarding Unenforceability
- C. Rental or Leasing of Lots
- D. Attorney's Fees
- E. Liberal Construction
- F. Number and Gender
- G. Binding Effect

all future owners. Definitions are outlined in Figure 7. Non-exclusive easements to the common areas are granted, which allows the association to give each owner usage rights, but also allows the association to limit guests and adopt rules and regulations for the common areas. The association can also borrow money to improve common and recreational areas and can grant utility easements.

Usually, some restrictions are imposed on the usage of the units. These may include needing specific authorization before putting up business signs or similar items. Parking is regulated for motorcycles, recreation vehicles, and guest vehicles. Maintenance and upkeep requirements are specified, including restriction on clotheslines, drainage to neighbor lots, and trash disposal.

The association is usually formed as a nonprofit corporation under the laws of the State of California. The articles of the original declaration prevail over any later adopted by-laws. The board of directors appoint or elect the officers and the governing body is usually composed of a least five members.

Each unit owner gets one vote. Voting is best handled by mailed written ballot, with the location and time of the meeting well publicized. Clear instructions should be given, both for those who want to attend and participate and for those who wish to vote by proxy. Mail-in ballots are very important to absentee owners who have rental units. The property manager usually handles the ballot preparation and distribution with the help of the voting/nomination committee.

The association has the power to levy assessments and enforce their payment by virtue of the original purchase agreement—each lot owner agrees to pay all dues, late charges, interest, attorney fees, and assessments. Regular assessments are the normal operating expenses, most of which are administered by the property manager. Any proposed budget, however, that exceeds the last year's budget by 20% usually requires a vote of approval by 51% of the members. Special assessments to defray large or unusual costs may be assessed as a lump sum or as installment payments. Interest is usually charged on the assessments between the due date and the time payment is received.

Figure 6

Association Definitions

"Articles"	The articles of incorporation of the Association, which include the articles that may be amended from time to time.
"Association"	The Home Owners Association, a California non-profit corporation, its successors and assigns.
"Board"	The board of directors of the Association.
"By-Laws"	The by-laws of the Association, which may be amended from time to time.
"Common Area"	Lot #________ of Tract #________, the streets abutting all lots of such Tract and all sidewalk areas. The common area shall be owned by the Association at the time of conveyance of the first lot within the development, and shall be free of any and all liens and encumbrances, excepting necessary easements for ingress, egress, and support utility easements.
"Declarant"	The limited partnership, or corporation owners, its successors and assigns, and all such successors and assigns who acquire or hold record title to all or any portion of the development for the development purposes.
"Lot"	Any numbered plot of land, together with the residential and other improvements thereon, as shown upon any recorded subdivision map of the development, with the exception of the common area.
"Member"	Every person or entity who holds a membership in the Association.
"Mortgage"	A mortgage or deed of trust encumbering a lot or other portion of the development. A "mortgage" shall also mean an installment sales contract as to a lot, or other portions of the development entered into under and pursuant to a sales contract. A "first mortgagee" is a mortgagee under a mortgage having priority over all other mortgages encumbering the same property.
"Owner"	Each person and entity holding a record ownership interest in a lot, including declarant. The term "owner" shall not include persons or entities who hold an interest in a lot merely as security for the performance of an obligation or as a contract purchaser.

The association has the right to suspend the voting rights and use privileges or assess monetary penalties for any violation of the declaration, articles, by-laws, rules, resolutions, or regulations. A 30-day suspension is not uncommon for a first violation, with a $100 penalty for a subsequent violation.

When a unit owner wants to sell his or her unit, he or she generally must notify the board, in writing, of the intent to transfer the interest. This usually must be within the first five days of the sale, and escrow normally performs this duty. This allows the board and property manager to figure the outstanding liens and to provide the prospective purchaser with a copy of the rules, regulations, and by-laws, which must have the written approval of the buyer prior to the close of escrow.

ROLE OF PROPERTY MANAGEMENT

The association has the authority to delegate its power, duties and responsibilities to committees or employees, including the hiring of a professional managing agent. The property manager handles the business operations and administers the association rules. These rules govern the use and enjoyment of the common area by the owner, family members, guests, invitees, and their family members, guests or invitees. The property manager must keep a copy of the rules posted in a conspicuous place in the common area (usually the clubhouse), and furnish a copy to each owner. The rules are amended, over time, usually with a 75% written vote. The property manager can be instrumental in making necessary recommendations for rules that need elimination or modification.

The property manager usually gets bids for the contract maintenance, i.e., pool, landscape, exterior painting. These bids are submitted to the Board for approval prior to incurring the expense. However, the manager also needs the authority to make emergency repairs, such as a broken water pipe.

The property manager receives, pays, and audits the utility bills. The insurance bids are often placed with the property manager, but a final presentation should be made at a board meeting to allow for questions. This applies to fire, liability, and errors and ommissions insurance coverage for the property manager and the board.

When a member of the association does not pay the dues bill for their assessed portion, the property manager has the obligation to notify the board of these delinquencies. This must be a written request, listing the unit, the amount due, the time period, and owner's name. There is usually a 20-day notice period before any action is taken. Trust deed holders also may request the property management to notify them in the event of default of association payments.

Meeting notices are usually published in a monthly or quarterly newsletter. The newsletter may also include articles of interest, bid information, a review of rules, and accounting data. The annual budget is mailed by the property manager with the newsletter. The operating statement, balance sheets, and operating information are contained in the budget.

The property management contract must give the property manager a clear directive regarding what he or she is responsible for and to whom he or she reports. Specific items to cover in the contract include the required procedures for handling funds and banking operations. The bank account is commonly in the name of the association and often requires two signatures on the account—the property manager and the association treasurer. Typically, an independent audit is performed on the books and the report is given directly to the board for review.

The approval process for expenses must also be clear. The manager may need no additional approval to pay a recurring expense that is included in the budget, such as the grounds maintenance. However, there are times when the actual expenses are more than the budget allowed (for example, an unusually high water bill). The property manager must know what steps to take in these circumstances.

The property manager needs to have guidelines for enforcing the association's rules and regulations and the power to impose penalties for violations. Without the power to penalize, the property manager can do little to maintain the integrity of the association's reputation.

It is vital that everyone understand the chain of authority. The property manager must take all directives from the board of directors of the association. Committee chairpersons need written board approval to give the property manager assignments and duties. The property manager cannot have 100 unit owners, and 50 tenants, and 10 committee chairpersons giving 160 potentially conflicting orders. The process must be clearly defined and constantly maintained.

Lastly, the contract must clarify the property management hours. Is the property manager expected to attend every board meeting, only business meetings, or only the business portion of some or all meetings? The number of hours included in the contract, the days and times they are to be scheduled, and what rate is paid for extra hours all needs to be clearly defined. A specific agreement makes operations work more smoothly for all parties, and maintains a more professional image.

CHAPTER 10–QUIZ

1. A townhouse is a type of:

   a. housing design
   b. condominium project
   c. cooperative
   d. planned unit development

2. A common area is that area which is owned by the:

   a. board of directors
   b. association
   c. developer
   d. property manager

3. A condominium owner owns:

   a. fee absolute simple title to a specific unit
   b. undivided interest membership in a homeowners' association
   c. shares of stock in a corporation
   d. Both a) and b)

4. A cooperative owner owns:

   a. fee absolute simple title to a specific unit
   b. undivided interest membership in a homeowners' association
   c. a share of stock in a corporation
   d. Both a) and b)

5. A planned unit development (PUD) owner owns:

   a. fee absolute simple title to a specific unit
   b. fee absolute simple title to the land under the unit
   c. an undivided interest in the common area
   d. All of the above

6. The powers of the association do not include the right to:

   a. inform the first trust deed holder of default in dues payments, if requested to do so in writing
   b. levy a $100 penalty to an owner who has tenants who have violated the association rules and regulations
   c. sell the unit without formal foreclosure procedures and expenses because the association holds legal title
   d. suspend the voting privileges of an owner who does not have their dues current and paid

7. The property management duties would not include:

   a. attending association board of directors meetings
   b. balancing the checkbook of the association
   c. completing annual CPA auditing verifications
   d. enforcing the rules and regulations of the association

8. The growth in popularity of housing ownership that includes belonging to an association is caused by all of the following except:

   a. affordability
   b. board interaction
   c. lifestyle changes
   d. maintenance-free ownership

9. The Institute of Real Estate Management (IREM) furnishes annual reports and information on:

   a. management agreement contract
   b. summary of expenses
   c. association rules and regulations
   d. association by-laws, and CC&Rs

10. The property manager gets his or her power and authority to act from:

    a. the association's CC&Rs
    b. the association rules and regulations
    c. the board of directors
    d. the property management committee

CHAPTER 10–QUIZ ANSWERS

1. a
2. b
3. c
4. c
5. d
6. c
7. c
8. b
9. b
10. a

11

Other Residential Property Management

References

Holland, Barbara. "Manage Small Properties Successfully—and Profitably." *Real Estate Today,* Sept. 1987.

Allen, George. "Managing the Manufactured Housing Community." *Journal of Property Management,* May/June 1988

Marshall Valuation Service. Marshall & Swift Publication Co., May 1981.

News a la C.A.R., November 1988.

Official California Apartment Journal, June 1988.

"The Graying of California." *California Real Estate,* Nov. 1988.

Last Chapter Review

The management of homeowner associations varies with the type of ownership unit, and this was reviewed in the last chapter. Condominiums, cooperatives, and planned unit developments were described, their governing structure explained, and the role of property management reviewed.

Chapter Overview

Specialized residential property management is an important, rapidly growing area of the California property management field. This chapter outlines the special knowledge required to manage single-family residences, mobile home parks, time-shares, recreational parks, housing for the elderly, and special purpose housing, such as senior communities, industrial housing, and dormitories.

Figure 1

WHERE YOU FIND RENTAL UNITS

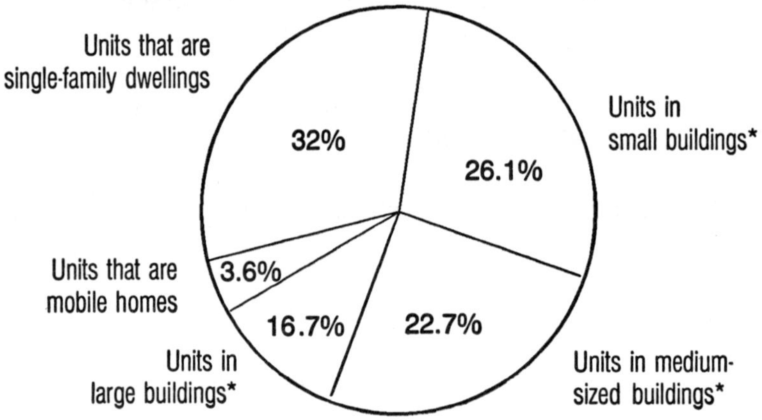

Percentages total more than 100 percent because of rounding.
*Small = 2-4 units; medium-sized = 5-19 units; large = 20 + units.
Source: U.S. Bureau of the Census, 1983 statistics

SINGLE-FAMILY RESIDENTIAL MANAGEMENT

Single-family homes are houses intended for use and occupancy by one family. They usually have amenities such as yards, garages, and a private entrance. They may be designed as a single- or multi-story home, a townhouse, or a row house. Single-family home density varies by type: three to eight houses per acre for homes, and six to fifteen per acre for row houses.

Market Activity

In 1985, there were 9.5 million renter-occupied, single-family homes—about 30% of all renter-occupied housing in the nation. From 1981 to 1985, 400,000 single-family homes were added to the rental supply each year. This was partly due to the high interest rates: higher interest rates meant bigger home payments. Many homeowners were unable to sell their homes as it became more difficult for buyers to qualify for home mortgages. Unsold units became rental units when owners were unable to sell them.

Once the property was converted to a rental property, the owner experienced the tax advantages of owning a rental unit. Both the tax depreciation (not available for owner-occupied homes) and the property appreciation (a forced savings account) benefitted the owner. Other investors increasingly turned towards single-family homes because they could no longer afford the payment for duplexes or triplexes. These investors soon discovered the advantages of single-family rental units.

Property management grew in this arena because many investors were reluctant to buy a rental property unless the brokerage company selling it arranged for the management after the sale. Brokers and property managers joined forces to service this segment of the market. For many real estate offices, the regular property management fees were a more steady source of income than commissions. These brokers encouraged less sophisticated investors, and those with less funds available, to buy single-family rentals.

Management

If a broker is arranging property management for a property after a sale, he or she must be sure all property managers are licensed and under direct supervision, in compliance with California Department of Real Estate requirements. The management office needs careful organization and well-developed policies. Even with a computerized accounting system to monitor the many management functions, the job can be difficult because of the numbers of properties and the distance between them. Management of single-family residential property is more completely discussed in Chapter 7.

Chapter Eleven

MOBILE HOME PARK MANAGEMENT

There are over 240,000 mobile home communities across the nation that contain about two million rental homesites. (The term "mobile homes" includes "manufactured homes;" these two terms are used interchangeably.) Approximately 60% of the 3.6 million occupied units on these two million sites are situated within these communities, with the remaining 40% situated on larger acreage plots or commercial lots. In California, just under one million people occupy units in the over 5,000 mobile home parks. California produces over 12,000 new units each year.

Advantages

The major reason for the growing use of the manufactured home unit is affordability. Used home prices in California average well over $125,000 statewide, while a new mobile home will vary from $20,000 to $50,000.

An additional benefit to manufactured home ownership is the tax deductibility of the interest payment. However, unless the homeowner also owns the land, there is no property tax deduction (as, for example, with a condominium unit). Mobile homes are taxed at a separate tax rate. If the unit was built before 7/1/80 and placed on a foundation, it is taxed by the county as personal property. If it was not placed on a foundation, it was treated as a pull-along trailer and taxed by the DMV at the time of sale, plus a sales/transfer tax. But, if it was built since 7/1/80, the unit is taxed at a rate set, administered, and collected by the California Department of Housing and Community Development (DOH). By writing the main DOH office, you can request the code sections, additional information, and local office addresses (shown at the end of this section).

An example of one DOH regulation is that they issue the permit required for a non-enclosed awning, rather than the local building department (which issues permits for home patio covers). This is because setback laws differ so widely. Cities usually have five-foot side and ten-foot rear minimum setbacks between property lines for homes. Mobile homes require only six feet between units, and only three feet between awnings and the neighboring unit.

Characteristics

In California, ownership of a manufactured home is similar to that of a recreational vehicle or auto, wherein title is by "pink slip" instead of a deed. The Certificate of Ownership shows the vehicle size, weight, class, and California Department of Vehicles (DMV) tag. When encumbered by a lien, the lender holds the title until final payoff, files the forms necessary to indicate payoff, removes the lender's name from the records, and releases full ownership of the unit.

A mobile home is manufactured, assembled, and finished at a factory. The difference between mobile homes and prefabricated homes is that "prefabs" are manufactured at a factory, but assembled and finished at the site.

Many mobile homes are, practically speaking, immobile because moving them is so costly. Special permits must be obtained to transport any unit over 8½' x 40' on a public road. A permit is required for each city the "oversize" load passes through, and a transportation permit is required for state highways. Front and rear escort vehicles are required to warn other drivers. The entire move is quite expensive. About 90% of the units never leave the mobile home park they are originally placed in, as they are usually sold as an 'in place' unit. This fact is very important to the property manager, who must enforce the rules of the park. Quick evictions are impossible. The property manager must enforce the rules and resolve problems without resorting to eviction, except in extreme cases.

New triple-wide units offer modern kitchens with built-in trash compactors, microwave ovens, dishwashers, disposals, ranges, ovens, and refrigerators. Washers and dryers are often included, as is forced air. Many have fireplaces, bay windows, carpets, drapes, and much more.

As of 1989, senior citizens may sell their homes and take their existing property taxes with them to a new property, without fear of reassessment. Because of this, manufactured home ownership is likely to become increasingly popular as those in densely populated city neighborhoods can afford to move to outlying areas. They will be able to sell their home in the more crowded, urban areas, and purchase land and a home in less populated areas. Entire mobile home communities are projected to enjoy a higher demand as a result of passage of Proposition 90 in November of 1988.

Development

Before deciding to develop a mobile home park, many factors must be considered. The developer must take into account the various hidden expenses of development: bringing utilities to the site, building storm drains, creating access roads, and performing traffic control and environmental impact studies. Local fees and assessments must also be taken into account. On-site costs include engineering expenses, including plans and specifications, a survey, architect and designer fees, public fees and permits. The site must be leveled for drainage and roughing out roads, excavation and hillside terracing must be completed, and individual unit sites must also be leveled. Street paving, patios, and walkways must also be completed.

Sewer costs include on-site lines and connections, and off-site connections to trunk lines, and possible sewage disposal systems or septic tank costs. Water costs are on-site mains, site service, sprinkler systems, and can include wells, pumps or off-site connections.

Gas costs include on-site piping, connections to buildings, off-site mains, and gas pumping in buildings. It may also include storage tanks and meters for propane distribution. Electrical costs include on-site conduit, electrical and telephone wiring to site outlets, street, area and building lighting, and off-site connections.

Permanent park facilities are a major part of the mobile home development. These include permanent structures for the clubhouse, laundry, restrooms, pool house, office, patios, barbecue, or other amenities. Entrance ornamentation, landscaping, and pools, tennis court, lakes and ponds are additional expenses, as well as recreational equipment, game tables, kitchen equipment, and furniture. Budgeting for advertising, promotional expenses and on-going management calls for expertise on the part of the property manager when planning a mobile home park.

The total costs of development are determined to calculate individual site costs and rents. To determine the gross area per unit, divide the entire improved area of the park by the number of units. Multipliers are given to adjust costs for differences from the base costs, as a quality rating for a park increases. An example of a 1981 valuation is shown in Figure 2.

Figure 2
1981 - Marshall and Swift Publication Co.,

MANUFACTURED HOUSING PARKS

Good Home

The good quality manufactured home will have an exterior finish of aluminum, plywood, or hardboard, sometimes a combination of two. The finish is often in various textures such as horizontal aluminum siding, board and batten, wood grain, etc. The base costs are for hardboard siding. Use percentage adjustments for variations from the base.

Walls are 4" thick and 7'6"to 8' high with ample fenestration consisting of numerous residential type sliding aluminum windows, a sliding door, and ornamentation around windows and entry.

Interior is of good quality prefinished plywood, cabinets and hardware are of good quality, and there are many extra interior appointments. Resilient flooring and carpeting are of good quality.

Heating has insulated perimeter ducts with cold air returns prepared for air conditioning. Add $ .75 to $1.30 per square foot for air conditioning.

Plumbing includes eight good quality fixtures, white or colored, and a plumbing rough-in in the base cost. The fixtures can include any of the following: lavatory, toilet, tub with shower over, tiled or modular stall shower, kitchen sink, laundry tray, water heater, and wet bar. The rough-in will typically consist of the water supply and waste for a laundry service. Adjust for more or less plumbing at $345 per fixture. For Roman tub, use the excellent quality lump sum plumbing adjustment, page 7.

Appliances, are not included and should be added from Section 12 or 42.

HOUSING COSTS (per square foot of floor area)

LENGTH	SINGLE WIDE				DOUBLE WIDE		
FEET	8	10	12	14	20	24	28
28	$29.31	$24.89	$21.77	$19.39	----	----	----
32	28.69	24.26	21.19	18.87	$28.67	$25.75	$23.89
40	27.69	23.25	20.25	18.02	26.38	23.68	21.60
44	27.27	22.83	19.85	17.67	25.73	22.98	20.90
48	26.90	22.45	19.51	17.36	25.15	22.35	20.27
52	26.56	22.12	19.20	17.07	24.64	21.80	19.71
56	26.25	21.81	18.91	16.82	24.17	21.30	19.22
60	25.96	21.52	18.66	16.58	23.74	20.83	18.76
64	25.70	21.26	18.42	16.36	23.34	20.42	18.35
68	25.45	21.02	18.20	16.16	22.98	20.04	17.97

For other than hardboard exterior wall finish, adjust the above costs as follows: shiplap aluminum siding, +3%; ribbed aluminum, −3%.

TRIPLE WIDE: Deduct 13% from the single-wide costs for a tagalong section; use full cost for the double-wide portion. For expandos and tip-outs see optional items.

Good Park

The typical good park is a manufactured housing park catering to the larger manufactured homes. It will accommodate large manufactured homes with private patios and gardens, and complete recreational facilities. Base area per site is 4,400 square feet and base number of spaces is 175.

ENGINEERING—Complete detailed plans and specifications, permits, fees, bonds, and survey $470

GRADING—Graded for drainage, view, and appearance,roads roughed in 415

STREET PAVING—Good 3" asphalt roadways on prepared base, 26 to 32 feet wide, edged or curbs, parking areas for visitors and extra cars 680

PATIOS AND WALKS—Home stands, patios, and car stands. Average 400 square feet of concrete per space, including walks around buildings and recreational areas 505

SEWER—4" service, 6" mains, 8" trunk, good code installation, well vented and trapped 510

WATER—4"-6" mains, good valve connection and hydrants at sites 465

GAS—Low pressure gas to all sites and buildings 265

ELECTRICAL—Underground conduit, 60 to 80 amperes per space. Good street lighting and lighted recreational areas. Costs include telephone connection boxes at sites and cable TV systems 770

BUILDINGS—Office, recreation, laundry 1,035

MISCELLANEOUS—Above-average landscaping and sprinklers, signs, masonry ornamentation and walls. Outdoor recreational facilities are not included and should be added from Sections 66 and 67 520

GOOD PARK—Cost per space $5,635

MODIFIERS

NUMBER OF SPACES	50	75	100	125	150	175	200	250	300
MULTIPLIER	1.17	1.12	1.08	1.05	1.02	1.00	.98	.96	.95

GROSS AREA PER SPACE	2,800	3,200	3,600	4,000	4,400	4,800	5,200	5,600	6,000
MULTIPLIER	.91	.93	.96	.98	1.00	1.01	1.03	1.05	1.06

For example, a 175-site park with no amenities might cost a total of $4000 per site to develop. A park with many features could cost $7000 per site. This park would offer lighted tennis courts, an adjoining golf course, pool, sauna, spa, club room, etc. Parks with many features are rated higher, and this rating is reflected in the multiplier. The property manager would take the site cost, the ongoing maintenance expenses, future reserves, and management costs and total the park costs. This total would be divided by the 175 sites for the manager to determine the monthly park space rental.

Government Regulation

State Law. Since June 1976, mobile homes are more closely regulated during construction. They must be manufactured to comply with the National Manufactured Home Construction and Safety Standards. The unit must receive agency approval from the Veterans Administration and Housing and Urban Development (HUD) office before mobile homes with VA- or FHA-insured loans can be sited.

The property manager must be aware of the special definitions assigned to mobile homes, as set by California laws. (Figure 3) In California, each unit owner must receive a copy of the current code every year, which is usually disbursed by the park manager.

The property manager needs to thoroughly review the mobile home inspection process. DOH enforces these rules and responds to complaints. The board of health files are generally open to the public and reviewing these sources should be included in the property manager's evaluation of prospective clients.

Federal Law. Until the fall of 1988, mobile home parks were segregated into groupings or areas within the park, for instance, senior citizen groupings, adults-only areas, or family areas. Or a park might have catered to only one of these groups. The passage of an amendment to the Federal Fair Housing Act changed this.

Under the new rules, park managers may not discriminate against tenants based upon any age restriction, other than seniors. Two separate seniors categories are set forth in the law, and the property manager must follow the designations closely to maintain the status legally.

Figure 3

California Civil Code Provisions
Mobilehome Residency Law

(Effective January 1, 1985)
NOTE: Bold type denotes new sections

Article 1. General

798 This chapter shall be known and may be cited as the "Mobilehome Residency Law." It shall apply only to a mobilehome that requires a permit to be moved on a street or highway.

798.1 Unless the provisions or context otherwise requires, the following definitions shall govern the construction of this chapter.

798.2 "Management" means the owner of a mobilehome park or an agent or representative authorized to act on on his behalf in connection with matters relating to a tenancy in the park.

798.3 "Mobilehome" is a structure designed for human habitation and for being moved on a street or highway under permit pursuant to Section 35790 of the Vehicle Code. Mobilehome includes a manufactured home, as defined in Section 18008 of the Health and Safety Code, but does not include a recreational vehicle, as defined in Section 799.24 of this code and Section 18010 of the Health and Safety Code or a commercial coach as defined in Section 18001.8 of the Health and Safety Code.

798.4 "Mobilehome park" is an area of land where two or more mobilehome sites are rented, or held out for rent, to accommodate mobilehomes used for human habitation.

798.6 "Park" is a mobilehome park.

798.8 "Rental agreement" is an agreement between the management and the homeowner establishing the terms and conditions of a park tenancy. A lease is a rental agreement.

798.9 "Homeowner" is a person who has a tenancy in a mobilehome park under a rental agreement.

798.10 "Change of use" means a use of the park for a purpose other than the rental, or the holding out for rent, of two or more mobilehome sites to accommodate mobilehomes used for human habitation, and does not mean the adoption, amendment, or repeal of a park rule or regulation. A change of use may affect an entire park or any portion thereof. "Change of use" includes, but is not limited to, a change of the park or any portion thereof to a condominium, stock cooperative, planned unit development, or any form of ownership wherein spaces within the park are to be sold.

798.11 "Resident" is a homeowner or other person who lawfully occupies a mobilehome.

798.12 "Tenancy" is the right of a homeowner to the use of a site within a mobilehome park on which to locate, maintain, and occupy a mobilehome, site improvements, and accessory structures for human habitation, including the use of the services and facilities of the park.

Article 2. Rental Agreement

798.15 The rental agreement shall be in writing and shall contain, in addition to the provisions otherwise required by law to be included, all of the following:

(a) The term of the tenancy and the rent therefore.

(b) The rules and regulations of the park.

(c) The language of the provisions of this chapter. A copy of the text of this chapter attached as an exhibit shall be deemed to satisfy the requirements of this section.

(d) A provision specifying that it is the responsibility of the management to provide and maintain physical improvements in the common facilities in good working order and condition.

(e) A description of the physical improvements to be provided the homeowner during his or her tenancy.

(f) A provision listing those services which will be provided at the time the rental agreement is executed and will continue to be offered for the term of the tenancy and the fees, if any, to be charged for those services.

(g) A provision stating that management may charge a reasonable fee for services relating to the maintenance of the land and premises upon which a mobilehome is situated in the event the homeowner fails to maintain such land or premises in accordance with the rules and regulations of the park after written notification to the homeowner and the failure of the homeowner to comply within 14 days. The written notice shall state the specific condition to be corrected and an estimate of the charges to be imposed by management if the services are performed by management or its agent.

(h) All other provisions governing the tenancy.

798.16 The rental agreement may include such other provisions permitted by law, but need not include specific language contained in state or local laws not a part of this chapter.

798.18 (a) A homeowner shall be offered a rental agreement for (1) a term of 12 months, or (2) a lesser period as the homeowner may request, or (3) a longer period as mutually agreed upon by both the homeowner and management.

(b) No such agreement shall contain any terms or conditions with respect to charges for rent, utilities, or incidental reasonable service charges that would be different during the first 12 months of the agreement from the corresponding terms or conditions that would be offered to the homeowners on a month-to-month basis.

798.19 No rental agreement for a mobilehome shall contain a provision by which the homeowner waives his or her rights under the provisions of Articles 1 to 8, inclusive of this chapter. Any such waiver shall be deemed contrary to public policy and void.

798.20 Membership in any private club or organization which is a condition for tenancy in a park shall not be denied on the basis of race, color, religion, sex, national origin, ancestry, or marital status.

798.22 (a) In any new mobilehome park that is developed after January 1, 1982, mobilehome spaces shall not be rented for the accommodation of recreational vehicles as defined by Section 799.24 unless the mobilehome park has a specifically designated area within the park for recreational vehicles, which is separate and apart from the area designated for mobilehomes. Recreational vehicles may be located only in the specifically designated area.

(b) Any new mobilehome park that is developed after January 1, 1982, is not subject to the provisions of this section until 75 percent of the spaces have been rented for the first time.

Article 3. Rules and Regulations

798.24 Each common area facility shall be open or available to residents at all reasonable hours and the hours of the common area facility shall be posted at the facility.

798.25 A rule or regulation of the park may be amended at any time with the consent of a homeowner, or without his or her consent upon written notice to him or her of not less than six months, except for regulations applicable to recreational facilities which may be amended without his or her consent upon written notice to him or her of not less than 60 days. Written notice to a new homeowner, whose tenancy commences within the required period of notice, of a proposed amendment shall constitute compliance with this section where the written notice is given to him or her before the inception of his or her tenancy

798.26 (a) Except as provided in subdivision (b), and notwithstanding any other provision of law to the contrary, the ownership or management of a park, subdivision, cooperative, or condominium for mobilehomes shall have no right of entry to a mobilehome without the prior written consent of the resident. Such consent may be revoked in writing by the resident at any time. The ownership or management shall have a right of entry upon the land upon which a mobilehome is situated for maintenance of utilities, for maintenance of the premises in accordance with the rules and regulations of the park when the homeowner or resident fails to so maintain the premises, and protection of the mobilehome park, subdivision, cooperative, or condominium at any reasonable time, but not in a manner or at a time which would interfere with the resident's quiet enjoyment.

(b) The ownership or management of a park, subdivision, cooperative or condominium for mobilehomes may enter a mobilehome without the prior written consent of the resident in case of an emergency or when the resident has abandoned the mobilehome.

798.27 (a) The management shall give written notice to all homeowners and prospective homeowners concerning the following matters: (1) the nature of the zoning or use permit under which the mobilehome park operates. If the mobilehome park is operating pursuant to a permit subject to a renewal or expiration date, the relevant information and dates shall be included in the notice. (2) The duration of any lease of the mobilehome park, or any portion thereof, in which the management is a lessee.

(b) If a change occurs concerning the zoning or use permit under which the park operates or a lease in which the management is a lessee, all homeowners shall be given written notice within 30 days of such change. Notification regarding the change of use of the park, or any portion thereof, shall be governed by subdivision (f) of Section 798.56. A prospective homeowner shall be notified prior to the inception of the tenancy.

798.28 The management of a mobilehome park shall disclose, in writing, the name of the mobilehome park owner upon request of a homeowner.

Article 4. Fees and Charges

798.30 The management shall give a homeowner written notice of any increase in his or her rent at least 60 days before the date of the increase.

798.31 A homeowner shall not be charged a fee for other than rent, utilities, and incidental reasonable charges for services actually rendered.

A homeowner shall not be charged a fee for obtaining a lease on a mobilehome lot for (1) a term of 12 months, or (2) a lesser period as the homeowner may request. A fee may be charged for a lease of more than one year if the fee is mutually agreed upon by both the homeowner and management.

798.32 A homeowner shall not be charged a fee for services actually rendered which are not listed in the rental agreement unless he or she has been given written notice thereof by the management, at least 60 days before imposition of the charge.

798.33 A homeowner shall not be charged a fee for keeping a pet in the park unless the management actually provides special facilities or services for pets. If special pet facilities are maintained by the management, the fee charged shall reasonably relate to the cost of maintenance of the facilities or services and the number of pets kept in the park.

798.34 (a) A homeowner shall not be charged a fee for a guest who does not stay with him or her for more than a total of 20 consecutive days or a total of 30 days in a calendar year. Such a guest will not be required to register with the management.

(b) A homeowner who is living alone and who wishes to share his or her mobilehome with one person may do so, and a fee shall not be imposed by management for such person. Such person shall be considered a guest of the homeowner and any agreement between the homeowner and such person shall not change the terms and conditions of the rental agreement between management and the homeowner. Such guest shall comply with the provisions of the rules and regulations of the mobilehome park.

798.35 A homeowner shall not be charged a fee based on the number of members in his or her immediate family. As used in this section, the "immediate family" includes the homeowner, his or her spouse, their parents, and their children.

798.36 A homeowner shall not be charged a fee for the enforcement of any of the rules and regulations of the park, except a reasonable fee may be charged by management for the maintenance of the land and premises upon which the mobilehome is situated in the event the homeowner fails to do so in accordance with the rules and regulations of the park after written notification to the homeowner and the failure of the homeowner to comply within 14 days. The written notice shall state the specific condition to be corrected and an estimate of the charges to be imposed by management if the services are performed by management or its agent.

798.37 A homeowner shall not be charged a fee for the entry, installation, hookup, or landscaping as a condition of tenancy except for an actual fee or cost imposed by a local governmental ordinance or requirement directly related to the occupancy of the specific site upon which the mobilehome is located and not incurred as a portion of the development of the mobilehome park as a whole. However, reasonable landscaping and maintenance requirements may be included in the park rules and regulations. The management shall not require a homeowner or prospective homeowner to purchase, rent, or lease goods or services for landscaping from any person, company, or corporation.

798.38 Where the management provides both master meter and submeter service of utilities to a homeowner, for each billing period the cost of the charges for the period shall be separately stated along with the opening and closing readings for this meter. The management shall post in a conspicuous place, the prevailing residential utilities rate schedule as published by the serving utility.

Article 5. Homeowner Meetings

798.50 The management shall permit meetings by homeowners or residents of a mobilehome in the park, or any or all of them, relating to mobilehome living or social or educational purposes to be held in any of the park community or recreation halls if the meeting is held at a reasonable hour and when the facility is not otherwise in use.

798.51 The management shall meet and consult with the homeowners, upon written request, within 30 days of the request, either individually, collectively, or with representatives of a group of homeowners who have signed a request to be so represented on the following matters:

(a) Amendments to park rules and regulations.

(b) Standards for maintenance of physical improvements in the park.

(c) Addition, alteration, or deletion of service, equipment or physical improvements.

Any collective meeting shall be conducted only after notice thereof has been given to all the requesting homeowners 10 days or more before the meeting.

Article 6. Termination of Tenancy

798.55 (a) The Legislature finds and declares that, because of the high cost of moving mobilehomes, the potential for damage resulting therefrom, the requirements relating to the installation of mobilehomes, and the cost of landscaping or lot preparation, it is necessary that the owners of mobilehomes occupied within mobilehome parks be provided with the unique protection from actual or constructive eviction afforded by the provisions of this chapter.

(b) The management shall not terminate or refuse to renew a tenancy, except for a reason specified in this article and upon the giving of written notice to the homeowner in the manner prescribed by Section 1162 of the Code of Civil Procedure, to remove the mobilehome from the park within a period of not less than 60 days, which period shall be specified in the notice. A copy of this notice shall be sent to the legal owner, as defined in Section 18005.8 of the Health and Safety Code, each junior lienholder, as defined in Section 18005.8 of the Health and Safety Code, and the registered owner of the mobilehome, if other than the homeowner, by United States mail within 10 days after notice to the homeowner, addressed to the legal owner, each junior lienholder, and the registered owner at their addresses, as set forth in the registration card specified in Section 18091.5 of the Health and Safety Code.

798.56 A tenancy shall be terminated by the management only for one or more of the following reasons:

(a) Failure of the homeowner or resident to comply with a reasonable rule or regulation of the park as set forth in the rental agreement or any amendment thereto.

(b) Conduct by the homeowner or resident, upon the park premises, which constitutes a substantial annoyance to other homeowners or residents.

(c) Failure of the homeowner or resident to comply with a reasonable rule or regulation of the park as set forth in the rental agreement or any amendment thereto.

No act or omission of the homeowner or resident shall constitute such a failure to comply unless and until the management has given the homeowner written notice of the alleged rule or regulation violation and the homeowner or resident has failed to adhere to the rule or regulation within seven days. However, if a homeowner has been given a written notice of an alleged violation of the same rule or regulation on three or more occasions within a 12-month period after the homeowner or resident has violated that rule or regulation, no written notice shall be required for a subsequent violation of the same rule or regulation.

Nothing in this subdivision shall relieve the management from its obligation to demonstrate that a rule or regulation has in fact been violated.

(d) Nonpayment of rent, utility charges, or reasonable incidental service charges; provided, that the homeowner shall be given a three-day written notice to pay the amount due or to vacate the tenancy. The three-day written notice shall be given to the homeowner in the manner prescribed by Section 1162 of the Code of Civil Prodedure. Such notice may be given at the same time as the 60 days' notice required for termination of the tenancy. Payment by the homeowner prior to the expiration of the three-day notice period, or payment by the legal owner, as defined in Section 18005.8 of the Health and Safety Code, any junior lienholder, as defined in Section 18005.3 of the Health and Safety Code, or the registered owner, as defined in Section 18009.5 of the Health and Safety Code, if other than the homeowner, on behalf of the homeowner prior to the expiration of 30 calendar days following the mailing of the notice to the legal owner, each junior lienholder, and the registered owner provided in subdivision (b) of Section 798.55, shall cure a default under this subdivision with respect to such payment. The homeowner shall remain liable for all payments due up until the time the tenancy is vacated. Cure of a default of rent, utility charges, or reasonable incidental service charges by the legal owner, any junior lienholder, or the registered owner, if other than the homeowner, as provided by this subdivision, may not be exercised more than twice during the term of the tenancy.

(e) Condemnation of the park.

(f) Change of the use of the park or any portion thereof, provided:

(1) The management gives the homeowners at least 15 days' written notice that the management will be appearing before a local governmental board, commission, or body to request permits for a change of use of the mobilehome park.

(2) After all required permits requesting a change of use have been approved by the local governmental board, commission, or body, the management shall give the homeowners six months' or more written notice of termination of tenancy.

If the change of use requires no local governmental permits, then notice shall be given 12 months or more prior to the management's determination that a change of use will occur. The management in the notice shall disclose and describe in detail the nature of the change of use.

(3) The management gives each proposed homeowner written notice thereof prior to the inception of his or her tenancy that the management is requesting a change of use before local governmental bodies or that a change of use request has been granted.

(4) The notice requirements for termination of tenancy set forth in Section 798.56 and 798.57 shall be followed if the proposed change actually occurs.

(5) A notice of a proposed change of use given prior to January 1, 1980, which conforms to the requirements in effect at that time shall be valid. The requirements for a notice of a proposed change of use imposed by this subdivision shall be governed by the law in effect at the time the notice was given.

798.57 The management shall set forth in a notice of termination, the reason relied upon for the termination with specific facts to permit determination of the date, place, witnesses, and circumstances concerning that reason. Neither reference to the section number of a subdivision thereof, nor a recital of the language of this article will constitute compliance with this section.

798.58. No tenancy shall be terminated for the purpose of making a homeowner's site available for a person who purchased a mobilehome from the owner of the park or his agent.

798.59. A homeowner shall give written notice to the management of not less than 60 days before vacating his or her tenancy.

798.60. The provisions of this article shall not affect any rights or proceedings set forth in Chapter 4 (commencing with Section 1159) of Title 3 of Part 3 of the Code of Civil Procedure except as otherwise provided herein.

Article 7. Transfer of Mobilehome

798.70. A homeowner may advertise the sale or exchange of his or her mobilehome or, if not prohibited by the terms of an agreement with the management, may advertise the rental of his or her mobilehome by displaying a sign in the window of the mobilehome stating that the mobilehome is for sale or exchange or, if not prohibited, for rent by the owner of the mobilehome or his or her agent. The sign shall state the name, address, and telephone number of the owner of the mobilehome or his or her agent and may be at least 12 inches in width and 12 inches in length.

798.71. The management shall not show or list for sale a manufactured home or mobilehome without first obtaining the owner's written authorization. The authorization shall specify the terms and conditions regarding the showing or listing.

Nothing in this section shall be construed as affecting the provisions of the Health and Safety Code governing the licensing of manufactured home or mobilehome salespersons or dealers.

798.72. The management shall not charge a homeowner or his or her agent a transfer or selling fee as a condition of a sale of his mobilehome within a park unless management performs a service in the sale. The management shall not perform any such service in connection with the sale unless so requested, in writing, by the homeowner or his or her agent.

798.73. The management shall not require the removal of a mobilehome from the park in the event of its sale to a third party during the term of the homeowners' agreement. However, in the event of a sale to a third party, in order to upgrade the quality of the park, the management may require that a mobilehome be removed from park where:

(a) It is less than 10 feet wide.

(b) It is more than 20 years old, or more than 25 years old if manufactured after September 15, 1971, and is 20 feet wide or more and the mobilehome does not comply with the health and safety standards provided in Sections 18550, 18552, and 18605 of the Health and Safety Code, and the regulations established thereunder.

(c) The mobilehome is more than 17 years old, or more than 25 years old if manufactured after September 15, 1971, and is less than 20 feet wide and the mobilehome does not comply with the construction and safety standards under Sections 18550, 18552, and 18605 of the Health and Safety Code, and the regulations established thereunder.

(d) It is in a significantly rundown condition or in disrepair, as determined by the general condition of the mobilehome and its acceptability to the health and safety of the occupants and to the public, exclusive of its age. The management shall use reasonable discretion in determing the general condition of the mobilehome and its accessory structures. The management shall bear the burden of demonstating that the mobilehome is in a significantly rundown condition or in disrepair.

798.74. The management may require the right of prior approval of a purchaser of a mobilehome that will remain in the park and that the selling homeowner or his or her agent give notice of the sale to the management before the close of sale. Approval cannot be withheld if the purchaser has the financial ability to pay the rent and charges of the park unless the management reasonably determines that, based on the purchaser's prior tenancies, he or she will not comply with the rules and regulations of the park. If the ownership or management rejects a purchaser as a prospective homeowner, the ownership or management shall inform the selling homeowner in writing of its reasons for the rejection.

798.75. An escrow, sale, or transfer agreement involving a mobilehome located in a park at the time of the sale, where the mobilehome is to remain in the park, shall contain a provision signed by the purchaser stating that, by such signature he or she has agreed to the terms of a rental agreement. A copy of a fully executed rental agreement signed by both the purchaser and park management will satisfy the requirements of this section. In the event the purchaser fails to execute the rental agreement, the purchaser shall not have any rights of tenancy.

798.76. The management may require that a purchaser of a mobilehome which will remain in the park, comply with any rule or regulation limiting residence to adults only.

798.77. No rental or sale agreement shall contain a provision by which the purchaser or homeowner waives his or her rights under this chapter. Any such waiver shall be deemed contrary to public policy and shall be void and unenforceable.

798.78. An heir or joint tenant who gains ownership of a mobilehome in the mobilehome park through the death of the owner of the mobilehome who is a homeowner shall have the right to sell the mobilehome to a third party in accordance with the provisions of this article, but only if all the homeowner's responsiblities and liabilities to the management regarding rent, utilities, and reasonable maintenance of the mobilehome and its premises which have arisen after the transfer of ownership to the heir or joint tenant have been satisfied up until the date the mobilehome is resold.

798.79. Any legal owner or junior lienholder who forecloses on his or her security interest in a mobilehome located in a mobilehome park shall have the right to sell the mobilehome within the park to a third party in accordance with the provisions of this article, but only if all the homeowner's responsibilities and liabilities to the management regarding rent, utilities, and reasonable maintenance of a mobilehome and its premises are satisfied by the foreclosing creditor through the date the mobilehome is resold.

Article 8. Actions, Proceedings, and Penalties

798.85 In any action arising out of the provisions of this chapter the prevailing party shall be entitled to reasonable attorney's fees and costs. A party shall be deemed the prevailing party for the purposes of this section if the judgment is rendered in his or her favor or where the litigation is dismissed in his or her favor prior to or during the trial, unless the parties otherwise agree in the settlement or compromise.

798.86. In the event a homeowner or former homeowner of a park is the prevailing party in a civil action against the management to enforce his or her rights under the provisions of this chapter, the homeowner, in addition to damages afforded by law, may, in the discretion of the court, be awarded an amount not to exceed five hundred dollars ($500) for each willful violation of those provisions by the management.

798.87. (a) The substantial failure of the management to provide and maintain physical improvements in the common facilities in good working order and condition shall be deemed a public nuisance. Notwithstanding the provisions of Section 3491, such a nuisance only may be remedied by a civil action or abatement.

(b) The substantial violation of a mobilehome park rule shall be deemed a public nuisance. Notwithstanding the provisions of Section 3491, such a nuisance only may be remedied by a civil action or abatement.

Article 9. Subdivisions, Cooperatives and Condominiums

799. As used in this article:

(a) "Ownership or management" means the ownership or management of a subdivision, cooperative, or condominium for mobilehomes.

(b) "Resident" means a person who maintains a residence in a subdivision, cooperative, or condominium for mobilehomes.

799.1 A resident may advertise the sale or exchange of his or her mobilehome or, if not prohibited by the terms of an agreement with the management or ownership, may advertise the rental of his or her mobilehome by displaying a sign in the window of his or her mobilehome stating that the mobilehome is for sale or exchange or, if not prohibited, for rent by the owner of the mobilehome or his or her agent. The sign shall state the name, address, and telephone number of the owner of the mobilehome or his or her agent, and may be at least 12 inches in width and 12 inches in length.

799.2. The ownership or management shall not show or list for sale a mobilehome owned by a resident without first obtaining the resident's written authorization. Authorization shall specify the terms and conditions regarding the showing or listing. Nothing contained in this section shall be construed to affect the provisions of the Health and Safety Code governing the licensing of mobilehome salesmen.

799.3 The ownership or management shall not require the removal of a mobilehome from a subdivision, cooperative, or condominium in the event of its sale to a party.

799.4. The ownership or management may require the right to prior approval of the purchaser of a mobilehome that will remain in the subdivision, cooperative condominium for mobilehomes and that the selling resident or his or her agent give notice of the sale to the ownership or management before the close of the sale. Approval cannot be withheld if the purchaser has the financial ability to pay the fees and charges of the subdivision, cooperative, or condominium unless the ownership or manager reasonably determines that, based on the purchaser's prior residences, he or she will not comply with the rules and regulations of the subdivision, cooperative, or condominium.

799.5. The ownership or management may require that a purchaser of a mobilehome which will remain in the subdivision, cooperative, or condominium for mobilehomes comply with any rule or regulation limiting residence therein to adults only.

799.6. No agreement shall contain any provision by which the purchaser waives his or her rights under the provisions of this article. Any such waiver shall be deemed contrary to public policy and void and unenforceable.

One senior group includes those age 55 or older (one resident in each unit must be at least 55). The property manager must maintain facilities and services geared for the needs of older persons, like ramps, card rooms, etc. The park must work towards and show intent to maintain at least 80% of the spaces for the senior citizen group, now or in the future, even if present occupancy is less than the necessary quota.

The second group includes those 62 or older, but everyone in the park must be over 62, not just one resident per unit. These types of mobile homes will become less common, because compliance will be more difficult.

Under the new rule, those with children cannot be discriminated against (except when the park is legally "senior" only). There are penalties for failing to adequately accommodate children. California state law, including the California Unruh Civil Rights Act, imposes penalties for failing to properly revise age restrictions, and for having outdated, unenforceable "Park Rules", even if no one tries to enforce them.

Management

The duties of the on-site manager include collecting rents, giving notices, enforcing the park rules, making bank deposits, and reading the utility meters, as shown in Figure 4.

The on-site park manager reports either to the off-site property manager or park owner. The on-site manager usually lives on the premises. Unlike apartment regulations, the law requires an on-site manager only if the park has 50 units or more. With larger parks, the office and living complex are often contained within the same unit, and the housing is included in the compensation package. The on-site manager may also receive free utilities as well as cash remuneration. It is important to comply with California minimum wage guidelines. Insurance and other benefits may also be included.

Lease Application. The mobile home application process differs greatly from that of an application for an apartment. A visual inspection of the prospect's mobile home is required before the tenant is permitted to move into the community. (Figure 5) An application usually includes at least two recent photographs of the unit taken from two different angles. The home must meet the age, size, and condition standards of the

Figure 4

Manager's Duties

- Read electric and gas meters (and water meters when installed) on or about the 22nd day of each month.
- Distribute rent statements and other papers to residents as needed.
- Receive and record rents. Managers agree not to accept cash. Only checks, cashier's checks, or money orders are accepted.
- Collect late and bad check fees as necessary.
- Deposit rents as received daily or within two days.
- Show and rent vacant spaces and houses.
- Have each new resident sign rental agreement, rules and regulations, emergency card, pet agreement, change of land use form, and other forms.
- Enforce park's rules and regulations and handle complaints as necessary.
- Clean laundry room, bathrooms, and area surrounding trash bins.
- Maintain regular office hours to be available for residents, prospective residents, service people, subcontractors, etc.
- Pick up paper and other trash on street and yards, regularly.
- Oversee details of move-ins and move-outs, with special attention to the placement and hook-up of the trailers.
- When a space becomes vacant, cap sewer and gas lines, clean and cut space to prepare for showing to prospective residents.
- Complete repairs to keep park in good maintenance and repair, including electrical and plumbing.
- Water and clean designated lawns and flower beds as needed.
- Supervise outside contractors who work on the property.
- Keep manager's office, trailer, and yard neat and clean as a model to the residents and others.
- Handle all phone and in-person inquiries.
- Any other duties as necessary to provide good management.
- Trim manager's trees, bushes, hedges by park sign, etc.

Figure 5

WMA

APPLICATION FOR RESIDENCY

IN Senator Mobilehome Park (COMMUNITY NAME)

Personal:

Name of Person Making Application: John Q. Resident

Phone Number: (916) 444-8847

Date: (of application)

Present Address: 1111 ANY STREET, ANYTOWN CA 95000 (City, State, Zip)

Social Security Number: 555-55-5555 Driver's License Number: N00000

Name(s) of Other Person(s) Who Will Be Occupying Space: Geraldine Q Resident

Relationship(s): SPOUSE

Social Security Number(s): 000-00-0000

Driver's License Number(s): N10000

Previous Residency:

Present Landlord or Mortgage Co.: XYZ Apartments Yrs.:

Address: 111 MAPLE ALLTOWN, CA 95810 (City, State, Zip) Phone

Monthly Rent or Mortgage Payment: $250.00

Prior Landlord or Mortgage Co.: ABC Apartments Yrs.:

Address: 200 GLEN, LAKEVIEW CA 92000 (City, State, Zip) Phone: 916-441-0000

Monthly Rent or Mortgage Payment: $150.00

Have you ever been asked to terminate your residency elsewhere, or have you ever been evicted?
☐ Yes ☒ No

If yes, please explain:

Have you ever lived in a mobilehome park before? ☐ Yes ☒ No

If yes, please explain: LIST INFORMATION IF APPLICABLE

Address:

Dates of Residency:

Latest Rent:

APPLICATION FOR RESIDENCY
Second Page

Vehicles:

Number of Automobile(s): 2 Boat(s): 1 Other: N/A

For your protection, we must have complete descriptions of all vehicles

Make: OLDS Model: Cutlass Year: 1984 License No: X00000 State: CA

Financed By: N/A Address: Phone:

Make: HONDA Model: Civic Year: 1987 License No: X00000 State: CA

Financed By: Bank of Trust Address: 12th & V streets Phone: 444-0000

Make: Bayliner Model: Sea Scout Year: 1979 License No: CF0000 State: CA

Financed By: Bank of Trust Address: 12th & V streets Phone: 444-0000

Employment:

Employer: MNO WIDGET Company Phone: 916-000-0000

Address: 000 MNO City: Sacramento State Zip: CA 95000

Position: SALESMAN Gross Monthly Salary $: 1800.00

Immediate Supervisor: Bob Buck Length of Employment: Yrs 8 Mos 2

Co-Resident's Employer: ENAMEL CITY Phone: 916-000-0000

Address: 2 BEAUTY LANE City: Sacramento State Zip: CA 95000

Position: MANICURIST Gross Monthly Salary $: 850.00

Immediate Supervisor: CANDY FILER Length of Employment: Yrs 6 Mos 4

Co-Resident's Employer: N/A Phone: —

Address: N/A City: — State Zip: —

Position: N/A Gross Monthly Salary $: —

Immediate Supervisor: N/A Length of Employment: Yrs — Mos —

Financial:

Name of Bank: BANK OF TRUST City: Sacramento Acct No: 0000-0000

☐ Checking ☐ Savings ☐ Loan

Name of Bank: BANK OF TRUST City: Sacramento Acct No: 0100-0000

☐ Checking ☐ Savings ☐ Loan

Credit Card: MASTER CHARGE Acct No: 000-00-0000 How Long: 10 yrs.

Credit Card: BARTONS Acct No: 0001.00-100 How Long: 2 yrs.

Credit Card: SANICS Acct No: 001-00-200 How Long: 5 years.

Net Worth (from back page): $29,000

APPLICATION FOR RESIDENCY
Third Page

References:

Business: Name: Mr Bob Buck City: Sacramento Phone: 916·000·0000

Name: Bille Todd City: San Francisco Phone: 415·000·0000

Personal: Name: GINNY JONES City: Sacramento Phone: 916·444·0000

Name: John Smith City: San Francisco Phone: 415·400·0000

Emergency:

Person(s) to notify in case of an emergency (other than co-resident):

Name: Josaphine Resident Relationship: ______

Address: 100 CANDY lane City: Sacramento State/Zip: CA 95000

Phone Number: 916 000-0000

Pets:

If you have dogs and/or cats, please provide following information

Name	Age	Type	Color/Description	Height	Weight
FIFI	7	Poodle	White/MINIATURE	18"	4 lbs.

Home or Recreational Vehicle to Occupy Space:

Mobilehome Make: Bayshore Net Size. Length: 60 Width: 14 Height: 11 feet

Year: 1979 Breaker Size: 40 amps License No.: N/A

Financed By: BANK OF TRUST HCD No.: ABC 1234

Serial No.: 10987654321

Current Location: 1121 L Street #400

Legal Owner Name/Address: Bank of Trust 100 Main Anytown

Registered Owner Name/Address: James Doe 400 Center St Sacramento

Junior Lienholder Name/Address (if any): (IF Applicable)

The undersigned understands and acknowledges that this Park is an "adult only"/"senior only" park with a minimum age requirement of ______ years of age or older. The undersigned hereby represents that the person(s) making application to reside in the Park are above the age requirement.

The undersigned requests the management to check the above credit references and representations. The undersigned acknowledges that in the event a rental agreement is executed by both the management and the undersigned, it is subject to approval by the management of the undersigned's mobilehome or recreational vehicle as provided in the Rental Agreement.

The undersigned represents and warrants that the above information is true and correct and has been made for the purpose of informing the management of the park. The management has permission to verify any and all information offered on this application.

APPLICATION FOR RESIDENCY
Fourth Page

The undersigned understands that in the event that any of the above information cannot be verified by the management of the Park, that the management of the Park has the right to deny the application. The undersigned further understands that Prospective Residents shall have no rights of tenancy until a Rental Agreement has been signed by the Park management and the prospective resident.

APPLICANT John Q Resident

APPLICANT Geraldine Q Resident

APPLICANT ______

NET WORTH STATEMENT

ASSETS		IN DOLLARS (OMIT CENTS)	LIABILITIES		AMOUNT (OMIT CENTS)
CASH	BANK/OFFICE NAME & NO: Bank of TRUST Branch 280	3,000	NOTES PAYABLE TO BANKS	BANK OFFICE NAME & NO: Bank of TRUST Branch 280	3,000
				Bank of Cityside	8,000
STOCKS AND BONDS	NONE		OTHER NOTES & ACCOUNTS PAYABLE	Real Estate Loans	N/A
				Sales Contracts & Chattel Mtgs	N/A
				Loans on Life Ins. Policies	N/A
NOTES RECEIVABLE (COLLECTIBLE)	Relatives & Friends	N/A	TAXES PAYABLE	Current Year's Income Taxes Unpaid	N/A
				Prior Year's Income Taxes Unpaid	N/A
	Trust Deeds & Mortgages	N/A		Real Estate Taxes Unpaid	N/A
REAL ESTATE	Improved	N/A	OTHER LIABILITIES	Unpaid Interest	
	Unimproved	N/A		Credit Cards	$1,000
	Leasehold Interest Owned	N/A			
LIFE INSURANCE	Cash Surrender Value	$15,000		TOTAL LIABILITIES	$12,000
OTHER PERSONAL PROPERTY	BOAT	$3,000	NET WORTH CALCULATION	TOTAL ASSETS	$41,000
	CAR	5,000			
	CAR	10,000		TOTAL LIABILITIES	$12,000
	TOTAL ASSETS	41,000		NET WORTH	$29,000

park. A copy of the Certificate of Title, along with the purchase contract, should also be attached to the application, in case of tenant abandonment or nonpayment of rent.

For new move-ins, park rules typically include the requirement that the skirting (siding installed around the foundation) be in place within 30 days. Earth anchors and steel straps holding the unit in place are also common requirements. The property manager provides new resident packets for new move-ins showing park activities, organization, and social events, and furnishes them with any newsletter or calendar available.

A new resident receives a copy of the Park Rules and agrees to follow them. If a tenant is selling the unit, he or she must have prospective buyers approved by the park management before the transfer is consummated. Failure to comply risks eviction of the home and the new owner.

Utilities. The park often sells utilities in conjunction with the park rental space. The park may have one or two central meters, and the park manager reads the tenant usage. Usage is billed to each unit owner, and collected with the rent payment. The property manager keeps an ongoing administrative record of these charges and payments (Figure 6). The property manager cannot charge for utilities unless they are separately metered. If there are separate meters for gas, electricity, water, and sewer, these costs can be passed through to the tenant. The property manager needs to schedule meter checks; the law requires that the meters be calibrated every ten years.

Why bother with utilities? Because the park buys at the wholesale rate and sells it to tenants at the retail rate. Thus the park owner can realize a profit, after deducting the administration, maintenance, and servicing costs, plus meter purchase price.

Some parks are changing from master meter to individual meters, others are doing the reverse. These decisions are determined by business objectives, area utility costs, projected profits, and management style. However, the property manager must give six months prior written notice to all residents for any proposed change in any services. So, the lead time for the desired results is a major consideration when taking action.

Leases. In California, the property manager must offer a one-year lease to all mobile home tenants. The standard rental agreement would cover the due date, intended use, attorney's fees, and include a clause stating "time is of the essence", in addition to the rent amount. Most California communities have mobile home rent control. (Figure 7).

Figure 6

STATEMENT

Bellflower Trailer Haven
9847 Flora Vista St.; 16234 Bellflower Blvd.
Bellflower, CA 90706 • (213)866-3683

Resident ______________________________ Space #__________

Rent: From ____________________ To ____________________

Utility Charges (billing is for previous month)

Meter Readings

	Present	Previous	Difference	Billing Factor	Usage		
Date							
Gas							
Edison							
Water							
					Total Due		

Rent is Payable in Advance
Check, Money Order or Cashier's Check

Dates Present __________ Previous __________ #Of Days __________
Meter Reads Present __________ Previous __________
Difference (CCF) x__________ = __________
Billing Factor Therms

Customer Charge	________	Days	@	$ .10192	= . . .$	
Lifeline	________	Therms	@	.46484	= . . .	
Tier II	________	Therms	@	.71810	= . . .	
Tier III	________	Therms	@	.81810	= . . .	
State Regulatory Fee	________	Therms	@	.00034	= . . .$	________
					City Tax	________
					Total Billing (Gas)	________

(See other side for total billing)

Figure 7 **California Communities with Rent Control**

Jurisdiction	Affected Mobilehome Parks	Affected Mobilehome Spaces	Coverage	Allowable CPI and Percent of Increase	How Adopted	Vacancy Decontrol	Date Passed
Alameda County	22	712	†	Automatic 5%	Ordinance	No	12/85
Arroyo Grande	5	498	†	Lesser of 8% or 75% of CPI	Ordinance	No	5/86
Beaumont	8	459	†	75% of CPI	Ordinance	Yes	10/84
Benicia	4	317	†	Rent Review Commission	Ordinance	Yes	9/78
Berkeley	0	0	‡	Set by Board	Initiative	No	11/78
Beverly Hills	0	0	‡	Variable formula related to CPI	Ordinance	Yes/to market	3/79
Calistoga	5	569	†	Rent Review Commission	Ordinance	No	8/84
Camarillo	4	747	†	Mediation—arbitration	Ordinance	Yes	12/81
Capitola	8	623	†	50% of CPI+limited pass-throughs	Ordinance	No	11/79
Carson	28	2,565	†	Set by Board	Ordinance	No	8/79
Carpinteria	7	866	†	75% of CPI	Ordinance	No	3/82
Cathedral City	10	2,064	†	Rent Review Commission	Initiative	Yes to avg. rent	3/83
Chino	5	554	†	66% of CPI	Initiative	No	8/83
Cloverdale	4	165	†	Rent Review Commission	Ordinance	No	6/86
Clovis	6	582	†	Rent Review Commission	Ordinance	Yes	9/78
Cotati	3	106	‡	Set by Board	Initiative	No	11/79
Daly City	1	501	†	Rent Review Commission	Ordinance	No	6/80
Delano	4	310	†	50% of CPI	Initiative	No	11/84
East Palo Alto	4	274	‡	Set by Board	Initiative	No	11/83
Fairfield	9	883	†	Rent Review Commission	Ordinance	No	11/84
Fontana	13	684	†	60% of CPI	Ordinance	No	5/85
Fremont	3	726	†	Greater of $10 or 3% to 6% of CPI, or 60% of CPI	Ordinance	No	1/87
Gardena	28	1,388	†	Binding arbitration	Ordinance	Yes	3/87
Gilroy	4	336	†	Lesser of 5% or 80% of CPI	Ordinance	Yes	5/87
Hayward	16	2,160	‡	Lesser of 3% to 6% or 60% of CPI	Ordinance	No	2/80
Hemet	20	2,805	†	Rent Review Commission	Initiative	Yes	5/79
Indio	6	528	†	75% of CPI	Initiative	Yes to avg. rent	3/84
La Verne	8	1,762	†	Lesser of 7% or 100% of CPI	Ordinance	$25	10/84
Lancaster	27	2,584	†	Binding arbitration	Ordinance	Yes	3/85
Lompoc	7	654	†	Lesser of 5% or 75% of CPI to 10%	Ordinance	No	12/83
Los Angeles	78	7,716	‡	Automatic 4%	Ordinance	10%	8/78
L.A. County	(Phased by	Out) Supv.)	‡		Ordinance		7/79

†—Mobile Home Only *‡—All Units*

California Communities with Rent Control

Jurisdiction	Affected Mobilehome Parks	Affected Mobilehome Spaces	Coverage	Allowable CPI and Percent of Increase	How Adopted	Vacancy Decontrol	Date Passed
Los Gotos	2	137	‡	70% of CPI	Ordinance	Lesser of 10% or $25	10/80
Merced	3	574	†	8% or 100% of CPI (lesser amount)	Ordinance	Yes	5/82
Mono County	Sunseted		†		Ordinance		5/83
Montclair	8	620	†	6% or 80% of CPI (lesser amount)	Ordinance	No	11/85
Moorpark	4	270	†	75% of CPI	Ordinance	No	9/83
Moreno Valley	7	809	†	65% of CPI—5-8% range	Ordinance	Equal to previous CPI	12/84
Morgan Hill	9	875	†	75% of CPI	Ordinance	No	3/83
Morro Bay	15	641	†	75% of CPI	Ordinance	$10.00	8/86
Napa Repealed	by Voter	Initiative	†		Ordinance		12/82
Oakland	3	49	‡	6%	Ordinance	Yes	9/80
Oceanside	20	2,401	†	CPI up to 8% or NOI (net operating income)	Ordinance	No	5/82
Oxnard	25	2,780	†	Lesser of 3% to 8% or 75% of CPI	Ordinance	Yes $15	3/83
Palm Desert	4	676	†	75% of CPI	Ordinance	No	4/80
Palm Springs	14	2,242	‡	75% of CPI	Ordinance	No	4/80
Palmdale	15	1,455	†	Set by Board	Ordinance	No	10/85
Paramount	19	1,442	†	100% of CPI	Ordinance	Yes	7/87
Pismo Beach	2	412	†	Lesser of 8% or 75% of CPI	Ordinance	No	4/81
Rancho Mirage	6	882	†	75% of CPI	Ordinance	No	7/82
Redlands	8	684	†	Lesser of 6% to 9% or 75% of CPI	Ordinance	Yes 10%	12/82
Rialto	18	1,963	†	Rent Review Commission	Ordinance	No	7/78
Riverside County	124	12,376	†	Rent Review Commission	Ordinance	Yes/to highest park rent	8/83
Rocklin	3	384	†	Graduated CPI	Ordinance	Yes/10% or $20	5/82
San Francisco	1	56	‡	Automatic 7%	Ordinance	Yes	6/79
San Jose	70	11,435	‡	Automatic 5%	Ordinance	No	7/79
San Juan Capistrano	7	1,209	†	110% of CPI x expenses or modified CPI	Ordinance	No	3/79
San Lius Obispo City	15	1,551	†	75% of CPI	Ordinance	No	4/82
San Luis Obispo Cty.	40	2,408	†	60% of CPI	Initiative	Issue being litigated	6/84
San Marcos	17	3,216	†	CPI or NOI	Ordinance	Yes	11/80
Santa Barbara City	16	1,487	†	75% of CPI	Ordinance	Yes 10%	9/84
Santa Barbara Cty.	15	960	†	75% of CPI	Ordinance	No	10/79
Santa Cruz Cty.	36	2,212	†	50% of CPI+ limited pass-throughs	Ordinance	No	1/79
Santa Monica	3	286	‡	Set by Board	Initiative	Set by Board	4/79

†—Mobile Home Only *‡—All Units* *Apartment Journal, June, 1988*

Security deposits for mobile home parks are governed by the same rules as deposits for apartments. The security deposits may not exceed an amount equal to two months' rent, in addition to any first month's rent collected. Tenant deposits are not required to be kept in an interest-bearing account. Effective January 1, 1989, security deposits on space rentals may only be demanded before occupancy, and no additional security deposits may be demanded after initial occupancy. If a park changes ownership, the new owner may not then require deposits from those tenants who made no original deposit. Also, if rents have increased over time, the property manager may not ask for the deposit to be increased to match the new, higher rents.

A tenant may give a written request to the property manager demanding a refund of any security deposit paid. If the tenant meets the specified criteria, the deposit must be refunded. To meet the criteria, the tenant must have made payment within five days of the due date for the previous twelve months, including rent, utility and service charges.

The lease provision prohibiting subletting or assignment is very important. If the park tenant could assign the lease, the property manager would have to sue the unit owner to enforce park rules. The agreement should also specify that the property manager must give the resident a minimum of 60 days' notice for rent increases.

The mobile home rental agreement has clauses not found in many other leases. For example, the park is responsible for maintaining services to residents. The tenants are responsible for site maintenance. The property manager gives a seven-day notice to the tenant for Notice for Repairs. The park must approve subsequent purchasers of units prior to transfer.

If the property manager or unit owner wishes to remove a mobile home and terminate the tenancy, he or she must comply with the Mobile Home Park Residency Law. Because the cost to move a unit is so prohibitive, the law places certain restrictions on the process. The property manager must give the tenant 60 days prior written notice of an intent to terminate. The tenant need only give the property manager 30 days' notice of the intent to vacate. (Figure 8).

Enforcement. To enforce the park rules and rental agreement, the property manager must be familiar with the use of several forms. One problem common to mobile home parks is animals; they should be registered with the park office for identification purposes (Figure 9).

Figure 8

THREE (3) DAY NOTICE TO PAY RENT OR QUIT AND SIXTY (60) DAY NOTICE TO TERMINATE POSSESSION

TO: John Q. & Geraldine Q Resident
(Resident's Name)

and to all Residents or occupants in possession of 1979 Bayshore, Decal #ABC 123

(description of mobilehome)

located at the premises herein referred to and commonly known as Senator Mobilehome Park, 1121 L Street, #400, Sacramento, CA 95814
(Park Name/Address/Space No.)

THIS IS TO NOTIFY YOU that there is now due and unpaid rent in the total sum of $200 at the rental rate of $200 per month, being the rent from Feb. 1, 1988, to Feb. 29, 1988

WITHIN THREE DAYS after the service on you of this Notice, you are hereby required to pay the said rent for the premises to the park owner or manager, or the owner of said premises will institute legal proceedings against you to declare the forfeiture of the rental agreement under which you occupy the said premises and to recover possession of said premises, together with court costs and attorneys fees. You are further notified that the undersigned elects to and does declare the forfeiture of your rental agreement under which you hold possession of the above-described premises if the rent is not paid within three (3) days after service on you of this Notice.

THIS NOTICE IS INTENDED AS A THREE DAY NOTICE TO PAY OR QUIT AS PROVIDED BY CALIFORNIA LAW.

THIS IS TO FURTHER NOTIFY YOU that pursuant to the rental agreement and parks rules and regulations under which you now hold possession of the above-described premises, you agreed to abide and conform with the rental agreement and the park rules and regulations.

Pursuant to California Civil Code 798.56d you are hereby notified that the above acts or omissions constitute a failure on your part to comply with the park's rental agreement and rules and regulations

THEREFORE, THIS IS TO NOTIFY YOU THAT if you do not pay the rent specified above within three days, you are required to quit said premises within sixty (60) days after service of this Notice upon you and deliver up possession of same to the park owner or manager or legal proceedings for unlawful detainer will be instituted against you by the owners of the premises to declare said rental agreement forfeitured, as of this date, and recover possession of said premises, together with court costs and attorneys fees.

THIS NOTICE IS INTENDED AS A SIXTY DAY NOTICE TO TERMINATE POSSESSION AS PROVIDED BY CALIFORNIA LAW.

YOU ARE FURTHER NOTIFIED THAT by this Notice the undersigned elects to and does hereby declare the forfeiture of said rental agreement for your failure to abide by and conform with said rental agreement or rules and regulations as hereinbefore specifically enumerated.

Dated: 2/6/88 — J. M. Manager
Park Management

cc: Legal Owner Bank of Trust

(Other) James Doe (registered owner)

Figure 9

PET AGREEMENT AND RULES

Senator Mobilehome Park
(Park Name)

Resident(s) must obtain written permission from Management to keep a house pet in this Park and must execute this Pet Agreement and Rules. Resident(s) understands and agrees that the following is the only pet allowed in the above-named Park pursuant to the Park's Rules and Regulations and that no pet of any guest of a Resident is allowed in the Park.

- ☑ One small dog, defined as "small" when fully mature.
- ☐ One cat.
- ☐ One small house pet, defined as "small" when fully mature.
- ☐ Other ______

Resident(s) agrees to comply with any state or local governmental law, regulation or ordinance governing the proper inoculation and licensing of any pet allowed to remain in the Park.

Resident(s) also agrees to the following:

1. If a dog is allowed in the Park:
   a. Disturbances such as barking, snarling, growling, etc. which will annoy your neighbors is cause for revoking permission to keep your pet.
   b. Any dog, when not inside your mobilehome or contained within a fenced yard (if permitted by the Park's Rules) must be on a short leash.
2. Regardless of the type of pet:
   a. No pet is to invade the privacy of anyone's homesite, flowerbeds, shrubs, yard, etc.
   b. No pets are permitted in the clubhouse, recreation area, common areas, laundry room, etc.
   c. Droppings must be picked up and disposed of daily.
   d. If a resident loses a pet, written permission must be acquired from Management before replacing the pet.
   e. ______

The Park encourages pets to be spayed or neutered. However, in the event of offspring, the Management must be notified and written permission must be obtained for the offspring to stay in the Park for an interim period.

Further, Resident(s) understands that he and/or she is responsible for any damage to Park property or the property of other residents caused by the pet, including waste and any disturbances or annoyances caused within the Park.

I HAVE READ THE ABOVE PET AGREEMENT AND RULES AND AGREE TO ABIDE BY ITS TERMS AND PROVISIONS. I UNDERSTAND THAT VIOLATION OF ANY OF THESE RULES IS CAUSE FOR REVOKING PERMISSION TO KEEP A PET.

Dated: 12/31/87   John Q Resident (Resident)

Dated: 12/31/87   Geraldine Q Resident (Resident)

Permission is given to the above Resident(s) to keep the following described pet at

1121 L street # 400
(Address/Space No.)

TYPE Poodle WEIGHT 4 lbs. AGE 7 COLOR white

NAME Fifi DISTINGUISHING MARKS Brown SPOT ON EAR

RABIES VACCINATION # 4064 LICENSE # NZ1601

Dated: 12/31/87   J M. Manager (Park Management)

Failure to properly maintain the rental space requires a 14-day notice to allow the tenant to cure the problem before the park gets the work done and bills the resident. The property manager regularly handles complaints, and the disposition of these complaints should be put in writing. (Figure 10).

The most serious problem with tenants is the non-payment of rent or other fees. The property manager must serve a three-day notice for lack of rent or utility payment. If the resident does not pay, an unlawful detainer action must be filed before the tenant can be evicted. The best way to avoid an eviction situation is to develop adequate criteria for screening tenants. For example, a minimum standard might be that a resident's income must be three times the sum of the park rent, utilities, and mobile home payment, if any. When a tenant fails to pay the rent, the property manager should immediately notify the lender on the unit of any legal proceedings begun. The bank often keeps up the park space payment during unit foreclosure proceedings.

If tenants cannot meet their financial obligations, they may simply abandon the unit in the park. The property manager cannot just enter the unit and take possession, nor dispose of the mobile home. Any lender must first be notified, as they have a grace period of 120 days prior to repossession. They may issue a writ of restitution, bringing rent current, and resell the unit in its existing place, with park approval of the purchaser.

Organizations

A California organization that protects mobile home park tenants' rights is the Golden State Mobilehome Owners (GSMO). They assist park residents in the areas of rent control, discrimination, and unfair practices. For example, if a park owner decided to go out of business and close down a park, this group might be instrumental in having the owner meet the legal requirement of performing a relocation study to determine the effects on the residents. In addition, many cities keep older parks and discourage change of use permits because these parks meet the state and federal quotas for affordable housing. GSMO and cities work to obtain funds for residents to offset the cost of moving if a park is closed.

A California organization geared at serving the needs of the park owner is the Western Mobile Home Association. The main office can refer you

Figure 10

To be completed by resident in full

RESIDENT OBJECTION FORM

While we are attempting to insure a harmonious community atmosphere, sometimes incidents occur which infringe on your enjoyment of the park.

In order to remedy the situation when appropriate, we request all complaints or suggestions be submitted to Management in writing.

TYPE OF COMPLAINT:

☐ Park Facilities ☐ Park Management

☑ Other park residents

If against a particular person.

Name Rodney Resident

Space No. or Address 1121 L St. # 398

Detail incident, complaint or problem.
(specify date, time, place.)

ON 1/2/88 at 9p.m. Rodney Resident was speeding through the park & honking horn so as to Cause the Neighbors alarm + disturb our rest.

What action do you think is appropriate?

Talk to Rodney and tell him to respect neighbors & that the park won't tolerate this action.

Because of repeated complaints, in extreme cases, eviction proceedings may be initiated against an offending park resident. In compliance with California law it may be necessary to use this complaint for documentation purposes. Consequently we cannot insure complete confidentiality.

John Q Resident — Your Signature | 1/3/88 — Date

John Q. Resident — Please Print Name | 400 — Space #

OFFICE USE ONLY — DISPOSITION ______

to the local chapter. Membership is reasonable, and has remained at $8 per space for the past three years. Membership benefits include distributing data on current, pending, and new laws affecting the business of mobile homes and related matters. Their publication, *The Bulletin,* carries current articles of information. They provide members with current forms, from rental agreement and application, to proof of service. They furnish copies of the Health and Safety Code and the Mobile Home Residency Law to owners. They have a manager referral placement system that can mail 25 resumes to interested owners. They counsel people on written policy, qualifications for residents, discrimination, and more.

For more information, the following are helpful sources:

National Manufactured Housing Federation
1015 15th Street, N.W.
Washington, D.C. 20005

Department of Housing (DOH)
6007 Folsom Boulevard
Sacramento, California 95819

Manufactured Housing Institute
1745 Jefferson Davis Highway
Chicago, Illinois 60601

Western Mobilehome Association
1121 L Street, Suite 400
Sacramento, California 95814

RECREATION MANAGEMENT

One of the fastest growing markets in California is the leisure time real estate market. Long-term vacation real estate ownership is attractive because of the tax benefits. Short-term vacation real estate (time-shares) are attractive because they offer the owner the chance to get out of the crowded city for a long weekend. These reasons, along with the increasing population and mild California climate, have spurred the demand for leisure property.

Leisure properties used to be limited to places like Hawaii, Colorado ski areas, or Florida beaches. They were predominantly resort properties set up as condominiums. When the owner wasn't using the unit, it was subleased to tenants.

The owners benefited because they could claim the unit as income-producing property and take advantage of the tax benefits. The Tax Reform Act of 1986 changed this. Some types of recreation ownership have lost their tax benefits. For example, for time-shares, the interest is deductible only as consumer interest, which will no longer be deductible in 1991. The property taxes are not deductible, and no depreciation is allowed on time-share ownership. However, owners can take advantage of the deductibility of mortgage payments on a second home if the property is a motor home that meets the specified criteria, such as having a full bathroom.

Condohotels

A forerunner to the present time-share system was the popular *condohotel*—hotel rooms sold to seasonal occupants on a contract basis. The owner got the room for one month, and agreed to have the property manager sublet it for the balance of the year at resort rates. They were managed like hotels, including daily maid service.

Time-Shares

Modern *time-shares* evolved by keeping the most popular features of the condohotel system and adding amenities to meet the present market demand.

Ownership. Time-share ownership is frequently divided into one-week segments. One unit could be owned by 52 owners, each occupying a unit for one week. A 100-unit complex would have 5,200 owners, each owning a one-week interest, but not owning a particular unit. Instead, they would have "the undivided 1/5200th interest in and to the" time-share group.

The units are typically sold by unit size rather than by specific unit. Ownership of a one-bedroom, a two-bedroom suite, or an economy/bachelor unit is transferred in the title. The owner has "the exclusive right to use and occupy a specified suite type as delineated on the map" which is attached to the document as Exhibit A. The rules and regulations are attached as Exhibit B.

The ownership includes a non-exclusive right to use the common area as shown on the map, but only during the "season" or specified unit ownership time period. Owners are specifically prohibited from using common area amenities during non-season periods.

A unit sells for a specific, lump-sum payment. The cost depends upon the demand for an area, and the cost of real estate at that location. California land costs are higher than almost any other state's, but are far less expensive than many international and resort spots. Although luxury California units are well over $30,000, an average price in California ranges from $15,000 to $20,000, with bachelor units in off-season times with few amenities as low as $8,000. When compared to the price of second home ownership ($100,000 or more), time-shares are considerably more affordable. Annual costs run about $500 per year—$300 for dues to cover maintenance and management, plus $200 for property taxes.

One attractive feature of time-shares is the ability to trade the ownership location and date for a different place or time. If you own two weeks at a California beach resort, you could use one of those weeks in California, and trade the second week for a week at a ski resort. Or, you could trade both, and take one week in Hawaii and another in the Bahamas. Or, you could just "bank" the time. This is done by putting your time into a reserve, letting someone else use your week, and using your week at a later time. This is often done to add weeks together for longer stays, such as for European visits.

Companies specialize in these placements, and have published directories with as many as 1,200 different locations available. Some typical locations include: all sections of the U.S., including Alaska and Hawaii, the Caribbean, Canada, Mexico, Europe, South America, the Middle East, the Canary Islands, Africa, Asia, and Australia. Users should be aware that these geographic areas have many specific resorts available within them to chose from.

For the international traveler, many additional rules apply. When guests arrive, the property manager may provide customs data to the guests. Another difference between countries are baths and kitchen facilities. A kitchen in one unit may be just like home, and in another may be only a bar refrigerator and a microwave or toaster oven.

Management. One of the manager's duties is preparing a proposed budget for the directors to approve. (Figure 11). When approved, the property manager typically mails assessments to all owners at the beginning of each year (all fees are due at the beginning of the year, not just when the unit is occupied).

Typically, the manager distributes a newsletter to members. It lists the activities schedule, such as exercise classes, tennis matches, golf or water lessons, tours, bike trails, excursions, and associated events. Travel package offerings are often available.

On-site management usually gets about 2½% of the budget for managment, off-site management gets about 8%. However, to make the unit available to others, the leasing fee is 25% of the rental amount. For example, on a $100 per night resort rental, the owner would receive $75 and the agent $25 for the placement.

Property management of timeshares involves supervising the on-site maintenance crews to assure user comfort. When an owner has only one week a year, and that is the hottest week at the resort, the property manager can be assured that taking four days to repair an air conditioner will be unacceptable. Regular checks for preventative maintenance are even more important than corrective maintenance.

Management operations include overseeing maid services. Some resorts offer daily service, just like a hotel. Most, however, provide service only a once a week, or between guests. Other areas of concern are security, parking, the front desk, the gift shop, the restaurant, and recreational areas.

The property manager needs special expertise to handle time-shares. As the market grows, the techniques will become less pioneering and more standardized.

Figure 11

Tamarack Beach Resort Vacation Owners Association
1988 Operating Budget

Description		Annually	Monthly
INCOME			
Maintenance Fees		793,046	66,087.17
Late Charges		1,700	141.67
Billing Charges		12,000	1,000.00
Beach-Break		23,000	1,916.67
Miscellaneous		500	41.67
Interest		1,700	141.67
General Fund		36,000	3,000.00
Rental		2,700	225.00
Activities		39,441	3,286.75
	Total Income	910,087	75,840.58
DISBURSEMENTS			
Administration			
Insurance			
Directors & Officers		979	81.58
Fidelity Bond		7,126	593.83
Fire & Liability		60,230	5,019.17
Group Health		3,319	276.58
Worker's Compensation		19,725	1,643.75
	Subtotal Insurance	91,379	7,614.92
Payroll			
Activities Director		18,000	1,500.00
Assistant Manager		15,300	1,275.00
Front Desk		64,500	5,375.00
Housekeepers		72,000	6,000.00
Housekeepng Supervisor		19,200	1,600.00
Guest Services		21,600	1,800.00
Laundry Manager		7,200	600.00
Maintenance Assistant		8,100	675.00
Maintenance Supervisor		19,200	1,600.00
Resort Manager		22,500	1,875.00
Payroll Taxes—FICA		19,200	1,600.00
Payroll Taxes—Unemployment		13,425	1,118.75
	Subtotal Payroll	300,225	25,018.75

Tamarack Beach Resort Vacation Owners Association
1988 Operating Budget

Description	Annually	Monthly
Other Administrative		
Accounting Fees (Sole)	2,000	166.67
Accounting Fees (Common)	2,378	198.17
Activities	35,728	2,977.33
Advertising	2,096	174.67
Bad Debt—Deed Backs/Bankruptcy	2,500	208.33
Computer Reservation System	8,971	747.58
Equipment Lease (Office)	4,444	370.33
Legal Fees	1,761	146.75
Licenses, Permits & Fees (Sole)	3,600	300.00
Licenses, Permits & Fees (Common)	838	69.83
Management Fees (Common)	16,722	1,393.50
Management Fees (Sole)	62,000	5,166.67
State/Corporate Taxes	951	79.25
Supplies, Printing, Postage (Sole)	8,000	666.67
Supplies, Printing, Postage (Joint)	3,354	279.50
Telephone System Lease	12,241	1,020.08
TV/VCR Lease	15,000	1,250.00
Van	4,611	384.25
Subtotal Other Administrative	187,195	15,599.58
Total Administrative	578,799	48,233.25
Services		
Elevator Service	2,934	244.50
Grounds Maintenance (Common)	7,450	620.83
Maintenance Contracted (Common)	11,888	990.67
Maintenance Contracted (Sole)	1,500	125.00
Patrol	5,310	442.50
Pest Control	922	76.83
Rubbish Removal	2,515	209.58
Total Services	32,519	2,709.92

Tamarack Beach Resort Vacation Owners Association
1988 Operating Budget

Description	Annually	Monthly
Supplies		
Cleaning	16,768	1,397.33
Coffee	2,515	209.58
Furnishing & Equipment	3,000	250.00
Gas & Mileage Reimbursement	1,509	125.75
Grounds (Common)	476	39.67
Hardware (Common)	3,170	264.17
Hardware (Joint)	1,677	139.75
Linen	5,500	458.33
Office (Joint)	7,965	663.75
Office (Sole)	1,000	83.33
Paint	838	69.83
Pool/Spa	4,024	335.33
Room	500	41.67
Uniforms	3,605	300.42
Video	3,500	291.67
Total Supplies	56,047	4,670.58
Utilities		
Cablevision	6,500	541.67
Electricity (Common)	26,153	2,179.42
Electricity (Units)	29,800	2,483.33
Gas	13,710	1,142.50
Telephone	1,174	97.83
Telephone (800 Number)	10,480	873.33
Water (Irrigation)	713	59.42
Water (Units)	4,192	349.33
Total Utilities	92,722	7,726.83
Total Operating Expenses	760,087	63,340.58
Reserves		
Reserves	150,000	12,500.00
Total Reserves	150,000	12,500.00
Total Expenses & Reserves	910,087	75,840.58

Maintenance Fees: One-Bedroom Unit—$298.00 Per Week
Two-Bedroom Unit—$358.00 Per Week

Chapter Eleven

Recreational Vehicle Park

The recreational vehicle park has met with widespread acceptance in California. Its popularity stems from the shortage of weekend camp areas within a reasonable driving time, rather than any tax benefits of ownership. The California climate and crowded cities encourage use of these parks by a wide range of diverse people.

Characteristics. Park membership usually carries with it the ability to trade sites among various parks. During the few winter months when camping is too cold for the local weekenders, "Snow Birds" from the east and north flock to the milder California campgrounds.

At first glance, these parks seem like little more than campgrounds where overnight stays are rented on a per night basis. Many campgrounds have reservation programs and a referral network, so they do appear to be similar to recreational parks. Due to the method of ownership, however, these parks are far from being just a campground.

The purchaser has a recorded lease giving him or her an "Undivided Leasehold Estate" in the recreational vehicle club. The club issues 99-year leases and allows the owner to sell or assign the leasehold interest to subsequent purchasers. Members also receive ownership of an "Undivided Interest" in the real property owned by the club (the common areas). These ownership rights are recorded at the County Recorder's Office where the property is located, not where the owner resides.

A park with 800 physical sites will typically restrict sales to no more than 5,000 owners. Each owner receives an assigned time on a rotating basis. For example, an owner may receive preference for every fifth week, on a year-round basis. For their weekend, an owner may reserve the time for themselves and an additional space for a guest. The member and guest get priority over all other members wanting to use the facility at that time. The members who want to use the park on a non-assigned weekend would have to wait until a few days before the weekend to make their reservation on a space-available basis. These members would have priority over guests of non-assigned members.

The cost of membership ranges between $5,000 and $10,000, with dues of about $500 a year. Guests pay a separate $10-$15 per night for park use if they go with a paid member. Some persons leave their trailer in the park storage yard, at an average cost of about $3 per day, plus a $10 set up/take down fee. Other services that may be offered for a fee include winterizing, towing, and servicing the vehicles. Special group camping rates are also available with reservations.

Management. The property manager is responsible for administering absentee ballots, sending budget figures to members, and billing dues and fees. Enforcement of the park rules is a primary concern. Rules often include age restrictions with family members. Some facilities may be for adults only, if they have an area such as a teen center or a children's section available as well. Facilities can include bike trails, pools, stocked trout pond, playground, pool tables, shuffleboard court, horseshoe pit, laundry facilities, and much more. Rules on campsite occupancy and guest usage must be adhered to by members and their guests.

The property manager also handles equipment usage and damage. Parks prohibit firearms, weapons, and liquor. Fires, noise, pets, non-licensed recreational vehicles, and non-licensed drivers are prohibited as well.

Capital expenditures are necessary to maintain the quality of the park, and the property manager takes part in these projects. The park dues pay for these major expenses. The property manager participates in projects such as the replacement, repair, or purchase of: picnic tables, energy saving lighting, pool heater, underground cable television, paving, ice machines, well drilling, computer system, recreational equipment, etc.

The property manager must review the by-laws, rules and regulations of the park, as well as the Recreational Park Occupancy Law (Figure 12). Conflicts between the law and the park rules should be noted and the Governing Board informed in writing. Then an amendment should be passed to take care of the discrepancies.

Many management opportunities will arise in the area of recreational property for those skilled in the special requirements of this unique and growing market.

HOUSING FOR THE ELDERLY

Housing for the elderly is a rapidly growing market. Yet less than 15% of California's 325,000 real estate licensees focus on servicing the needs of those 55 years or older. By 1990, the number of California seniors is expected to increase by 28%. By 2010, one in every four Americans will be 55 or older.

Figure 12

RECREATIONAL VEHICLE PARK OCCUPANCY LAW

Many mobilehome park operators become involved — by necessity — with RVs and trailers and the laws that relate to them. Consequently, we have reprinted the RV Park Occupancy Law (ccc 799.20 et seq.). Additional copies are available by request from WMA's Sacramento office.

Recreational Vehicle Park Occupancy Law
California Civil Code Article 1
General Provisions

799.20. This chapter shall be known and may be cited as the "Recreational Vehicle Park Occupancy Law."

799.21. Unless the provisions or context otherwise requires, the following definitions shall govern the construction of this chapter.

799.22. "Defaulting occupant" means an occupant who fails to pay for his or her occupancy in a recreational vehicle park or who fails to comply with reasonable written rules and regulations of the recreational vehicle park given to the occupant upon registration.

799.23. "Occupant" means the owner or operator of a recreational vehicle who has been an occupant in a recreational vehicle park for less than 30 days.

799.24. (a) "Recreational vehicle" means a motor home, slide-in camper, travel trailer, park trailer, truck camper, or camping trailer, with or without motive power, designed for human habitation for recreational or emergency occupancy.

(b) "Camping trailer" means a vehicular portable unit mounted on wheels and constructed with collapsible partial sidewalls which fold for towing by another vehicle and unfold at the campsite and designed for human habitation for recreational or emergency occupancy.

(c) "Motor home" means a vehicular unit built on or permanently attached to, a self-propelled motor vehicle chassis, chassis cab or van, which becomes an integral part of the completed vehicle, designed for human habitation for recreational or emergency occupancy.

(d) "Slide-in camper" means a portable unit, consisting of a roof, floor and sides, designed to be loaded onto and unloaded from a truck and designed for human habitation for recreational or emergency occupancy. A "slide-in-camper" means a truck camper.

(e) "Travel trailer" means a portable unit, mounted on wheels, of such a size and weight as not to require special highway movement permits when drawn by a motor vehicle and for human habitation for recreational or emergency occupancy.

(f) "Park trailer" means a trailer coach, designed for human habitation for recreational or seasonal use only, which meets all of the following criteria:

(1) It contains 400 square feet or less of gross floor area measured at the maximum horizontal projects. However it may not exceed 12 feet in width or 40 feet in length in the traveling mode.

(2) It is built on a single chassis.

(3) It may only be transported upon the public highways with a permit.

(4) It is constructed in accordance with the Standard No. A119.5 of the American National Standards Institute, as it may be changed by department's regulations. (Section 799.24 of the Civil Code.)

799.25. "Recreational vehicle park" means either of the following:

(a) An area or tract of land, within an area zoned for recreational use, where one or more lots are occupied by owners or users of recreational vehicles or tents and which is customarily occupied for temporary purposes and where there is displayed in plain view on the property a sign indicating that the recreational vehicle may be removed from the premises for the reasons specified in Section 799.22 and containing the telephone number of the local traffic enforcement agency.

(b) An area or tract of land or a separate designated section within a mobilehome park where one or more lots are occupied by owners or users of recreational vehicles used for travel or recreational purposes and where there is displayed in plain view in that area or tract of land or separate section within a mobilehome park a sign indicating that the recreational vehicle may be removed from the premises for the reasons specified in Section 799.22 and containing the telephone number of the local traffic enforcement agency.

799.26 "Tenant" means the owner or operator of a recreational vehicle who has been an occupant in a recreational vehicle for 30 or more consecutive days.

799.27. The rights created by this chapter shall be cumulative and in addition to any other legal rights the manager or owner of a recreational vehicle park may have against a defaulting occupant or tenant, or that a tenant or occupant may have against the manager or owner of the recreational vehicle park.

799.28. Nothing in this chapter shall apply to a mobilehome as defined in Section 798.3.

799.29. No occupant registration agreement or tenant rental agreement for a recreational vehicle shall contain a provision by which the occupant or tenant waives his or her rights under the provisions of this chapter, and any such waiver shall be deemed contrary to public policy and void.

Article 3. Removal of Recreational Vehicles of Defaulting Occupants

799.35. As a prerequisite to the right of an owner or manager of a recreational vehicle park to have a defaulting occupant's recreational vehicle removed from the lot which is the subject of the registration agreement between the recreational vehicle park and the occupant pursuant to Section 799.38, the owner or manager shall serve a 72-hour written notice as prescribed in Sections 799.36 and 799.37. A defaulting occupant may correct his or her payment deficiency within the 72-hour period during normal business hours.

799.36. The 72-hour written notice shall be served by delivering a copy to the defaulting occupant personally. Delivery of the 72-hour notice to a defaulting occupant who is incapable of removing the occupant's recreational vehicle from the park because of a physical incapacity shall not be sufficient to satisfy the requirements of this section. For such defaulting occupants and those with recreational vehicles which are not motorized or cannot be moved by the occupant's vehicle, the default shall be cured within 72 hours, but the date to quit shall be no less than seven days after service of the notice.

799.37. The written 72-hour notice shall state that if the defaulting occupant does not remove the recreational vehicle from the premises of the recreational vehicle park within 72 hours after receipt of the notice, the owner or manager of the park has authority pursuant to Section 799.38 to have the recreational vehicle removed from the lot to the nearest secured storage facility.

799.38. The owner or manager of a recreational vehicle park, subsequent to serving notice to the city police or county sheriff, whichever is appropriate, and after the expiration of 72 hours after service of the written 72-hour notice in the manner specified in Section 799.36, may cause the removal of a defaulting occupant's recreational vehicle parked on the premises of the recreational vehicle. Such a notice shall be void five days after the date of expiration.

799.39. The owner or manager of a recreational vehicle park who causes the removal of a defaulting occupant's recreational vehicle, and the individual or entity who removes such vehicle, shall exercise reasonable and ordinary care in removing such vehicles to the storage area. The owner or manager of a recreational vehicle park shall have a lien upon the recreational vehicle and the contents therein for the proper charges due from a defaulting occupant. Such a lien shall be identical to that authorized by Section 1861, and shall be enforced as provided by Sections 1861 to 1861.7, inclusive. Disposition of any possessions abandoned by an occupant at a recreational vehicle park shall be performed pursuant to Chapter 5 (commencing with Section 1980) of Title 5 of Part 4 of Division 3.

Article 4. Recreational Vehicle Park Tenants

799.45. The owner or manager of a recreational vehicle park shall not terminate or refuse to renew a tenancy except upon the giving of a written notice to the tenant in the manner prescribed by Section 1162 of the Code of Civil Procedure to remove the recreational vehicle from the park within a period as specified by this section, which period shall be specified in the notice.

(a) In the case of a tenant who has continuously resided in the park for less than nine months after January 1, 1980, such notice need not state cause for termination but must provide not less than 30 days' notice of termination of the tenancy.

(b) In the case of a tenant who has continually resided in the park for nine or more months after January 1, 1980, such termination shall be made pursuant to Article 6 (commencing with Section 798.55) of Chapter 2.5 of Title 2 of Part 2 of Division 2.

(c) Evictions pursuant to this article shall be subject to the requirements set forth in Chapter 4 (commencing with Section 1159) of Title 3 of Part 3 of the Code of Civil Procedure, except as otherwise provided herein.

799.46. A tenant of a recreational vehicle park shall give notice of intent to vacate consistent with that required of the park owner or operator.

799.47. The owner or manager of a recreational vehicle park shall have a lien upon the recreational vehicle and the contents therein for the proper charges due from a defaulting tenant. Such a lien shall be identical to that of the apartment keepers lien authorized by Section 1861a, and shall be enforced as provided therein. Disposition of any possessions abandoned by a tenant at a recreational vehicle park shall be performed pursuant to Chapter 5 (commencing with Section 1980) of Title 5 of Part 4 of Division 3.

799.48. Except as otherwise specifically provided by this chapter, the provisions of Article 1 (commencing with Section 2.5 of Title 2 of Part 2 of Division 2 shall apply to tenants who have continually resided in the recreational vehicle park for nine months or more after January 1, 1980.

Article 5. Actions and Proceedings

799.50. In any action arising out of the provisions of this chapter, the prevailing party shall be entitled to reasonable attorney's fees and costs. A party shall be deemed a prevailing party for the purposes of this section if the judgment is rendered in his or her favor or where the litigation is dismissed in his or her favor prior to or during the trial, unless the parties otherwise agree in the settlement or compromise.

799.51. In the event that a tenant, resident, occupant, or a former tenant, resident, or occupant is the prevailing party in a civil action against the owner or operator of a recreational vehicle park to enforce his or her rights under the provisions of this chapter, the tenant, occupant, or resident, in addition to damages afforded by law, may, in the discretion of the court, be awarded an amount not to exceed five hundred dollars ($500) for each willful violation of these provisions by the owner or operator.

Senior housing includes existing housing, new construction, and buildings that can be converted to accommodate the elderly. Senior housing encompasses condominiums, planned unit developments, low-rise apartments , garden or walk-up apartments, high-rise apartments, mobile home parks, and resort communities.

What are seniors looking for? Clean air, a safe and secure neighborhood, proximity to friends and family, affordability, and housing that fits their lifestyle. This lifestyle may be very athletic and active; or, coupled with health and age conditions, may necessitate constant care. Seniors are often attracted to areas where price ranges allow them to pay all cash. If financing is required, they want fixed-rate loans. Counties that allow seniors to park their recreational vehicle or mobile home on their own lot, with access for a boat and trailer, are popular.

Definitions

It is difficult to discuss this specialized market without defining "elderly." Compared to the 55-year-old, the 75-year-old senior has an entirely different set of physical needs, background, musical tastes, habits, likes and dislikes. Compared to the 75-year-old, the 95-year-old, who is a full generation ahead, has still different physical needs, habits, likes and dislikes.

The **empty-nester** group, those aged 55 to 64, will grow 109% between 1985 and 2020. Over five million will reside in California. The **young-old,** aged 65 to 74, will increase by 127% from 1985 to 2020, surpassing the three million mark. Both of these groups enjoy the highest levels of income of any prior group.

The **elderly,** age 75 to 84, have significantly lower incomes, and a higher likelihood of disability. The **older-old** are those over age 85. This segment has more service-oriented housing needs to meet increasing health requirements.

Special Considerations

As of 1988, 48% of California's senior population is found in the greater Bay Area and Los Angeles Area. This represents over 1.36 million people. Until now, seniors faced substantial financial hardships if they wanted to move out of these highly populated urban areas.

Two-thirds of these people own the homes they reside in, 80% being mortgage-free. They survive on limited incomes, averaging about $25,000. Under Proposition 13, the taxes on the homes they own are based on 1978 tax rolls. A typical annual property tax bill might be $360 a year, or $30 a month. If they sell their home and purchase a smaller one at $70,000, their new property tax bill would run $875 a year ($70,000 x 1.25%), or $72.92 a month—a 143% increase in their expenses. Even though their present house may be too large for them to maintain, they couldn't afford to move.

With the passing of Proposition 90 in November 1988, a senior can now purchase outside the county they presently reside in, anywhere in California, and keep their old tax bill. The only criteria is that the senior must apply to and be accepted by the county they're moving to. This will allow a large number of seniors to gain mobility and freedom of choice, instead of the present condition where 49% of those over 55 who bought homes moved within the same city or county, often because they had to.

A 1987 survey by the Institute of California Real Estate Research indicated that of those over age 55 who purchased a residency, 55% bought single-family residences, 24.8% manufactured homes 12.8% condominiums, and 5.5% multi-family income property. Nearly 38% migrated to California from outside the state.

The availability of affordable housing ranked most important among senior renters. This is because many older renters face substantially higher housing expenses in relation to their incomes than do senior homeowners. Senior renters also realize that rents will increase in the future, especially in areas of higher demand.

Tax Benefits. The major tax benefit for seniors is the once-in-a-lifetime capital gains exemption, which allows seniors to exclude up to $125,000 of gain on one property. To obtain this benefit, the person must have lived in the home three of the last five years.

A second benefit is California Proposition 60, which allows seniors to transfer their tax base to a new home of equivalent or lesser value in the same county. This state law was, of course, increased in force by the passage of Proposition 90, discussed earlier.

Another tax benefit program for seniors includes the property tax deferment program, which allows low-income seniors to defer all property taxes until the time they sell their home.

Finance Options. Finance options have drastically changed for this emerging market. Sale-leaseback and shared equity arrangements are popular. This is because the elderly homeowner can sell all or part of the home in return for a monthly income and lifetime residence rights. Deferred maintenance loans are available so older homeowners can borrow money for repairs without having to pay off the loan until the home is sold. Cash poor but equity rich seniors can take advantage of a reverse annuity mortgage (RAM), where the senior homeowner gets a loan (in the form of monthly payments), which is repaid when the home is sold.

Types of Senior Housing

These special tax and finance options allow property managers to provide several optional plans for senior housing. One type of senior housing program is the **group home.** Occasionally developed by a private concern (such as a religious organization), this is an arrangement where unrelated seniors live under one roof and share all the expenses. The management can be by one of the members/users, or by an outside management firm.

Convalescent homes and **nursing facilities** are more like hospitals, in that they are a continuous care facility. They provide a medical staffperson and various lifesupport services geared for older or infirm seniors. They offer physical therapy, housekeeping services, and dietary help. The medical field administers these facilities rather than a real estate property manager.

Congregate care facilities are set up like an apartment building or condominium. They feature the regular housing amenities offered by other apartments or condos, with additional assistance when needed, such as meal service and occasional medical assistance. They are run by professional property management personnel.

Retirement hotels have been around for some time. Formerly they were restricted to older, downtown buildings that could not attract higher paying tenants. Today, they are built specifically for the senior group. The property manager should have training in the specialized hotel-restaurant management field. These retirement hotels offer meals, maid service, and special activities, and are popular in resort and sunbelt areas of the United States.

Senior apartment buildings are like any other apartment house and are handled by property managers. Tenants have separate living units, but are all seniors. These buildings usually provide some special programs, but each apartment has its own kitchen, and each tenant cleans and cares for his or her own unit.

Retirement centers are usually housed within a single building. They offer scheduled local transportation, beauty/barber shop, coin-operated laundry facilities, exercise and art classes, library, patios and lounge areas, game rooms, social programs and even widescreen television. They do not allow food or kitchens within the individual rooms. A central dining room prepares three meals daily, plus a 24-hour snack bar is available. Daily maid service is also available.

Retirement communities are not set up to offer any medical or daily living support. They are primarily geared for the lifestyle and recreational needs of seniors. They may be set up as a manufactured home, condominium, or planned unit development. Or, they may be within a single building, offering single rooms, double rooms, or suites. Modern fire protection and 24-hour security features are popular. Emergency call systems are also popular. Each of these rooms offer features such as individually controlled heating and air conditioning.

The kinds of housing seniors demand requires highly specialized real estate skills. Both public housing and private groups seek property managers to oversee operations. The property manager deals with family members and social workers, in addition to the demands of the residents themselves. This property management field has considerable room for growth, innovation, improvements, and formalized organization.

SPECIAL PURPOSE RESIDENTIAL HOUSING

Institutional housing is developed as a means of support for another entity. The primary concern is not to maximize cash flow, but to provide benefits for the select group it serves. Each specialized group makes its own demands upon the property manager.

Dormitories accommodate students and faculty at colleges and universities. Their purpose is to maintain a quality of life for this group and benefits usually include matching roommates to split the per user room cost. Group study/conference rooms, desks, and bunks are standard furnished features. Each floor usually has a leader who reports maintenance/repair or other needs of their floor to the building supervisor, who in turn reports to the housing officer. Interpersonal conflict resolution skills are as neccessary as maintenance expertise. These leaders may get some college unit credits for their role in learning the property management skills needed for ongoing building user coordination. The housing officer is the ultimate property management authority on the housing issues, and requires considerable expertise and skills to effectively handle this type of housing.

Military housing is usually run by military staff personnel. In many areas, however, this is coordinated through local property management personnel who help locate affordable off-base housing. Because of the property managers' ability to report rent payment defaults to the tenant's superior officer, rent collection is usually easier. Income is more fixed, with high demand around military installations. California has many coastal military operations, with hundreds of miles of beach and harbors that are government owned. Inland valley installations are also frequent, and entire communities have developed housing just to meet these needs. Property managers running these buildings need general management skills.

Industrial housing is provided by private corporations to meet the needs of employees. Examples are apartments developed for the Alaska pipeline workers. Mobile home parks in the Middle East became fenced-in American cities within foreign nations. Recreational vehicle parks in South America were built to accommodate the needs of the U.S. dam and road workers within jungles or near overcrowded cities. Industrial housing is run by professional property managers.

The property managers have to meet the owner's goal of maintaining employee comfort, appeasing family members, minimizing operational expenses and satisfying a group of diverse needs. Good support personnel help maintain successful institutional housing.

CHAPTER 11 QUIZ

1. When you are not the property owner, which of the following is required when managing single-family residences?

   a. A permit from DOH
   b. A real estate license from DRE
   c. A certificate from HUD
   d. A user fee from DMV

2. Manufactured housing parks may not discriminate in any of the following areas EXCEPT when dealing with:

   a. adults only
   b. senior citizens
   c. handicapped persons
   d. families

3. Which of the following do not have a California Resident Occupancy Law?

   a. Mobile home parks
   b. Recreational vehicle parks
   c. Apartments.
   d. Condominiums

4. An on-site manager is required, by law, to manage a:

   a. 100-unit mobile home park
   b. 10-unit apartment house
   c. 100-unit condominium
   d. 10-unit planned unit development

5. A tenant of a manufactured housing unit must receive a copy each year of:

   a. the association Rules and Regulations
   b. the Park By-laws and Amendments
   c. California Civil Code laws
   d. DOH license and permits

6. Managing time-shares includes overseeing:

   a. subtenant activities and Certificates of Ownership
   b. personnel such as maid service, park towing, and maintenance crews
   c. preventative maintenance, corrective maintenance, and equipment repair
   d. highway tax, trade license, and association fees

7. Recreational vehicle parks:

   a. require little property management
   b. are unpopular due to their higher cost
   c. have problems because they cannot be traded for or linked to other parks
   d. appeal to both retired persons and local weekend users

8. Which of the following would be LEAST likely to use the services of a real estate property management expert for senior citizens?

   a. Convalescent home
   b. Seniors apartment building
   c. Retirement centers
   d. Retirement communities

9. Institutional housing does not usually include:

   a. dormitories
   b. time-shares
   c. military housing
   d. industrial housing

10. Which of the following is NOT a special senior citizen tax benefit that the property manager should be familiar with?

    a. A one-time $125,000 capital gains tax exemption
    b. California's Proposition 60 and 90 for property tax transfer
    c. The property tax deferment program
    d. A RAM or sale-leaseback/shared equity tax

CHAPTER 11 QUIZ ANSWERS

1. b
2. b
3. d
4. a
5. c
6. c
7. d
8. a
9. b
10. d

12
Maintenance and Repairs

References

Downs, Jr., James C. *Principles of Real Estate Management.* 12th ed. Chicago: Institute of Real Estate Management, 1980.

Forms. Sacramento California Apartment Association, 1984.

"Appliance Efficiency." *CPM Aspects.* [Chicago: Institute of Real Estate Management.] Sept 1987.

Last Chapter Review

While property managers are involved with apartment complexes, office buildings, and shopping centers, a major area of growth in the industry will be single-family residential units, mobile home parks, recreational parks and housing for the elderly. The last chapter described and reviewed the many elements of these specialized areas of residential property management.

Chapter Overview

The most time-consuming phase of property management is maintenance and repairs. Preventing and correcting the variety of maintenance problems requires expertise in many areas (which are reviewed in this chapter). Also, using the right personnel for the job can save time and money. This chapter discusses basic building elements, energy considerations, security and safety, fire, and the various appliances that the property manager is responsible for.

GENERAL CONSIDERATIONS

Maintenance is the primary responsibility of the property manager. If buildings are maintained by means of a regular schedule, this phase of the business is an orderly procedure. The goal needs to be "management by design" not "management by crisis." Even emergency repairs can be routinely handled if guidelines are set up beforehand to minimize inconvenience and keep costs within reason.

When the property was purchased, the owner should have received detailed information on the age and condition of the property, including utility and service systems, appliances, and fixtures (as was discussed in Chapter 4). Subsequently, information regarding the on-going replacement and repair should be available in the detailed depreciation schedule, discussed in Chapter 4.

When the property manager takes on the responsibility of managing a building, a walk-through of each unit and the maintenance areas will verify and update information on the current status.

> **Example:** A window air conditioner may not be shown on any prior records, yet the property manager can see there is one installed when she walks through the units. The walk-through and inquiry reveals that it was installed by the tenant and is not serviced by the management company. But, it could affect the power load on the building's electrical system, which affects management maintenance.

Maintenance
The repairs, replacement, and services necessary to preserve assets, while maintaining the budget, meeting the owner's goal, and satisfying tenant and building needs.

Asset Life vs. Economic Life

There is a real difference between the actual life or age of a building and its economic life or age. The old adage "More buildings are torn down than fall down" is very true. Some buildings, though relatively new, are in such bad shape that they have a limited economic (useful) life left. Other buildings, because of effective maintenance, can enjoy a long economic life even though they are actually very old buildings.

Economic Life
The period of time that an asset can be used in the production of income and services.

The economic life of the building has a great deal to do with how much it will cost to maintain and repair it. By determining the present condition of the building, the property manager can give the owner a fairly accurate prediction of maintenance costs for the budget. The property manager who sees a 20-year-old apartment stove, purchased used ten years ago for $50, should know that repairing it may exceed the cost of a new, more energy-efficient model.

Physical Life
The period of time an asset actually stands physically, which can be shortened or prolonged through maintenance.

Many times the property manager has the responsibility of educating the absentee owner on the building's present condition and need for the repairs. At the same time, he or she must temper the tenants' demands and soothe their grumblings about disrepair.

While the property manager has to keep the existing owner and tenant happy, he or she also has a moral obligation to maintain the asset for future owners and tenants. Temporary, quick-fix treatments may increase short-term profits at the expense of long-term resale price, or additional maintenance expenses.

Example: An owner may have a policy of only repainting units when vacant, and lose existing long-term tenants as a result.

> Or, an owner may not want to bother with maintaining appliances, window coverings, and carpet, so all units come with wood floors, bare windows, and no appliances. The rents will be $100 to $200 per month less, and the resale price $10,000 to $20,000 less per unit, because the owner avoids the $2,000 initial cost to install these items, and the $200 per year to maintain them. This is in addition to the lost rents because it is harder to attract tenants to stripped units.

Types Of Maintenance

Maintenance falls into five main categories: custodial maintenance, corrective maintenance, preventive maintenance, deferred maintenance, and emergency maintenance.

Custodial Maintenance. Custodial maintenance is often performed by the on-site staff or by a hired firm. These duties are in the realm of housekeeping: keeping office hallways, restrooms, elevators, and common areas clean. Model units must be kept dust free and ready for showing. Common area pools, parking areas, recreational centers, laundry areas, and mailbox spots must be kept litter free to maintain a good building image. Those involved in this on-going building maintenance include companies who do the pool service, vending machines and laundry equipment, pest control, gardening/groundskeeping, and maid service. All of these services should be on routine schedules. The off-site manager, on-site manager, and tenants should have a copy of the schedule (or it can be posted in a common area) for trash collection, gardening, and other activities so they can inform work crews of any work needed.

> **Example:** On a Thursday morning as I'm getting ready to drive to work, I notice a puddle of water where I have to step into the car. I see the water's coming from a leak at the base of a sprinkler pipe. Since I know the gardener is scheduled to come on Friday before noon, I can tell him about the broken sprinkler head and hopefully get if fixed the next day. This saves the gardener from having to make a separate trip to make the repair.

Corrective Maintenance. Corrective maintenance includes the on-going, regular repairs necessary to maintain an asset. These repairs include responding to normal wear and tear, changing burnt-out light bulbs, replacing missing screens, broken windows, faucet washers, etc. The work may be done by a handyman, the on-site manager, or outside labor. A primary goal is to stay within the budget allocation. Most corrective maintenance is caused because of a neglected preventive maintenance program. It should be performed on a routine, scheduled basis.

Preventive Maintenance. Preventive maintenance is the process of replacing or repairing items identified during routine building inspections before they become emergencies or corrective maintenance. This would include checking cracked pavement, corroded pipes, worn out floor and window coverings, tree trimming, deck and roof coverings, toilet ballcocks, etc. The goals of preventive maintenance include: detecting problems before they become emergencies; planning the expenses to avoid budget overrides; and forestalling major replacement by on-going minor repairs and upkeep. A system of review should be maintained for each building (Figure 1).

Deferred Maintenance. When ordinary maintenance is postponed to a later date, it is called deferred maintenance. Deferred maintenance has a negative effect on both the value and the usefulness of an asset. The most common cause of deferred maintenance is inadequate funds to make the necessary repairs. Maintenance may be put off until the property is refinanced, generating enough funds to make the repairs. Or maintenance may be delayed until rents are increased to support the increased expenses. Too often, however, work is postponed until the property is sold, and the work must be completed as a part of the closing of escrow. Either the buyer or the lender may demand repairs before the transaction closes. Typical items needing repair are roofs or decks, and repairing termite/dryrot damage. Sometimes work is required to renew an insurance policy. Common repairs include removing graffiti, repaving cracked surfaces to avert trip-and-fall liability, and securing stairs and handrails.

The property manager should alert the building owner of deferred maintenance when he or she begins managing, and schedule maintenance as soon as possible.

Emergency Maintenance. If regular inspections are considered unnecessary, or minor repairs are postponed, emergency maintenance is often the result. Infrequent or unforeseen repairs that need immediate

Figure 1

BUILDING MAINTENANCE

ADDRESS *123 Elm* **FILE#** *88-271*

	DATE	UNIT# LOCATION	VENDOR ACTION	COST	•	►	
	1/88	*Walk way*	*Trim trees*	*$200*	✓		*#72*
	3/88	*All units*	*Smoke detector battery*	*$100*	✓		*#13*
	4/88	*Pool-basement*	*Oil pumps*	*$30*	✓		*#15*
	5/88	*All units & exterior*	*Bug spray*	*$300*			*#47*
	5/88	*All units*	*Replace screens*	*$800*			*#39*
	7/88	*Laundry room*	*Replace hoses*	*$30*	✓		*#41*
	9/88	*Storage area*	*Drain water heaters*	*$25*	✓		*#9*

• PREVENTATIVE
► CORRECTIVE

	J	F	M	A	M	J	J	A	S	O	N	D
A/C FILTERS			✓						✓			
HTG. FILTERS									✓			
WASHERS			✓									
POOL EQUIPMENT			✓									
LAUNDRY				✓								
WINDOWS				✓								
DRAPERY					✓							
PAINTING					✓							
DOORSTOPS									✓			
DOWN SPOUTS									✓			
SMOKE DETECTOR				✓								
FIRE EXTINGUISHER				✓								

attention also fit into this category. Examples include cleaning leaves and other materials out of gutters in the fall to avoid water backups and interior water damage. Also, frozen or broken water pipes is an emergency that may not have been avoided if the area rarely gets cold enough to freeze water.

Often, emergency repairs (such as a broken water pipe) don't have to be fixed at 7 a.m. on a holiday or Sunday—at triple-time repair rates. Ask the tenant if they will be home all day. They may be unwilling to stay home to wait for a plumber, or be planning on visiting friends or family anyway. In that case, calmly reassure the tenant that everything's going to be all right and direct them to the main water valve that you showed them when they moved in. Instruct them to leave it off all day, turn it on briefly in the morning when they have to get ready for work, then turn it back off until the plumber arrives first thing Monday morning—at regular pay. The property manager should have regular checklist procedures to follow for leaking roofs, plumbing, fires, and other disasters, such as the frequent California earthquakes.

The professional property manager makes routine drive-by inspections, and informs the tenant, in writing, about the areas that need attention (Figure 2). It is best to give at least as many compliments as work requests.

In addition, the property manager should keep a continuous repair report on each unit managed (Figure 3). By keeping individual sheets on each unit, the property manager can produce an ongoing maintenance log should the tenant use a defense of lack of habitability in a pending eviction proceeding. The log is also valuable when the building is to be sold—it will help the purchaser set up new maintenance schedules, in addition to being part of the process of valuing the building. The main reason for the log, however, is so the property manager can look back and review all maintenance on a per unit basis with the owner to make a budget, repair, or replacement decision.

All maintenance should have written work orders. (Figure 4). These serve as written invoices for the IRS and for the owner's records.

Maintenance Personnel. Many different people perform maintenance and repairs on a building. Many property owners have property managers deal with the asset management, tenant relations, and marketing efforts on their building. The owners may retain the duties of maintenance and repair, except for emergencies (and then only if the owner is

Figure 2

Dear Resident of ______*123 Elm Street*______:

A drive-by inspection was done on ___*2*___/___*18*___/___*89*___ by an agent of our firm, and the following conditions were found:

______ Front/real yard needs:
  ____ Water
  ____ Mowed/edged/weeded
  ____ Debris or trash needs to be cleaned up.
______ Driveway needs oil-slick cleaned off or removed
______ Front door needs to be cleaned or repaired.
__✓__ Auto needs to be removed from lawn or *blocking neighbor's garage*
______ Broken/damaged sprinkler needs to be repaired.
______ Shrubbery is overgrown. Please trim.
__✓__ Animal(s) on premises. Please remove. *Cat sleeping in window.*
______ Mail box needs repair.
______ Exterior fixtures need repairing.

The following vehicles appeared at the premises:

86 Taurus ICFD491
84 Toyota Pickup TGU883

Comments: *Your cooperation in making these corrections is appreciated. I'll call on you in one week to finalize this.*
The flowers you put in by the front door are very nice looking.

Figure 3

Repair Problem Report/Office

82-271 BLDG UNIT #	DATE-BY WHOM	PROBLEM	"REPROBOF" WORKMAN
Apt J	*3/88—Tenant*	*Replace smoke detector battery*	*#13—John 561-3421*
Apt J	*5/88—Mgr.*	*Sprayed for ants & fleas*	*#47—Cory 486-2232*
Apt J	*5/88—Mgr.*	*Replace rusted, torn & missing screens*	*#39—Joe 664-7778*
Apt J	*9/88—Mgr.*	*Changed air filters*	*#On—site*
Apt J	*9/88—Mgr.*	*Replace 3 doorstops*	*#Handyman*
Apt J	*10/88—Tenant*	*Repaired broken waterpipe to stool*	*#Superintendent*

Figure 4

SUNBELT*

Call Taken By ____________ Schedule For ________ ☐ Morning ☐ Afternoon ☐ Evening Completion Promised ____________

☐ Home Call ☐ Carry In

Customer			Phone	Date
Street			City	
Bill To		Above ☐	Type of Unit	
Make	Model #		Serial #	
Dealer	Date Purchased		Parts ☐ Warranty ☐ COD	Service ☐ Warranty ☐ COD

Service Requested

	Parts and Material	Amount		Summary of Charges		
				MATERIAL		
				TAX		
				SERVICE CALL OR PICK-UP-DELIVERY		
				LABOR OR FLAT RATE		
				MILEAGE		
				CARRYING CHARGE		
				TOTAL		
				Service Performed		
				Date	On / Off	Shop Serviceman
				☐ No one home Date Completed ________		

Signature ____

I hereby acknowledge the satisfactory completion of the above described work.

Workmanship performed and materials replaced on this repair are warranted for thirty days from date completed. Parts not replaced are not guaranteed.

* DISCLOSURE: A family member of D. Grogan may have a financial interest in Sunbelt.

unavailable). This allows the owner to remain "active" for tax status, and keep abreast of the condition of the building.

One disadvantage of the owner performing maintenance duties is if the owner overrides property management policies and gets directly involved in tenant negotiations. The owner should remain the maintenance person only, if that is the arrangement. Many times the tenant may never know the maintenance person is the building owner. Problems arise because the owner may not report to the property manager when the work is completed, so the property manager has the burden of the follow up. Also, if the work takes too long to complete, or is poor quality, it is virtually impossible to fire the workman (owner) and get someone better qualified.

Another disadvantage is that the owner cannot deduct any expenses based on his or her own time for tax purposes. This can, however, be offset by the reduction in total building maintenance costs.

The owner may have a relative do most or all of the building repairs. For example, the owner's son may mow the lawns, or the owner's brother may paint the units. The disadvantage to this is the work may have a low priority. And when completed by unskilled labor, the work may have to be redone correctly later. The labor costs would be tax deductible, and some relatives are very conscientious in overseeing the owner's building.

If the owner delegates all maintenance to the property manager, the right worker for the job is a must. Staff maintenance personnel offer many advantages. The handyman or on-site manager should have the skills necessary to take care of most problems. They should provide full references and the property manager should be able to inspect their previous work before they are hired.

If the management company handles enough properties, a handyman can be kept busy on a full-time basis. Larger companies sometimes offer this potential cost reduction as an enticement to attract owners. The real savings is often never seen as there is a potential conflict of interest if the management company owns the maintenance company. Keeping good handymen busy with full work loads during slow periods could mean unnecessary work is being done. And, without outside bids, the owner cannot see any cost savings.

Some management companies have set up a mandatory monthly maintenance fee to offset the cost of routine work, such as faucet washers, door stops, air filters, alarm batteries, etc. The owner contributes regularly, so the work personnel have regular incomes. Extra and emergency repairs are billed separately. Since the management company has to maintain its own income, expenses, and profit center, there may be little, if any, savings to the building owner. The advantage, even at break even cost for the owner, would be the control the property manager would have over the work crew. The ultimate power to hire and fire can mean better service for tenants, prompter emergency turnaround time, and management-prioritized work orders. The Certified Property Manager's Code of Ethics of the National Association of Realtors (Chapter 15) dictates that the property manger must disclose the amount of profit and must get the prior approval of the owner if the maintenance company is owned by the management company.

Another method for time consuming maintenance supervision is where the property management company has a separate maintenance desk that all work is channeled through. To offset the cost of this personnel, the management company adds a flat amount, say 10%, above all work order billing. The incentive here is that this staff person gets quantity discounts from the vendors on their end of the billing. So, the owner gets a bill that is about the same amount, or very competitive.

There is no real control over the vendors, however, except the future expectation of work. Many vendors have far more work than they can already handle, especially in the heavily populated areas, so this added pressure can work as a negative incentive. When this happens, the management company often ends up using people new in the field, those unknowns who are trying to build a business, or apprentices rather than skilled work persons. The workers often use the big name management company to get their client base to increase, so their future will be retail pricing direct to the public, instead of wholesale prices to the property manager's maintenance desk.

The off-site manager can also perform the maintenance, in addition to managing it. Again, there can be a conflict of interest in keeping costs down when you write your own check and when no competing bids are obtained. There is, however, a good incentive for control. If the apartment isn't painted and cleaned up quickly, it cannot be rerented in a hurry, thus decreasing management fee income. And if the apartment is not rerented, no funds are available to pay for the materials and labor already expended for painting and cleaning.

The on-site manager frequently does maintenance work. This means an additional expense for liability coverage and workman's compensation insurance, in case of injury. The incentive is the same as for the off-site manager: filling the vacancy to get paid for the work and also a possible rent-up fee. The trick is in the training. Make sure the on-site manager knows when to call in an outside professional, so the owner doesn't pay twice—once when the on-site manager tried and failed to complete the work correctly, and again when the professionals present their bill.

Maintenance staff must deal with the question of whether they are employees or independent contractors. Written contracts should be signed that provide for the social security numbers, payroll deduction status and exemptions, and insurance coverage. It should outline who is responsible for tools, transportation to sites, equipment, materials, vehicle insurance, pagers, and parts. All labor and employment laws must be complied with.

As an alternative to staff positions, the property manager may wish to use only outside contractors for all work. This avoids the need for job descriptions, employee records and reporting, and maintaining volume business.

If outside contractors are used, the property manager should require proof that they are licensed, bonded, and insured. A criteria for hiring might be inspection of completed work and talking to references. The best reason for using an outside contractor is their level of expertise. They specialize in what they do, and they do it full-time. They have the right tools, equipment, and know where to get the parts to get the job done. They must be competitive in price or they couldn't stay in business.

Disadvantages include the lack of direct control over them and their work. They are often unable to do small jobs at all, and if they do them, their minimum trip-charge price is too high. The worst problem is the employees of the outside contractor. The property manager has no control over them, and they can cause many problems at the site.

Some owners have the tenant perform the maintenance functions. The tenant usually charges only for parts and little or nothing for the labor on their own unit. One injury, however, could offset any savings. The owner would need full insurance coverage, as with the on-site manager.

Some property managers allow tenants to do work on any unit, except the one they occupy, due to the potential conflict of interest—the tenant may end up constantly improving and upgrading his or her own unit. A written bid, like one used for any other work with any other workman, should be required. Figure 5 is a sample of the kind of work order that should be used for all repairs that are not emergencies.

> **Example:** At 8 p.m., December 2, the tenant phones the office, reporting a leaking pipe. The answering service connects the tenant to the particular property manager who is on call that evening (this function is rotated by office personnel). They determine that a pan under the bath sink will temporarily solve the problem.
>
> The next morning the property manager gets a workman to the property to bid the job. The workman phones the office for approval. The property manager calls the owner to discuss the work, the bid, and to ask the owner if any additional plumbing work should be done while the workman is on the premises. The owner approves the work by phone; the property manager informs the workman to do the work while at the property. A copy is mailed to the owner to sign and approve and return to the office, for the file. This keeps the owner very "actively" involved in the management process, for financial and tax purposes. The owner knows about the expense, in advance, and participated in the decision process immediately.
>
> To assist in keeping costs in control and the owner actively involved, the property manager may require all requests to be placed in writing (Figure 6). This shows the owner that the tenant, not the manager, initiated request for the service. The best part of this, on a similar form, is that the tenant signs off that the work is complete. As a standard policy, before any payment is issued, either the tenant should sign off, or the property manager should personally inspect the work, or both.

Each management company will probably have their own guidelines on the handling of the maintenance. For example, when receiving a repair request, a form letter may be dropped in the mail to clarify the property manager's position that if the problem is caused by the tenant, the owner will not be paying the bill. Also, the tenant should be notified that he or she must sign off on the work order. This gives the tenant power and control over the problem, to some extent, which they often appreciate.

Figure 5

Sunbelt Investments
P.O. Box 1659, Downey, CA 90240
(213) 861-3835

Workman: **Property Acct** # *88-271* **Property:**

Name *George Fernadez*	Tenant name *Joannie Forester*
Address *Box 7C*	Address *123 Elm Street* Apt# *4*
City *Redding* Phone *876-PIPE*	City *Redding* Phone *876-4332*
Your invoice # *391*	Directions: Thomas Map Coordinates
Today's date is *12-3-88*	*20B3 - N/Main - E/National Blvd*

– This Is A Written Estimate Of Service Or Repair Work –

The service/repair requested consists of the following list:

1) Drip/leak at hot water connection under bathroom sink
2) Check/change all washers (kitchen, bath & laundry)
3) Put blanket on hot water tank in garage.

I estimate the cost of the above listed work to be $ *62.50* and the estimate *is good for a period of 30, 45, 60 days from today.*
(circle one)

Dated: *Dec. 5, 1988* *By:* *George Fernandez* *(Workman's Signature).*

Date request received *12/2/88* Date to workman *12/3/88* Date to owner *12/4/88*
Date back from workman *12/4/88* Date work began *12/4/88* Date work done *12/4/88*

– Property Owner to Complete and Return –

I AUTHORIZE THE ABOVE WORK TO BE DONE AND ASSUME FINANCIAL RESPONSIBILITY FOR PAYMENT FOR WORK PERFORMED OR SERVICES GIVEN FOR MY PROPERTY.

Dated *December 5, 1988* Authorized Signature: *Matthew Andersen*

Figure 6

Dear Resident,

This is to acknowledge receipt of your request for repair work to be performed on the property you are renting. Please review the following items:

1. The name of the approved firm and their telephone number should have been given to you by now. They may contact you DIRECT.

2. Failure to keep an appointment you set with a vendor will obligate you to pay any trip/service charge fee that they bill for.

3. Should the workman not call you for an appointment, you may call them at their number. If they do not come, you are NOT authorized to obtain the services of any other firm. Let us know.

4. Only the work originally authorized is to be done. If the workman indicates that the maintenance problem has been caused by you (example: peach seed in the garbage disposal or diaper in the toilet), you are responsible to pay this bill.

5. When a workman has been given authority by this office to fix a toilet, and you have them also fix the kitchen sink, you are responsible for the extra bill over the amount he was sent for.

In addition, the workman will ask you to fill in the "Tenant Verification" portion of his copy of the work order, or he may ask you to sign off that the work is complete. Please assist him! The workman CANNOT receive payment without verification that the job is complete.

We hope this problem can be taken care of in a reasonably speedy time period without too great of an inconvenience to you. Further, we hope you do not encounter future maintenance problems during your occupancy.

Cordially,

Property Manager

Figure 7

Repair Rules

1. Is there any danger of bodily harm?
2. Is it an emergency?
3. Will delay to get approval create additional problems?
4. Is it under warranty or a maintenance contract?
5. Will repair cost 90% or more of a new replacement?
6. Who would the owner have make the repair?
7. What action am I authorized to take?
8. How much are you authorized to spend?
9. Who caused the problem and will pay to fix it?

In California, landlords must keep residential buildings intended for human occupancy in fit condition, and must repair all subsequent dilapidation (Civil Code Section 1941). The tenant is under an obligation to notify the landlord of a repair problem, and allow reasonable time for the repair to be made, usually 30 days. If the landlord has not cured the problem within the 30-day period, the tenant may make the repair him or herself or hire the work done, and deduct the amount of the repair work from the rent. The tenant may not spend more than one month's rent, nor repair and deduct more than twice in any 12-month period. However, tenants are not obligated to make any repairs. Instead, they may vacate the premises, and no further payment of rent is due. If the tenant is under a lease, rather than a month-to-month agreement, this would break the lease.

It is the building owner who must prove the habitability of the premises. The law (Civil Code Section 1941.1) has outlined the minimum dwelling requirements, although other conditions may be admitted as evidence of lack of habitability in any court action. The most frequent legal action is that of eviction for non-payment of rent, called an unlawful detainer (UD). To successfully defend the eviction action, the tenant would need to prove that one of several conditions exist:

Figure 8

Habitability For Tenantable Residential Dwelling

1. Effective waterproofing and weather protection of roof and exterior walls.
2. Unbroken windows and doors.
3. Plumbing facilities in good working order.
4. Gas facilities which conform to the law at the time of installation.
5. Water supply capable of producing hot and cold running water.
6. Appropriate fixtures connected to an approved sewage disposal system.
7. Heating facilities in good working order.
8. Electrical lighting in good working order.
9. Wiring and electrical equipment conforming to the law at time of installation.
10. Clean and sanitary building, grounds, and appurtenances at rental commencement.
11. All areas under control of the landlord kept free from accumulation of debris, filth, rubbish, garbage, rodents and vermin.
12. Adequate number of appropriate receptacles for garbage and rubbish, in clean condition and good repair at rental commencement.
13. Floors, stairways and railings in good repair.

(1) violation of any of the items shown in Figure 8,
(2) a public housing enforcement officer has given the owner written notice of an inspection, citing the obligation to abate the nuisance or to repair the substandard condition,
(3) the conditions cited have not been corrected within 60 days from notice, without good cause for delay, and
(4) the conditions were not caused by acts or omissions of the tenant.

The penalty for any landlord who collects rent or even demands the rent when the premises are untenantable are substantial (Civil Code Section 1942.4). The landlord is liable to the tenant for the actual damages, not less than $100 nor more than $10,000, the tenant's allowable court costs and reasonable attorney's fees, plus any additional punitive damages or other requirements the judge may impose—such as the recent cases where "slumlords" had to sleep in their own building for a specific period of time.

The landlord, however, may have valid defenses in the form of proof of violations by the tenant (Civil Code Section 1941.2). There is no duty on the part of the landlord to repair dilapidation if the tenant has substantially contributed to the problem, or has interfered with the landlord repairing the problem (Figure 9).

Tenant Habitation Obligations

1. Keep the premises occupied clean and sanitary.
2. Dispose of all rubbish, garbage, and waste from the unit in a clean and sanitary manner.
3. Properly use and operate all electrical, gas, and plumbing fixtures.
4. Keep all electrical, gas, and plumbing fixtures clean and sanitary.
5. Refrain from willfully or wantonly destroying, defacing, impairing, or removing any part of the structure or appurtenances.
6. Occupy and use the premises only for the intended or designed use.

The property management and maintenance crew should be trained to alert the building owner of any potential repair problems, not only to maintain the building value and keep ongoing operations running smoothly, but to avoid any possibility of other persons directing the business operations. Having to meet the demands of organized tenants, public health officers, and court orders is far more serious an undertaking than solving individual problems through planned maintenance.

Lastly, a misunderstood portion of many landlord/tenant relations is in the definition of "normal wear and tear." If the age and condition were noted in the owner's purchase and tax deduction records, they should be verified against each tenant move-in and move-out walk-through forms. Thus the ongoing allocation of costs between owner and tenant is substantiated by the property manager's building records.

> **Example:** If the apartment had new paint when the tenant moved in, the owner should not charge the tenant for normal fingerprints around the light switch plates, but should deduct for crayon and pencil marks on the walls.

MAJOR MAINTENANCE CATEGORIES

The property manager is responsible for the structure and operational elements of the building's exterior and interior. He or she must maintain the value of the asset in accordance with the owner's objectives. The property manager must advise the owner of required maintenance and repairs, current maintenance and repairs, or lack of proper maintenance and repairs. A solid construction background is very helpful to the property manager.

The following major maintenance categories are areas where property managers need a basic working knowledge.

Plumbing. The property manager needs to identify the apparent age and condition of toilet, garbage disposals, shower heads, hot water tanks, water softeners, pool pump and filter/heater, sprinkler system, laundry units, and water and sewage lines. Identification of potential problems can avert emergencies, including scheduling the replacement of washers. Tenants must know the location of the water main and gas shutoff valves, especially in earthquake-prone California.

Heating, Ventilating and Air Conditioning (HVAC). The HVAC system controls the movement and quality of air. The amount of humidity can drastically affect the office tenant computer lab, or restaurant clientele lunch crowd. The circulation pattern, thermostat control and dryness influences the productivity in the workplace a great deal. The property manager needs to understand duct work, floor and wall furnaces, boiler rooms, window/wall and central heat units, and central air cooling systems. The central unit repair person will not service window units, which are treated as appliances. The property manager must also evaluate and service the peripheral items that affect the human comfort zone of HVAC. These include double pane or tinted windows, canopies or lined drapes, and shades and other window coverings.

Electrical. The exterior elements consist of lead-in lines from the pole or underground cable conduit, and outside breaker box service. Interior core elements include power plants, pumps, motors, fans, elevator and lighting components. Interior unit elements include two- and three-prong outlets, light fixtures, kitchen and laundry appliance watt, amp and power needs, computer and business machine usage, and communication centers.

Old or faulty wiring calls for professional servicing to avert danger to human lives and to meet insurance requirements. Older buildings may still have wires run through glass tubes, fuses with a penny behind them, or extension cords running everywhere. The property manager should make a complete inspection and notify the owner of any potential problems. Each tenant should know where their fuse box is and know how to flip the breaker switch.

Roof. The elements of the roof consist of not only the covering and substructure bracing, but also the gutters, downspouts, and items such as television antennae, satellite dishes, roof air conditioning units, and solar panels.

California's climate ensures a low annual rainfall over a large portion of the state. Consequently, little attention is given to roofs until it is too late. High temperatures, dry winds, and extremely cool nights all put stress on roof materials. Whatever the roof composition—asphalt rolled roofing or shingles, wood shingles, clay tiles, rocks or aluminum—the lack of exterior care causes interior maintenance to be much more expensive. Water stains on interior ceilings and walls are hard to remove. The property manager must be able to visually inspect the various roofs, and have tar put around attached items before leaks occur.

General Work. Many general areas also need the attention of the property manager. Repairs to steps and porches can forestall replacing decks with magnasite surfaces. Handrails with proper metal angle iron prevents repairing large chunks of pulled away plaster. Doorstops in the bathroom prevent doorknob holes in the wall. Repairing the water damaged, lime soil line around the bottom of stucco prevents water seepage into the underlying surface, as does patching the mortar in cracked brick work.

Some maintenance items may meet resistance from the owner. A quick paint job for cosmetic appeal can be a property manager's headache; he or she will have to explain to the new owner the need for sandblasting to prepare the underlying surfaces. The same is true with treatment of exterior wood surfaces, garage doors, eaves and fascia boards, and unit doors.

Turnover. Making a unit ready to rent may require a considerable amount of work. The order of getting the work crews coordinated is critical in terms of downtime for the unit. The surface preparation and painting are the first item, followed by professional deep-cleaning of carpets, with general cleaning done last. The surfaces should not only be clean, substances should be used to make them shine. Speed and accuracy both count, whether it be scraping paint overspray off glass, or rehanging the clean, pleated drapes just back from the cleaners. The property manager knows no unit should be shown until it is completely ready to rent.

Building Exterior. The elements of the exterior building maintenance program consists of curb appeal, grounds, pool/spa, halls/walkways, and mail areas. Each common area has high traffic and multi-tenant use. Tenants can lose business if customers are turned off by building graffiti, littered parking lots, and dead landscaping. The building or center name, street numbers, and lettering should be neat, clean and freshly painted. Even native, natural flowers are better than dried up seasonal ones. Shrubs and lawns need periodic feeding, trimming and sprinkler adjustments. The signs posted by the pool areas cannot be chipped and faded. Waterscape is popular in many central buildings, with Koi ponds and lush landscaping, which cannot have green, slimy waterways. Junk mail accumulating in mail areas looks sloppy. The property manager knows the importance of good building exterior maintenance to the rent levels. A dated annual photo to an owner with a New Year's card is a subtle reminder to the absentee owner of the building's present condition.

Energy. The property manager is well aware of building utility costs and makes an effort to keep rising expenses in check, since rates increase even when usage goes down. The elements of the energy program include blankets for hot water tanks, automatic thermostats with timers, solar panels, hot water recirculating pumps, water conservation shower heads and fluorescent light bulbs.

One energy-related problem the property manager must deal with is the ongoing servicing and repairs needed by previously installed systems. In the past, tax credits were given for installing certain solar energy improvements. Rebates and tax incentives were often assigned to the company making the equipment installation. The service agreements and warranties too often expire the week before the property management agreement begins, and the original installing company is out of business. The property manager must locate qualified persons to service and maintain the system.

Another important element is the cost and time needed for tenant training. Showing tenants how to set the timer so the air conditioner comes on an hour before they arrive home after work saves on the life of the unit, rather than letting it run all day and all night when it is very warm. Putting water bags inside toilets saves on the water bill without obstructing usage.

Waste. An active waste management program consists of both a program to keep the common and sanitation areas clean, and controlling the use and disposal of toxic and asbestos materials. Many government agencies provide literature and training in these areas. The utility companies will go though a building to give advice on energy conservation and ways to decrease waste. The litter and disposal areas can have containers for glass, cans, paper and other recyclable trash handling. The Federal Asbestos Hazard Abatement Act of 1987 and January 1, 1987's California State Registration Law for asbestos removal contractors sets down guidelines for office workers and rental buildings with ten or more units. Both state and federal toxic waste laws regulate the storage, handling and disposal of the waste. The property management administers the waste reduction programs to meet government legal requirements and owner goals to reduce waste.

Appliances. The elements in an appliance maintenance program consist of air conditioner units, stoves and ranges, garbage disposals, dishwashers, built-in microwave and conventional ovens, trash compactors, clothes washer and dryer, and countertop blenders. When a tenant rents a unit with an older, used appliance, and the unit breaks down and the parts are impossible to locate or too expensive, the owner may not want to replace the unit. However, unless specified in the rental agreement, the tenant may give the owner no alternative but to reduce the rent for the decreased service being received or to replace the appliance. Some owners rent units with no appliances, and rent the appliances separately to the occupants. Some owners sell the appliances to the tenants with a provision to repurchase the appliance upon moveout for the same price, if it is in at least the same condition. The property manager needs to know the owner's objectives prior to marketing the units. The property manager reports the age and condition to the owner, along with an estimated replacement date and projected cost. In this way, consultation can be made on financing replacements, projecting capital expenditures and setting up depreciation schedules.

A 1987 publication on major appliances revealed many technological advances in appliances.

> **Example:** In 1972, a refrigerator cost an average of $141.57 a year to operate, and only $90.28 in 1985. Room air conditioners improved efficiency by 28% and reduced energy usage by 21%. Dishwashers had a 54% improved efficiency and 34% reduced energy usage.

The property manager may advise replacing older units with more modern units, which save energy costs and command higher rents. From the laundry room washer and dryers to under sink dormitory dishwashers, a lot of real changes have been made.

SECURITY AND SAFETY

As population grows in California, entire neighborhoods are changing in just a few short months. People resist change, and when tenants do not know the new neighbors, a fear of the unknown comes into place. People become more security conscious. Tenants want door, deadbolt, and window locks to secure their living unit. Tenants are willing to pay more rent for units with security bars on the windows and security screen doors. Tenants may even install them at their own expense for more security.

Should a building have security bars on the windows, however, check with the local fire department as to the safety in case of the need for an emergency exit in a fire. Make sure the property manager, on-site manager, and all tenants clearly know how to work a safety release on the barred windows to get out of the building to safety. In upper story buildings, the use and operation of escape ladders or fire escapes must be demonstrated to the tenants.

Businesses want secure employee parking areas, perimeter lighting and fencing, entry closed-circuit television monitors and shopping center patrol guards. Condo associations want security entry gates. Senior complexes want secured areas, plus the pager-monitoring devices for health safety.

These needs may be met with strictly mechanical or electronic devices. Staff personnel positions are common in many shopping malls. Outside contractors often patrol areas. Assistance from the local government is often available. The police will patrol buildings and areas upon request, if justified, and when available. Neighborhood alert programs are available through many local service organization areas. Schools offer safety booklets to local school children.

Security for personnel is another area where more is better. Training employees about their own personal safety is an important part of the property management orientation program. Various buildings and operations differ in many areas, but common rules benefit everyone. Some basic guidelines may include:

1. Never show a vacant unit alone.
2. Never have large amounts of cash on the premises.
3. Always know an escape route from your work station.
4. Know procedures for fire, flood, earthquake, burglary emergencies.

Another threat to tenants that must be prepared for is fire. The property manager must call the fire department in the area where the building managed is located to obtain their rules and regulations. Too often an owner lives in one city and the rental property is in the next city. The owner checks with his home city and is told that battery-operated smoke detectors are required. So, the owner picks up and installs units in both his or her home and rentals. Then a fire occurs, and the fire department cites the owner because the city required electrical, hard-wire smoke detectors. Then the insurance company cancels the policy because of owner negligence. The property manager must check with each city as to its separate laws.

The rental agreement should include a smoke detector agreement. Inspections by maintenance persons should be performed on a predetermined schedule. At the time of move-in, a detailed explanation of the safety value of smoke detectors should be explained to all tenants to encourage them to keep the system operable.

Fire extinguishers are required by law. They have a tag which shows the last service date, or date when next service is due. The property manager needs to log this in the maintenance schedule to make sure there are adequate numbers in the proper locations that are fully charged and operable. As they are often stolen, a glass front case in a metal enclosure is frequently used.

The best fire prevention is inspecting the building for common causes of fire and eliminating them. Some forested areas are subject to lightning fires, and the property manager can do little about natural causes. But California foothills have regular expectations of fires so that steps should be taken to prevent fires in these geographic locations. The removal of brush around structures, weed abatement, pumps from swimming pools to roofs, moisture-holding hillsides and similar programs can be enacted.

Most fires, however, are caused by people. Since fewer people smoke, in general, less smoking-in-bed fires have occurred, and those that have often do not get far due to smoke detectors. Another common cause of fire is inadequate, but not faulty, wiring. When tenants do not have enough outlets in a room, they buy cheap extension cords, which cannot carry the load. They are strung all over the house. The property manager should notice this when collecting the monthly rent, or when conducting a regular inspection. When a business runs a coffee pot, computer system, and photo machine, all off the same circuit, problems can be expected. In a home, a dishwasher, clothes washer and dryer, coffeepot, and microwave all run at the same time can overload a system and start a fire.

The property manager must inspect garage and storage areas to make sure flammable materials are not being stored on the premises. If the tenant in Apartment 3 is a gardener, make sure gasoline cans and lawn equipment full of gasoline and oil are stored elsewhere. If the tenant in Apartment F has a motorcycle and dune buggy, check to see if gasoline and oil are being improperly stored on the premises.

Gas lines to the hot water tanks, clothes dryers, and barbecues need to be inspected to determine that leaks are not occurring from oxidized, rusty pipes. If tenants own and install their own stoves, an inspection of the gas fittings and connections is warranted. All furnace pilot lights, fire boxes, and valves need to be a part of the scheduled maintenance program. With adequate prevention, danger can be avoided, lives can be saved, and fire averted.

Should there be a fire, however small (even just a burner or oven fire that the tenant puts out themselves), insist on a fire department written report and a written statement from the tenant(s).

The first step in any fire is to reach emergency personnel (DIAL 911) and assist humans. Don't forget to check on seniors, children, visitors, and pets, who may get confused on how to get to exits and safety. The occupants will need shelter, and a local motel may be the immediate answer if local relatives are not available. Always notify your local insurance agent as soon as possible. Take pictures, don't touch anything, and do not let anyone go into areas that government officials have sectioned off. Once the insurance company is involved, they usually walk the manager through reconstruction, handling tenant losses, and even rent payments. Insurance is discussed in more detail in Chapter 14.

CHAPTER 12–QUIZ

1. The period of time an asset can be used is:
   a. physical life
   b. maintenance
   c. repairs
   d. economic life

2. The process of replacing or repairing items identified during regular and routine building inspections is:
   a. corrective maintenance
   b. preventive maintenance
   c. deferred maintenance
   d. emergency maintenance

3. A main purpose for the building maintenance card is to:
   a. record unit work
   b. give the IRS records
   c. reduce emergencies by scheduling regular maintenance
   d. justify maintenance expenses to the building owner

4. The main reason for the drive-by inspection is to:
   a. indicate the condition on a specific date
   b. criticize the property manager's work
   c. alert the owner of a problem with the maintenance worker
   d. annoy the tenant

5. The office repair problem report:
   a. shows all work done on each unit, when, and by whom
   b. indicates the labor and material costs of maintenance
   c. gives a written work order
   d. is a maintenance invoice

6. The written estimate form:

   a. authorizes work to be done immediately
   b. lists details of repairs needed, including parts replacement
   c. is an invoice, accounting-billing system
   d. has owner authorization for financial responsibility

7. A form-letter for residential tenant repair requests should include:

   a. tenant authority to call a workman
   b. a vendor identification number from the approved vendor list
   c. tenant-caused damage responsibility for tenant payment of the bill
   d. date, time, and work which will be performed

8. Basic rules for reviewing a repair request would include:

   a. am I authorized by the owner to take action
   b. what is the estimated cost
   c. how much discount will be received
   d. when will the job be done

9. California laws dictate residential units as inhabitable when the:

   a. doorstops are gone
   b. window glass is broken
   c. floor coverings are worn
   d. window coverings are gone

10. The tenant is obligated to maintain:

   a. clean and sanitary premises
   b. stairways and railings
   c. fire extinguishers
   d. security bars

CHAPTER 12–QUIZ ANSWERS

1. d
2. b
3. c
4. a
5. a
6. d
7. c
8. a
9. b
10. a

13
The Management Office

References

"Job Skills for 1990". Information Society [Denver] 1982.

"California, Inc." California Business, June 1988.

Bergerud, Marly, and Jean Gonzales. *Information Processing Concepts*. New York: Wiley & Sons, Inc., 1981.

"Toward An Intelligence Beyond Man's." *Time*. Feb. 20, 1978.

Basile, Frank. "Study of Personality Styles in Property Management," *Journal of Property Management. Institue of Real Estate Management-National Association of Realtors [Chicago] July/August 1988.*

"Checklist for Going into Business." Small Marketers Aids, SMA 71 Washington: U.W. Small Business Administration, U.S. Government Printing Office 0-247-716, Office of Management and Budget.

DeCarlo, J., CPM. *California Real Property Management. Study Guide.*Sacramento: California Community Colleges, 1986.

Downs, Jr., James C. *Principles of Real Estate Management.* 12th ed. Chicago: Institute of Real Estate Management, 1980.

"Nine Steps to Avoid Burnout." *Real Estate Focus.* Fidelity Federal Savings and Loan, Vol. 1, No. 3.

Grogan, Donna. "Real Estate Property Management—Training and Education Needs in California Community College Curriculum". Master's Thesis. Pomona: California State Polytechnic University, Pomona, 1985.

Lapides, Paul D. *Managing Residential Real Estate. Boston: Warren, Groham & Lamont, 1986.*

Last Chapter Review

Maintenance can prolong the life of an asset. The last chapter reviewed the types of maintenance required to keep property in good repair. A discussion of the various maintenance personnel was outlined. Specific areas the property manager should know about were reviewed (and these included more than just plumbing, heating and electrical systems).

Chapter Overview

The form of ownership, management structure, and office location are all vital to the success of a property management business. Having the right equipment in the right place at the right time makes for a smooth operation. The management office records and forms are a mirror image of the entire property management operation, and their critical review is just as necessary for the mom-and-pop operation as the corporate property management office.

Any executive officer of a sound business knows that the efficiency and success of the office is dependent upon the directions received from "the powers that be," and that it is critical that leaders lead. The same is true for property management business operations.

OFFICE OWNERSHIP – MANAGEMENT FEES

Management fees are not set by law, but rather by custom within an area, such as Southern or Northern California, metropolitan area, or outlying semi-rural area; and by type of property, such as industrial or residential. All commissions are negotiable. Fixing the rate of commission would be in violation of federal anti-trust law. Below, some rough figures are given for some types of management fees, but these are not suggested or common rates.

Government

The largest single operator of real estate is the government. Managing the real and personal property owned by the federal, state, and local government involves many different types of agencies interfacing with their own departments. Many of these departments occupy leased space from the private sector, and the government's property manager deals with the lease negotiations and tenant improvements. As you might guess, government entities rent vast amounts of office building space.

The government is also the largest single landlord in the United States, controlling more residential units than any other source. Management of these properties is most often contracted out on a bid basis. The property manager hires the on-site managers, or building superintendents, to oversee the daily, on-site operations. In turn, the property manager reports to a government property administrator. The property manager needs to devote time to studying the government manuals, rules, and guidelines that must be followed. Operations are scrutinized for potential misappropriation of government project funds. Audits or accountability reviews are common. Government guidelines cover everything from tenant rent collections and eviction procedures to the mandated bid system for capital improvements and maintenance.

Property management fees run 2% to 5%, or are based on a flat "per unit" fee. For example, a Federal Housing Administration (FHA) property taken through foreclosure generates no income. The owner's goal is not to get a tenant, but to have it managed until it is disposed of at sale. Thus, a flat fee is commonly used, such as $15 to $50 per unit.

Government property management also includes managing properties held for receivership, probate, and litigation matters. Court-appointed attorneys often recommend property managers to handle the property for trustees or in cases where other matters are pending before the courts.

Corporate

Private businesses own many real estate holdings and require active property management. (One of the largest corporations in California is the Kaiser Permanente Medical Care System.) The property management division of these corporations often works closely with the property acquisition department to coordinate the many phases of corporate building development.

The property manager is usually a salaried staff position. The property manager must remember that the buildings are incidental to the business, and that user accommodations are more important than the real estate connection. Other corporate properties that require management include industrial employee housing, shopping malls, and office buildings, such as bank buildings. Corporations usually have large policy and procedures manuals, which mandate procedures to be followed. Performance reviews, salary reviews, and step/grade levels of pay are common for the property management personnel.

As an alternative, the property management position may be filled with contract personnel. Positions can begin with very low salaries at $15,000 to $25,000 for entry level, and go up to six-digit executive levels. Many non-salary benefits packages are often added to the job, such as paid vacations, medical and life insurance, and additional non-cash pay. Management fees are less likely to be based on a per unit basis of amount of rents collected, but if they are, management fees run 5% to 8% of collected rents.

These corporate owners are often banks, savings and loans, or insurance companies. Their goals may be to develop properties for long-term investment purposes, or their own use and occupancy. Or, they may want the properties emptied and made ready for bulk, wholesale liquidation of their Real Estate Owned (REO) properties to meet the government standards of their asset holdings. For this last purpose, they often use outside property managers on a fee basis because of the specific skills and expertise required. Outside management for REO properties is often best because of the corporate cost to set up and train a separate, temporary department that will, hopefully, be terminated upon disposition of the property.

Chains

The chain operations, with centralized training and operations, have several property management options. Like running dormitory-type fraternity houses throughout the state, but serving under one theme of control, the hotels are the largest of these business entities. Hotel and motel operations have many property management opportunities for managing both real and personal property. Recreational vehicle parks are also a growing management field of this kind.

Property managers usually need to attend college with a major in hotel-restaurant management to obtain the specific talents these employers seek. The property manager receives 3% to 6% of income when filling a contract position. As an entry-level employee, often a person must begin as an assistant on-site manager at about $1000 per month, then work up through the ranks, in order to receive $30,000 a year and up. Most positions include meals and other features of the hotel.

Franchises

The franchise operation is where independent business entities purchase a right to use a particular, identifiable business name. Money is paid for the future expectation of income generated from the franchise name. When the management company is a franchise operation, it is probably wholly owned by a franchised real estate office, where property management may be an aside business to accommodate the clients of the sales team. The property management income may offset the fixed office overhead, such as rent, franchise fees, etc. Many other non-residential property managements are also being franchised, such as mini-warehouse storage operations (e.g., PS Storage).

The type of property being managed would greatly influence how the business is run, as well as the franchise requirements and restrictions. Franchises have the advantages of pooled funds for advertising, a referral network, and structured business direction. A disadvantage is that if one business makes a customer unhappy, it passes along that bad name to other franchise operations. There is also the lack of complete control of the office when policies are dictated from another source. If it is part of another business, the management direction is too often not focused on the property management operation. And the capital needed to increase the property management department sometimes is seen as siphoning off funds needed for the "real" business, so budget requests are overridden, or shoved to a back burner.

The property manager can make a great deal more money in franchise operations. The management operation may receive a 25% referral fee income for each property sold when referred by the property manager. The management side may have to pay the sales team a fee for the referral, say $10 to $100 per unit, depending upon the income. The property manager may begin at as little as $500 per month, as a draw against future commission. A commission fee is often 5% to 10% of collected rents as office income. The broker gets ⅓, the property manager gets ⅓, and ⅓ goes to office expenses, such as computer data processing and accounting operations.

This is becoming the fastest growing and most popular field of privately owned property management firms. The partnership property management company is usually set up where the owner of a suitable office building, several brokers, and property managers join together to operate a property management business. Each person contributes $1000 to $25,000 to buy into the company, depending upon the income size of the firm and the number of investors. They each share the "profit" as an annual bonus, or as a credit in the fees for their own units.

For example, this arrangement can be where a commercial broker, industrial broker and residential broker are tired of unhappy clients or tired of giving away potential income. They want their clients to be very pleased with how smooth the rentals are running so the client will want to buy more. They are tired of losing business because someone they cannot control does not manage the property according to the owner's objectives. They are tired of watching management fee income go out the window.

The brokers may also have a partnership joint venture in an escrow company, insurance brokerage company, and maintenance company. The property management office must be allowed to operate as a separate entity to maximize its profit potential.

The property manager may be a salaried person at $25,000 the first year, until sufficient income from partners generates additional income. The building owner gets a guaranteed tenant, and also gets the space rental income, plus a potential year-end bonus from the profits. The management company gets the guaranteed management income from the building being operated where the management company is situated. Management fees are similar to any other office building fee structure, ranging from 5% to 10% of collected rents.

Sole Proprietor

The individual who owns and operates his own rental income business usually starts with only a few units. A desk in the private home of the building owner is typical, with a file cabinet for documents. Some owners find it easier to have a separate business telephone number, answering machine, and remote pager as their number of units managed increases, in order to stay on top of emergency repairs. An answering service, where calls can be cross-connected may also be used.

The sole proprietor usually owns a mobile home park, or only one residential building, often with an on-site property manager. If there is an on-site, business is conducted in the manager's apartment. If not, no specific location is used, other than the building location. No management fee income or expense can be made, as the IRS does not allow "sweat equity" and management to be deducted for tax purposes.

OFFICE LOCATION

There is an old saying that: "The first three most important elements to a piece of real estate are location, location, and location." This is also true of the real estate property management office. The location is a direct result of the office ownership structure and the type of buildings being managed, for both residential and non-residential properties.

A common site is at the managed building itself. A portion of the structure is dedicated to the business office operations. Both office buildings and many malls have a leasing office, as do larger apartment complexes. This office is used as a place to write rent receipts, receive repair requests, arrange to show vacant units, and handle many management functions that are easier to perform on-site.

For the on-site resident manager, the office is often a part of the apartment living unit. As part of the employment agreement, however, it should be made clear that the manager's desk and possibly a file cabinet be in a separate area, to establish the professional office. Many buildings have areas that are under-utilized, near the laundry room or a storage room, that can hold a desk and chair for an office.

Off-site property management offices vary according to the type of operation. Hotel operations have on-site business offices and off-site corporate headquarters offices. A real estate franchise may have the office in some portion of the real estate office. The chain may have limited on-site office space, but mainly operate from a separate business office. Private property management operations most frequently operate as a stand-alone business, with a separate location.

Many considerations govern the choice of the office location. One major consideration is access. This includes access not only for the property manager to quickly circulate to and from properties, but also for clients and customers. The property manager who is too remote from the properties does not inspect the building as frequently as a closer proximity would encourage. Traveling is a waste of the office's most valuable asset: time. In addition, if it is too far for prospective tenants to locate the office, units may stay vacant longer. Owners will not travel far to a remote office location, nor will reliable workmen, in order to get work orders.

If the property manager handles hundreds of units for a single owner, or just a few owners, there is no need for an off-site office. All business can be handled through the on-site manager at the building itself. A separate business telephone number, call forwarding and answering machine, computer, photo machine, and desk fit into this efficient operation. Efficiency means reasonable rates to the owner in the form of overhead cost savings.

If the property manager handles many single-family residential units and duplexes, where on-site office facilities are not plausible, the business office should be located on a high visibility corner of a major traffic artery. The property manager can even offer the building owner a greatly reduced management fee for use of the building, as a tenant.

Thus the property manager can get a prime location (perhaps at reduced costs) and generate more business. Often, the property manager will get a group of investors to purchase a good office building site and the property manager will manage the syndication property at the same time as the other property management accounts.

The property manager should base the office location on function: all too often prestige and ego determine the office location. If the property manager has many professional owners visiting the office, a facility matching their expectation is warranted. However, when an owner of 12 units walks into an office that looks like it costs more than the owner's own home, that small investor may feel that the 10% to 12% management fee could certainly be less if the office was less ostentatious. Most owners don't want to visit the office—a simple phone call following receipt of the monthly written statement is usually enough. If an owner does want monthly face-to-face discussion, he or she will have to be charged fees above the regular rate to offset the additional time they require.

If you must have an office, and many property managers do, make sure the office hours are posted, and that it is manned during those hours. Owners often drop in without any appointment. Since the owners may be senior citizens who are having their units managed while traveling, the owners may not even have known they would arrive back in town before they're already there. With no phone in their motorhome, they will not call. If they arrive at 8:00 a.m. at the real estate office, which has posted hours of 8:00 a.m. to 8:00 p.m., and the agents are all showing property, or the property manager is doing drive-by property inspections, they'll get very irritated. This is especially true for those who have a vacancy and feel that if the office is closed for them, it is closed for prospective tenants as well.

Other considerations for location include nearness to support businesses, such as the bank, post office, stationary store, and similar complimentary businesses. Parking can be a major issue, as tenants and vendors need to have frequent and easy access. Exterior building signs and lighting can be prohibited in many newer glass and chrome structures and advertising lost.

LAYOUT AND EQUIPMENT

The physical layout of the management office should be determined by functionality. This means the layout of furniture and equipment is designed to match the person using it, and not vice versa. Get a job description of the user first, then determine the equipment needed. Determine the frequency that the equipment will be used—daily, weekly, monthly, quarterly. Lastly, set up the office furniture to match the user and equipment in a sensible workflow pattern.

Standard office equipment consists of such items as a typewriter, tables, chairs, answering machine, postage meter and mailing area, telephones, dictation equipment, computer, fax machine, bookcases, conference table, lunch room, reception/waiting room area, and restrooms (Figure 1). The easiest way to see what works best is to review a poor example. An office that is difficult to work in is one that has any of the following features:

1. Walking through an office to get to another room, as it disrupts both workers.
2. Coffee pot located where receptionist must leave work station to get herself or clients refreshments, leaving rent receipts, office equipment, and phone unmanned.
3. Having to walk past a person's desk to use commonly used equipment, like typewriter or photo machine.
4. Inadequate counter space and trash receptacles for working around the photo machine.
5. File cabinets with commonly used forms located other than next to the photo machine, typewriter work center.
6. Inadequate lighting over work areas.
7. Frequent need to get up to get something, instead of caster and matted floor surfaces between heavy work areas.
8. Looking across a working desk, with stacks of distractions, when talking with anyone—employees or clients.
9. No conference or meeting place.
10. Library and reference materials in dark backroom where it takes a special effort to reach them.
11. Inability to see the front door.
12. Lack of apparent security in money receipting area.
13. Entry not specifically sectioned off with waiting area.

Figure 1

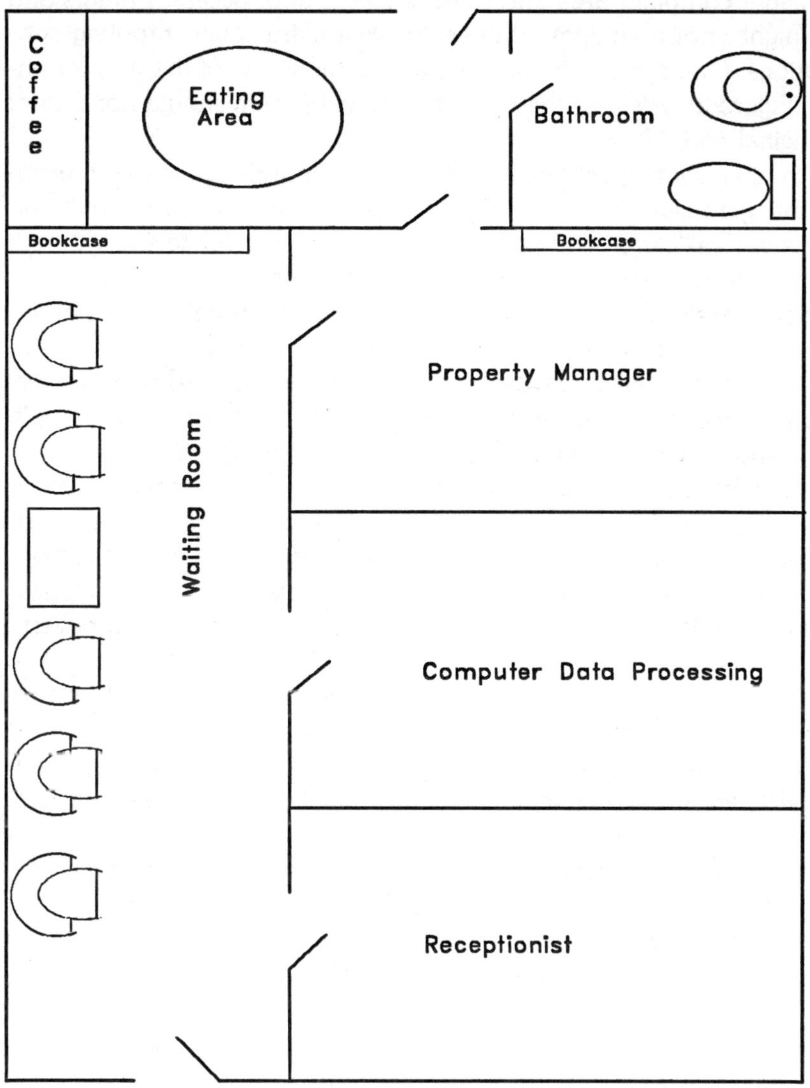
Coffee
Eating Area
Bathroom
Bookcase
Bookcase
Property Manager
Waiting Room
Computer Data Processing
Receptionist

The office layout should include locked offices, ceiling security camera, secure computer area and safe, and rear door access. Printers and other higher noise equipment need to have extra sound proofing considerations. One person should not have to move out of the way for another (Figure 2). Also, as the office grows, expansion should not disrupt the original core.

An open room layout with partitions is a poor design, as each property manager relies heavily on telephone communications while in the office. As voices "carry" and phones ring, the noise level gets to where it is hard to concentrate because of the distractions.

Some areas of the office require a more thorough examination. One is the communications center. When in the office, messages previously inputed into an electronic mail terminal can be read and answers sent back. With a fax machine, on-site managers can send rental applications and receipts by wire, along with the rental agreement.

Voice pagers, number pagers, and vibrating pagers make the property manager available to the office from virtually any business location. Number codes, like "911" means an emergency, or "32" means the on-site manager at 3215 Queen Street, or "1" means the office supervisor needs you—this signal communication can make the job easier for everyone.

Car phones are helping many managers stay in touch with the office personnel, on-site managers, property managers, tenants, and prospective tenants more easily. In the 1990s, a property manager can work with an answering service and a portable phone to handle telephone communications.

Arranging for dictating and secretarial services in the communications center can really help the property manager. When traveling to and from properties, meetings, and court appearances, the property manager can dictate reports. With the proper organization, the transcription can be on his or her desk within a relatively short time.

Another area needing special examination is the computer system. With executive work stations, the property manager has access to the word processing system for letters, form letters, and agreements (such as rental agreements) where templates are set up so that only the name,

Figure 2

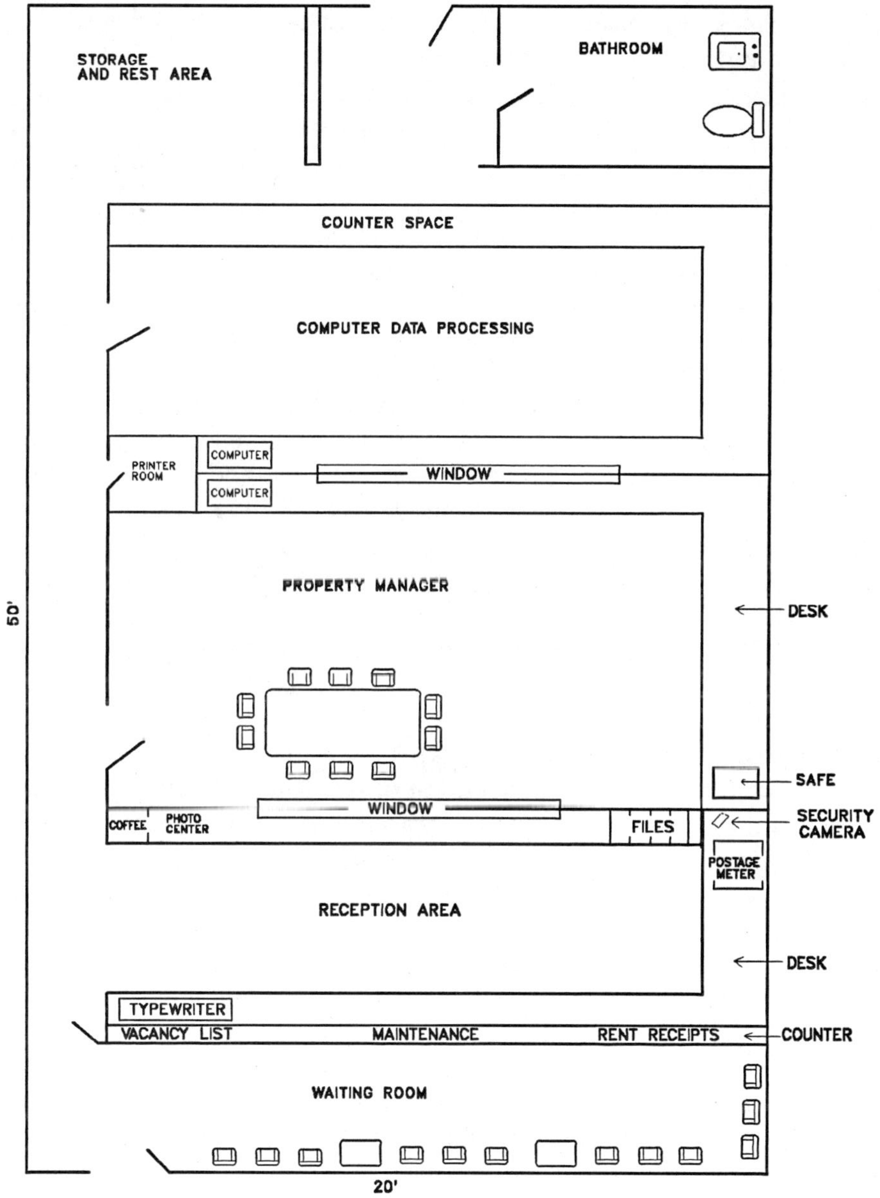
STORAGE AND REST AREA
BATHROOM
COUNTER SPACE
COMPUTER DATA PROCESSING
PRINTER ROOM
COMPUTER
COMPUTER
WINDOW
PROPERTY MANAGER
DESK
SAFE
SECURITY CAMERA
COFFEE
PHOTO CENTER
WINDOW
FILES
POSTAGE METER
RECEPTION AREA
DESK
TYPEWRITER
VACANCY LIST
MAINTENANCE
RENT RECEIPTS
COUNTER
WAITING ROOM
50'
20'

rent amount, and address are needed. Data base mailing labels, automatic rent increase notices, and computer accounting to check an owner's checkbook balance before authorizing payment of a bill will be automatic functions of these work areas.

Executive Work Station
A touch-sensitive panel or keyboard with a visual display terminal that networks into a computer system to allow collection, dissemination, communication, and retrieval within an organization, and linked by modem to the world.

The data processing computer system can be an in-house mainframe, mini- or microcomputer. The system may be stand-alone individual terminals, or a linked, multi-user system. Outside computer services are also available to property management firms where a pick up and delivery arrangement is used for hard copy. Their method of charging can run 25% to 33% of the management fee income generated. Banks are offering computer services also. They may use a fee charge schedule, such as $.25 per check, $.10 per receipt, and $1.00 per page for hard copy reports.

In addition to merely inputing data, the data processing department should balance and maintain the trust account bank balances. The reports of income and expenses for the month and year must be in understandable terms to the building owner (Figure 3).

Through the use of a modem, the on-site manager can input rents gathered at the on-site office and sent to the property management office. A printer would not be needed at the on-site location, as data would be sent only one way. A keyboard terminal could send electronic mail messages, data processing figures, and word processing quickly via modem. If the on-site had a printer, however, the off-site office could send the rental agreements, three-day notices, and rent increase notices that would be prepared at the management firm end.

Lastly, ergonomics is an important key to the success of the operation. If the desk top is too low, workers develop a backache from leaning over it. Or, if the chair back gives the wrong support, other problems develop. Tables at the correct working height with good lighting make the

Figure 3

OPERATING STATEMENT

Sunshine Realty

12345 Oceanview Drive, Oceanview, CA 55555

ACCOUNT	MONTH TO DATE	%	YEAR TO DATE	%
INCOME				
Rental income	$1,025.00	95%	$2,050.00	95%
Parking income	$50.00	5%	$100.00	5%
Cleaning income	$0.00	0%	$0.00	0%
Late Fee income	$0.00	0%	$0.00	0%
Other income	$0.00	0%	$0.00	0%
TOTAL INCOME:	$1,075.00	100%	$2,150.00	100%
EXPENSES				
Accounting	$0.00	0%	$0.00	0%
Advertising	$0.00	0%	$0.00	0%
Cleaning	$0.00	0%	$0.00	0%
Depreciation	$0.00	0%	$500.00	23%
Electricity	$0.00	0%	$0.00	0%
Garden	$35.00	3%	$70.00	3%
Gas	$4.59	0%	$7.84	0%
Insurance	$0.00	0%	$0.00	0%
Legal	$0.00	0%	$0.00	0%
Maintenance	$0.00	0%	$0.00	0%
Management	$125.00	12%	$250.00	12%
Miscellaneous	$0.00	0%	$0.00	0%
Replacement	$0.00	0%	$0.00	0%
Services - outside	$0.00	0%	$0.00	0%
Supplies	$0.00	0%	$0.00	0%
Taxes	$0.00	0%	$0.00	0%
Telephone	$0.00	0%	$0.00	0%
Trash removal	$0.00	0%	$0.00	0%
Water	$0.00	0%	$0.00	0%
OPERATING EXPENSES:	$164.59	15%	$827.84	38%
OPERATING PROFIT:	$910.41		$1,322.16	
Interest - notes	$0.00	0%	$0.00	0%
Mortgage int. - 1st	$722.00	67%	$1,444.50	67%
Mortgage int. - 2nd	$0.00	0%	$0.00	0%
TOTAL INTEREST EXP:	$722.00	67%	$1,444.50	67%
TOTAL EXPENSES:	$886.59	82%	$2,272.34	106%
NET INCOME:	$188.41		– $122.34	

Current cash balance: $1,050.15

workplace a pleasant environment. Employee comfort is a must. This may include name plates, uniforms, their name in an office directory, or similar items that increase job comfort.

OFFICE PERSONNEL

When discussing any business, one must start from the top down. This means a careful evaluation of the ownership set-up and the purpose for the business entity. Starting, running, and managing a business has great risks. A checklist to determine and understand potential problems can avert disaster (Figure 4).

When hiring, recruiting and training personnel, the owner should look for those job skills that round out the operation. Different people can cover different bases to make a successful business. Some important skills to look for include: evaluation and analysis, critical thinking, problem solving, organization and reference, creativity, decision making with incomplete information, and communication. Personal styles vary, and fitting the right person to the right job helps ensure success. Studying body language and the like can help a leader effectively manage an organization.

Organizational Chart

One basic business ingredient is a pre-planned organization chart that begins with a statement of the business objective. If you don't have a goal, how do you know when you've reached it? Each leader will have his or her own idea of how an organizational chart works in the firm. Such charts will vary with the size and types of properties being handled.

For the one-person office there needs to be pre-planned criteria for when a second person comes on-board; what part of the business each will handle; and clearly defined duties. One example may be that upon reaching 100 units, or $5,000 per month income, a second person will be hired. The broker owner will handle all owners, the trust account, marketing, legal matters (including court evictions), association meetings, a quarterly newsletter to all owners, and the office management.

Figure 4

BEFORE YOU START

Do I have previous property management experience?

Am I willing to work long hours for low pay to get started?

What business training and schooling have I had?

Do I know how much capital I will need to start the business?

Where can I get more capital should I need it?

Has my banker reviewed my financial statement?

Has my banker reviewed my projected business plan?

Have I reviewed this ventury with my attorney? Accountant? Insurance agent?

What is my competition? How many, how are they doing, where are they?

Who are my customers? What is my target market?

What are my previous successes? Failures? Pleasures? Irritations?

Should I start my own business or buy out an existing concern?

Who do I need to help me? Employees? Family? Contractors? Team players?

The second person will handle all tenants, including placing and canceling ads for vacancies, showing units, move-in and move-out, rental agreements, three-day notices, rent increases, and maintenance ordering and inspections. When a third position becomes warranted, a computer accounting/communications center will be established. This person's responsibilities will be to make bank deposits, write all checks, balance all checkbooks (office and trust accounts), print owner statements and process owner bills, give the owner management reports on the company and owner's accounts, give the tenant manager reports on vacancies, advertising, and work processing rental forms, etc. (Figure 5).

One key factor to remember in any organization structure, especially the smaller ones, is a business disease called burnout. It can happen in any firm at any level. But, in an office of only one or two people, there is no backup. A month off to cure the problem can be fatal to the firm. An alternative to this problem in the small organization is to "spin the organizational chart." Switch jobs every six months or a year, just for the diversion. Employee tedium is avoided by letting them see light at the end of the tunnel. It also helps the firm because as each new person attacks a position, he or she brings a fresh perspective and new ideas.

At the other end of the spectrum are the larger organizations with many properties and property managers. These larger firms have branches for various different state operations, plus divisions for commercial, industrial, office building, and residential properties. Each division has departments for specialty areas. An example of such a large firm would reflect the economies of scale achieved when combining functions and job duties for a firm with many units (Figure 6).

Policy Manual

A critical element to a successful business organization is the policy manual. The contents should include the organizational chart, employee and personnel policies, job descriptions, accounting and office policies, company policy, company services and benefits, and employee security and safety regulations (Figure 7). It is the same throughout all branches, divisions and departments of the firm. A policy manual may be divided in any manner, such as the following four areas:

Figure 5

ORGANIZATIONAL CHART

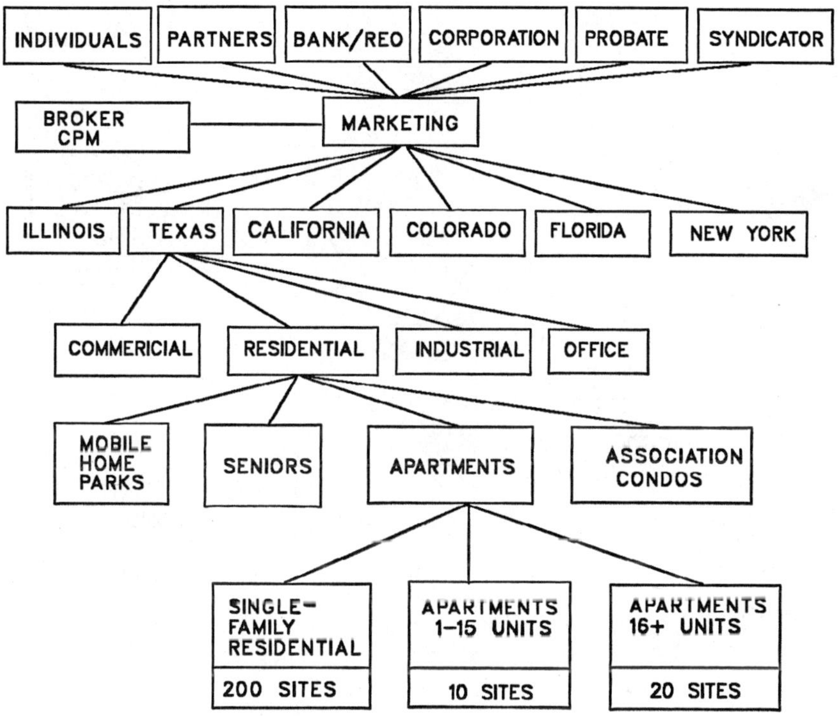

MANAGEMENT OFFICE

Computer Accounting	Office Support	Property Management
Receipts	Communications	On–site managers
Banking	Word processing	Maintenance
Audit	Forms maintenance	Tenants
Operating statements	Legal desk	Owners
Data report	Vacancy desk	Associations

Figure 6

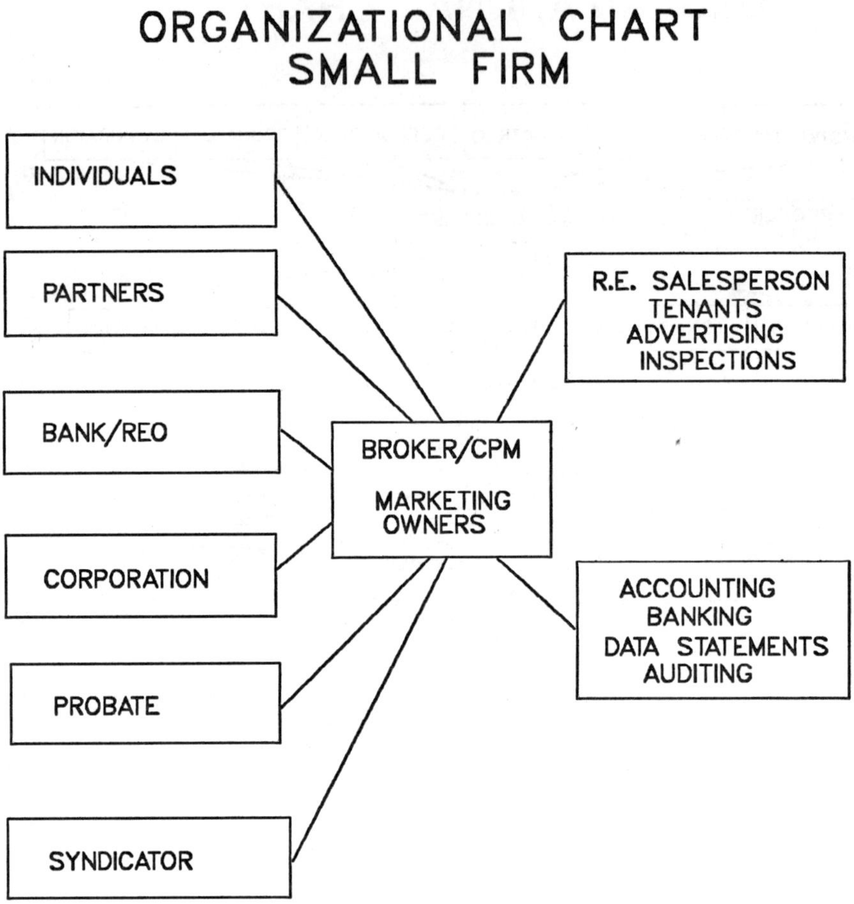
ORGANIZATIONAL CHART
SMALL FIRM
INDIVIDUALS
PARTNERS
BANK/REO
CORPORATION
PROBATE
SYNDICATOR
BROKER/CPM
MARKETING
OWNERS
R.E. SALESPERSON
TENANTS
ADVERTISING
INSPECTIONS
ACCOUNTING
BANKING
DATA STATEMENTS
AUDITING

Figure 7

1. General rules of employment (hours, holidays, vacation)
2. Policies of the organization (public relations, employee attitudes, employee future)
3. Job descriptions (duties, responsibilities, chains of command)
4. The firm (history of the business, objectives of the enterprise)

Policy Manual
The rules of the business.

The procedures manual varies between different divisions as to the particulars needed to run the day-to-day operations of that segment of the business. The purpose of the manual is to lay out interrelations between phases of operations, using forms, steps to processing data, and types of materials to be used (Figure 8).

Procedure Manual
A step-by-step course of action that shows how to get things done.

The best set up, no matter what the size of the business, is to have a loose-leaf notebook where current updates, revisions, and additions can be easily and quickly accessed. As each step of the business expands and grows, the basic outlines can also be expanded. As each new position gets settled, the specific job description can be written.

Staffing

The heartbeat of the company is the staffing. As a service organization, the business depends upon people. To affect results, the work assignments should be outlined clearly in written job descriptions. They can be part of the policies and procedures manuals. One person may fill several positions until income and responsibilities warrant breaking up the job for additional staff. A brief review of some job descriptions is outlined below (Figure 9).

Figure 8

Figure 9

JOB DESCRIPTIONS

Broker/Certified Property Manager

1. Develop NEW business.
2. Maintain ongoing banking relations.
3. Establish community and political ties.
4. Serve on Association Board positions and chairing committees.
5. Direct the business.
6. Attend staff meetings.
7. Set and direct goals.
8. Create enthusiasm and creativity.
9. Monitor delegated authority.
10. Oversee assets and increase net worth.

Director of Operations

1. Solicit NEW business.
2. Establish personnel policies.
3. Supervise staff.
4. Approve business income/expense.
5. Conduct performance reviews.
6. Dissolve conflict and administer discipline.
7. Implement procedures.
8. Set management fees, referral commissions, and charges for services.

Leasing Agent

1. Solicit NEW business.
2. Examine vacant units.
3. Prepare rental comparison analysis for property manager.
4. Write, place, and cancel advertising.
5. Complete move-in and move-out inspection.
6. Examine application to rent credit forms.
7. Review data and approve data.
8. Show property.
9. Hold advertized open houses.
10. Prepare and have contracts signed.
11. Maintain prospects.

Legal Desk

1. Solicit NEW business.
2. Prepare and serve three-day notices, signed by the property manager.
3. Prepare and serve all rent increase notices approved and signed by the property manager.
4. Coordinate court trial dates for all property managers.
5. Maintain the legal calendar.
6. Review and maintain all current forms for the property managers in conjunction with the firm's attorney and office manager.
7. Prepare rental agreements and legal contracts from templates.

Property Manager

1. Solicit NEW business.
2. Review manager reports.
3. Inspect properties and units.
4. Review vacancy report.
5. Approve owner's monthly operating statement.
6. Approve work and maintenance.
7. Review rent collections, deliquencies, three-day notices, and rent increases.
8. Approve move-in and move-out reports and order security deposit refunds.
9. Maintain landlord/tenant and office relations.

Unit Inspector

1. Solicit NEW business.
2. Measure new units and vacancies.
3. Serve legal notices.
4. Install smoke detectors.
5. Install management company sign on property.
6. Meet marshall for lock-out.
7. Re-key units and make duplicate keys.
8. Report move-out maintenance walk-through.

Janitor

1. Solicit NEW business.
2. Perform custodial tasks.
3. Be caretaker for "curb appeal" appearance.
4. Maintain orderly and clean lobby and hallways.
5. Refill supplies stock for common restrooms, recreational room, kitchen, etc.
6. Notify pool, gardener, and other maintenance personnel of problem areas.
7. Keep property manager informed on building status.
8. Winterize and summerize the property systems.

Purchasing Agent

1. Solicit NEW business.
2. Order all company supplies.
3. Order all on-site supplies for the properties.
4. Catalog and maintain supply inventories.
5. Approve all vendor and supplies payments, then forward to property manager for approval.
6. Maintain list of wholesale discounters.
7. Keep data on labor costs.
8. Prepare purchasing budget.

Service/Maintenance clerk

1. Solicit NEW business.
2. Handle all incoming repair requests.
3. Disburse written work orders and purchase orders.
4. Schedule vendors, staff, and contractor work.
5. Obtain property manager approval for payment, after property manager signs off inspection of the work.
6. Maintain lists of approved vendors.
7. Comply with government requirements for worker identification and necessary forms.
8. Coordinate all work with tenants.
9. Obtain estimates and bids for work.

Job Descriptions
The functions and responsibilities of work assignments that a person will perform which includes specific duties.

Training and Development

Interests change, skills become obsolete, individual and organizational expectations differ, job assignments change, and morale varies. This creates the need to develop a well-trained workforce. Most property management training and education programs are designed to improve immediate performance for particular workers, with the most common being on-the-job training.

All employees should receive an orientation. Topics should cover job expectation, duties, functions, insurance, emergencies and the like. Basic skills, including mathematics and communications, should be reviewed to insure proper rent receipt data and telephone techniques. Functional and technical training should be emphasized, which consists of a review of accounting techniques, report interpretation, marketing and advertising, supplies handling, and general operations.

General management should give guidance on the building owner's goals, the building's history, neighborhood image, past management, and the firm's philosophy. In addition, handling subordinates should be discussed so there are clear lines of authority.

A well-defined list of priorities is required for all on-site personnel. A general discussion of the firm's position regarding ethics should also be included. (Ethics is discussed in Chapter 15.) Other areas that might be incorporated into a comprehensive training program may include assertiveness, time management, avoiding burnout, alternative career preparation for future responsibilities, and other specific information.

The ongoing training and development of property management personnel can be carried out in a number of ways. Correspondence courses, such as real estate law and self-study workbooks for legal forms, are ways of training personnel. Attending conferences or workshops given by trade associations is another way personnel can learn how to correctly complete an application to rent credit form, or review preventative maintenance for a swimming pool. Adult and regional occupational schools (ROP) have developed programs to train people on computer accounting and maintenance. Community colleges offer courses on bookkeeping, accounting, property management, and real estate law.

Employing a variety of training techniques is helpful. Knowledgeable personnel reduce mistakes, create an atmosphere of job satisfaction, and give off a professional image to the clients and residents. A well-qualified, reliable employee gives the property owner and the tenants peace of mind, as well as putting many extra dollars into the building income each year. A wise training and development program also assures that personnel are already waiting to fill future vacancies.

A 1985 study of Real Estate Property Management Training and Development Education Needs in California Community College Curriculum was distributed to three groups: community college and university students enrolled in a property management course and working in the property management field, property managers in property management offices, and real estate agents doing property management in the real estate sales office. The respondents were asked information concerning their current activities and their education (Figure 10). The results indicate many duties for which specific training skills need to be incorporated into the training program.

Management often feels that personnel will somehow get the training they need to improve their on-the-job skills. This naive management attitude gives the competition the advantage. Most people working within the field of property management have not had many of the courses needed to aid in their performance on the job (Figure 11).

Employment Forms

Both the federal and state government require certain forms to be completed and maintained for personnel, in addition to any company-required records. At the federal level, persons must complete W-2 and 1099 taxpayer identification information. At the state level, workers need to complete a Department of Real Estate transfer form and the Broker/Salesperson employment contract. Many firms also require

Figure 10

Current Property Management Duties Performed				
Duties	College Students	Property Managers	Real Estate Agents	Total
Place advertising	15	12	7	34
Show vacant units	19	12	9	40
Clean vacant units	5	4	3	12
Type correspondence	9	5	8	22
Clean common areas	2	4	0	6
Serve notices	14	10	2	26
Use accounting system	8	12	8	28
Give financial advice	8	7	7	22
Appear in court	9	8	4	21
Make bank deposits	10	8	7	25
Complete rental agreement	28	12	10	50
Complete walk-thru	18	9	8	35
Set rent rate amount	14	15	9	38
Quote rent rate prices	24	14	9	47
Make repairs	5	5	5	15
Order supplies	4	8	6	18
Open/sort mail	4	4	6	14
Collect rent(s)	15	11	6	32
Do credit check	9	12	7	28
Refund deposits	7	10	6	23
Write newsletter	2	1	0	3
Solicit property	10	9	4	23
Attend meetings	8	12	4	24
Balance checkbook	7	1	8	16
File legal forms	7	6	4	17
Handle insurance	4	7	6	17
Handle escrows	18	2	11	31
Syndicate/develop	4	6	1	11

Figure 11

Courses Respondents Have Taken

Course	College Students	Property Managers	Real Estate Agents	Total
R.E. law	32	14	14	60
R.E. economics	23	11	10	44
R.E. appraisal	26	13	13	52
R.E. finance	29	10	15	54
R.E. practice	20	11	13	44
R.E. principles	45	11	16	72
R.E. property management	30	14	8	52
Escrow/title	6	6	5	17
Ethics/prof.	4	10	10	24
R.E. investment	11	6	6	23
R.E. math	7	6	2	15
Business law	6	7	6	19
Business math	4	7	2	13
Business communications	4	5	2	11
Business English	6	4	5	15
Accounting/bookkeeping	9	8	7	24
Computer accounting	2	4	2	8
Credit administration	2	0	1	3
Principles of business	3	4	6	13
Typing/business machines	3	5	6	14
Marketing	3	5	6	14
Salesmanship	4	6	4	14
Insurance	2	2	0	4

forms in case of an emergency, and insurance information for licensing and bonding purposes. Basic employment applications are commonly required for all positions, and resumes may be part of the processing for management positions.

Some positions require time cards, as was discussed in Chapter 8, Figure 1. Other positions require dealing with collective bargaining, such as office workers or tradesmen (e.g., plumbers or electricians). A credit report on all personnel may be part of the job. Completion of payroll deduction forms are part of the multitude of paper work required, including verification of citizenship (Chapter 8, Figure 5), medical history, and the like. Job performance and employee behavior need to be part of the original job description. Minimum wage and hours worked should be stated. The employment form should include any job requirements of licensing or bonding, and possible causes for termination.

Compensation is normally a separate attachment to the basic contract, as each job and its rate would vary according to that particular job. Benefits vary widely in property management. They can include paid vacation, discounted rents, discounted pricing purchases, or a company car. Some typical salary ranges can run:

Receptionist/Switchboard/Clerk Trainee-Minimum wage to $5.00 per hour;
Unit Inspector-Minimum wage to $4 per hour, plus $.22 per mile, or company car and $1 per notice posted/served, or $3 per notice personally served;
Janitor-$500 per month, plus one-third apartment rent;
Purchasing Agent/Service Clerk/Maintenance Clerk-$6 to $10 per hour;
Legal Clerk-$8 to $12 per hour;
Leasing Agent-$100 per unit rented, commission only.

Employee vs Independent Contractor

The employee relationship is normally understood by most individuals. The employer exercises control over the job to the extent of duties, hours, how tasks are performed, the order of work, assignment completion, etc.

An independent contractor relationship, however, is not so easily understood. The broker enters into a contract with the property owner to manage the property. The broker has the freedom to choose to accomplish the work personally, or by substituting other workers. The broker has multiple employment arrangements with more than one property owner. The broker's expenses and income are not those of the property owner. Either party can terminate the contract by giving the other party notice. The property owner has no right to control the manner in which the broker performs the task.

Independent Contractor
A person who renders services for a specified result under the control of a principal as to result and not as to the means by which such result is accomplished . . . *California Labor Code Section 3353*

The distinction between an employee and an independent contractor is important for federal and state income tax, social security tax withholding, worker's compensation, unemployment insurance, and other purposes. The real estate licensed salesperson status is determined by the facts of the employment, not by the title on the employment contract. The facts may include some of the following:

- Who provides the tools?
- Are instructions given on how to do the job?
- Is training provided by either party?
- Do both parties have an equal right to terminate the relationship?
- Are specific work hours required?
- Is payment by hour, week, month, tasks, the job?
- Who pays business and travel expenses?
- Are written or oral reports part of the job?
- What is the reporting process for accountability?

One reason for so much confusion on the employment status is that a licensed real estate salesperson could be an independent contractor for purposes of unemployment insurance, worker's compensation and tax withholding, while they are an employee for California real estate law purposes. Court decisions have uniformly held that a real estate salesperson is not an independent contractor:

> "A real estate salesman cannot contract in his own name...he can only be employed by a licensed real estate broker..., he cannot be employed by...any person other than the broker under whom he is at the time licensed..., and his license must remain in possession of his broker employer...who risks the supervision over the activities of his salesmen." *(Resnik v. Anderson and Miles, 109 Cal. App. 3rd 569.)*

MANAGEMENT COMPANY RECORDS

The major concern of all business entities is management of the company dollar. Without the economic benefits of potential profit, the management company could not remain in existence. The office manager is responsible for maintaining the income stream for operations. Annual budgets are prepared for forecasts, and compared to stabilized funding.

The income can be generated as a stand-alone property management fee, or as a part of other operations. As a stand-alone unit, the income can be management fees generated from properties managed, or a flat contract fee.

> **Example:** For a building that generates $50,000 a year income, the property management income could be $50,000 x 5% = $2,500 per month, or it could be a flat fee of $2,000 per month.

Many brokers, however, have the property management income equal the overhead costs to have the property management company manage the units of the broker, at no expense to the broker. This is done to retain control over the units and to defray the costs.

When the property management is part of another operation, the management fee is often treated differently than if it had to support itself, as a stand-alone unit. For corporate-owned property, the management has no income, per se. The building budget projected a $30,000 expense for managing the building, and the entire management organization has to work within this budgeted amount. The budget expense of the building becomes the management company income, from which the company operational expenses are allocated.

Another management fee structure is when the property management operation is part of another business. Typically, a real estate brokerage sales office will maintain property management accounts to generate only enough income to pay the overhead costs of the real estate office. These include the office rent and the employee cost for the property management department in addition to the office utilities. In this situation, the licensed real estate agents quote the prices, show the vacancies if there is no on-site manager, and negotiate leases. The property manager/secretary handles all trust account banking, types the rental agreements, prepares the legal notices (Pay or Quit, Rent Increases), and disburses owner's operating statements, all under the direct supervision and control of the broker.

The purpose is to provide a means to manage the various properties owned directly by the broker and agents in the office, or in partnership with clients, or as a direct service to clients for property they purchase through the sales office. Thus, the department does not have to be a profit-making operation, but is thought of rather in terms of break-even analysis. While generating more commissions from property sales and exchanges, and caring for the agent/broker properties, total income may not be a big profit center ideal, but rather compliment the other business operations.

Expenses

Expenses should be thought of as those outflows necessary to produce the income. They often may be reviewed in the context of long-term results. Workers may have unrealistic expectations of what should be provided. To be paid top salary, with maximum benefits, and also be high-tech too, may not be a short-term result the company can afford. If the property manager wants the firm to lay out the initial high front-end expenses of portable lap-top computers with forms in the memory, short-term pay increases may not be possible. In addition to the cost to develop and deliver training for the high-tech operations, there are on-going costs, such as the rates for portable telephone/communications link systems.

Efficient operations and streamlining are as vital to monitor within the expense analysis as is alleviating unnecessary expenses. Cutting basic necessities is unwise. The cost to train a new person for a position often exceeds the cost to give the former person a raise. The management must balance these wisely and make the executive decisions that will make the firm successful.

Budgets

A typical operating budget is shown below (Figure 12). Every business should prepare, maintain, and analyze a budget.

The management company has to see that the worker's compensation insurance for each property and for the company personnel is fully paid. Taxes for unemployment insurance and social security are mandated. The government often puts these expenses on the management company instead of the building owner, and the property manager must re-allocate the expense to the individual building owner.

Almost every city in California requires a separate business license fee for any city where a sign for a company is placed on the building—whether it be a "business" sign, a "for rent" sign or a "for sale" sign. The license fee is determined by total revenue dollars generated in that city. The property manager must allocate the total expense for the one license required for that city back to each property owner according to their proportional cost. Most cities require a business license fee for a laundry room, based upon a minimum fee or the total income of that business.

The operating ratios of any business vary by industry. A property management company executive should review its bank's standards for line-of-credit guidelines as one source of what's acceptable within their field. Another source is the Standards & Poors business rating system. An excellent rating for business guidelines to try to follow is the Dunn & Bradstreet business standard. Using these three as an initial base, the office manager can usually get the property manager and broker approvals for budgets.

PROPERTY MANAGEMENT COMPANY
MARKETING DEPARTMENT

G/L	INCOME/MONTH	January	February	March	April	May	June	July	August	September	October	November	December	TOTAL
202	Commissions Sales													
	(4/mo.@ $2000/ea)	8000.00	8000.00	8000.00	8000.00	8000.00	8000.00	8000.00	8000.00	8000.00	8000.00	8000.00	8000.00	96000.00
203	Commission—Leasing													
	(10/mo.@ $20/ea)	0.00	0.00	0.00	0.00	0.00	0.00	2000.00	2000.00	2000.00	2000.00	2000.00	2000.00	12000.00
204	Maint. Repair Fees	0.00	0.00	0.00	0.00	0.00	0.00	0.00	0.00	0.00	0.00	0.00	0.00	0.00
205	Management Fees													
	(1 mo.@$43/ea)	1720.00	1075.00	6450.00	6450.00	8600.00	8600.00	10750.00	10750.00	10750.00	10750.00	10750.00	10750.00	97395.00
206	Finders Fee	0.00	0.00	0.00	0.00	0.00	0.00	0.00	0.00	0.00	0.00	0.00	0.00	0.00
207	Late Fees	0.00	0.00	0.00	0.00	0.00	0.00	0.00	0.00	0.00	0.00	0.00	0.00	0.00
208	Referral Fees	300.00	0.00	150.00	150.00	200.00	200.00	250.00	250.00	300.00	3000.00	300.00	300.00	2700.00
211	Set-up Fee	500.00	300.00	1000.00	1000.00	1500.00	1500.00	2000.00	2000.00	2000.00	2250.00	2250.00	2250.00	18550.00
	25 owners @ $50 - 1250													
	10 owners @ $100 - 1000													
	TOTAL INCOME	10520.00	9375.00	15600.00	15600.00	18300.00	18300.00	23000.00	23000.00	23050.00	23300.00	23300.00	23300.00	226645.00

G/L	EXPENSES/MONTH	January	February	March	April	May	June	July	August	September	October	November	December	TOTAL
302	Commissions Paid													
	Salespersons	2400.00	2400.00	2900.00	3500.00	4000.00	4000.00	5000.00	5000.00	5000.00	5000.00	5000.00	5000.00	49200.00
	Unit Average	0.00	0.00	0.00	1500.00	3000.00	3000.00	3750.00	3750.00	3750.00	3750.00	3750.00	3750.00	30000.00
303	Lease Fee Paid													
	$500/mo. + $50/unit	0.00	0.00	0.00	0.00	0.00	0.00	1000.00	1500.00	2000.00	1000.00	1200.00	1500.00	8200.00
305	Management Fees Paid	0.00	0.00	0.00	0.00	0.00	0.00	0.00	0.00	0.00	0.00	0.00	0.00	0.00
306	Finders Fee Paid													
	In-House Refunds	100.00	150.00	200.00	250.00	300.00	350.00	400.00	450.00	500.00	550.00	600.00	650.00	4500.00
307	Late Fees Paid	0.00	0.00	0.00	0.00	0.00	0.00	0.00	0.00	0.00	0.00	0.00	0.00	0.00
315	Bonus	0.00	0.00	495.00	495.00	745.00	745.00	995.00	995.00	995.00	995.00	995.00	995.00	8450.00
320	Finders Fee	150.00	300.00	600.00	900.00	1200.00	1500.00	2100.00	2100.00	3000.00	3000.00	3000.00	3000.00	20850.00
322	Referral Fee	50.00	50.00	50.00	50.00	50.00	50.00	100.00	100.00	100.00	100.00	100.00	100.00	900.00
324	Rebate to Owner	40.00	40.00	80.00	160.00	200.00	240.00	320.00	400.00	400.00	400.00	400.00	400.00	3080.00
325	Appraisal Fee	0.00	0.00	0.00	0.00	0.00	0.00	0.00	0.00	0.00	0.00	0.00	0.00	0.00
329	Payroll													
		2500.00	2500.00	2650.00	2650.00	2700.00	2800.00	2750.00	2750.00	2750.00	2750.00	2750.00	2750.00	32300.00
	Admin. Asst.	1200.00	1200.00	1200.00	1280.00	1300.00	1300.00	1300.00	1300.00	1400.00	1400.00	1400.00	1400.00	15600.00
	Dept. Secretary (2)	1892.00	1900.00	2000.00	2100.00	2200.00	2300.00	2400.00	2500.00	2600.00	2700.00	2800.00	2900.00	28292.00
330	Contract Labor	0.00	0.00	2250.00	2534.00	2576.00	2626.00	2500.00	2500.00	2500.00	2500.00	2500.00	2500.00	24986.00
332	Membership Dues													
340	Refund to Owner	0.00	0.00	0.00	0.00	0.00	0.00	0.00	0.00	0.00	0.00	0.00	0.00	0.00
380	Deburse From Trust	0.00	0.00	0.00	0.00	0.00	0.00	0.00	0.00	0.00	0.00	0.00	0.00	0.00
401	Rent	500.00	500.00	500.00	500.00	500.00	500.00	500.00	500.00	500.00	500.00	500.00	500.00	6000.00
402	CAM													
	Telemarketing													
	PMN Paper													
404	Util-Electric	100.00	100.00	100.00	100.00	100.00	100.00	100.00	100.00	100.00	100.00	100.00	100.00	1200.00
405	Util-Natural Gas	50.00	50.00	50.00	50.00	50.00	50.00	50.00	50.00	50.00	50.00	50.00	50.00	600.00
406	Util-Water/Sewer	100.00	100.00	100.00	100.00	100.00	100.00	100.00	100.00	100.00	100.00	100.00	100.00	1200.00
407	Util-Refuse Service	0.00	0.00	0.00	0.00	0.00	0.00	0.00	0.00	0.00	0.00	0.00	0.00	0.00
408	Util-Combo	0.00	0.00	0.00	0.00	0.00	0.00	0.00	0.00	0.00	0.00	0.00	0.00	0.00
409	Telephone Service													
	100/mon/salesperson	200.00	500.00	250.00	350.00	400.00	400.00	500.00	500.00	500.00	500.00	500.00	500.00	5100.00
415	Maintenance Service	100.00	100.00	100.00	100.00	100.00	100.00	100.00	100.00	100.00	100.00	100.00	100.00	1200.00
417	Pest Control	0.00	0.00	0.00	0.00	0.00	0.00	0.00	0.00	0.00	0.00	0.00	0.00	0.00
418	Answering Service	100.00	100.00	100.00	100.00	100.00	100.00	100.00	100.00	100.00	100.00	100.00	100.00	1200.00
419	Bottled Water	0.00	0.00	0.00	0.00	0.00	0.00	0.00	0.00	0.00	0.00	0.00	0.00	0.00
420	Labor/Mater. Repairs	50.00	50.00	50.00	50.00	50.00	50.00	50.00	50.00	50.00	50.00	50.00	50.00	600.00
430	Legal Services	100.00	100.00	100.00	100.00	100.00	100.00	100.00	100.00	100.00	100.00	100.00	100.00	1200.00
431	Data Processing	0.00	0.00	0.00	0.00	0.00	0.00	0.00	0.00	0.00	0.00	0.00	0.00	0.00
432	Admin. Service	500.00	500.00	500.00	500.00	500.00	500.00	500.00	500.00	500.00	500.00	500.00	500.00	6000.00
620	Accounting Service	100.00	100.00	100.00	100.00	100.00	100.00	100.00	100.00	100.00	100.00	100.00	100.00	1200.00
441	Computer Hardware	100.00	100.00	100.00	100.00	100.00	100.00	100.00	100.00	100.00	100.00	100.00	100.00	1200.00
442	Computer Software	50.00	50.00	50.00	50.00	50.00	50.00	50.00	50.00	50.00	50.00	50.00	50.00	600.00
443	Computer Publication	0.00	0.00	0.00	0.00	0.00	0.00	0.00	0.00	0.00	0.00	0.00	0.00	0.00
444	Supplies-Computer	100.00	100.00	100.00	100.00	100.00	100.00	100.00	100.00	100.00	100.00	100.00	100.00	1200.00

445	Repairs-Computer	25.00	25.00	25.00	25.00	25.00	25.00	25.00	25.00	25.00	25.00	25.00	25.00	300.00
	Marketing Supplies													
	Microfishe	0.00	0.00	75.00	75.00	75.00	75.00	75.00	75.00	75.00	75.00	75.00	75.00	750.00
	REDI-Cross Director	0.00	0.00	0.00	0.00	0.00	0.00	0.00	0.00	0.00	0.00	200.00	200.00	200.00
453	Advertising													
	Yellow Pages	300.00	300.00	300.00	300.00	300.00	300.00	300.00	300.00	300.00	300.00	300.00	300.00	3600.00
	Pennysaver Cover	250.00	250.00	250.00	250.00	250.00	250.00	250.00	250.00	250.00	250.00	250.00	250.00	3000.00
	Property Mgmt News	0.00	150.00	0.00	150.00	0.00	150.00	0.00	150.00	0.00	150.00	0.00	150.00	900.00
	Key Chains	0.00	0.00	0.00	500.00	0.00	0.00	0.00	0.00	0.00	0.00	0.00	0.00	500.00
	Apt. Assn. Journal	300.00	300.00	300.00	300.00	300.00	300.00	300.00	300.00	300.00	300.00	300.00	300.00	3600.00
	IREM/CAR/Board	100.00	0.00	0.00	100.00	0.00	0.00	100.00	0.00	0.00	100.00	0.00	0.00	400.00
	Daily Breeze	100.00	100.00	100.00	100.00	100.00	100.00	100.00	100.00	100.00	100.00	100.00	100.00	1200.00
	Press Telegram	100.00	0.00	100.00	100.00	100.00	100.00	100.00	100.00	100.00	100.00	100.00	100.00	1100.00
	LA Times	100.00	0.00	100.00	100.00	100.00	100.00	100.00	100.00	100.00	100.00	100.00	100.00	1100.00
	Misc. Adv.	200.00	200.00	200.00	200.00	200.00	200.00	200.00	200.00	200.00	200.00	200.00	200.00	2400.00
454	Promotions (give away)	200.00	0.00	0.00	0.00	0.00	500.00	0.00	0.00	0.00	0.00	500.00	0.00	1200.00
455	Education	100.00	0.00	0.00	350.00	0.00	0.00	0.00	350.00	0.00	0.00	0.00	0.00	800.00
456	Flags/Banners/Signs	0.00	0.00	200.00	0.00	0.00	0.00	200.00	0.00	0.00	0.00	0.00	0.00	400.00
458	MLS/Board/IREM Dues	0.00	0.00	24000.00	0.00	0.00	0.00	0.00	0.00	0.00	0.00	0.00	0.00	24000.00
459	Listing Fee	100.00	100.00	100.00	100.00	100.00	100.00	100.00	100.00	100.00	100.00	100.00	100.00	1200.00
460	Misc. Sales Exp.	40.00	25.00	150.00	150.00	200.00	200.00	250.00	250.00	250.00	250.00	250.00	250.00	2265.00
461	Publications	10.00	10.00	10.00	25.00	25.00	25.00	50.00	50.00	50.00	50.00	50.00	50.00	405.00
465	Donations	20.00	20.00	20.00	20.00	20.00	20.00	50.00	50.00	50.00	50.00	50.00	50.00	420.00
467	Forms-Mgmt. Contract	40.00	25.00	150.00	150.00	200.00	200.00	250.00	250.00	250.00	250.00	250.00	250.00	2265.00
	Flyers/Printing	200.00	200.00	200.00	200.00	200.00	200.00	200.00	200.00	200.00	200.00	200.00	200.00	2400.00
	Photocopy Supplies	50.00	50.00	50.00	50.00	50.00	50.00	50.00	50.00	50.00	50.00	50.00	50.00	600.00
468	Supplies Office	100.00	150.00	100.00	150.00	100.00	200.00	100.00	200.00	100.00	200.00	100.00	200.00	1700.00
469	Notery Expenses	0.00	0.00	0.00	250.00	0.00	0.00	0.00	0.00	0.00	0.00	0.00	0.00	250.00
470	Postage/Mailings	760.00	760.00	760.00	760.00	760.00	760.00	760.00	760.00	760.00	760.00	760.00	760.00	9120.00
	PMN Brochure													
	Letters													
490	Vehicle Expense	0.00	0.00	50.00	100.00	100.00	100.00	200.00	200.00	200.00	200.00	200.00	200.00	1550.00
499	Misc. Operating Exp.	20.00	20.00	20.00	20.00	20.00	20.00	20.00	20.00	20.00	20.00	20.00	20.00	240.00
501	Business License	0.00	0.00	0.00	0.00	0.00	0.00	0.00	0.00	0.00	0.00	0.00	0.00	0.00
503	Prof. License/Fees	0.00	0.00	0.00	0.00	0.00	0.00	0.00	0.00	0.00	0.00	0.00	500.00	500.00
507	Membership Dues	0.00	0.00	0.00	0.00	0.00	0.00	0.00	0.00	0.00	0.00	0.00	500.00	500.00
513	Insurance-Auto	0.00	0.00	0.00	0.00	0.00	0.00	0.00	0.00	0.00	0.00	0.00	0.00	0.00
514	Insurance-Medical	140.00	140.00	140.00	140.00	140.00	140.00	140.00	140.00	140.00	140.00	140.00	140.00	1680.00
515	Insurance-Workmans	50.00	50.00	50.00	50.00	50.00	50.00	50.00	50.00	50.00	50.00	50.00	50.00	600.00
516	Insurance-Liability	0.00	0.00	0.00	0.00	0.00	0.00	0.00	0.00	0.00	0.00	0.00	0.00	0.00
517	Insurance-Bonds	0.00	0.00	0.00	0.00	0.00	0.00	0.00	0.00	0.00	0.00	0.00	0.00	0.00
518	Insurance-Fire	0.00	0.00	0.00	0.00	0.00	0.00	0.00	0.00	0.00	0.00	0.00	0.00	0.00
519	Insurance-Contents	0.00	0.00	0.00	0.00	0.00	0.00	0.00	0.00	0.00	0.00	0.00	0.00	0.00
610	Taxes-Payroll	503.00	504.00	527.00	536.00	558.00	576.00	580.00	590.00	608.00	617.00	626.00	635.00	6860.00
612	Taxes-Property	0.00	0.00	0.00	0.00	0.00	0.00	0.00	0.00	0.00	0.00	0.00	0.00	0.00
615	FIT (see G/L 610)													
616	SIT (see G/L 610)													
617	FICA (see G/L 610)													
618	SDI (see G/L 610)													
620	Tax Prep. (see G/L 432)	0.00	0.00	0.00	0.00	0.00	0.00	0.00	0.00	0.00	0.00	0.00	0.00	0.00
725	Gasoline	0.00	0.00	0.00	0.00	0.00	0.00	0.00	0.00	0.00	0.00	0.00	0.00	0.00
730	Travel Expenses	0.00	0.00	50.00	250.00	0.00	0.00	50.00	250.00	0.00	0.00	50.00	250.00	900.00
	Total (Non-Cash)	500.00	650.00	500.00	650.00	500.00	650.00	756.00	756.00	500.00	650.00	500.00	650.00	7262.00
	EXPENSES TOTAL	14290.00	14369.00	42652.00	23140.00	24594.00	26002.00	29665.00	30905.00	31723.00	31232.00	31791.00	33400.00	333763.00
	NET OPERATING INCOME	- 3770.00	- 4994.00	- 27052.00	- 7540.00	- 6294.00	- 7702.00	- 6665.00	- 7905.00	- 8673.00	- 7932.00	- 8491.00	- 10100.00	-107118.00

Audits

Audits are a very important part of the business. The first, personnel audits, can be performed by in-house personnel, or by paid specialists. Don't rely on feedback alone, as typically only negative comments reach management's ears. Outside persons are more objective and specially trained to check on how the on-site managers handle a vacancy, janitorial building "curb appeal" results, telephone inquiry, and repair request response. The biggest problem with personnel audits is the lack of allocation of funds in the budget to do the job.

Monetary audits should be ongoing. The person who writes the checks should balance the bank statement one month, then switch the next month with the person who makes the deposits. Every quarter, a supervisor should perform the task. Once a year, an accountant can independently audit the account. Any accounting department termination should have an audit before the termination is complete. This rotation method helps morale, relieves job boredom, and assures a better maintenance of accurate books.

The broker's trust account must comply with many specific requirements. It is important that all personnel working with the trust account(s) be properly trained on the details of the documentation process.

The *Business & Professions Code* defines the trust account responsibilities in *Section 101(e)*. Basic rules include keeping one owner's funds separate from another owner's funds. Another rule is keeping any owner's funds separate from the funds of the broker. Commingling is a serious violation. Another serious violation is called conversion, when the broker actually uses an owner's funds for his or her own purposes. The California Department of Real Estate requires that the trust account be balanced at least once every 30 days.

A new California Real Estate Commissioner regulation, *Regulation 2831.2,* effective April 1988, for brokers who deposit trust funds into a trust fund bank account is that they must now reconcile their trust fund records at least once a month. Two records that must be reconciled are the "Record for all Trust Funds Received and Disbursed" (Regulation 2831) and "Separate Beneficiary Records" (Regulation 2831.1).

Trust Fund
A bank account which physically segregates client funds from broker's own funds.

In addition to maintaining complete records for owner income and expenses (Figure 13), the property manager handles tenant deposit funds. Both *AD2289* and *Civil Code Section 1950.5* cover residential property, and *1950.7* covers non-residential security deposits. Specific areas covered by the law on deposits include:

- All deposit money is refundable, no matter what it's called (i.e., key deposit, cleaning fee, waterbed deposit, pet deposit).
- The claim of the tenant to this money comes before any creditors of the landlord (i.e., bankruptcy, foreclosure).
- Allowable deductions from a deposit are unpaid rent, tenant-caused damages, repairs, or cleaning.
- The landlord must furnish a written statement showing the amount received, the amount spent (if any), and the amount disbursed to the tenant.
- All deposits must be returned to the tenant, with the proper accounting, within two weeks after the premises were vacated.
- Bad faith retention of deposits may subject the landlord to a $200 cost, plus the actual damages caused to the tenant.
- Tenant deposit money transferred to another party requires that the tenant receive the name, street address, and telephone number of where the funds are held.
- The maximum deposit on an unfurnished unit is first month's rent plus two month's rent (total three months), and on furnished units is first month's rent plus three month's (total four months).

As a matter of practice, owners want an itemized list of income, and a rent roll, showing who paid, how much, and when they paid. The property manager likes to review the date paid to determine the quality of the tenant. The owner also wants to see an itemized list of checks

	CONDITION			
	MOVE-IN		MOVE-OUT	
Bedrooms	#1	#2	#1	#2
Doors and Locks	OK	OK		
Carpeting	NEW	NEW		
Floors & Baseboards	OK	OK		
Walls and Ceiling	OK	OK		
Windows and Screens	OK	OK		
Draperies	NONE	NONE		
Electrical Fixtures	OK	OK		
Electrical Switches, Outlets	OK	OK		
Closets, Doors, Tracks	GOOD	GOOD		
Misc. SMOKE DETECTOR	(1) NEW	(1) NEW		

Bedrooms	#3	#4 or NONE	#3	#4 or ____
	NONE			
Doors and Locks				
Carpeting				
Floors & Baseboards				
Walls and Ceiling				
Windows and Screens				
Draperies				
Electrical Fixtures				
Electrical Switches, Outlets				
Closets, Doors, Tracks				
Misc.				

Bathrooms	#1	#2	#1	#2
Doors and Locks	OK	NONE		
Floors & Baseboards	OK			
Walls and Ceiling	OK			
Windows and Screens	OK			
Window Covering	NONE			
Shower, Tub	CLEAN			
Shower Door, Curtain	NONE			
Toilet	CLEAN			
Sink, Medicine Cabinet	CLEAN			
Plumbing Fixtures	OK			
Electrical Fixtures, Fan	OK			
Electrical Switches, Outlets	OK			
Towel Racks	LOOSE			
Misc. TILE COUNTERTOP	1 TILE CHIPPED			

Other Items				
Heating	OK			
Air Conditioning	NONE			
Patio, Balcony	DIRTY			
Yard Areas	NONE			
Fencing	NONE			
Garage or Carport	LEAVES			
Misc. NEW UNIT DOOR LOCKS	NEW			
LAUNDRY ROOM	CLEAN			

UNIT INSPECTED AND ACCEPTED AS NOTED	UNIT INSPECTED AND VACATED AS NOTED
Date ____________	Date ____________
Signature of Tenant	Signature of Tenant
Signature of Landlord/Agent	Signature of Landlord/Agent

Reprinted with permission, California Association of Realtors®.

The bank balance is positive (+$100), but this is the illegal act of COMINGLING. Owner Jones used owner Smith's money to make the 4/1 mortgage loan payment, because one of Jones' tenants rent checks bounced.

paid, date paid, and payable to whom. Owners review the income and expense statements, as do the property managers. It is part of the responsibility of the accounting department to review the trust account records, passing them along to the property manager to review prior to distribution to the property owner.

The government also has banking requirements that must be met. These include who may sign on the account, signatory identification, opening accounts with taxpayer identification numbers, minimum daily balances, title held on the account, business teller machine deposits, holding period from time funds are deposited until the bank allows them to be available for use, endorsement stamps and how the backs of checks are endorsed. Most banks will not open an account in a business name without seeing proof of the actual, recorded DBA ("Doing Business As") Fictitious Name from the county recorder.

The property manager is usually assigned the task of seeing that the data is available in a timely manner for the preparation of tax returns. With on-site managers and employees, quarterly payroll tax forms must be completed and filed by specific dates to avert penalties. Annual tax returns and W-2, 1099, DE3 and similar forms must be supervised to see that they are done for all payroll.

Payroll records must be kept for annual audits, such as worker's compensation insurance, as well as taxes. Liability insurance, error's and omission's insurance, and other payroll records are used for premium calculations.

Client and Customer Records

Tenant security deposit itemization statements should be kept for a minimum of seven years from the date the management company ceased managing the property, if the management company collected the original deposits or if deposits were disbursed to another person from notification of transfer. Records retention should be kept according to specified company policy (Figure 14).

Monthly bills and disbursement statements can be handled in several ways. Some operations choose to close out all records every month and send the owner the original invoice, a copy of the check, and the

Figure 14

	Years Retained
1. Administration:	
☐ Property acquisition	5-7 years after sale
☐ Deeds and mortgages	Permanent
☐ Management agreement	3-5 years after termination
☐ Contracts and other legal documents	3-5 years after termination
☐ General management matters	5-7
☐ Routine correspondence	2-5
☐ Employee personnel files	10-Permanent
☐ Payroll registers	10
☐ Time cards/records	3-7
☐ Payroll tax reports and payment receipts	7-10
☐ Employee expense reports	3-5
☐ Personnel evaluations	7-10
2. Maintenance Files:	
☐ General work orders and logs	3-5
☐ Equipment repairs and maintenance	3-5 years after disposal
☐ Renovation and rehabilitation	7-10
☐ Property additions	Permanent
3. Resident Management Files:	
☐ Policies and rules	3-Permanent
☐ Accounts receivable details	7-10
☐ Legal filings and records	3-10
☐ Resident correspondence	1-10
4. Marketing and Leasing:	
☐ Market research and plans	5-7
☐ Marketing and leasing records	3-10
☐ Leases	3-5 years after termination
5. Financial Records:	
☐ General ledger	Permanent
☐ Supporting ledgers/journals	10-Permanent
☐ Financial statements	3-Permanent
☐ Financial workpapers	1-7
☐ Copies of invoices	7-10
☐ Bank statements and cancelled checks	7-10
☐ Bank reconciliations	7-10
☐ Cash receipts and disbursements records	7-10
☐ Inventory records	5-7
☐ Fixed assets records	Permanent
☐ Insurance policies and records	3-7 years after termination
☐ Tax returns	7-Permanent
☐ Tax workpapers	7-Permanent
☐ Tax correspondence	5-Permanent

	By	Date
Prepared	______	______
Prepared	______	______
Reviewed	______	______

statement on a monthly basis. This eliminates management company storage problems if many accounts are handled. The disadvantage is that the property manager must either bear the cost to photocopy the invoices to keep a copy in the file for reference, or bear the cost to transfer the data to a maintenance log sheet, or else have no way to reference back billing data. In practical application, also, the owners may often misplace their storage of this necessary tax information and will consequently ask the property manager to obtain a duplicate bill.

Another method of handling client bills and invoices is to send the owner a monthly operating statement, showing funds received and itemized expenses, but not to give copies of the actual bills. All bills are kept at the management company. The year-end accounting statement, showing cumulative annual income and expenses has all bills for the year attached, so that it is one complete package for the owner to review and forward to the tax preparer.

Using this latter method, it is also common for these management company operations to include a comparable market analysis indicating the current approximate value of the property, and the owner's equity position in order to analyze the investment. From this data, the tax preparer or property manager/real estate sales and exchange department can calculate the owners' return on their investment. It may be time to trade up, pull out equity to purchase more, sell, or determine how much longer to keep the property.

The handling of company books, audit materials, bank records, tenant accounting and owner statement data brings up the need to analyze filing, storage, and retrieval of the information. The location of storage should be somewhat fire proof and secure, yet accessible. If storage is offsite, such as at a mini-warehouse storage facility, it may be very inconvenient to get to the data, and may waste the time of expensive employees. If the location is on-site, such as a basement, moisture can get into the paper and cause mildew on the records; or when using attics, mice and silverfish eat paper quickly. If the archives are stored on the premises, the floor space rent per square foot may be very costly, in addition to the fact that it may be in the way of workers who need the space to generate new business and process current business. Storage may be file cabinets of folders, computer discs, microfilm, magnetic tape, telephone message books, rent receipts, tax and government filing forms, cancelled checks, books, former personnel records.

NEW MANAGEMENT ACCOUNT FORMS

Many forms are used to process an account through the management company operation. All may be done by a single person, such as in a one-broker business. They may each be done by different departments and personnel, crossing state lines, computer linked, or by manual sheets. Completing this necessary paperwork is part of the business.

Management Inquiry

It takes many inquiries to produce enough appointments to get new business on a regular basis. Prior to obtaining a new account, many prospects will make inquiries about management company services. Some prospects are not interested immediately, but are setting up future arrangements for their business affairs. Some prospects are owners inquiring about how to handle their own rental problem, and these may be distinct client possibilities. Others are actually shopping around, while some inquire just to see what the services offer, as many income-producing property owners do not know what property management involves. Some have misconceptions about the services, so they call to ask. Few owners call and want to immediately sign a contract within the hour—unless one spouse has just had a stroke, or the property was found vacant over the weekend and there is an immediate need to handle an eviction or vacancy.

All inquiries should be logged on some kind of form, and filed for future reference. For multi-location operations, the business manager may want to call up daily inquiries on a computer through the use of modem data transfer to a central marketing department to have a daily count of future business. Larger firms use 3 x 5 or 5 x 8 cards because of the size and ease of filing, handling, sorting, and storage. Medium-sized to smaller firms may wish to use 8½ x 11 page sheets in a log book (Figure 15).

The purpose is to be able to retrieve the data immediately should the owner call back again. Even if a different person takes the next call, the caller and marketing person pick up the conversation as if this call is

Figure 15

Management Inquiry

Inquiry Date: ____________ Time: ____________ By: ____________

Inquiry Name(s) __________________ Phone work: (____)__________

Owner's address________________________ Home: (____)__________

City _______________ State _______________ Zip _______________

Rental Property Address(es) ______________________________________

____

____

Directions to the Property ____

Number of Units _______ House _______ Condo _______ Apt. _______

Bedrooms: _____ Baths: _____ Yard: _____ Air: _____ Garage: _____

Rent Not Less Than $_______/Month Fees Quoted: Mgmt $25/_______%

Leasing Fee $_________ + $_________

One-Shot $_________ + $_________

Brochure mailed out on ____________

Property Profile Ordered: ___________ Owner Letter #1 out on _________

Owner Letter #2 out on _________

Owner Letter #3 out on _________

Owner Letter #4 out on _________

Reason Owner is Renting Property: _________________________________

__________________________________ VACANT BY: __________

REMARKS: ____

____

____

FOLLOW-UP: ____

____

______________________________ TAKEN BY: ____________________

an extension of the original one, without much disruption. In addition, the marketing department staff will use the inquiry form to follow up on future mailings (Figure 15) along with telephone follow up to the potential client.

New Account Set-Up

A new account folder should include not only a copy of both the inquiry data and the signed management contract, but many other items. A property profile shows the way title was taken and the signatures of those with title. These signatures should be checked against the signature on the management contract to see that an authorized person gave the management company the necessary powers to act. On an eviction, tenants can challenge this and the proper contractual authority may have to be proven to a judge.

Management company data sheets should be included which show if the management company or owner pays lenders, utilities, vendors, etc. The data sheet should list full name, address, phone number, account numbers, due dates, late date, penalty, contact, balance due, interest rate, and other pertinent information (Figure 16). A sheet should also contain data on the tenant(s): name, address, billing address, phone numbers, due date, deposits, history, last rent raise, rent increase calculation, etc. Building data should include past income and expense records, owner's attorney, accountant, and insurance agents.

All new accounts need a signed letter from the owner authorizing the release of data and showing the power to act. If the management company is taking over existing tenants, an introduction letter is appropriate (Figure 17). A summary sheet may list quick staff reference data to be distributed within the management office (Figure 18).

Additional new account file data could include a picture of the property, schematic/floor plan/layout of the property, units and lot, infrastructure, streets, utilities, etc.

All contracts should also be included in the file: tenant rental agreements, laundry room contract, pool service and gardener contract, etc.

Figure 16

New Property Information Data *To Property Manager*

	Date	Who
1. Contract Signed by Property owner................	________	________
2. Contract Signed by Our Firm Authorized Person......	________	________
3. Copy of Contract Sent Back to Owner..............	________	________
4. Receipt for Owner's Deposit Funds to Open Acct.	________	________
5. Owner Code # Given	________	________

Property Address: ______________________ Owner Code #________

City: ______________________ State: ________ Zip: ________

Units Numbered: ______________________________

6. Owner Information:

Owner's Name(s) ______________ ______________

Address ______________ ______________

City_____State _______ Zip _______ City_____State _______ Zip _______

Home Phone (_____)__________ Home Phone (_____)__________

Work Phone (_____)__________ Work Phone (_____)__________

7. Management Information:

Owner's Maximum Expense Allowance ....$________

Owner's Permanent Operating Reserve Account ....$________

Monthly Management Fee ....________% or $________

One-Time Set Up Fee ....$________

8. Other Information: ______________________________

____

____

____

____

____

____

9. Unit #A ________________ Copy of Rental Agreement ________________
   Unit #B ________________ Copy of Rental Agreement ________________
   Unit #C ________________ Copy of Rental Agreement ________________
   Unit #D ________________ Copy of Rental Agreement ________________
   *(List additional units on back side of this page)
10. Keys #A _______ Rent Paid To What Date________________________
    #B _______ Rent Paid To What Date________________________
    #C _______ Rent Paid To What Date ________________________
    #D _______ Rent Paid To What Date ________________________
11. Tenant's Names:
    Unit #A__________________________ Phone: ________________________
    Unit #B__________________________ Phone: ________________________
    Unit #C__________________________ Phone: ________________________
    Unit #D__________________________ Phone: ________________________
12. Copy Of All Rent Increases & 3-Day Notice to Pay or Quits
13. Equipment Warranties
14. All Repair & Maintenance Receipts For This Calander Year
15. Copy Of All Tenant Rental Applications/Credit Reports
16. List Of Repairmen/Service Companies/Other Bills
    Condo Association: ____
    Pool Service: ____
    Gardener: ____
    Laundry Room: ____
17. Other Comments/Special Instructions: ____________________________
    ____
    ____
    ____
    ____

New Property Information Data— *To Accounting*

Property Street Address ______________________ Owner Code ________

\# of Units ____________ City: ____________ Zip: ____________

1. FIRST TRUST DEED HOLDER: ______________________________

   Mailing address: ______________ City ______________ Zip: ________

   Loan # __________ Pymt.: __________ @ ______ % Balance $ __________

2. SECOND TRUST DEED HOLDER: ______________________________

   Mailing address: ______________ City ______________ Zip: ________

   Loan # __________ Pymt.: __________ @ ______ % Balance $ __________

3. THIRD TRUST DEED HOLDER: ______________________________

   Mailing address: ______________ City ______________ Zip: ________

   Loan # __________ Pymt.: __________ @ ______ % Balance $ __________

4. FOURTH TRUST DEED HOLDER: ______________________________

   Mailing address: ______________ City ______________ Zip: ________

   Loan # __________ Pymt.: __________ @ ______ % Balance $ __________

5. INSURANCE COMPANY: ______________________________

   Mailing address: ______________ City ______________ Zip: ________

   Policy # ________ Agent: __________ (____) ________ Type: Fire, Liab., Equit., (Circle One)

6. INSURANCE COMPANY: ______________________________

   Mailing address: ______________ City ______________ Zip: ________

   Policy # ________ Agent: __________ (____) ________ Type: Fire, Liab., Equit., (Circle One)

7. UTILITY COMPANIES: (Circle the ones the owner pays):

   Electric __________ (______) __________ Gas __________ (______) __________

   Water __________ (______) __________ Trash __________ (______) __________

   Sewer __________ (______) __________ Telephone __________ (______) __________

8. Mgmt Firm to pay the property taxes? (Circle One) Yes No
   (Send a copy of the last bill).

I acknowledge receipt of a copy of this form and certify that the facts are true and correct under penalty of perjury; Any items left blank at this date will be furnished by owner within 30 days.

Dated: ______________________ Owner: ______________________

Figure 17

Dear Resident:

The Owner of the property you rent has hired our firm to handle the management and daily operations of the property. We will collect the rents, serve notices for non-payment of rent, and handle maintenance, eviction, and repair problems that you may have from time to time.

All future rental payments are payable to our firm. Rents should be in the form of cashier's check or money order ONLY, as we explained the dangers of dealing with cash on the premises. Pay your rent to no other persons. We will send you a receipt. Make rent payable to:

To: Sunbelt Investments— (Your Apt #)
P.O. Box 1659
Downey, CA 90240

We look forward to being of service to you, and the opportunity we will have in working with you in the future. Please do not hesitate to contact us if you have any questions.

There is no need for an On-Site Manager to handle these units. You may call the office at (213) 861-3835 to report any problems or needs that you may have. We have forms for you to fill out for any repair request that you may have. In order for the workman to be paid, you need to sign off that the work is completed. You will need to be present to let in workmen for repairs, as we do not use pass keys.

If no one is in the office when you call, please leave a message with your name and address and your message on the answering machine, along with your telephone number. We have many properties, so do not just say "Apt. 1" without a street name. We will always try to get back to you within the shortest possible time. For a true emergency, there is "911" or the utility companies.

WE WILL BE ON THE PREMISES FOR RENT COLLECTION ON THE FIRST OF THE MONTH BY 6:00 PM OR SERVE NOTICES TO PAY RENT.

Cordially,

Property Manager

Figure 18

		MARKETING DEPARTMENT								NEW ACCOUNTS					PROPERTY MANAGEMENT DEPARTMENT	
Owner Name Date Signed	Address City	No. Units #	Scheduled Rents $	%	Scheduled Fee $	Collect From Owner $	Set Up Fee $	Reserve $	Max Exp $	Date/# Code# Date/DP	Total Collect Rents $	Collected Fee $	Special Notes (V)acant (E)viction Coupont	Projects Transfer Date	Date Rec'd	Property Supervisor

Management Contract

The most important form is the legally binding contract, called the Management Agreement. It states the terms and conditions for employment. The purpose of the Management Agreement is to formalize the understanding between the parties. A careful review of each portion of the contract is necessary.

Most firms use pre-printed contracts. Several excellent forms are in use. The National Association of Realtors, Institute of Real Estate Management contract is regularly reviewed by national professionals. It is the most formalized contract, consisting of many pages. The California Association of Realtors has a two-sided, one-page contract that contains less contract clauses, but easily breaks down various options for fee structure. Stationary stores carry standardized forms, but check the copyright date for current validity. The Apartment Association is recommended when looking for any contract regarding rental property.

It is best to have the legal council for the management company review all portions of the management contract, as they will be called upon to defend it. Remember, don't violate copyright laws if you try to write your own management contract.

One method used by larger firms is to have all clauses in a computer data bank, that may be deleted or used as negotiated, so each contract is individually customized. This program does, however, have certain "boilerplate" clauses that cannot be altered, such as for liability or indemnity. This allows the marketing person and property owner to specifically negotiate such items as: use of lockbox, fees, reserves, maximum expense, etc. The management contract should contain clauses which cover all of the following:

- **Names.** Complete, legal names and contact of all parties.
- **Agent powers.** Delegation of authority and restrictions, including the right to hire, fire, and train the owner's personnel.
- **Owner responsibility.** Powers retained by the property owner, or those the management company will not take.
- **Money.** The fees, commissions, and related costs by the owner. The agent handling and reporting of owner funds.
- **Third-party responsibility.** Government audit and reports, on-site personnel, insurance, brokerage, etc.

The property management contract may include some agreement for the future sale or exchange of the property. This listing arrangement may be a part of the contract, or it may be a separate agreement realty form. In either event, any reference to the broker/owner sale, now or in the future, requires that two additional contracts be part of the necessary paperwork—the agency relationship and the real estate transfer disclosure statement, which are both reviewed in Chapter 14.

The management contract termination should include specifics such as future time costs for court appearances, accounting reports, insurance audit, etc. These will probably differ depending on whether the contract is terminated by the owner or by the management company. Forecasting future services must be a portion of the consideration.

INCREASING MANAGEMENT OFFICE BUSINESS

A professional manager can increase income by increasing the volume of business handled by the firm. As was discussed earlier, fee management accounts can be solicited from individual owners. Professional business referrals can increase activity—referrals by tax preparers, attorneys, developers, syndicators, etc. Brokerage houses can increase accounts through their real estate sales and exchange activity. An additional method is to buy existing accounts from other firms, or to purchase another business entity entirely.

Buying Existing Accounts

Trust in the integrity and capability of individuals within a firm should be the foremost goal for any property manager. This is especially true for referral business. Solid credentials help a business maintain credibility within the business community and is necessary to get a call from another business thinking about divesting itself from its property management accounts.

Some businesses are not in the management business exclusively, and may handle some aspects of management for their clients. These firms may be in the tax-preparation business, assisting on investments such as real estate, and using their computer account equipment to process units. Insurance brokerage persons may handle a limited number of accounts. The real estate sales office, however, manages the greatest number of units managed of any business that is not exclusively a property management company.

It is not unusual for these firms to handle anywhere from 10 to 100 owners, representing under 130 units. It is not a profitable business until about 200 units are being handled. When firms primarily in a non-property management industry handle over 20 units they are taking vital business time away from their main objectives. At 75 to 120 units, they are often losing money because of the management. These reasons often prompt the business owner to consider selling off these units.

Good references make good referrals. If word gets around the Chamber of Commerce, banking operations personnel, real estate board office, and similar local businesses that you purchase accounts, this will help encourage others. If your reputation for fairness is well communicated, along with your professional image, prospects will at least listen to your solicitation, even if not presently interested in selling. It establishes future leads. A brochure should outline your referral policy (Figure 19).

The agreement to purchase accounts should contain specific terms regarding future business. If the client wants to sell the property in the future, have a written broker agreement specifying that the former unit manager (seller) gets 100% of the commission for the sale. Alternative plans can be that the seller gets 80% of the commission and the buyer gets 20%, as a referral fee for keeping the client in contact for the future transaction. Or, the seller can receive a 20% referral fee on any future sale of this unit, or purchase of additional units, and the buying property manager gets 80% of the commission. It is also common to have other commission splits, such as a 50/50 split on all future transactions with the same client.

Aside from commissions on purchase and sale by the client, there is also the purchase price of the actual accounts. One common method is to pay a flat fee dollar amount, such as $300 to $600 per unit. This rate would include all rights to the future business of the owner and the units in regards to the management fee income, separate from any sales commission agreement.

Figure 19

Ask the following agents who have kept their listing after our services:

- Anita Jepson
  Happy Home Realtors, Upland
- Larry Jones
  Jones Investments, Riverside
- Jerry Garcia
  Sunshine Home Finders, San Diego
- Barbara Jorgenson
  Dream Home Realtors, San Jose
- Steve Girmant
  Neighborhood Realtors, Chino

Other references on file

Office meetings available by appointment

WANTED!

REFERRALS

REWARD

Professional Property Management
XXX-XXXX

DON'T LOSE THAT CLIENT!

ESCROW PROBLEMS?
Get that client off your back. Yes, we can rent the property for a short term to help cover costs.

INVESTOR BUYS UNITS AND EXPECTS YOU TO GET A TENANT INTO PROPERTY . . . FOR FREE?
Third-party expertise gives you credibility when you hire the Specialists in the rental market.

YOUR OWN RENTAL PROPERTY VACANT?
Get large deposits and thorough investigation on prospective tenants.

TOO BUSY WITH BUY/SELL SITUATION?
Hire us to do what we do best, while you do best what earns you the most;buying/selling/exchanging/tax/escrow.

DEAL FELL THRU?
Owner has to go — faces vacancy? Let us rent it now while you save listing for later. Give us the place to sign and we'll GUARANTEE it in writing.

*Free Dinner for Two for Referral
*Plus Future Listing Saved for You!!

RENTING MORE NOW, BUT ENJOYING IT LESS?

You can charge 6% of a year's lease to find a tenant, and after you lease the unit, we can take over the full-time day-to-day operations while we keep you posted for your future sale.

You can handle your client when you put them into and out of the property and you hire us to handle the tenant/rental/inspection/maintenance period.

You can charge 6% of a year's lease, then hire us to find the tenant on our flat fee arrangement–
$250 for any rent over $650/month
$200 for rent $500 to $649/month
$150 for rent under $500/month
YOU KEEP THE DIFFERENCE!

Call us for any special service we can offer to you.

XXX-XXXX

Purchasing A Business

There are many benefits to purchasing an existing property management business. The business is already in place and operational. Changes can be made, over time, but these are easier to implement than starting from scratch. The furniture, equipment, personnel, office location, and visibility in the community are already in place. There is existing income from the first day. Marketing efforts are spent on radiating confidence to existing owners, while soliciting new accounts to add to the base, rather than having to go into the marketplace to solicit each new account.

The purchase of the entire property management business is similar to the purchase of any other business, in that it should be escrowed under the bulk sales contract transfer. The sales price may include trade fixtures, for which the seller would produce an itemized inventory description, including furniture and equipment, using a bill of sale to convey title to the property. The purchaser would have to file a new fictitious business name, DBA (doing business as), while the seller could file an Abandonment of DBA. This should be done even if the purchaser plans to use another name for the business, so that the seller cannot sell the old name to anyone else, or open another business by the same name. A covenant not to compete in the same business for a period of five years within a ten-mile radius of the business being sold should be part of the sales contract.

Several business operations require special attention. The timing for the sale should correspond with the accounting cycle of the business. One superior method is for the old and new business to run side-by-side for the last month of changeover. This prevents clients from being lost in the transfer, since each management agreement is a personal contract between the broker and property owner. It is not transferrable. Each owner must sign a new management agreement with the purchaser of the business, and the seller of the business should assist in this process. In addition, the trust account funds are not transferrable to another broker, and each owner must approve the balance, as the seller would write a check payable in the property owner's name, which needs to be endorsed by that owner so it can be deposited into the new purchaser's trust account.

Specific agreements between the parties would include the terms of a pre-sale agreement and a post-sale agreement. The handling of vendors, such as inspection prior to payment of ongoing bills, is an important business matter. Legal cases that are in progress should be specified, because the seller may have to be available to appear in court as the person who prepared and/or served notices affecting the tenancy that is in dispute.

The terms of the sale affect the cooperation between the parties a great deal. If the seller wants an all-cash buyout or lump sum payment, the price is often lower. This price can be determined as was discussed above, at $300 to $600 per unit, for each 12-month remaining contract, and prorated for each portion left. Another method is to pay 50% of the remaining contract management fee. Some firms use three to six months of the present management fees, but these do not take any future rent increases into account in the price.

If the seller carries back a loan for any portion of the purchase price, then all parties have the incentive to maximize future profits so the buyer stays liquid enough to make the payment to the seller. The buyer should not squander company assets by sudden changes, which decreases income. When the buyer handles any escrow sale for any management account, the balance of the funds due the seller for that account should be paid in full at the close of escrow. Under a partial cash and partial loan arrangement, the seller should consult his or her tax preparer to determine the amount of tax that must be paid upon the sale of the business. The payment on the note can be interest only, with a balloon due at a future date, fully amortized, or tied to the business income and payments spread over several years. A good business analyst can give guidelines, as can business bankers and business tax specialists, on measuring the value of a business.

In addition to the account values, however, is that intangible asset, called "goodwill", which is much more difficult to determine. This is the ongoing expectation of future business, based upon the past reputation with the industry and community. This should be valued separately.

CHAPTER 13–QUIZ

1. A good office layout would include all of the following except:

   a. a conference table and reception area/waiting room
   b. a bookcase library for reference materials
   c. walking through an office to get to another room
   d. security on rent receipts and office forms

2. Before starting any business, a checklist would include the:

   a. amount fees can be cut to obtain business contacts
   b. ability to borrow from relatives
   c. number of accounts that can be taken from the property management company last worked for
   d. willingness to work long, hard hours to get started

3. Organizational charts:

   a. are set by the Institute of Real Estate Management
   b. have rigid standards for clearly defined structures for all management company operations
   c. vary according to size of company, and number of units.
   d. would be the same for all company policies

4. Divisions for a policy manual would include all but which of the following?

   a. Owner's name, address, and telephone number
   b. History of the business and business objective
   c. Job duties, descriptions, and responsibilities
   d. General rules of employment

5. Most property managers:

   a. write a newsletter to the property owners
   b. have taken a course in real estate principles and law
   c. have studied insurance and credit
   d. clean common areas

6. The facts used to determine independent contractor or employee include which items listed below?

   a. Who owns the auto driven to work?
   b. Who provides the tools?
   c. How many total hours worked?
   d. What is the mode of business travel?

7. A broker trust account:

   a. must be reconciled at least once a month
   b. can have one owner with a negative balance and another owner with a positive balance, so long as the total bank balance is a positive number
   c. has to give owners a monthly statement of their funds
   d. requires tenants to receive monthly accounting of their deposit funds

8. Management agreement contracts should be retained for how many years after termination of the working relation?

   a. two-five years
   b. three-five years
   c. five-seven years
   d. ten years

9. The purpose of the management inquiry sheet is to:

   a. be able to retrieve data for call backs
   b. price management unit fees
   c. set up ongoing file folder processing
   d. get all necessary data to manage the property

10. The management contract should include clauses covering:

    a. fees, powers, responsibilities
    b. authority, property expenses, powers
    c. rent rates, fees, authority
    d. hours, vacation, duties

CHAPTER 13–QUIZ ANSWERS

1. c
2. d
3. c
4. a
5. b
6. b
7. a
8. b
9. a
10. a

14

Property Management Legal and Insurance Aspects

References

Kimball, T.C. "Beware of Eviction Delay Firms!" *California Rental Housing,* Fall 1988.

Fisher, Colleen. "How Fair is Fair Housing?" *Units,* Sept./Oct. 1988.

Last Chapter Review

The last chapter outlined managing a property management office. We discussed choosing the office location on the basis of the type of property managed and the structure of office ownership. Management fees, the physical office layout and its equipment, and office policies and procedures were also discussed. Company records and forms were examined, in addition to the management contract and management accounts.

Chapter Overview

Making your way through the legal maze and insurance hurdles in today's business world can seem overwhelming. This chapter outlines the steps necessary to prepare and serve legal notices, terminate a tenancy, and process an eviction. Laws and court cases are reviewed in many areas of practice, as well as the rules regarding discrimination. Insurance types, coverages, the parties, and the property managers' duties are also outlined.

PROPERTY MANAGEMENT AUTHORITY

One of the most difficult jobs of the property manager is to identify and maintain the authority of all parties. The manager must educate all office personnel on the organizational chart so that internal work flows in a smooth pattern. Likewise, external contacts also have clear lines of authority that the property manager must work within.

The management company, of course, gets its power to act through the management contract. This document spells out the responsibilities and duties of both the owner and the management firm. By contracting for services, the owner actually relieves him or herself of many areas of liability regarding the property, as much of the burden has been transferred to the property manager.

The management company takes the entire bundle of duties and delegates specific tasks to various persons. These may include in-house employees who handle money, accounting, filing, etc. Or the tasks may be delegated to outside, hired contractors, such as a phone answering service, maintenance, and leasing agents. The powers of authority in these relationships come from the employment agreement.

Education

The property manager must educate all employees and independent contractors as to their responsibilities, and also as to what is not their responsibility. This means that the property owner must be educated about the laws of the rental market (what is illegal), as well as the duties and obligations of property ownership. The property manager must also educate the tenants as to their duties and obligations while renting the property. This education is often done on an individual basis, situation by situation. Some management companies use newsletters to help disseminate educational information. Apartment association magazines are excellent sources of information on these matters.

Education also means training oneself on the newest laws, projected industry direction, and economic, financial, and management techniques. This helps property managers remain industry experts in this very specialized field of real estate. Continuing education courses, articles, *CPM Aspects*, and the *Journal of Property Management*, plus annual Institute of Real Estate Management compiled data all contribute to this growth.

The property manager's authority includes the training of all on-site managers. In-house orientation and training classes are an excellent way to accomplish this goal. Audio-visual cassettes accompanied by training manuals can be an effective way to train managers on such subjects as: effective advertisements, showing vacancies, qualifying prospects, telephone techniques, etc. Seminars are more costly, but no training may be costlier still.

Communications

Communications are part of the property manager's responsibilities. These can include recording devices, newsletters, training seminars, and personal contact. We have already outlined many good communication devices for all parties. Owners like prompt monthly accounting statements, annual property market evaluation, rent grid comparisons to know current market conditions, and a periodic property condition report or photograph. Tenants appreciate tips like a water-saving guide, and prior notice of intent to enter the premises.

Staff, vendors, and contractors appreciate communication concerning how well they are carrying out their authority and responsibility. Two positive comments for every negative one makes for good interpersonal development. Performance reviews can be guidelines for future training. Reviewing the written assignment of duties can show management if they are on base or whether corrections and adjustments need to be made. Reviewing the owner's goals and objectives annually is an excellent method of assessing performance to try to produce the desired results.

LEGAL SYSTEMS AND EVICTION STEPS

Legal System

California and the Southwest evolved in a different manner than the rest of the United States. Our laws are a combination of the feudal system (where the sovereign set all the rules), the English common law (created by the courts), the allodial system (where individuals hold title ownership rights), and Spanish law (where custom and usage by and among the people are used). These have caused both oral and written agreements to influence the handling of property management in California.

Because of the wide range of legal background sources leading to the formation of present-day California laws, it is no wonder that many individuals become confused about the law, especially real estate law. The first basic understanding is that California law may not be in conflict with, or go against federal law, based upon the U.S. Constitution and all its amendments. These include all federal laws, regulations, and court decisions. However, many subject areas are not covered by federal law, so state laws in these areas are controlling.

The second basic concept is that California has a separate state constitution and its own state laws, regulations, and court decisions. State agencies may enforce both state and federal laws.

The third concept is that local ordinances vary from county to county and city to city. But local laws and regulations may not violate state and federal legal sources. Local officers cite and enforce both state and federal legal sources, in addition to their own local regulations.

Interpretation Of Laws

The most misunderstood area concerns the differences that arise because of varying interpretations of laws. Property managers must learn that the intent of the law is not the letter of the law. A specific, written law can often be understood in more than one way. The circumstances and events, relationship of the parties, local customs, and the political arena can influence the outcome of any matter heard before a judge.

When a judge renders a decision, it is based upon that judge's experiences, past cases heard, articles read relating to the matter, other court cases, and the way the case is presented.

Most individual property owners have infrequent contact with the courts. Because of the volume of units handled for owners, property managers are often more current on getting through the legal maze. Property managers know which attorneys specialize in process serving and eviction proceedings. It cannot be emphasized strongly enough the importance of knowing about the different courts and judges who hear these cases.

It is extremely important to know if the judge or court commissioner is known as usually being pro-tenant or pro-landlord. Case decisions are an individual judge's opinion, like an appraisal is an appraiser's opinion. Persons with frequent court dealings get to know which judges favor which issues.

Most property managers are well aware that in busy California courts you are often asked to have someone other than a judge hear the case. When a case is called, you may have a court commissioner hear the case. This person is usually a local attorney who practices law in the area. He or she may have had years of experience hearing landlord/tenant cases, or may be inexperienced in this specialized area of the law. Only those in frequent contact with local court cases could give advice on how these individuals are likely to decide a case. A decision would need to be made on whether the case should be heard by the commissioner, or if it would be better to request a judge.

The Eviction Process

The following guide outlines many steps necessary in a legal eviction. Only the most common procedures and laws are introduced in this text. Laws change frequently and local procedures may vary, so you should consult your attorney or property managers' and apartment association for specific information on local ordinances, customs, and procedures.

While some of these steps take place long before you begin an eviction process, it's important that they be done properly so you have the correct documentation when you go to court. For example, it is important that you established the proper landlord-tenant relationship with the rental agreement (discussed in Chapter 8). Oral agreements on residential month-to-month tenancies are enforceable, but rentals for one year or more must be in writing.

All legal documents must be properly served. The Declaration of Service was also reviewed in Chapter 8, along with the Notice to Pay Rent, and Notice of Change of Terms. It is important to note that all of these legal documents must get into the hands of the tenant without any burden put upon the tenant to sign for receiving the documents. Personal service is preferred; and in lieu of this, prepaid, first-class mailing is allowable when service was to another person or when the document was also posted on the premises. Remember: both the person serving and the person receiving the notice must be at least 18 years of age.

Termination of tenancy begins when service of a 30-Day Notice of Termination of Tenancy is used, asking the tenant to voluntarily leave. This form should be used 30 days before the end of a lease or any month-to-month agreement. When the tenant moves, and gives back possession of the keys, the tenancy is terminated.

The next step if payment is not received within the prescribed time or the tenant refuses to vacate the premises, is to file an action with the court. A tenant cannot be evicted without a court order. The landlord must give the tenant notice that he or she wants to end the tenancy before the court action can be filed. The Three-Day Notice to Pay or Quit is used for this purpose.

The date the notice is served upon the tenant cannot be counted in the three-day time period. If the rent was not received on the first of the month, and if the notice was served on the second day of the month, the three days would be the third, fourth, and fifth of the month. The tenant could pay rent on the fifth and stop further action under the use of a Three-Day Notice to Pay or Quit. If the tenant failed to pay by the fifth, the matter could be filed with the courts on the sixth day of the month.

The plaintiff—property owner or property manager-cannot serve the court papers. (The person bringing the court action is called the plaintiff.) Instead, the sheriff, marshal, or a process-server serves the Summons and Complaint upon the person being sued (the defendant). The legal action for non-payment of rent or to obtain possession of the premises of real property is called an Unlawful Detainer action (UD).

The court action can be filed by the property owner or an attorney. Of course, a property manager cannot practice law and should avoid giving legal advice to the property owner. The property manager can prepare the rental agreement, the Notice to Pay or Quit, the Termination of Tenancy, and the Proof of Service that will be used in court. The property manager can appear in court as a witness to the identity of the parties named in the rental agreement, and who was served with the legal papers.

The tenant has the right, under a Notice to Pay or Quit, to remedy the problem by simply paying the rent within the prescribed time. After the Summons and Complaint has been served by a disinterested third party, the tenant still has the right to file an Answer to the Complaint within five days. This action by the tenant causes the court clerk to set a trial date so that all parties can have their day in court, and a judge can hear testimony by witnesses and by the parties. After the case is heard, it may take days before a judgment is rendered on the outcome of the case.

If the judge rules in favor of the tenant, the landlord may not evict the tenant for at least 180 days (six months). If the judge rules in favor of the landlord, someone must file a "Writ of Possession" with the marshal's or sheriff's office. They, in turn, serve a Notice to Vacate the premises upon the tenant(s), giving the tenant five days to leave. If the tenants are still on the premises after five days, they will be physically removed from the property by the sheriff or marshal (NOT the property manager). The property manager should have someone present to change the locks. The marshal or sheriff will inventory any personal property left on the premises, which the landlord becomes responsible for, and the tenant has the right to recover. The marshal or sheriff will post a large red paper notifying all persons that the previous tenants may not set foot on the property or else they may be jailed for trespass.

An owner may wish to handle the eviction him or herself, without a property manager or attorney. The owner would file the necessary papers with the court clerk for small claims court. The court date is usually set for about 45 days from the date first filed, then after an owner is successful, the judgment is stayed for another 20 or more days. In

California metropolitan cities with heavy court loads, expect 60 to 90 days for this type of case. The filing fees and court costs run less than $50, as opposed to an attorney who specializes in evictions who may charge about $300 (which includes the court costs and fees).

In addition to the time and fee, the most significant difference between a municipal court and a small claims court is that in small claims court neither party may have an attorney present to represent them. Also, if the landlord loses because of the issues or legal technicalities (such as incorrect paperwork), he or she may not appeal the decision. It is over and done with. If the tenant loses, however, they may file an action to appeal the matter to a higher court, where the action could have been handled originally. The tenant can then have an attorney represent them, so the landlord would be well advised to also have one.

The Court Case

In the following sample case, the tenant is evicted for non-payment of rent. The property manager completes the initial eviction form and sends the original to the eviction attorney, a copy to the property owner, and keeps a copy for the office file and internal follow up (Figure 1).

The attorney prepares the Summons and Complaint. These are served on the non-paying tenant (defendant) by the attorney's court-approved process server. A copy of these papers and the Declaration of Service of these papers is then filed with the court clerk.

At this point the tenant has two options. He or she can just move and the case will be dismissed. The landlord or property manager takes possession and goes on with the business of re-renting the unit. This matter could be completed within two to three weeks.

The tenant's other option is to file an "Answer" to the Complaint (Figure 2). This is where the tenant claims to have reasons for the non-payment of rent and requests a day in court to be able to explain the matter. The reasons may be valid or not and if they are invalid, the tenant will not be successful at the trial. In Los Angeles Municipal Court, there were over 7,000 claims of possession heard in one year, with the vast majority held invalid.

Figure 1

To: *Ronald Jansen, Attorney*	For: *Sandra Pollard*
123 First Avenue	*2014 Crestview Drive*
Anywhere, CA 90301	*Somewhere, CA 90242*
(213) 671-1234	*No Phone*

Please begin EVICTION on the above tenant.

Enclosed is:	Send us:
Check #*1271* For $*300.00*	Date Complaint Filed ______
✓ 3-Day Notice *10/3/89*	Date U.D. Served ______
✓ Proof of Service *10-4-89*	Default:
✓ Rental Agreement *9/21/88*	Date Requested ______
✓ Change in Terms of Tenancy *12/1/89*	Date Entered ______
	Opposed: Date Answered ______
✓ Credit Application *9/18/88*	Date Trial Requested ______
✓ Picture I.D. *Driver's License*	Court Date ______
✓ Rent Ledger/Past pymt record	Trial Time ______
	Marshal:
__/__/__-__:__ Lock Out Date/Time	Date to Marshal ______

COMMENTS

1-When we tried to serve and she was inside door, she slammed the door in server's face. Copy mailed to tenant 10/4/89

2-She was in car accident, so autos are rentals

3-She has other people "visit" but I cannot get any names.

4-Picture ID is enclosed as she will AVOID service.

Figure 2

CLAIMANT OR CLAIMANT'S ATTORNEY *(Name and Address):* Jean Sampson, 842 Roanoke, Somewhere, CA 90243 — TELEPHONE NO.: None — ATTORNEY FOR *(Name):* Sandra Pollard	FOR COURT USE ONLY
Insert name of court, judicial district or branch court, if any, and post office and street address: Downey Municipal Court, 8206 E. Third Street, Downey, California 90241	
PLAINTIFF: Denise White	
DEFENDANT: Sandra Pollard	
ANSWER-Unlawful Detainer	CASE NUMBER: 89C000

1. This pleading including attachments and exhibits consists of the following number of pages: 2
2. Defendants *(name):* Sandra Pollard

   answer the complaint as follows:
3. Check ONLY ONE of the next two boxes:
   a. ☒ Defendant generally denies each statement of the complaint. *(Do not check this box if the complaint demands more than $1,000.)*
   b. ☐ Defendant admits that all of the statements of the complaint are true EXCEPT:
      (1) Defendant claims the following statements of the complaint are false *(use paragraph numbers from the complaint or explain):*

      ☐ Continued on Attachment 3.b.(1)
      (2) Defendant has no information or belief that the following statements of the complaint are true, so defendant denies them *(use paragraph numbers from the complaint or explain):*

      ☐ Continued on Attachment 3.b.(2).
4. AFFIRMATIVE DEFENSES
   a. ☒ *(nonpayment of rent only)* Plaintiff has breached the warranty to provide habitable premises. *(Briefly state the facts below in item 4.k.)*
   b. ☐ Plaintiff waived, changed, or canceled the notice to quit. *(Briefly state the facts below in item 4.k.)*
   c. ☒ Plaintiff served defendant with the notice to quit or filed the complaint to retaliate against defendant. *(Briefly state the facts below in item 4.k.)*
   d. ☒ Plaintiff has failed to perform his obligations under the rental agreement. *(Briefly state the facts below in item 4.k.)*
   e. ☐ By serving defendant with the notice to quit or filing the complaint, plaintiff is arbitrarily discriminating against the defendant in violation of the constitution or laws of the United States or California. *(Briefly state the facts below in item 4.k.)*
   f. ☐ Plaintiff's demand for possession violates the local rent control or eviction control ordinance of *(city or county, title of ordinance, and date of passage):*

(Briefly state the facts showing violation of the ordinance in item 4.k)

(Continued)

Form Approved by the Judicial Council of California
Effective January 1, 1982
Rule 982.1(95)
76A506 CI194JC (12) PS-284

ANSWER-Unlawful Detainer

CCP 425.12

COURT TITLE: White vs. Pollard	CASE NUMBER 89C000

ANSWER-Unlawful Detainer Page two

g. ☐ Plaintiff accepted rent from defendant to cover a period of time after the date stated in paragraph 8.b. of the complaint
h. ☐ *(nonpayment of rent only)* On *(date):* defendant offered the rent due but plaintiff would not accept it.
i. ☐ Defendant made needed repairs and properly deducted the cost from the rent, and plaintiff did not give proper credit.
j. ☐ Other affirmative defenses. *(Briefly state below in item 4.k.)*
k. FACTS SUPPORTING AFFIRMATIVE DEFENSES CHECKED ABOVE *(Identify each item separately.)*

4a. Leaky faucets, and no gardener as provided for in the rental agreement.
4c. Notice to quit was served because Defendant complained about plumbing.
4d. No gardener and the landlord has failed to keep the plumbing in good working order.

☐ Continued on Attachment 4.k.

5. OTHER STATEMENTS
a. ☐ Defendant vacated the premises on *(date):*
b. ☒ Defendant claims a credit for deposits of $ 1075.00
c. ☒ The fair rental value of the premises in item 12 of the complaint is excessive *(explain): because of the condition of the premises*
d. ☐ Other *(specify):*

6. DEFENDANT REQUESTS
a. that plaintiff take nothing requested in the complaint.
b. costs incurred in this proceeding.
c. ☒ reasonable attorney fees.
d. ☒ other *(specify): such other and further relief as the court may deem just and proper.*

Jean Sampson — *Jean Sampson*
(Type or print name) — (Signature of defendant or attorney)

(Type or print name) — (Signature of defendant or attorney)

(Each defendant for whom this answer is filed must be named in item 2 and *must sign this answer unless represented by an attorney.)*

VERIFICATION

(Use a different verification form if the verification is by an attorney or for a corporation or partnership.)
I am the defendant in this proceeding and have read this answer. I declare under penalty of perjury under the laws of the State of California that this answer is true and correct.

Date: *10-20-89*

Sandra Pollard — *Sandra Pollard*
(Type or print name) — (Signature of defendant or attorney)

Page two

Anytime an Answer is filed, the courts must set a trial date so the case can be heard in court (Figure 3). The date of trial, averages about 30 days from the date the Three-Day Notice to Pay or Quit was served.

Before you go to court, all of the following persons need to be available to give testimony and present evidence during the trial. The landlord's side needs the owner, or an appointed agent, the property manager, plus the person who served the Summons and Complaint, plus any persons needed to document issues that arose in the Answer. In the Answer shown in Figure 2, the records for plumbing and the maintenance person who performed the work would need to be there, in addition to the gardener. Photographs of completed work, signed and dated by workmen, would be good, plus a photo of the grounds. The tenant's side would need witnesses as to the conditions and photographs of the lack of maintenance, plus an attorney, if one is used.

When you appear at the trial date, a court calendar will be posted, showing all the trials that day, and which department, division or courtroom the matter will be heard in. Go to that place to see the name of the person presiding. In large courts, a commissioner will assign all the cases to different rooms throughout the building. In small courts, it may be heard by this person. Ask your attorney whether the matter will be heard by a judge or commissioner. Ask the attorney about the past record of who is on the case (pro-tenant or pro-landlord).

There is always a risk in having a case heard in court; you could lose the trial. The courts prefer the parties to resolve the issues among themselves, if at all possible. Attorneys always, just prior to trial, talk with the opposing side to try to work out some agreement. If they do not agree, everyone goes inside the courtroom to have the case heard by the proper authorities.

If, however, everyone agrees on a settlement, a Stipulation is drawn up (Figure 4). This document spells out the terms and conditions that the parties agreed to between themselves. It is signed by the plaintiff (landlord) and defendant (tenant) and submitted to the judge for approval. Everyone goes into the courtroom, and the attorney gives the paper to the clerk to give to the judge to review. It is common for the judge to read the Stipulation out loud so it is officially part of the court records, and ask the tenant if he or she understands and agrees to what it says.

Figure 3

NOTICE OF TRIAL	IN THE MUNICIPAL COURT OF Downey JUDICIAL DISTRICT COUNTY OF LOS ANGELES, STATE OF CALIFORNIA 8206 Third St., Downey, CA 90241	Case Number 89C000

Denise White v. Sandra Pollard

Plaintiff(s) Defendant(s)

To Ronald Jansen Attorney(s) for Denise White
To Jean Sampson Attorney(s) for Sandra Pollard
To ______ Attorney(s) for ______
To ______ Attorney(s) for ______

*JURY You and each of you will please take notice that the above-entitled cause has been set for TRIAL BY *COURT on Nov. 10, 1989 at 9:30A M. in Division F of the above-named court located at Downey Municipal Court 8206 Third St., Downey, CA 90241 .

Dated October 28, 1989 By B. Gutierrez, Deputy
Clerk of the aboved-named Court

* strike out inappropriate word

NOTE: Please notify clerk at once if reporter is desired. Jury Fees must be deposited at least 25 days before trail pursuant to 631 C.C.P.

CLERK'S CERTIFICATE OF SERVICE

I hereby certify that I am the Clerk of this court, not a party to this cause; that I served a copy of this NOTICE on the below date, by placing a copy thereof in separate sealed envelope(s) addressed to:

Ronald Jansen
123 First Avenue
Anywhere, CA 90301

Jean Sampson
842 Roanoke
Somewhere, CA 90243

at the address shown by the records of this Court, and by then sealing said envelope(s) and depositing same with postage fully prepaid thereon, in the United States mail at Downey California.

Elaine Osborne ,Clerk

Dated October 28, 1989 By B. Gutierrez, Deputy

76N630—CI-26—(Rev.8/78) NOTICE OF TRIAL C.C.P.594.20155

Figure 4

<table>
<tr><td>MUNICIPAL COURT OF CALIFORNIA, COUNTY OF LOS ANGELES
LOS ANGELES JUDICIAL DISTRICT

(X) METRO (✓) DOWNEY BRANCH

ADDRESS:</td><td rowspan="3"></td></tr>
<tr><td>PLAINTIFF:
DENISE WHITE</td></tr>
<tr><td>DEFENDANT:
SANDRA POLLARD</td></tr>
<tr><td>STIPULATION FOR JUDGMENT — UNLAWFUL DETAINER</td><td>CASE: #89C000</td></tr>
</table>

IT IS HEREBY STIPULATED BY AND BETWEEN THE PLAINTIFF(S) Denise White

AND DEFENDANT(S) Sandra Pollard THAT PLAINTIFF BE AWARDED RESTITUTION OF THE PREMISES LOCATED AT 2014 Crestview Dr., Somewhere, 90243 CALIFORNIA AND THAT A MONEY JUDGMENT BE GRANTED IN FAVOR OF PLAINTIFF(S) AS FOLLOWS: 1,000.00 RENT; $ -0- DAMAGES; $ 300.00 ATTORNEY FEES, AND COSTS IN THE SUM OF:$ -0- .

STAY OF EXECUTION AS TO ( ) POSSESSION Writ to issue forthwith, but no lock-out until December 10, 1989, providing defendant pays $750.00, by Cashier's Check or Money Order, by 5:00 p.m. on 11/10/89. If not paid then Plaintiff is entitled to an immediate Writ of Possession.

*Defendant states that she is the only adult residing on the premises.

STAY OF EXCECUTION AS TO ( ) MONEY JUDGEMENT

Sum of 750.00 receipt is acknowledged

DATE: 11-10-89	*Denise White* PLAINTIFF/~~ATTORNEY~~	*Ronald Jansen* ~~PLAINTIFF~~/ATTORNEY
DATE: 11-10-89	*Sandra Pollard* DEFENDANT/~~ATTORNEY~~	*Jean Sampson* ~~DEFENDANT~~/ATTORNEY

I/WE THE DEFENDANT(S) UNDERSTAND THAT I/WE HAVE THE RIGHT TO: (1) HAVE AN ATTORNEY PRESENT; (2) NOTICE AND HEARING OF ANY DEFAULT OF TERMS OF THE STAY OF EXECUTION; (3) I/WE GIVE UP THE ABOVE RIGHTS.

✓ YES S.P. (INITIAL) ______ NO ______ (INITIAL)

JUDGMENT IS HEREBY ORDERED ON ALL TERMS OF THE FOREGOING STIPULATION

DATE: 11/10/89

Marian Leckir
JUDGE/COMMISSIONER

CIV M-582 (7/85)

Upon completion of this step, the judge signs the Stipulation and it goes to the court clerk.

If there is no Stipulation, the case goes to trial. If the landlord wins, the clerk files the case into the court records, and then the papers are prepared for the marshal's office to serve. This can take from one day to three weeks, depending upon court workload, holidays, the attorney, the court size, and the follow up by the property manager.

The Writ of Possession is the document giving the marshal the power to physically evict the tenant, should he or she still be in possession (Figure 5). At this point the property owner has only a few remaining problems that the tenant can cause. For example, the tenant could file bankruptcy, which would stop the eviction until the matter is heard in the federal bankruptcy courts. This process takes an extra two to four weeks to have the Unlawful Detainer judgment matter released from the bankruptcy court so that the landlord can regain possession of the premises.

The marshal serves the Notice to Vacate and Notice to Occupants (Figure 6A). This legal document notifies the occupants of their rights. If any occupants lived at the property before, during, and after the court action, but were not named in the court action, they can file an Arrieta Claim. (Figure 6B). The marshal will not give legal possession to the owner until there is a hearing to determine the validity of the claim and the judge gives instruction to the marshal to take action. If the claim of the unnamed tenant is upheld by the judge, this person must be served with a notice to leave the premises, properly prepared and served, and a second eviction proceeding begun.

As with any document served upon tenants, a Declaration of Service would have to be completed by the marshal (Figure 7). This indicates the time and date that the clock would begin running. The date of service is not counted. From the date of service, the tenants have five days to move their belongings. The property manager is notified by the marshal of the date and time to be at the premises to take possession.

At the appointed time, should the property appear occupied, the marshal will call for a backup unit, if two officers did not originally come to the property. The occupants are ordered to immediately leave the premises or they will be jailed for contempt of court.

Figure 5

ATTORNEY OR PARTY WITHOUT ATTORNEY *(Name and Address):* TELEPHONE NO.: (213) 671-1234
☐ *Recording requested by a return to:*
Ronald Jansen
123 First Avenue
Anywhere, CA 90301
☒ ATTORNEY FOR ☒ JUDGMENT CREDITOR ☐ ASSIGNEE OF RECORD

FOR RECORDER'S USE ONLY

NAME OF COURT: Downey Municipal Court
STREET ADDRESS: 8206 E. Third Street
MAILING ADDRESS: Same
CITY AND ZIP CODE: Downey, California 90241
BRANCH NAME:

PLAINTIFF: Denise White
DEFENDANT: Sandra Pollard

WRIT OF ☐ EXECUTION (Money Judgment)
☒ POSSESSION OF ☐ Personal Property
☒ Real Property
☐ SALE

CASE NUMBER
89C000

FOR COURT USE ONLY

1. To the Sheriff or any Marshal or Constable of the County of Los Angeles
You are directed to enforce the judgment described below with daily interest and your costs as provided by law.
2. To any registered process server: You are authorized to serve this writ only in accord with CCP 699.080 or 715.040.
3. *(Name):* Denise White is the
☒Judgment creditor ☐ assignee of record
whose address is shown on this form above the court's name.
4. Judgment debtor *(name and last known address):*

Sandra Pollard
2014 Crestview Dr.
Somewhere, CA 90243

☐ additional judgment debtors on reverse
5. Judgment entered on *(date):* 11/10/89
6. ☐ Judgment renewed on *(date):*
7. Notice of sale under this writ
a. ☒ has not been requested.
b. ☐ has been requested *(see reverse).*
8. ☐ Joint debtor information on reverse.

9. ☒ See reverse for information on real or personal property to be delivered under a writ of possession or sold under a writ of sale.
10. ☐ This writ is issued on a sister-state judgment.
11. Total judgment.................. $
12. Costs after judgment (per filed order or memo CCP 685.090...... $
13. Subtotal *(add 11 and 12)*......... $________
14. Credits......................... $________
15. Subtotal *(subtract 14 from 13)*..... $________
16. Interest after judgment (per filed affidavit CCP685.050 .... $
17. Fee for issuance of writ .... $
18. Total *(add 15, 16, and 17)* .... $________
19. Levying officer: add daily interest from date of writ *(at the legal rate on 15)* of .... $
20. ☐ The amounts called for items 11-19 are different for each debtor. These amounts are stated for each debtor on Attachment 20.

(SEAL)

Issued on *(date):* DEC. 20, 1989 Clerk, by Carolyn Sue Palicte, deputy

-NOTICE TO PERSON SERVED: SEE REVERSE FOR IMPORTANT INFORMATION-

(Continued on reverse)

Form Approved by the Judicial Council of California
EJ-130 (Rev. January 1, 1987)
76W791 CI-75JC (11)(Rev. 1/87) PS 1-87

WRIT OF EXECUTION

CCP 699.520, 712.010, 715.010

Figure 5, page 2

SHORT TITLE: White vs. Pollard	CASE NUMBER: 89C000

Items continued from the first page:

4. ☐ Additional Judgement debtor *(name and last know address):*

7. ☐ Notice of sale has been requested by *(name and address):*

8. Joint debtor was declared bound by the judgment (CCP 989-994)
   a. on *(date):*
   b. name and address of joint debtor:

   a. on *(date):*
   b. name and address of joint debtor:

   c. ☐ additional costs against certain joint debtor *(itemize):*

9. ☐ *Writ of Possession or Writ of Sale)* Judgment was entered for the following:
   a. ☒ Possession of real property. The complaint was filed on *(date):* 10/14/89
      The court will hear objections to enforcement of the judgment under CCP 1174.3 on the following dates *(specify):* TO BE DETERMINED BY THE COURT
   b. ☐ Possession of Personal Property
      ☐ If delivery cannot be had, then for the value *(itemized in 9e)* specified in the judgmont or supplemental order.
   c. ☐ Sale of personal property
   d. ☐ Sale of real property
   e. Desicription of property:

      2014 Crestview
      Somewhere, CA 90243

-NOTICE TO PERSON SERVED-

Writ of execution or sale. Your rights and duties are indicated on the accompanying Notice of Levy.

Writ of possession of personal property. If the levying officer is not able to take custody of the property, the levying officer will make a demand upon you for the property. If custody is not obtained following demand, the judgment may be enforced as a money judgment for the value of the property specified in the judgment or in a supplemental order.

Writ of possession of real property. If the premises are not vacated within five days after the date of service on the occupant or, if service is by posting, within five days after service on you, the levying officer will remove the occupants from the real property and place the judgement creditor in possession of the property. Personal property remaining on the premises will be sold or otherwise disposed of in accordance with CCPPP 1174 unless you or the owner of the property pays the judgment creditor the reasonable cost of storage and takes possession of the personal property not later than 15 days after the time the judgment creditor takes possession of the premises. A Claim of Right to Possession form accompanies this writ.

EJ-130 (Rev. January 1, 1987) **WRIT OF EXECUTION** Page two

Figure 6A

MARSHAL OF MUNICIPAL COURTS
LOS ANGELES COUNTY

NOTICE TO VACATE

CASE NUMBER: *89C000*

TO: Judgement debtor, members of the judgment debtor's household, and any occupants holding under the judgment debtor

By virtue of a **Writ of Possession of Real Property,** a copy of which is attached,

YOU ARE HEREBY ORDERED TO VACATE THE PREMISES DESCRIBED IN THE WRIT NOT LATER THAN: *12-26*, 19*89*

MARSHAL'S DIVISION (*Name, Address, and Telephone Number*)

940-8932
MARSHAL'S OFFICE
8206 East Third Street
Downey, California

ROBERT F. MANN, MARSHAL

By: ______________________
Deputy

Date: *12-21-89*

NOTICE TO OCCUPANTS

IF YOU ARE NOT NAMED in the attached writ and if you claim a right to possession of the premises described in the writ based upon the fact that you were in possession on or before the date of filing of the unlawful detainer (eviction) action, YOU MUST ACT AT ONCE.

You must claim a legal right to possession with the Marshal's Office, or you will be removed by the Marshal's deputies at the time of the eviction.

TO CLAIM YOUR RIGHTS, if any, you must complete the attached **Claim of Right to Possession** form in which you state under penalty of perjury that you were in possession of the subject premises on or before the date of filing of the unlawful detainer action. You can complete and SUBMIT THE CLAIM FORM

(1) at the Marshal's Office located at the address above before the date of eviction, **or**
(2) at the premises at the time of the eviction.

If you do not complete and submit the form (and pay a filing fee or file the appropriate form for proceeding in forma pauperis if you cannot pay the fee), YOU WILL BE EVICTED along with the parties named in the writ.

- GIVE THE CLAIM FORM to the Marshal at the address above. *(Do not take or send the claim form to the court.)*
- **TO OBTAIN A COURT HEARING**

1. You must PAY A FILING FEE OF $ *24.00* directly to the court *(see attached writ for the address)* within 48 hours after you give the claim form to the Marshal. *(INCLUDE THE CASE NUMBER ON ALL DOCUMENTS.)*
2. IF YOU CANNOT PAY THE FEE, you must file with the court the appropriate form for proceeding in forma pauperis. *(Ask the court clerk for the form "Application for Waiver of Court Fees and Costs.")* You must file that application form within 48 hours after you give the claim form to the Marshal.
3. IF YOU MAIL to the court the fee for the application for waiver, you must make sure the envelope is postmarked within 48 hours after you give the claim form to the Marshal. *(Write the case number on your check, money order, or application form.)*
4. IF YOU DO NOT pay the fee or file an application for waiver of the fee, you will not have a court hearing and YOUR CLAIM OF RIGHT TO POSSESSION WILL BE DENIED.

[Rev. January 1, 1988]
76P475

NOTICE TO VACATE
and
NOTICE TO OCCUPANTS

ccp 715.010, 715.020, 1174.3

Figure 6B

CLAIMANT OR CLAIMANT'S ATTORNEY *(Name and Address):* TELEPHONE NO.: ATTORNEY FOR *(Name):*	FOR COURT USE ONLY
NAME OF COURT: STREET ADDRESS: MAILING ADDRESS: CITY AND ZIP CODE: BRANCH NAME:	
PLAINTIFF: DEFENDANT:	
CLAIM OF RIGHT TO POSSESSION AND NOTICE OF HEARING	

HEARING DATE:	TIME:	DEPT. OR DIV.:	ROOM:	CASE NUMBER:

Complete this form only if ALL of these statements are true:
1. **You are NOT named in the accompanying form called Writ of Possession.**
2. **You occupied the subject premises on or before the date the unlawful detainer (eviction) action was filed.** *(The date is in the accompanying Writ of Possession.)*
3. **You still occupy the subject premises.**

(For levying officer use only)
Completed form was received on
Date:__________ Time:__________
By:____________________

I DECLARE THE FOLLOWING UNDER PENALTY OF PERJURY:

1. My name is *(specify):*
2. I reside at *(address):*
3. The address of "the premises" subject to this claim is *(address):*
4. On *(insert date):* ____________, the landlord or the landlord's authorized agent filed a complaint to recover possession of the premises. *(This date is on the accompanying Writ of Possession.)*
5. I occupied the subject premises on the date the complaint was filed *(the date in item 4)*. I have continued to occupy the subject premises ever since.
6. I was at least 18 years of age on the date the complaint was filed *(the date in item 4)*.
7. I claim a right to possession of the subject premises because I occupied the premises on the date the complaint was filed *(the date in item 4)*.
8. I was not named in the Writ of Possession.
9. I understand that if I make this claim of possession, a court hearing will be held to decide whether my claim will be granted.
10. If I submit this claim form, a COURT HEARING will be held as follows:

(To be completed by the levying officer)
Date of hearing: Time: Dept. or Div.: Room:
Address of court: **DATE AND TIME TO BE SET BY COURT CLERK UPON THE PAYMENT OF COURT FEES**

NOTICE: If you fail to appear at this hearing you are likely to be evicted.

(continued on reverse)

[Rev. January 1, 1988]
76C216PN2

CLAIM OF RIGHT TO POSSESSION AND NOTICE OF HEARING

CCP 715.010, 715.020, 1174.3
ORIGINAL/COURT COPY

CLAIM OF RIGHT TO POSSESSION (Continued)

11. Rental agreement. I have *(check all that apply to you):*
- a: ☐ an oral rental agreement with the landlord.
- b: ☐ a written rental agreement with the landlord.
- c: ☐ an oral rental agreement with a person other than the landlord.
- d: ☐ a written rental agreement with a person other than the landlord.
- e. ☐ other *(explain):*

I declare under penalty of perjury under the laws of the State of California that the foregoing is true and correct.

WARNING: Perjury is a felony punishable by imprisonment in the state prison

Date: ► ______________________________
(SIGNATURE OF CLAIMANT)

____
(TYPE OR PRINT NAME)

NOTICE: If your claim to possession is found to be valid, the unlawful detainer action against you will be determined at trial. At trial, you may be found liable for rent, costs, and, in some cases, treble damages.

NOTICE TO OCCUPANTS

IF YOU ARE NOT NAMED in the attached writ and if you claim a right to possession of the premises described in the writ based upon the fact that you were in possession on or before the date of filing of the unlawful detainer (eviction) action, YOU MUST ACT AT ONCE.

You must claim a legal right to possession with the Marshal's Office, or you will be removed by the Marshal's deputies at the time of the eviction.

TO CLAIM YOUR RIGHTS, if any, you must complete this **Claim of Right to Possession** form in which you state under penalty of perjury that you were in possession of the subject premises on or before the date of filing of the unlawful detainer action. You can complete and SUBMIT THIS CLAIM FORM

(1) at the Marshal's Office located at the address on the **Notice to Vacate** before the date of eviction, **OR**

(2) at the premises at the time of the eviction.

If you do not complete and submit this form (and pay a filing fee or file the appropriate form for proceeding in forma pauperis if you cannot pay the fee), YOU WILL BE EVICTED along with the parties named in the writ.

- GIVE THIS CLAIM FORM to the Marshal at the address on the **Notice to Vacate.** (Do not take or send this claim form to the court.)
- **TO OBTAIN A COURT HEARING**
  1. You must PAY A FILING FEE of: **$** directly to the court *(see attached writ for the address)* within 48 hours after you give this claim form to the Marshal. *(INCLUDE THE CASE NUMBER ON ALL CHECKS AND DOCUMENTS.)*
  2. IF YOU CANNOT PAY THE FEE, you must file with the court the appropriate form for proceeding in forma pauperis. *(Ask the court clerk for the form "Application for Waiver of Court Fees and Costs.")* You must file that application form within 48 hours after you give this claim form to the Marshal.
  3. IF YOU MAIL to the court the fee or the application for waiver, you must make sure the envelope is postmarked with 48 hours after you give this claim form to the Marshal. *(Write the case number on your check, money order, or application form.)*
  4. IF YOU DO NOT pay the fee or file an application for waiver of the fee, you will not have a court hearing and YOUR CLAIM OF RIGHT TO POSSESSION WILL BE DENIED.

[Rev. January 1, 1988] CLAIM OF RIGHT TO POSSESSION AND NOTICE OF HEARING PAGE TWO

Figure 7

MARSHAL OF MUNICIPAL COURT
LOS ANGELES COUNTY

Case #___*89C000*__________

On ___*12-29-89*___ at *11:22 a.m.*__, I enforced the court order upon which this endorsement appears by placing the plaintiff in possession of the described premises.

ROBER F. MANN, MARSHAL

by ______________________________, Deputy

Penal Code § 419 makes it a misdemeanor for any person who, after removal by court order, returns to settle, reside upon, or take possession of such lands.

In the event evicted individuals reenter the property in violation of Penal Code § 419, present this document with the attached copy of the writ of possession to the responding local law enforcement agency.

76S864D (rev 7/86)

If the tenants were unable to have all their personal property removed from the premises, the marshal will go through the property prior to allowing the owner or manager into the unit. The property manager must then determine if the value of the property is more or less than $300. An itemized inventory of the items must be sent to the tenant. Care, storage, and recovery of the items must be accounted for by the landlord (Figures 8a and 8b). This notice must, again, have a Declaration of Service prepared. For an accurate inventory, it is wise to cluster the items into photographs should future disputes arise. The owner may not keep the tenant's personal property to offset rents, cleaning costs, or reimbursement for damages to the real property.

LEGAL ASPECTS OF EMPLOYMENT

Many of the property management personnel requirements were discussed in Chapter 13. The following discussion is geared to other areas, especially for those who manage their own property.

The property owner may be ultimately liable to persons hired by the off-site property manager, on-site manager, or other independent contractors. Thus owners need a general, working understanding of the elements that could affect them and their property. It is important to know the various rights and protections that persons have under the law. A temporary worker, such as a gardener, painter, or clean-up person may be determined to be an employee by government agencies, unions, and current laws.

One federal law requires all persons who make payment to any other person for $600 or more in one tax year to file forms and report that income to the government. The payer must provide an IRS 1099 form with the individual's social security number or federal "95-" taxpayer I.D. number. There are penalties for failure to comply. The payer must withhold 20% of the payment and send these funds directly to the IRS if unable to obtain the tax numbers, or be subject to fines.

Owners sometimes have conflicting records within a 12-month period where, for example, they managed their own property in January, February, March, and April; then they hired an on-site manager for May, June, July, August, September, and October; then hired an

Figure 8A

NOTICE OF RIGHT TO RECLAIM ABANDONED PERSONAL PROPERTY

(Value *more* than $300.00)

TO: ____

All former residents (tenants and subtenants) full names

When you vacated the premises situated in the City of ____________________,
county of__________, State of California, designated by the number and street as:
____,
Apt. ________, the following personal property remained: (see description below).

Unless you pay the reasonable cost of storage for all the below-described personal property and take possession of the property which you claim, not later than 18 days after this Notice is deposited in the mail, this personal property may be disposed of pursuant to Civil Code Section 1988.

If you fail to reclaim the property, it will be sold at a public sale after notice of the sale has been given by publication. You have the right to bid on the property at this sale. After the property is sold and the cost of storage, advertising, and sale is deducted, the remaining money will be paid over to the county. You may claim the remaining money at any time within one year after the county received the money.

DATE OF MAILING OF THIS NOTICE: ____________________
DATE OF EXPIRATION OF THIS NOTICE: ____________________

You may claim this property at:

____

Address where property may be claimed

____

Owner/Agent

THE ABANDONED PERSONAL PROPERTY IS DESCRIBED AS FOLLOWS:

Figure 8B

NOTICE OF RIGHT TO RECLAIM ABANDONED PERSONAL PROPERTY

(Value *less* than $300.00)

TO: ____

All former residents (tenants and subtenants) full names

When you vacated the premises situated in the City of ________________, county of__________, State of California, designated by the number and street as: ____,

Apt. ________, the following personal property remained: (see description below).

Unless you pay the reasonable cost of storage for all the below-described personal property and take possession of the property which you claim, not later than 18 days after this notice is deposited in the mail, this personal property may be disposed of pursuant to Civil Code Section 1988.

Because this property is believed to be worth less than $300.00, it may be kept, sold, or destroyed without further notice if you fail to reclaim it within the time indicated below.

DATE OF MAILING OF THIS NOTICE: ____________________

DATE OF EXPIRATION OF THIS NOTICE: ____________________

You may claim this property at:

____

Address where property may be claimed

____

Owner/Agent

THE ABANDONED PERSONAL PROPERTY IS DESCRIBED AS FOLLOWS:

off-site, professional management company for November, December, and thereafter. Within this calendar year, the management company would not need to provide a federal IRS 1099 form for the gardener who earns $125 per month, as the management company records show only $250 total earnings paid for the year. The first manager, for the summer months, may not have known about the rules; or, they may not provide these records on property they don't manage at year end; or, they feel it is not part of what they are paid to provide and feel that it is the owner's reporting problem. However, they paid $125 per month for six months. They would be required to report the gardener's $750 earnings as it is over the $600 per year exempt status. They would need to file the form which includes the gardener's taxpayer identification number, or be subject to a fine of $50 for not providing the contractor with a 1099, and a $50 fine for not filing the earnings with the IRS. The property owner, however, would be responsible for the entire $125 per month for the 12 months, for a total of $1800. The penalty for the owner who did not file would be $50 for not filing the necessary IRS form, plus $180 ($1800 x 10%) for not sending the gardener his 1099.

The necessary tax filing forms, even for one person, are part of the property management business. The person may be an employee or an outside contractor (different forms are required for each type of status). The following is a brief summary of current rules, which are subject to change with each tax year.

Employees–For employees where payroll deductions are subject to earnings, a table is provided (Figure 9). On the state level, the employer must provide a quarterly filing form (DE3) reporting earnings to the Employment Development Department in Sacramento (EDD), and an annual form showing total yearly earnings on the proper form (DE43) with the W2 forms attached for all wage earners. On the federal level, the employer must file a quarterly earnings form (941) with the IRS in Fresno, and an annual form (940) for total yearly income for all persons, attaching a copy of the W2 form for all employees.

Non-employees–For non-employees (independent contractors), it is necessary to file state and federal forms. The state requires filing (596) with the Franchise Tax Board in Sacramento and copies of the 1099, showing earnings. The federal government requires an annual transmittal of their form (W3) to indicate social security taxes through

TAX TABLE — REVISED JANUARY 1, 1989

And Other Employee Deductions [2]

Figure 9

STEP1 Multiply TAXABLE EARNINGS[3] for the Pay Period by the appropriate FACTOR

	Calendar Month or School Month (Factor)	Half Month [1] or Bi-Weekly (Factor)
If the employee has only 10-month assignments	10	20
If the employee has any 11-month assignment and has NO 12-month assignment	11	22
If the employee has any 12-month assignment	12	24

NOTE: If an employee receives more than one salary warrant during a pay period, Step 1 must include all earnings. Multiply the total of earings for this warrant plus earnings of any other warrants paid the same period. After the last step, deduct the taxes paid on the previous warrant(s).

FEDERAL

STEP 2 Reduce the result of STEP 1 by $2,000 times the number of exemptions claimed by the employee

STEP 3 Use FEDERAL Table "A" SINGLE or MARRIED to compute taxes on result of STEP 2

TABLE "A"
FEDERAL ANNUAL TAX

SINGLE person—including head of household

If the amount of wages is Not over $1,100 .... The amount of income tax to be withheld shall be: 0

Over—	But not over—		of excess over—
$ 1,100	—$ 19,650	15%	—$ 1,100
$ 19,650	—$ 46,000	$ 2,782.50 plus 28%	—$ 19,650
$ 46,000	—$105,430	$10,160.50 plus 33%	—$ 46,000
$105,430	....	$29,772.40 plus 28%	—$105,430

MARRIED person—

If the amount of wages is Not over $3,200 .... The amount of income tax to be withheld shall be: 0

Over—	But not over—		of excess over—
$ 3,200	—$ 34,150	15%	—$ 3,210
$ 34,150	—$ 78,050	$ 4,642.50 plus 28%	—$ 34,150
$ 78,050	—$192,120	$16,934.50 plus 33%	—$ 78,050
$192,120	....	$ 54,577.60 plus 28%	—$192,120

STEP 4 Divide result of STEP 3 by factor used in STEP 1, round answer up

[1] Federal Tax withheld from half month payments is limited to 32% of taxable earnings.

STATE

STEP 2 If the result of STEP 1 is equal to or less than the following there is no state tax. Otherwise proceed to STEP 3.
MARRIED - 0 or 1 exemption - $6,110
- 2 or more exemptions - $12,230
SINGLE - $6,110, UNMARRIED HEAD OF HOUSEHOLD - $12,230

STEP 3 STANDARD DEDUCTION
MARRIED - 0 or 1 exemption - $1,966
- 2 or more exemptions - $3,932
SINGLE - $1,966, UNMARRIED HEAD OF HOUSEHOLD - $3,932

STEP 4 ESTIMATED DEDUCTION ALLOWANCES
Reduce the result of STEP 3 as follows:
$1,000 for each estimated deduction allowance

STEP 5 Use State Table "B" SINGLE, MARRIED, or HEAD OF HOUSEHOLD to compute taxes on the result of STEP 4.

TABLE "B"
STATE ANNUAL TAX

SINGLE person
If the taxable income is:

Over—	But not over—	Computed tax is:	Of amount over—
$ 0	$ 3,818	$ 0.00 plus 1%	$ 0
$ 3,818	$ 9,048	$ 38.18 plus 2%	$ 3,818
$ 9,048	$14,278	$ 142.78 plus 4%	$ 9,048
$14,278	$19,822	$ 351.98 plus 6%	$14,278
$19,822	$25,052	$ 684.62 plus 8%	$19,822
$25,052 and over		$1,103 plus 9%	$25,052

FEDERAL AEIC
(ADVANCED EARNED INCOME CREDIT)

Available only to eligible employees filing Form W-5.
There will be no AEIC if the result of STEP 1 is greater than:
$19,340 for unmarried head of household or married without spouse filing certificate
$ 9,670 for married with both spouses filing certificates

Otherwise proceed to STEP 2 below.

STEP 2 Using the amount of earnings from STEP 1, compute the amount of the AEIC from Table (a) or (b) below.

AEIC ANNUAL TABLE

(a) UNMARRIED HEAD OF HOUSEHOLD or MARRIED Without Spouse Filing Certificate

If the amount of wages (before deducting withholding allowances) is		The amount of payment to be made shall be:
Over—	But not over—	of excess over—
$ 0	$ 6,500	15% of wages
$ 6,500	$10,240	$910.00
$10,240	$19,340	$910.00 less 10% of wages in excess of $10,240
$19,340		$0

(b) MARRIED With Both Spouses Filing Certificates

If the amount of wages (before deducting withholding allowances) is		The amount of payment to be made shall be:
Over—	But not over—	of excess over—
$ 0	$3,250	14% of wages
$3,250	$5,120	$455.00
$5,120	$9,670	$455.00 less 10% of wages in excess of $5,120
$9,670		$0

STEP 3 Divide the result of STEP 2 by the factor used in STEP 1.

MARRIED person
If the taxable income is:

Over—	But not over—	Computed tax is:	Of amount over—
$ 0	$ 7,636	$ 0.00 plus 1%	$ 0
$ 7,636	$18,096	$ 76.36 plus 2%	$ 7,636
$18,096	$28,556	$ 285.56 plus 4%	$18,096
$28,556	$39,644	$ 703.96 plus 6%	$28,556
$39,644	$50,104	$1,369.24 plus 8%	$39,644
$50,104 and over		$2,206.04 plus 9%	$50,104

UNMARRIED HEAD OF HOUSEHOLD
If the taxable income is:

Over—	But not over—	Computed tax is:	Of amount over—
$ 0	$ 7,636	$ 0.00 plus 1%	$ 0
$ 7,636	$18,096	$ 76.36 plus 2%	$ 7,636
$18,096	$23,326	$ 285.56 plus 4%	$18,096
$23,326	$28,870	$ 494.76 plus 6%	$23,326
$28,870	$34,100	$ 827.40 plus 8%	$28,870
$34,100 and over		$1,245.80 plus 9%	$34,100

STEP 6 Reduce result of STEP 5 by Table "C" State Tax Credit Table
Only include personal allowances - exclude estimated deduction allowances.

TABLE "C"
STATE TAX CREDIT TABLE

Allowances	0	1	2	3
Single	0.00	52.00	104.00	**
M or H	0.00	52.00	104.00	**

** Plus $52.00 for each exemption above 2

STEP 7 Divide result of STEP 6 by factor used in STEP 1, round answer up

[2] Other Employee Rates: STRS 8%, Social Security 7.51% on wages up to $48,000. PERS 7% on wages if *not* in social security. If in social security, monthly wages less $133.33 times 7% *or*, if wage is less than $400, wage times .6667 times 7%. Note: These tax tables are only issued when income tax changes occur - If other employee deduction rates change, tables are not reissued.
[3] Taxable earnings - gross pay, less tax sheltered annuities (TSAs), and employee retirement if the employer has implemented employer retirement "pickup."

Salinas, California. All earnings are listed on either the 1099 Miscellaneous form or the 1099 NEC (Not Employee Compensation) and filed with the IRS in Fresno. You must complete an annual 1096 to report the total amount, and attach the 1099's.

Others–Two particular earning groups need special review. Many property owners contact AARP (American Association of Retired Person) for prospects to perform management functions, as these persons often have the time and skills to do maintenance and manage income-producing properties. Seniors may earn up to $8800 in 1989 and not reduce their social security income payments. These earnings receive special consideration and are subject to certain wage taxes.

Another group is low-income persons with children, who file W5 forms. These are persons who earn under $10,000 a year. Typically, in positions of on-site managers, these persons get to stay home with their children, yet derive income by working from their home. They may be an unmarried head of household, or married (subject to special spouse filing). Instead of having all the taxes taken out of their income as they go through the year, they are in a special category called Federal Advanced Earned Income Credit (AEIC) where they get the tax credit back as they go through the year so they may increase their day-to-day income to support their family, rather than get a lump sum refund the next year.

The property of these income-property owners is often located in various areas, rather than in just a single jurisdiction. As investors diversify their portfolio, they are interacting with various on- and off-site managers throughout California. Property owners must evaluate their combined rental business income for all properties to see what category of personnel compensation status they may fall into. For federal tax purposes, if the owner's rental business income grosses over $250,000 per year, all persons working on the property are employees, and the state categorizes everyone as employees irrelevant of the income, especially on-site managers, or any hourly worker.

LEGAL ASPECTS OF HOUSING

Many federal, state, and local laws affect the rental industry. Some of the major laws will be reviewed in more detail here, but all are based upon the underlying foundation of the Constitution.

Discrimination

The law (both state and federal) prohibits discrimination in housing on the basis of race, color, religion, national origin, ancestry, sex, marital status, family status, or physical handicap. This includes all aspects of housing—appraisal, financing and loans, advertising, sales, and industrial, commercial, and residential income-producing rental property.

You cannot refuse to rent or deal with any person based on the special classifications listed above. You cannot make different terms, deposits, rental amounts, or conditions for different persons. You cannot advertise that housing is available to only certain persons, except for special senior status discussed earlier. You cannot deny the use of real estate services. Activities such as blockbusting and steering violate discrimination laws.

Blockbusting
The illegal act of attempting to induce the sale or rental of property, based on statements that persons of a particular race, creed, color, sex, or national origin are moving into the neighborhood.

Steering
The illegal act of directing prospective real estate clients to specific properties, neighborhoods, or areas based upon their race, sexual preference, accent, appearance, customs, or religion.

To help eliminate discrimination in all your rental business, you should have uniform and consistent policies for all persons, as was described in detail in Chapter 8. You may set specific guidelines to show sufficient income to meet rent payments. You may require credit and unlawful detainer credit checks on all applicants. You may set the deposit amount by formula. You may refuse to rent to persons with pets (except specially trained dogs, such as seeing-eye canines for the handicapped).

The Fair Housing Amendment Act of 1988 was approved 94 to 3 by a U.S. Senate vote to set federal guidelines, as local and state laws vary so vastly. The familial status will make it illegal to have sections or floors of buildings designated as "adult only." This law does not set any guidelines on the maximum number of persons that may occupy the unit. Violations are acts of discrimination.

Handicapped
Any person who is at a disadvantage in their capacity to perform because they are impaired by physical disability or mental deficiency.

It is illegal to refuse to rent to handicapped persons who otherwise meet your eligibility criteria. It is legal to set criteria for guide and service dogs, whether they be housed with the trainer or permanent placement person.

New construction criteria include wheelchair-width passage to ground floor units and access to common/public use areas. This would include turnaround space in kitchens and bathrooms, accessible routes through the unit, and accessible light switches, plugs, and environmental controls. For existing units, the owner may not prohibit the handicapped person from making reasonable modifications to allow them full enjoyment of their unit, when done at the tenant's expense, conforming to local building permit laws, and if the unit is returned to its original condition when vacated.

Violations will be heard by a jury trial or a Housing and Urban Development (HUD) administrative law judge. Victims of discrimination can be awarded actual damages, injunctive relief, attorney's fees, and fines. A $10,000 fine is given for a first violation, $25,000 if two or more violations occurred within the past five years, and $50,000 if two or more violations occurred within the past seven years.

Safety

Although the California Occupational Safety and Health Act (OSHA) has been disbanded, the federal OSHA still investigates workplace safety. Some employee unions are concerned with practices in the work areas of their members. The maintenance personnel in industrial and commercial environs are particularly involved with the hazards of maintaining, removing, and replacing both asbestos and insulation materials. Construction sites require safety hats for the protection of the workers. All areas of remodeling, repairing, and management should comply with the applicable laws.

Notices

Many state and federal rules and regulations apply to any business operation, including the business of managing rentals. These laws require that certain notices be posted in a conspicuous place at the job site.

The HUD Equal Housing Opportunity poster should be located at the management office and at the rent-paying site of each building. The office hours of the business office should be posted so they are visible when the office is locked and closed.

Employee safety rules, housing rules, pool rules, and equipment use rules should all be clearly visible. Minimum wage laws, and other required legal employment documents are regularly mailed to those who possess tax identification numbers as employers.

INSURANCE

Protection

There are many controversial issues regarding insurance coverage in dealing with California real estate transactions. One feature stands out, however, and that is the fact that if a tenant or other person's own insurance covers the problem, and that person is satisfied with the outcome, the best results occur. If the person is unhappy with the conclusion, they always look for "deep pockets" to sue. To avert this insurance-management problem, the property manager tries to advise all parties to have adequate coverage.

The property manager should review the coverage of the property owner to see the coverages the owner should have, compared to actual coverage, and should comparison shop for basic rates, deductibles, premium rates, exclusions and similar considerations.

Property managers must also assess their own coverage. This would include an analysis of whether they should maintain their own coverage, or be a part of the property owner's coverage. Due to potential conflict of interest issues on some management decisions, certain specific areas of coverage should be separate, such as the cost of and choice of an attorney in an owner/manager dispute.

The property manager is certainly expected to review and make recommendations regarding the coverage for the property being managed. This requires special knowledge and expertise. The owner expects the manager to be able to advise on the selection of insurance brokers, evaluating risks, overseeing losses, and averting the need for claims.

The property manager must also have expertise in protecting the rights of tenants and advising them on many areas of insurance coverage. Some leases do not require the tenant to produce proof of insurance coverage, but the wise property manager reviews the insurance coverage with the tenant, clarifying what is NOT part of the property owner's coverage. There are many types of tenant insurance policies, and the tenant needs to be advised that the owner of the residential property cannot cover the loss of the tenant's personal property. Other nonresidential tenants must show insurance coverage as part of their lease—i.e., glass breakage, business interruption, etc. Advising tenants about coverage for their guests and invitees warrants careful consideration as part of the management practices.

Existing Coverage

The property manager should have a good working relationship with several insurance brokers. Through experience—the management of a number of properties and a thorough review of each owner's policy, coverage, and premium, a good knowledge of rates, claims handling and insurance analysis will come naturally to the property manager. For example, the manager will quickly learn that the lowest price is not much of a bargain if the claims loss payoff is poor. And the nicest agent is of little value if most items needing to be covered are specific exclusions.

Typically, when a building is purchased the prospective buyer is required to furnish an insurance policy to obtain approval for the loan. The request for the insurance coverage is made by the escrow officer as part of the transaction (Figure 10).

When a property manager takes on an account for management, a copy of the existing insurance policies should be part of the management contract. Some owners are reluctant to give out this information because they think the property manager may change the policy, agent, or coverage. The property manager needs to dispel potential fears by reassuring the owner that insurance companies require the owner's signature to change policy coverage.

The property manager should only deal with "A" rated companies, those with ongoing working track records with at least one major independent company and several chain firms. There are times when it becomes necessary to get quick, temporary, immediate coverage, or specialized types of coverages.

Insurance issues are subject to frequent change by the voters and the state legislators. Many future insurance changes will be a result of the ongoing controversy over costs, coverage, and claims. Due to these potential changes, some firms are leaving the California market, while others are catering to the market demands. While some firms are only keeping existing policies and not writing new California business, others are actively seeking to offer services to individuals—not only to meet lender requirements, but also to actually aid the clients. Because of these changes, the professional manager keeps several irons in the fire.

Penalties

Many penalty fees and related charges can be averted with a thorough understanding of insurance. Building coverage is typically much larger than for the owner's home, so a policy for $10,000 is not unusual.

Figure 10

INSURANCE INFORMATION STATEMENT

Your lender will require an original fire insurance policy in an amount equal to or greater than your loan balance, prior to the closing of your escrow, and will require that the premium be paid through escrow, or that your agent furnish paid receipt if paid by you directly.

Please furnish us with the information as indicated below as soon as possible in order to expedite the closing of your escrow:

☐ I will request my agent, set forth below, to contact you regarding insurance coverage.

Name ____

Address ____

____

Telephone (_____) __________________________________

Insurance Company/Agency ____________________________

I have been quoted annual premium of approximately $__________ for the following coverage:

☐ Homeowners $____________ ☐ Standard Fire $____________

☐ I will select my insurance agent later, and will deliver or cause to be delivered to you such policy, in time to meet the lender's requirements.

________________________ ________________________

________________________ ________________________

If the policy is paid in installments, expect a finance fee of $500 to $1000 additional expense. If the policy is cancelled early, a penalty fee is also charged.

Lender Requirements

Each mortgagee requires a certificate of insurance, showing the collateral for the loan being covered. The building owners have the right to choose their own coverage. However, should the owners fail to have proof of property insurance, a clause in the loan terms allows the lender to provide and place their own coverage, irrespective of rate, and to bill the owner along with the loan payment. Hazard and liability insurance are often the only types of coverage. The coverage meets the loan amount, but rarely is adequate to cover the equity in the property. The lender will need the insured's name, policy number, loan number, agent's name and agent number, agent's address, and telephone number, master company name, address, and telephone number.

Most insurance policies contain a mortgagee clause which makes the proceeds for a loss or claim payable to the insured and the lender, so all must sign off in event of a claim's loss.

Indemnification/Exclusions

To indemnify is to make good a loss: to replace or repair or pay for the extent of a loss. "All-risks" insurance covers losses caused by all perils, except those specifically excluded in the contract. An exclusion is a provision in an insurance contract stating a situation in which insurance is not afforded under the contract. For example, damage caused by a flood may be specifically excluded from a policy.

Deductible

A clause in a policy providing that the insurer will pay only that amount of any loss that is in excess of a specified amount. The insured must cover the balance. By increasing the deductible amounts, you can save a lot of money in premiums.

Types Of Coverage

Fire. Fire insurance protects against losses caused by fire, and usually includes losses caused by lightening. Check for exclusions. Extended coverage also covers losses caused by windstorm, explosion, riot, aircraft, smoke, and other items.

As of January 1, 1986, all single-family and factory-built dwellings must have working smoke detectors. As of January 1, 1987, working smoke detectors must be installed in common stairwells and in each unit of multiple-dwelling units, including duplexes, lodging houses, apartment complexes, hotels, motels, condominiums, time-share projects, and stock cooperatives. Failure to comply with this California law could mean not only citation by the local fire/health department, but also cancellation of insurance policies.

Liability. Liability insurance is intended to cover both damages and expenses connected with alleged or actual owner liability. Coverage should include claims against the insured for damages arising from the business premises or operations.

By May 1988, 17 insurance companies left California and four were forced to leave because of low reserves caused by high negligence awards under liability policies. Insurance companies inspected buildings and informed owners that they would cancel the policy if the owner failed to resolve cited items (such as graffiti painted on carport walls and cracks in sidewalks). The rule has been to prove what the "reasonable and prudent" landlord would do in like circumstances. (Figure 11)

Errors & Omissions/Rent Loss/Bond/Additional Insured. Insurance coverage should include the errors and defaults of the property managers and staff, loss of rents during a repair period, and additional living expenses provided to house occupants due to property damage (i.e., hotel costs), and coverage for financial loss due to dishonesty of employees or losses caused by acts or omissions of the principal. The property managers, lenders, and building owners should all be on the policy as the insured, or as named additional insured.

Figure 11

LIABILITY NEGLIGENCE

The Reasonable and Prudent Care Landlord would:

1. Clear trash receptacles and dumpsters from buildings.
2. Clear grease, oil spots, and puddles from driveways, carports, and walkways.
3. Post signs in or on halls, stairways, doors, pool:

   "Watch your Step" "No Lifeguard on Duty"
   "Use Handrail" "No Trespassing"
4. Never allow loose carpets or rugs where someone could slip.
5. Never allow loose banisters or railings
6. Always have well-lighted stairways, halls, door, and parking areas.
7. Never allow tenants to keep any "ferocious" animal or pet on the premises.
8. Dispose of or secure any "attractive nuisance" from children or the mentally incompetent.
9. Never have unkept grounds or slovenly appearances on the property.

Co-insurance. This is an arrangement where the property is insured for less than its full value. If the property manager keeps the current market value policy coverage, a concession is given on the premium rate at 60%, 80% or similar amounts.

Glass Coverage/Sprinkler Leakage. Insurance where the insured agrees to replace or pay for damaged glass and to pay certain incidental costs relating to glass is called glass insurance. Commercial leases often require tenants to provide proof of glass coverage as a term for the lease, as well as sprinkler leakage insurance. This covers accidental leakage or discharge from a sprinkler system due to causes other than fire.

Worker's Compensation. Worker's compensation is insurance against liability imposed on an employer by the Worker's Compensation Law, which is a statute that imposes benefits and coverage to employees injured or killed in the course of and because of their job. Rates have drastically changed in the recent past. (Figure 12). California law requires insurers to surcharge policies to settle unpaid claims in the event of company insolvencies. The burden of proof rests with the employer to prove that the injured individual was not an employee. The state treats on-site, resident managers as employees. The state can fine you $100 per employee (maximum $10,000) for failing to carry Worker's Compensation. In case of injury there is a 10% penalty, plus the benefits you would have to provide, which include all medical expenses, loss of income for the worker, $2,000 funeral expense for the family of the worker and up to $95,000 death benefit, plus rehabilitation and vocational retraining costs. Always review all personnel (employees and independent contractors) with your insurance agent.

If a loss occurs, take pictures, determine the extent of the loss, and notify your agent immediately. When determining the loss, remember that you will have to prove all claims. In conclusion, don't buy insurance you don't need, but make sure you have adequate coverage.

Figure 12

California Worker's Compensation Rates

Rating Classification	1984	1988	1989
8810 Clerical Office Employees	.53	.74	.78
9015 Building Operation— All employees 9014 Building Operation— By owner or lessee	7.64	11.72	11.11
8741 Real Estate Agencies— Employees engaged out-side of office, including sales 8742 Collectors or Outside— Salespersons		.92	.84

CHAPTER 14–QUIZ

1. The initials "U.D." relate to:

   a. mortgage information
   b. uninsured determination matters
   c. condominium rules and restrictions
   d. an unlawful detainer/eviction action

2. A stipulation refers to a/an:

   a. insurance clause
   b. loan term
   c. legal settlement
   d. rental agreement

3. An Arrieta Claim pertains to:

   a. a maintenance and repair claim
   b. persons not named in an eviction action
   c. an insurance claim
   d. personal property claims of tenant for improvements

4. An independent contractor would be involved with which form:

   a. 1099
   b. W-2
   c. DE3
   d. 941

5. The illegal act of directing prospective persons to particular areas or neighborhoods based upon their race is:

   a. blockbusting
   b. steering
   c. Section 8
   d. segregation

6. Rent loss insurance covers:

   a. rents lost in a tenant eviction
   b. court costs and fees in a tenant eviction
   c. rents lost because of a building fire
   d. Both a) and b)

7. A certificate of insurance is required by a/an:

   a. mortgagee
   b. tenant
   c. landlord
   d. attorney

8. Worker's Compensation Insurance contains:

   a. clauses excluding graffiti
   b. a surcharge for claims of insolvent companies
   c. stock options for coinsured lack of losses
   d. exclusion for glass and water problems

9. Should a tenant who owes rent move, leaving $500 worth of personal property on the premises, the landlord may:

   a. sell the property and apply the funds to the rent due
   b. hold the items until the tenant pays the rent due
   c. store, advertise, publish, and sell the items, sending the proceeds to the county
   d. store, advertise, publish and sell the items, sending the proceeds to the nearest relative or the state

10. In an unlawful detainer action the tenant files the:

    a. Answer
    b. Summons and Complaint
    c. Notice to Pay or Quit
    d. Notice of Trial and Stipulation

CHAPTER 14–QUIZ ANSWERS

1. d
2. c
3. b
4. a
5. b
6. c
7. a
8. b
9. c
10. a

15

Property Management In Review

References

The IREM-OC Newsletter. January 1988; Chapter 91.

"Business executives face ethical questions daily." In: *CPM Aspects*. Chicago: Institute of Real Estate Management; August 1987; XIX(7).

Last Chapter Review

The legal and insurance aspects of management were reviewed in the last chapter. The legal steps in an eviction were discussed in some detail, and the employment laws were outlined regarding employee, manager, tenant, and owner's authority, rights and responsibilities. The various types of insurance coverage were discussed as to types of protections.

Chapter Overview

The management of any real property is the culmination of actions and reactions between many groups of individuals. This chapter reviews the professional property manager, the professional organizations of property managers, the professional landlord/tenant relationship, and the ethics of management.

THE PROFESSIONAL MANAGER

The licensed real estate broker is the central player in the management business. Many licensed real estate salesperson licensees have the knowledge and experience required to be a good property manager, they merely have not taken the time to obtain a broker's license. This is sometimes due to the shield of liability that comes from working under a broker instead of being one. Other times it is because these individuals like managing the buildings, but don't want to be responsible for the business operations (responsibility for year-end W-2 and 1099 forms, tax preparation, building rent, balancing the trust account, etc.). Some good salespersons don't want the extra expense that comes with a broker's license. In any event, property managers must be brokers or work under licensed brokers to perform their duties.

The professional property manager has education in management skills, auditing, communications, writing skills, marketing, advertising, contracts, negotiations, human relations, accounting, and law. They have experience in construction, maintenance, repairs, equipment, and materials. These persons have developed techniques for giving market evaluations, estimating value, projecting rents, estimating the feasibility of new projects, and giving advice on project conversions and property use alternatives.

The property manager oversees all phases of operation of the rental business and reports back to the property owner. The owner matches the findings and recommendations to goals for the property and ability to meet the financial demands. Together they develop a professional plan of operation that's carried out by the manager.

The professional property manager, like any other worker, has outside interests, family and friends, and likes reasonably regular working hours. But the field of property management has many emergency situations that require a willingness to be available when tenants are home (often nights and weekends), and when emergencies arise. Individuals attracted to this area must have a lot of confidence in themselves and the ability to advise others. They must also possess the ability to work with frequent interruptions, changes in plans, occasional hostility, and the ability to work and reason with government agencies.

PROFESSIONAL MANAGEMENT ORGANIZATIONS

The property manager is involved with various professional organizations, according to the particular type of property being managed. Earlier, the individual organizations were reviewed so that you could contact the specific group of choice. There are organizations for those managing shopping centers, industrial property, residential property, mobile homes, office buildings, and the like.

IREM

One organization that addresses all areas of professional property management on a nationwide basis is the National Association of Realtors management branch, called the Institute of Real Estate Management (IREM). This organization was founded in 1933 (after the depression when lenders became the owners of many foreclosed properties). Institutions and professionals found that there was no formalized property management expertise available on a nationwide basis. One community would have an excellent trained manager, and another area would have no one who knew anything about property management. These professionals developed a criteria for membership. The high standards they imposed and their candidate-training process has led to today's superior level of professional management.

IREM offers professional designations to an individual licensee, to a company who meets the qualifications, and to non-licensee on-site resident managers. IREM members receive many benefits, such as the periodical they publish addressing current issues of concern—asbestos, rent control, maintenance, etc. Their articles are kept as reference materials by various individuals and firms. Membership in this national organization aids in networking issues, and gives all members a collective voice in matters affecting real estate.

CAR

The California Association of Realtors, through its local Real Estate Boards, is a professional organization that lends itself to many property managers. Each Board has local community leaders, and fosters political interaction, community involvement, and government interest that affect the property management job. The Board can help the property manager with anything from how to get approval for a permit to stucco-coat a building, to knowing which local insurance agent has the best rates.

The Board has many committees that the property manager should be involved with. For example, the education committee can help the licensed property manager obtain continuing education hours for license renewal. The computer committee can assist in the management decision as to whether to have a computer that not only does word processing, but also provides a link to the Board computer to access comparable sales prices and compatible unit rental rates.

Miscellaneous Organizations

Other professional organizations that the professional property manager should be associated with include the Chamber of Commerce and Better Business Bureau. These groups not only assist in local connections, but are also helpful in obtaining discounts to their members and providing the names of good, reliable vendors—plumbers, electricians, gardeners, etc.

THE PROFESSIONAL LANDLORD

Many property owners are self-made entrepreneurs who have mowed their own lawns, painted their own units, and collected their own rents. Although growing in numbers, few individuals purchase property and hire all the management from day one. On the other hand, nonindividual ownership—syndications, corporations—have always tended to hire management. These facts lead to a wide divergence in owners, and each landlord will have a different view of his or her role.

The professional property manager expects to work with a professional landlord/owner. The manager cannot be expected to be available by telephone to answer questions on a regular basis after 10:00 p.m. on weekdays, nor on Sunday. The landlord should have a regular method of communicating with the manager—not on an as-needed basis, but on a planned schedule. Their agenda should include discussing money matters, tenants, maintenance, and projected business changes. This is the time when bids the manager obtained and had previously mailed to the owner for review, are discussed. The status on evictions and collections are rarely part of this process, as the owner receives notice of all legal progress. However, projected rent increases and budget differences are good materials to consider discussing at this time. The meeting can be in person quarterly or annually, and by telephone monthly or as scheduled.

The professional landlord does not ask the manager to participate in illegal activities for the landlord. For instance, an owner should not expect the property manager to participate in his or her accepting the highest bid, then hiring a lower bidder to complete a job, and pocketing the difference. Instructions to use persons who are not legal citizens or real estate licensees or contractors to perform work on the property cannot be tolerated. Orders to rent to a particular group or not to rent to particular groups of people are not acceptable, either.

The professional landlord must give directions regarding the property that are legal, reasonable and good business. The landlord who gives poor, unacceptable or illegal orders will find that because of the confidentiality of the relationship, the professional property manager cannot "turn them in" and the only alternative is for the manager to "fire" the landlord. The manager who cannot follow the commands of the landlord has no alternative but to sever the ties in order for the manager to keep his or her license, credentials, and professionalism.

THE PROFESSIONAL TENANT

The tenant who keeps their tenant/property manager relationship on a professional level will have less aggravation and be better able to cope with the interaction between the parties. The professional tenant should strive to maintain integrity in all situations.

The tenant should not make major alterations (painting white latex walls with high-gloss, black enamel is a major change) to the decorating, structure, or rental use without notifying the landlord for prior approval.

This may be necessary in order to obtain permits, or to meet insurance and lender requirements.

The tenant should know management's financial criteria, and what he or she qualifies for in terms of rent, assessments, and other deposits and expenses that he or she takes on with the rental unit. Evictions can often be avoided if the tenant has laid out his or her finances and knows the limitations. The professional tenant obtains estimates from the local utility companies on the expected amount of recurring expenses for these items. The tenant should budget these as a regular part of the monthly expenses, in addition to the rent due. An example of a tenant budget is shown in Figure 1. If inadequate disposable funds are available for housing, alternatives need to be reviewed. They may include moving to smaller, less expensive quarters, obtaining roommates, or decreasing other expenses.

Figure 1

Budget—*How much can I afford?*

Per Month

INCOME		+ $______
Food	$______	
Transportation	$______	
Clothing	$______	
Insurance	$______	
Medical	$______	
Savings	$______	
Installment debt	$______	
Fun	$______	
	Less Expenses	− $______
LEFT TO SPEND ON HOUSING		= $______
Heating	$______	
Electric	$______	
Water	$______	
Trash	$______	
Telephone	$______	
THE AFFORDABLE AMOUNT OF RENT TO PAY		$______
	Amount of rent presently paying	______

Low- and moderate-income families may be eligible for public assistance programs and should be advised by the property manager to check with the local Housing Authority. Often the handicapped, seniors, and other persons qualify for programs but may be too proud to apply for assistance, or they do not know it is available. Tenants need to seek out all means that are available to them.

The Housing Voucher Program is the newest addition to many county Housing Authority rental assistance programs. The program is funded by the U.S. Department of Housing and Urban Development, and is administered by the local Housing Authority office. Because of the very high rent levels in many California communities, many persons were unable to obtain assistance of any kind, because the maximum amounts of the program rents and deposits was far below the minimum level that a property would command in the marketplace.

Unique aspects of the Housing Voucher Program that appeal to both owners and tenants include:

1) The contract rent of the unit is NOT limited to HUD's Fair Market Rents, allowing the amount of rent to be negotiated between landlord/property manager/tenant.
2) Tenants may choose to pay above 30% of their adjusted gross income towards rent. The family pays the difference between the unit rent and the government portion.
3) The government portion of the rent is payable directly to the owner on behalf of the family, so payments are guaranteed and timely.
4) The unpaid rent and damage protection is one month's contract rent minus the security deposit paid by the family.
5) Annual rent increases are not limited by any amount set by the government. The tenant and landlord are responsible for yearly negotiations.

Regular aspects of the Housing Voucher Program include the unit's regular inspection for Housing Quality Standards of decent, safe and sanitary conditions. The lease must be a 12-month contract signed by all parties.

Section 8 rent under HUD contracts aids the handicapped, elderly, and lower income families. Their program revolves around the HAP anniversary date—the date the tenant contract was approved by HUD for the tenant rent to begin. Annual increases are based upon HUD's annual adjustment factor (AAF), and a list of proposed fair market rent schedules can be obtained from the nearest HUD office. Other government programs are available and local agencies may assist in these other areas.

Professional tenants know their rights and seek to keep up to date on matters concerning the landlord/tenant relationship. For instance, the right of tenants to form collective bargaining units has evolved. Groups such as the National Tenant Organization inform and educate tenants on their rights. Legal Aid helps negotiate tenants' legal rights. Rent strikes command the attention of any landlord or manager. Government agencies, such as health, safety, and building departments assist in keeping persons from inhabiting dilapidated properties that do not meet the criteria for human occupancy and collection of rents. Rent Control governs rents, deposits, and rent raises.

ETHICS

Business honesty, or *ethics,* does not have to conflict with business operations. Most good business leaders are ethical and they rely upon their reputation to stay in business for the long run, with their foundation premised upon their having sound business ethics.

There are always conflicts between people's interpretation of what ethics consists of, and whether it borders on religion, or if it includes morals. Controversy surrounds the issue of whether ethics can even be taught to adults. This text is not attempting to address these issues, but to state the rules and regulations surrounding the written Code of Ethics that the professional property manager agrees to abide by.

Ethics are not inflexible rules that managers must follow. They are solutions applied to situations that professionals find themselves in, where a dilemma confronts them, and where they attempt to resolve the problem. To arrive at the solution, people generally follow one of the four following models:

1) They use the "Golden Rule" to guide them with concern for others.
2) They put profit first, in the basic free-enterprise system style where they believe that profit benefits everyone, so it must be the reasonable way.
3) They look at issues in the "live and let live" way that if it does not harm others, it must be okay.
4) They take those actions that accomplish the greatest good for the greatest number of people, even if a few suffer.

The misconceptions about ethics are usually found in the following five areas:

1) You cannot mix morality and profit. The mentality here is that if a person achieved wealth and success, they must be money-hungry, unscrupulous persons—therefore, profit is not predicated upon hard work.
2) Black and white vision. All business issues can be clearly defined as good or bad, right or wrong, ethical or immoral. As business persons today know in the complicated international markets, what is standard business practice in one area is completely against all business acceptance in another area, and vice versa. The gray areas of business are always harder for everyone to deal with, including managers. The executive is paid to make these judgment calls, and is responsible for the results.
3) Success requires unethical behavior. This attitude is based upon the misconception that the American heroes of business were successful only by being insensitive to others in the business world and community, and by backbiting and backstabbing, and using spies to steal ideas.
4) Ethics equals social responsibility. Social pressures are sometimes placed heavily upon the business community, but a business can still succeed by doing what is right and ethical. Some firms encourage ethical behavior, others ignore the issue and do not educate their employees concerning ethical behavior.

5) The law and ethics are equivalent. Many times, in fact, there is conflict between what the law says a business must do, and what a business manager ethically wants to do (i.e., the conflict between property manager wanting to give the homeless an empty building in cold, rainy weather, but the law ruling it uninhabitable for human occupancy).

The best way to handle ethics is to educate all personnel. It should be a part of their original orientation of what is and what is not acceptable with the company. It should be a written part of all job descriptions. When a worker signs on and receives a copy of the job description, and has a brief training session on the issues surrounding ethics, more job success is experienced.

Most frequently, people fail to use good ethics and good judgment when they are under stress, pressure from peers, in a panic, or handling a crisis. There should be written daily operations describing many phases of the property management field of employment to avoid these kinds of situations. These should review sample cases covering some of the regular, recurring issues that the person will have to deal with. In this manner, a discussion and exchange of reasoning can become a regular part of training.

The National Association of Realtors has a written *Code of Ethics* (Figure 2). A good guideline to use is their publication *Interpretations of the Code of Ethics,* which gives examples of conduct (Figure 3).

In addition to the *Code of Ethics*, the National Association of Realtors has their *Standard of Practice Relating to Articles of the Code of Ethics,* which were set forth by the Professional Standards Committee and approved by the Board of Directors. (Figure 4).

Figure 2

Code of Ethics and Standards of Practice
of the NATIONAL ASSOCIATION OF REALTORS®

Preamble. . .
Under all is the land. Upon its wise utilization and widely allocated ownership depend the survival and growth of free institutions and of our civilization. The REALTOR® should recognize that the interests of the nation and its citizens require the highest and best use of the land and the widest distribution of land ownership. They require the creation of adequate housing, the building of functioning cities, the development of productive industries and farms, and the preservation of a healthful environment.

Such interests impose obligations beyond those of ordinary commerce. They impose grave social responsibility and a patriotic duty to which the REALTOR® should dedicate himself, and for which he should be diligent in preparing himself. The REALTOR®, therefore, is zealous to maintain and improve the standards of his calling and shares with his fellow REALTORS® a common responsibility for its integrity and honor. The term REALTOR® has come to connote competency, fairness, and high integrity resulting from adherence to a lofty ideal of moral conduct in business relations. No inducement of profit and no instruction from clients ever can justify departure from this ideal.

In the interpretation of this obligation, a REALTOR® can take no safer guide than that which has been handed down through the centuries, embodied in the Golden Rule, "Whatsoever ye would that men should do to you, do ye even so to them."

Accepting this standard as his own, every REALTOR® pledges himself to observe its spirit in all of his activities and to conduct his business in accordance with the tenets set forth below.

ARTICLE 1
The REALTOR® should keep himself informed on matters affecting real estate in his community, the state, and nation so that he may be able to contribute responsibly to public thinking on such matters.

ARTICLE 2

In justice to those who place their interests in his care, the REALTOR® should endeavor always to be informed regarding laws, proposed legislation, governmental regulations, public policies, and current market conditions in order to be in a position to advise his clients properly.

ARTICLE 3

The REALTOR® should endeavor to eliminate in his community any practices which could be damaging to the public or bring discredit to the real estate profession. The REALTOR® should assist the governmental agency charged with regulating the practices of brokers and salesmen in his state. (Revised 11/87)

ARTICLE 4

To prevent dissension and misunderstanding and to assure better service to the owner, the REALTOR® should urge the exclusive listing of property unless contrary to the best interest of the owner. (Revised 11/87)

ARTICLE 5

In the best interests of society, of his associates, and his own business, the REALTOR® should willingly share with other REALTORS® the lessons of his experience and study for the benefit of the public, and should be loyal to the Board of REALTORS® of his community and active in its work.

ARTICLE 6

The REALTOR® shall seek no unfair advantage over other REALTORS® and shall conduct his business so as to avoid controversies with other REALTORS®. (Revised 11/87)

ARTICLE 7

In accepting employment as an agent, the REALTOR® pledges himself to protect and promote the interests of the client. This obligation of absolute fidelity to the client's interests is primary, but it does not relieve the REALTOR® of the obligation to treat fairly all parties to the transaction.

ARTICLE 8
The REALTOR® shall not accept compensation from more than one party, even if permitted by law, without the full knowledge of all parties to the transaction.

ARTICLE 9
The REALTOR® shall avoid exaggeration, misrepresentation, or concealment of pertinent facts relating to the property or the transaction. The REALTOR® shall not, however, be obligated to discover latent defects in the property or to advise on matters outside the scope of his real estate license.

ARTICLE 10
The REALTOR® shall not deny equal professional services to any person for reasons of race, creed, sex, or country of national origin. The REALTOR® shall not be party to any plan or agreement to discriminate against a person or persons on the basis of race, creed, sex, or country of national origin.

ARTICLE 11
A REALTOR® is expected to provide a level of competent service in keeping with the standards of practice in those fields in which the REALTOR® customarily engages.

The REALTOR® shall not undertake to provide specialized professional services concerning a type of property or service that is outside his field of competence unless he engages the assistance of one who is competent on such types of property or service, or unless the facts are fully disclosed to the client. Any person engaged to provide such assistance shall be so identified to the client and his contribution to the assignment should be set forth.

The REALTOR® shall refer to the Standards of Practice of the National Association as to the degree of competence that a client has a right to expect the REALTOR® to possess, taking into consideration the complexity of the problem, the availability of expert assistance, and the opportunities for experience available to the REALTOR®.

ARTICLE 12

The REALTOR® shall not undertake to provide professional services concerning a property or its value where he has a present or contemplated interest unless such interest is specifically disclosed to all affected parties.

ARTICLE 13

The REALTOR® shall not acquire an interest in or buy for himself, any member of his immediate family, his firm or any member thereof, or any entity in which he has a substantial ownership interest, property listed with him, without making the true position known to the listing owner. In selling property owned by himself, or in which he has any interest, the REALTOR® shall reveal the facts of his ownership or interest to the purchaser.

ARTICLE 14

In the event of a controversy between REALTORS® associated with different firms, arising out of their relationship as REALTORS®, the REALTORS® shall submit the dispute to arbitration in accordance with the regulations of their Board or Boards rather than litigate the matter.

ARTICLE 15

If a REALTOR® is charged with unethical practice or is asked to present evidence in any disciplinary proceeding or investigation, he shall place all pertinent facts before the proper tribunal of the member board or affiliated institute, society, or council of which he is a member.

ARTICLE 16

When acting as agent, the REALTOR® shall not accept any commission, rebate, or profit on expenditures made for his principal-owner, without the principal's knowledge and consent.

ARTICLE 17

The REALTOR® shall not engage in activities that constitute the unauthorized practice of law and shall recommend that legal counsel be obtained when the interest of any party to the transaction requires it.

ARTICLE 18

The REALTOR® shall keep in a special account in an appropriate financial institution, separated from his own funds, monies coming into his possession in trust for other persons, such as escrows, trust funds, clients' monies, and other like items.

ARTICLE 19

The REALTOR® shall be careful at all times to present a true picture in his advertising and representations to the public. The REALTOR® shall also ensure that his status as a broker or a REALTOR® is clearly identifiable in any such advertising.

ARTICLE 20

The REALTOR®, for the protection of all parties, shall see that financial obligations and commitments regarding real estate transactions are in writing, expressing the exact agreement of the parties. A copy of each agreement shall be furnished to each party upon his signing such agreement.

ARTICLE 21

The REALTOR® shall not engage in any practice or take any action inconsistent with the agency of another REALTOR®.

ARTICLE 22

In the sale of property which is exclusively listed with a REALTOR®, the REALTOR® shall utilize the services of other brokers upon mutually agreed upon terms when it is in the best interests of the client.

Negotiations concerning property which is listed exclusively shall be carried on with the listing broker, not with the owner, except with the consent of the listing broker.

ARTICLE 23

The REALTOR® shall not publicly disparage the business practice of a competitor nor volunteer an opinion of a competitor's transaction. If his opinion is sought and if the REALTOR® deems it appropriate to respond, such opinion shall be rendered with strict professional integrity and courtesy.

The Code of Ethics was adopted in 1913. Amended at the Annual Convention in 1924, 1928, 1950, 1951, 1955, 1956, 1961, 1962, 1974, 1982, 1986, and 1987.

Figure 3

Case #16-1, Profit on Supplies Used in Property Management:

REALTOR® A, as a property manager, bought at wholesale prices, janitor supplies used in the cleaning and maintenance of an office building which he managed for his client, Owner B. In his statements to Owner B, he billed these supplies at retail prices.

The practice came to the attention of Owner B who filed a complaint against REALTOR® A with the local Board of REALTORS® charging unethical conduct in violation of Article 16 of the Code of Ethics.

In questioning during the hearing called by the Board's Professional Standards Committee, REALTOR® A's defense was that the prices at which he billed these supplies to this client were no higher than prices which Owner B had been paying prior to putting the property under REALTOR® A's management. Subsequently, it was clearly established that no disclosure of this profit on supplies used in property management had been made, and also that in proposing the management contract, REALTOR® A had held out to Owner B the inducement of attainable economies in operation.

REALTOR® A was found by the Committee to be in violation of Article 16.

Case #16-2, Manager's Use of Client's Property for Vending Machines:

REALTOR® A managed Client B's large apartment building, and made an arrangement under which coin-operated vending machines were placed in a basement corridor of the building.

On an inspection, six months after the machines were installed, Client B observed them and raised a question as to the propriety of REALTOR® A's action in installing them, and deriving some revenue from them, without his knowledge and consent. REALTOR® A's response was that he had considered the arrangement under which the machines were brought in as a service to the tenants and in no way adverse to the owner's interests. He told Client B that he did derive some small revenue from them, which had not been remitted because he felt that this revenue no more than compensated him for his time in arranging for installation of the machines and maintaining contact with the firm that operated them. He suggested that Client B seek a formal ruling on any ethical consideration involved by submitting the matter to the Professional Standards Committee of the Board of REALTORS® .

Accordingly, Client B did so, indicating that the question was being raised at the suggestion of REALTOR® A in order to establish a clearcut finding in the matter. The Committee then held a hearing on the matter which established that 1) REALTOR® A had not consulted his client at the time he authorized installation of the machines; 2) that revenue derived from operation of the machines had been retained by REALTOR® A; 3) that Client B had been furnished no information whatever in the matter until he observed the machines in his own periodic inspection of the building.

It was the conclusion of the Committee on Professional Standards of the local Board that, whether or not the presence of the machines was a service to the tenants, the giving of authority for their installation was in effect a rental of the space they occupied; that, in the absence of any disclosure to the owner, REALTOR® A was in violation of Article 16 of the Code of Ethics.

Case #16-3, Management Responsibility in Relation to Manager's Enterprises:

REALTOR® A managed a large apartment building for his client, Owner B. After the building had been under his management for two years, REALTOR® A acquired a vacant site adjacent to the building and developed it as an automobile parking terminal with monthly rates set at $15. REALTOR® A advised Owner B of this action, feeling that it would be advantageous to the building and Owner B indicated that he, too, felt this development was favorable to him.

Six months after establishing the parking lot, REALTOR® A raised his monthly parking rate to $22. When this came to the attention of Owner B, he filed a complaint against REALTOR® A with the Board of REALTORS® charging that the parking rate increase represented an unethical attempt on the part of REALTOR® A to profit by Owner B's investment in the apartment building; that REALTOR® A should have raised rents in the building but had instead transferred the rent increase to an increased rate in his parking lot.

A hearing was called on the complaint before the Board's Professional Standards Committee. In the hearing REALTOR® A presented data tabulating monthly parking rates in the general area of his enterprise, which showed that $22 was about the average prevailing rate for similar facilities in the area. He also presented a tabulation of rents which showed that the rent schedule in Owner B's building was relatively high in comparison with similar rental accommodations in the area.

After careful review of this data, the Committee concluded that REALTOR® A's parking lot enterprise had involved no expenditure of Owner B's funds; that his action in establishing this business had met with Owner B's, approval at the outset; that REALTOR® A's exhibits demonstrated that there was no merit to Owner B's contention that a justified rent increase had been shunted into an increase in parking rates; that Owner B had no valid claim for participation in the enterprise of REALTOR® A; that Owner B's interests had in no sense been betrayed; that the proximity of the parking area continued to be an asset to Owner B's building; that REALTOR® A was not in violation of Article 16.

Figure 4

Standards of Practice

Relating to Articles of the Code of Ethics
(Adopted through November 12, 1980)

The Standards of Practice relating to the Code of Ethics are "interpretations" of various Articles of the Code of Ethics and are not a part of the Code itself. The proper relationship between the Standards of Practice and the Code of Ethics is set forth in the following advisory opinion by the Board of Directors of the National Association:

"In filing a charge of an alleged violation of the Code of Ethics by a REALTOR® , the charge shall read as an alleged violation of one or more Articles of the Code. A Standard of Practice may only be cited in support of the charge."

The Standards of Practice are only supplementary to, and do not replace, the "numbered cases" found in *Interpretation of the Code of Ethics*. A Standard of Practice is a statement of general prinicple related to an Article of the Code of Ethics to guide REALTORS® and REALTOR-ASSOCIATES® as to the professional conduct required in the specific situation described by the Standard of Practice, whereas each of the "numbered cases" in *Interpretations of the Code of Ethics* presents a set of particular facts alleging a violation of the Code of Ethics, and describes the conclusion determined on merit by the Professional Standards Committee as related to the particular facts of the case.

As additional Standards of Practice are adopted, Member Boards and Board Members will be advised of their adoption.

Standard of Practice 4-1

"The REALTOR® shall not misrepresent the availability of access to show or inspect a listed property."

Standard of Practice 7-1

"The REALTOR® shall receive and shall transmit all offers on a specified property to the owner for his decision, whether such offers are received from a prospective purchaser or another broker."

Standard of Practice 7-2

"The REALTOR®, acting as listing broker, shall submit all offers to the seller as quickly as possible."

Standard of Practice 7-3

"The REALTOR®, in attempting to secure a listing, shall not deliberately mislead the owner as to market value."

Standard of Practice 7-4

(Refer to the Standard of Practice 22-1, which also relates to Article 7, Code of Ethics.)

Standard of Practice 7-5

(Refer to Standard of Practice 22-2, which also relates to Article 7, Code of Ethics.

Standard of Practice 9-1

"The REALTOR® shall not be a party to the naming of a false consideration in any document, unless it be the naming of an obviously nominal consideration."

Standard of Practice 9-2

"The REALTOR®, when asked by another broker, shall disclose the nature of his listing, i.e., an exclusive right to sell, an exclusive agency, open listing, or other."

Standard of Practice 9-3

(Refer to Standard of Practice 7-3, which also relates to Article 9, Code of Ethics.)

Standard of Practice 9-4

"The REALTOR® shall not offer a service described as 'free of charge' when the rendering of a service is contingent on the obtaining of a benefit such as a listing or commission."

Standard of Practice 9-5

"The REALTOR® shall, with respect to the subagency of another REALTOR®, timely communicate any change of compensation for subagency services to the other REALTOR® prior to the time such REALTOR® produces a prospective buyer who has signed an offer to purchase the property for which the subagency has been offered through MLS or otherwise by the listing agency."

Standard of Practice 11-1

"Whenever a REALTOR® submits an oral or written opinion of the value of real property for a fee, his opinion shall be supported by a memorandum in his file or an appraisal report, either of which shall include as a minimum the following:

1. Limiting Conditions
2. Any existing or contemplated interest
3. Defined value
4. Date applicable
5. The estate appraisal
6. A description of the property
7. The basis of the reasoning including applicable market data and/or capitalization computation

"This report or memorandum shall be available to the Professional Standards Committee for a period of at least two years (beginning subsequent to final determination of the court if the appraisal is involved in litigation) to ensure compliance with Article 11 of the Code of Ethics of the NATIONAL ASSOCIATION OF REALTORS®."

Standard of Practice 11-2

"The REALTOR® shall not undertake to make an appraisal when his employment or fee is contingent upon the amount of appraisal."

Standard of Practice 12-1
(Refer to Standard of Practice 9-4, which also relates to Article 12, Code of Ethics.)

Standard of Practice 15-1
"The REALTOR® shall not be subject to disciplinary proceedings in more than one Board of REALTORS® with respect to alleged violations of the Code of Ethics relating to the same transaction."

Standard of Practice 16-1
"The REALTOR® shall not recommend or suggest to a principal or a customer the use of services of another organization or business entity in which he has a direct interest without disclosing such interest at the time of the recommendation or suggestion."

Standard of Practice 19-1
"The REALTOR® shall not submit or advertise property without authority, and in any offering, the price quoted shall not be other than that agreed upon with the owners."

Standard of Practice 19-2
(Refer to Standard of Practice 9-4, which also relates to Aricle 19, Code of Ethics.)

Standard of Practice 21-1
"Signs giving notice of property for sale, rent, lease, or exchange shall not be placed on property without the consent of the owner."

Standard of Practice 21-2
"The REALTOR® obtaining information from a listing broker about a specific property shall not convey this information to, nor invite the cooperation of a third party broker without the consent of the listing broker."

Standard of Practice 21-3
"The REALTOR® shall not solicit a listing which is currently listed exclusively with another broker unless the listing broker, when asked by another broker, refuses to disclose the nature and current status of such

listing; i.e., an exclusive right to sell, an exclusive agency, open listing, or other."

Standard of Practice 21-4

"The REALTOR® shall not use information obtained by him from the listing broker, through offers to cooperate received through Multiple Listing Services or other sources authorized by the listing broker, for the purpose of creating a referral prospect to a third broker, or for creating a buyer prospect unless such use is authorized by the listing broker."

Standard of Practice 21-5

"The fact that a property has been listed exclusively with a REALTOR® shall not preclude or inhibit any other REALTOR® from soliciting such listing after its expiration."

Standard of Practice 21-6

"The fact that a property owner has retained a REALTOR® as his exclusive agent in respect of one or more past transactions creates no interest or agency which precludes or inhibits other REALTORS® from seeking such owner's future business."

Standard of Practice 21-7

"The REALTOR® shall be free to solicit a listing in respect to any property which is 'open listed' at any time."

Standard of Practice 21-8

"Unless otherwise precluded by law, the REALTOR® may discuss with an owner of a property which is exclusively listed with another REALTOR® the terms upon which he would accept a future listing upon the expiration of the present listing provided the owner initiates the discussion and provided the REALTOR® has not directly or indirectly solicited such discussion."

Standard of Practice 22-1

"It is the obligation of the selling broker as subagent of the listing broker to disclose immediately all pertinent facts to the listing broker prior to as well as after the contract is executed."

Standard of Practice 22-2

"The REALTOR®, when submitting offers to the seller, shall present each in an objective and unbiased manner."

Standard of Practice 24-1

"The purpose of Article 24 is to discourage salespersons from breaching their agreements with the REALTORS® by whom they are employed or with whom they are affiliated. Its further purpose is to prevent REALTORS® from inducing salespersons to breach such agreements.

"Article 24 must not be construed as precluding a REALTOR® from making an offer of employment or affiliation to the salesperson of another REALTOR® at any time or on any terms he deems appropriate. Any use of Article 24 to limit the opportunities for employment or affiliation available to salespersons is improper and a violation of Article 24.

"Article 24 is infringed only in the case where a REALTOR® solicits the services of a specific employee or independent contractor salesperson of another REALTOR® who is under a written agreement. A general announcement by a REALTOR® that he is interested in expanding his staff and invites qualified persons to call or write him is not a solicitation violative of Article 24. Nor would a REALTOR® be required by Article 24 to notify the REALTOR® with whom salespersons responding to such general announcement are associated."

The California Association of Realtors has the *California Code of Ethics and Arbitration Manual,* which contains the membership duties and the methods of enforcement at an Ethics Hearing and Arbitration of Disputes. This publication contains the many forms that may be used to ajudicate a matter at the local Board level. Some of the items included are titled:

Notice to Respondent,
Outline of Procedure for Hearing,
Notice of Right to Challenge
Qualification of Panelist,
Acknowledgment of Rule of Procedure,
Decision of Panel of the Committee,
Proof of Service of Civil Subpoena
Notice of Hearing,
Complaint,
Reply,
Certificate of Qualification,
Arbitration Agreement,
Arbitration Subpoena,
Award of Arbitrators.

Special training and expertise is needed for a person to qualify to hear matters brought before them.

The *Institute of Real Estate Management Code of Professional Ethics of the Certified Property Manager* is the one paper that all persons associated with the property management should sign and agree to as part of their employment process (Figure 5).

Figure 5

Institute of Real Estate Management Code of Professional Ethics of the Certified Property Manager®

Introduction

To establish and maintain public confidence in the honesty, integrity, professionalism and ability of the professional property manager is fundamental to the future success of the Institute of Real Estate managment and its members. This Code and performance pursuant to its provisions will be beneficial to the general public and contibute to the continued developement of a mutually beneficial relationship among CERTIFIED PROPERTY MANAGERS®, REALTORS®, clients, employers and the public.

The Institute of Real Estate Management as the professional society of property managers seeks to work closely with all other segments of the real estate industry to protect and enhance the interests of the public. To this end, members of the Institute have adopted and, as a condition of membership, subscribe to this Code of Professional Ethics. By doing so, they give notice that they clearly recognize the vital need to preserve and encourgage fair and equitable practices and competiton among all who are engaged in the profession of property management.

Those who are members of the Institute are dedicated individuals who are sincerely concerned with the protection and interests of those who come in contact with the industry. To this end, members of the Institute have subscribed to this Professional Pledge:

> I pledge myself to the advancement of professional property management through the mutual efforts of members of the Institute of Real Estate Management and by any other proper means available to me.
>
> I pledge myself to seek and maintain an equitable, honorable and cooperative association with fellow members of the Institute and with all others who may become a part of my business and professional life.

I pledge myself to place honesty, integrity and industriousness above all else; to pursue my gainful efforts with diligent study and dedication to the end that service to my clients shall always be maintained at the highest possible level.

I pledge myself to comply with the principles and declarations of the Institute of Real Estate Management as set forth in its By-laws, Regulations and this Code of Professional Ethics.

1. Fiduciary Obligation to Clients

A CERTIFIED PROPERTY MANAGER® shall at all times exercise the utmost business loyalty to the interests of his or her clients and shall be diligent in the maintenance and protection of the clients' properties. In order to achieve this goal, a CERTIFIED PROPERTY MANAGER® shall not engage in any activity which could be reasonably construed as contrary to the best interests of the client or the client's property. The CERTIFIED PROPERTY MANAGER® shall not represent personal interests divergent or conflicting with those of the client, unless the client has been previously notified in writing of the actual or potential conflict of interest, and has also in writing assented to such representation. A CERTIFIED PROPERTY MANAGER®, as a fiduciary for the client, shall not receive, directly or indirectly, any rebate, fee, commission, discount or other benefit, whether monetary or otherwise, which has not been fully disclosed to and approved by the client.

2. Disclosure

A CERTIFIED PROPERTY MANAGER® shall not disclose to a third party confidential information which would be injurious or damaging concerning the business or personal affairs of a client without prior written consent of the client, except as may otherwise be required or compelled by applicable law or regulation.

3. Accounting and Reporting

A CERTIFIED PROPERTY MANAGER® shall at all times keep and maintain accurate accounting records concerning the properties managed for the client, and such records shall be available for inspection at all reasonable times by each client. A CERTIFIED PROPERTY MANAGER® shall cause to be furnished to the client at intervals to be agreed upon with the client, a regular report in respect to that client's properties.

4. Protection of Funds and Property

A CERTIFIED PROPERTY MANAGER® shall at all times exert due diligence for the protection of client's funds and property in the possession or control of the CERTIFIED PROPERTY MANAGER® against all reasonably foreseeable contingencies or losses.

5. Relations with other Members of the Profession

A CERTIFIED PROPERTY MANAGER® shall not make, authorize or otherwise encourage any unfounded derogatory or disparaging comments concerning the practices of other CERTIFIED PROPERTY MANAGERS®. CERTIFIED PROPERTY MANAGERS® subscribing to this Code shall not exaggerate or misrepresent the services offered by him or her as compared with competing CERTIFIED PROPERTY MANAGERS®. Nothing in this Code, however, shall restrict legal and reasonable business competition by and among CERTIFIED PROPERTY MANAGERS®.

6. Contract

The contract, if any, between a CERTIFIED PROPERTY MANAGER® and his or her client shall provide for the specific terms agreed upon between the parties and shall be in clear and understandable terms, including a general description of the services to be provided by and responsibilities of the CERTIFIED PROPERTY MANAGER®.

7. Duty to Firm or Employer

A CERTIFIED PROPERTY MANAGER® shall at all times exercise the utmost loyalty to his or her employer or firm and shall be diligent in the maintenance and protection of the interests and property of the employer or firm. The CERTIFIED PROPERTY MANAGER® shall not engage in any activity or undertake any obligation which could reasonably be seen as contrary to the obligation of loyalty and diligence owed to his or her employer firm, and shall not recieve, directly or indirectly, any rebate, fee, commission, discount or other benefit, whether monetary or otherwise, which could reasonably be seen as producing a conflict with the interests of his or her employer or firm. A CERTIFIED PROPERTY MANAGER® shall at all times exercise due diligence for the protection of the funds of his or her employer or firm against all reasonably foreseeable contingencies or losses and shall as agent of his or her employer or firm exercise the highest degree of responsiblity for safekeeping and preservation of these funds.

8. Preserving and Protecting Property of the Client

It shall be the duty of the CERTIFIED PROPERTY MANAGER®, as a skilled and highly trained professional, to competently manage the property of the client with due regard for the rights, responsibilities and benefits of the tenant. A CERTIFIED PROPERTY MANAGER® shall manage the property of his or her clients in a manner which takes due regard for his or her obligations to conserve natural resources and to maximize the preservation of the environment.

9. Compliance with Laws and Regulations

A CERTIFIED PROPERTY MANAGER® shall at all times conduct his or her business and personal activities with knowledge of and in compliance with applicable federal, state and local laws and regulations, and shall maintain the highest moral and ethical standards consistent with membership in and the purposes of the Institute of Real Estate Management.

10. Continuing Professional Education

A CERTIFIED PROPERTY MANAGER®, in order to assure the continued retention and further growth and development of his or her skills as a professional, shall utilize to the highest extent possible the facilities offered to him or her for continuing professional education and refinement of his or her management skills.

11. Incorporation of the NATIONAL ASSOCIATION OF REALTORS® Code of Ethics

The Code of Ethics of the NATIONAL ASSOCIATION OF REALTORS®, as in effect, from time to time is incorporated by reference into this Code and in relevant parts shall be binding on CERTIFIED PROPERTY MANAGERS® as other articles of this Code.

12. Enforcement

Any violation by a CERTIFIED PROPERTY MANAGER® of the obligations of this Code shall be determined in accordance with and pursuant to the terms of the Bylaws and Rules and Regulations of the Institute of Real Estate Management. Disciplinary action for violation of any portion of this Code shall be instituted by the Institute of Real Estate Management in accordance with the Bylaws and Rules and Regulations established by the Governing Council of the Institute. The result of such disciplinary action shall be final and binding upon the affected CERTIFIED PROPERTY MANAGER®, and without recourse to the Institute, its officers, councillors, members, employees and agents.

Article 1 - Fiduciary Obligation to Clients. This states that the Certified Property Manager (CPM) has the utmost business loyalty to the interests of the client, not to the interests of the CPM. Any potential or actual conflicting interest must be fully disclosed in writing to the client and must be approved by the client. This means that if the painter does 20 units and the building exterior and offers to do the property manager's personal residence, or the on-site manager's personal residence at no charge, or at the cost of paint only, or at a reduced rate, it would require the owner's approval. This would also be true of the gardening services, rug shampooing, plumber, pool service, and any other services.

Article 2 - Disclosure. This requires that all office personnel keep client information confidential. If a receptionist gets a call asking how much an occupied unit is rented for, they should not disclose this information. It may be a neighboring owner who is about to have a vacancy or a rent increase and they want to establish area rents. It may be an appraiser checking comparables in the local area. Or, it may be the current owner's ex-wife's attorney securing information on the income of the owner, and a subsequent increase in support payments may have to be paid because of the property manager's slip of the tongue.

Article 5 - Relations with Other Members of the Profession. This covers property managers who exaggerate the services they offer to clients. It also covers misrepresenting their services or stating bad things about the competition. If a manager has only had experience as an unlicensed manager of a condominium association and indicates that he or she has the qualifications equal to a licensed person, he or she may be under scrutiny to prove that expertise.

Article 6 - Contract. This calls for the written management agreement to be worded in easy-to-understand words, not big, fancy, long words. The contract is to be written so that the owner/layman may read and decipher the terms of the agreement without having to hire an attorney.

Article 7 -Duty to Firm or Employer. The items covered here are exactly the same as those disclosures necessary to be made under the provisions in Article 1, discussed above, except they are not directed to the Broker. This article covers all persons who work for the owner through a broker or through a management company or directly for the owner.

Article 11 - National Code of Ethics. This clause binds the manager to be held for and accountable to the National Association of Realtors by including their Code of Ethics as part of this Code of Ethics. This makes the parties responsible for both sets of rules.

CHAPTER 15–QUIZ

1. The professional property manager has:

   a. education
   b. experience
   c. application
   d. All of the above

2. The professional landlord:

   a. gives direction
   b. lets the manager handle everything
   c. personally reviews all aspects of management
   d. uses only a CPA, CFP, and CPM

3. The Institute of Real Estate Management aids in:

   a. communications with owners
   b. communications with tenants
   c. networking on issues
   d. listing approved vendors

4. Affiliation with the local Board of Realtors:

   a. joins members with the local Apartment Association
   b. affects interests of the property management job
   c. authorizes the member to use the Certified Property Manager logo (CPM)
   d. certifies the member as an AMO

5. The professional tenant knows:

   a. their budget limitations and rights
   b. that arbitration waives all their rights
   c. their rights are limited to mediation
   d. that a non-licensee cannot get sued

6. Which is not involved in tenant rent assistance?

    a. Housing Authority
    b. Housing Voucher Program
    c. Health & Urban Division
    d. Section 8

7. The National Tenant Organization (NTO):

    a. rules and negotiates
    b. informs and educates
    c. bargains and presides over
    d. litigates and instructs

8. Ethics matters in business are most likely to be:

    a. the same as ethics in family, home and personal life
    b. in gray areas rather than strictly black and white
    c. arbitrary, subjective, and cannot be trained
    d. must come from the home in early family life to be valid

9. A professional property manager must:

    a. obtain approval from the client for a non-monetary benefit
    b. get three competitive bids before approving any work
    c. pledge themselves to pay for contingencies and losses
    d. agree to abide by the findings of a Code of Ethics trial

10. A Certified Property Manager, when discussing the previous property management operation, would emphasize:

    a. the prior firm's lack of professional qualifications
    b. the audit trail you will perform to seek a trial against them
    c. the excessive spending they did using their vendors
    d. the quality of service that he or she can offer

CHAPTER 15–ANSWER KEY

1. d
2. a
3. c
4. b
5. a
6. c
7. b
8. b
9. a
10. d

Glossary

Accredited Resident Manager (ARM). A designation conferred by the Institute of Real Estate Management to those qualified as resident on-site managers.

Advertising. Buying space in a newspaper, magazine, or other medium used to attract public attention to a particular item for sale or lease, or to a particular organization's services.

Affidavit of service. A sworn statement that an eviction notice has been properly served.

Agent. A person who enters into a fiduciary relationship with another party and is authorized to act for that party.

Amortization. Gradually reducing the book value of an asset by depreciating it over a period of time. Or, gradually paying off a debt by making regular payments of principal and interest.

Anchor tenant. A major tenant in a shopping center that attracts other businesses to the center as well as consumers.

Appraisal. An estimate of value of a particular item at a particular point in time.

Assessment. An amount charged against each condominium owner or building tenant to pay the building's operating costs.

Assignment. Transfer of a party's rights under a contract. For example, a tenant may transfer his or her right of possession in a property to a third party.

Automatic renewal clause. A lease provision that ensures renewal of the lease automatically unless the tenant or the landlord gives the other party notice of an intent to terminate.

Blight correction. Rehabilitating deteriorated residential properties.

Block grant program. A federal revenue-sharing program where direct grants are given to local governments for developing urban communities.

Board of directors. The people who govern a corporation (including condominium corporations).

Break-even point. The point at which a property's gross income equals its total operating costs.

Budget. A detailed plan providing for the use of funds available to a specific property over a specific period of time.

Building Owners and Managers Association International (BOMA). An international organization of office building owners and managers that encourages professionalism with educational programs and publications.

Bulk purchasing. When supplies are bought in large quantities (and stored for later use) in order to cut operating costs for a property.

Business cycle. The ups and downs of increasing and decreasing economic prosperity. The cycle consists of four phases: expansion, recession, contraction, and revival.

Business park. A development of offices/warehouses usually devoted to a similar use. Sometimes referred to as an office park.

Bylaws. Corporate regulations that set out the specific procedures for handling routine corporate matters.

Cancellation option. A lease clause giving the tenant the option to cancel at the end of a specific period of time.

Capitalization. The method of converting a property income into value.

Cash flow. The amount of cash available after all operating expenses and mortgage payments have been made.

Cash flow statement. A yearly financial report showing the cash available return after paying the annual expenses, mortgage payments, and taxes.

Cashier. The person in the property management firm who collects and records all income, bills accounts, and draws buildings' payrolls.

Certified Apartment Maintenance Technician (CAMT). Designation awarded by the National Apartment Association (NAA) for certain courses of study.

Certified Property Manager (CPM). The professional designation given by the Institute of Real Estate Management to those who distinguish themselves in the areas of education, experience, and ethics.

Classified advertisement. Line ads that announce space for rent, usually appearing in a special section of a newspaper

Co-insurance clause. A common provision in insurance policies that limits the liability of the insurance company to that proportion of the loss that the amount of insurance bears to a percentage of the value of the property.

Common area. Space used by all tenants/owners of a building, such as lobbies, corridors, and stairways; in a condominium, the property in which a unit owner has an undivided interest.

Common expenses. The costs of operating, managing, maintaining, and repairing a condominium's common areas and administering the condominium association.

Community shopping center. A retail shopping center, covering approximately 100,000 to 250,000 square feet, that offers convenience items, apparel, and home furnishings, and often features one main anchor tenant (a department or variety store).

Conditions, covenants, and restrictions (CC&Rs). Private restrictions placed by a subdivider (or condominium association) on lots or units within a subdivision, limiting the use of the property.

Condohotel. A residential building in which seasonal occupants purchase hotel rooms on a contract basis for a limited period of time and sublease them for the remaining part of the year.

Condominium. A type of ownership consisting of a separate interest in an individual unit combined with an undivided interest in common areas.

Condominium association. The body that governs the condominium: every unit owner automatically belongs to it.

Consultation. A service offered to owners whose properties don't require ongoing management, but who do need advice on certain problems, such as modernization.

Consumer price index. An index compiled by the U.S. Bureau of Labor and Statistics that compares prices of certain items to prices from a selected base year: it measures inflation.

Contract services. Maintenance duties carried out by outside laborers (as opposed to employees) on a regular basis for a fee.

Controllable expense. An operating expense within the management's control.

Cooperative. In a cooperative, the individual owner purchases shares in the corporation that owns the building, and receives a proprietary lease on the individual unit and the right to use the common areas.

Corporation. An artificial person, consisting of an association of individuals, but regarded by the law as a single person, separate from the individuals.

Corrective maintenance. Ongoing repairs that are made to a building and its equipment to restore it to good operating condition.

Cost approach. Estimating a property's value by adding the value of the land to the cost of reproducing the improvements, and then deducting depreciation.

Credit agency. A firm that prepares credit checks on prospective tenants for property owners or managers. They usually charge a fixed fee per report.

Curb appeal. The impression of a property, good or bad, when it is seen from the street while driving.

Default. The failure to meet a legal obligation (usually contractual) when due.

Deferred maintenance. Ordinary maintenance that is put off (through lack of funds, neglect, etc.) that reduces a property's use and value.

Deflation. An economic condition when there is less money available and goods are relatively scarce.

Department of Housing and Urban Development (HUD). A government agency authorized to help improve the housing conditions in the United States; it oversees the FHA (Federal Housing Authority) which insures home mortgages.

Depreciation. Loss of value due to any cause, including physical deterioration, functional obsolescence, or economic obsolescence.

Deteriorating neighborhood. An area where buildings are in a state of disrepair and transience is high.

Developing neighborhood. A neighborhood that is growing, with recently constructed buildings and stable families.

Direct-mail advertising. Promoting a product by mailing letters, cards, or brochures directly to potential customers. Its success relies heavily on accurate, specialized mailing lists.

Direct management costs. Expenses attributed directly to the management functions of a property's operation.

Director of leasing. The person in a property management firm who markets and leases the property.

Display advertisement. A large advertisement (usually with graphics) in a newspaper designed to market a new property. Used most often for large residential complexes, commercial buildings, and industrial space.

Dun & Bradstreet. A credit reporting agency that publishes credit ratings for many corporations and businesses.

Economic life. The period during which improved property will yield a return over and above the rent due to the land itself.

Economic rent raise. An increase in rent justified by supply and demand.

Employee policy manual. A handbook given to all employees stating job descriptions, company policies, and rules and regulations.

Environmental Protection Agency (EPA). A government agency that regulates air and water pollution, noise abatement, and waste treatment.

Equity. The difference between the value of a piece of property and the charges against it.

Escalation clause. A clause in a lease or mortgage providing for the adjustment of payments or interest in the event of certain contingencies, such as changes in taxes or the interest rate.

Established neighborhood. A sound, healthy, fully developed neighborhood with stable families and social institutions.

Eviction. Dispossession, expulsion, or ejection of someone from property. May be either actual, a physical removal from the premises; or constructive, a violation by the landlord of the covenant of quiet enjoyment, as by shutting off the water or electricity.

Eviction notice. A written notice to a tenant to pay the rent immediately or leave the premises within a specified time.

Fair Credit Reporting Act. Legislation requiring a property manager to tell applicants when a credit agency is used to investigate their credit.

Feasibility study. A report summarizing the potential profitability of a proposed real estate project. It includes consideration of land costs and physical features of the land, requirements of the project, projected income, and estimated expenses.

Federal Housing Administration (FHA). An agency created by the National Housing Act of 1934 to insure home mortgages through a federal mortgage insurance program (the Mutual Mortgage Insurance Program).

Federal housing policy. Legislation that affects government housing agencies and the programs they administer.

Financial analysis. The complete evaluation of a property's worth as an investment; includes valuation, depreciation, tax benefits, and cash flow calculations.

Fixed expense. A property management expense that remains the same, regardless of rental income.

Flat fee. A set dollar amount per year or per month.

Foreclosure. Legal action instituted by the mortgagee, in the county where the property is located, whereby property used as security for a debt is sold to satisfy the debt following default by the debtor.

Garden apartment. A low-rise building designed for multi-family living, usually located in a suburban area.

General partner. The member of a limited partnership who manages the business and is liable for all its debts.

Gross floor area. The total floor area of a property, including the common area.

Gross leasable area (GLA). The total floor area designed for the occupancy and exclusive use by tenants.

Gross lease. A lease in which the tenant pays a fixed rental amount and the owner pays all the operating expenses of the property.

Gross sales. The total sales made by a retail tenant. A proportion of the tenant's gross sales is due the landlord as part of the rent under a percentage lease.

Ground lease. The property owner leases the property to a tenant who constructs his or her own building on the site. Also called a land lease.

Heating, ventilating, and air-conditioning (HVAC) system. The system that regulates the distribution of heat and fresh air through a building.

Highest and best use. The use that at the time of appraisal is most likely to produce the greatest net return from the property over a given period of time.

High-rise apartment. A multi-family residence several stories high, about 300 units, usually located in a major metropolitan area where space is at a premium.

Household. All persons, related or not, who occupy a housing unit.

Housing and Community Development Act of 1974. Legislation that authorized the Section 8 and community development block grant programs.

Housing and Urban Development Act of 1965. Legislation that created the U.S. Department of Housing and Urban Development (HUD).

Housing unit. Any unit that constitutes separate living quarters.

Income and expense report. A monthly financial report showing the property's income, operating expenses, and the amount remitted to the owner.

Income approach. A method of appraising property basing the value upon the net amount of income produced by the property. Also called the capitalization method.

Index escalation clause. A clause in a lease providing for rental increases based upon the changes in a specified index, usually the Consumer Price Index.

Indirect influence. The effect of monetary, fiscal, and credit policies on housing.

Indirect management costs. Expenses in a property's budget that are partially attributable to the operation of the management department.

Industrial park. A development designed to accommodate light manufacturing tenants.

Industrial real estate. Property used for the processing and manufacture of goods.

Inflation. The economic condition when the money supply increases (and its value decreases) associated with rising wages and costs.

Infrastructure. The man-made features of a neighborhood, such as roads, highways, sewage and drainage systems, and utility facilities.

Institute of Real Estate Management (IREM). A professional association affiliated with the NATIONAL ASSOCIATION OF REALTORS® for those who meet standards of experience, education, and ethics.

Institutional advertising. Advertising focused on improving the reputation or increasing the public's recognition of a particular company.

Institutional property. Office buildings owned and occupied by the same corporation.

Insurance. Coverage by contract whereby one person undertakes to guarantee another against losses caused by a specific event in exchange for the payment of a premium.

Job description. Written description of the requirements of a particular job, the duties involved, how they are to be performed, and their importance.

Joint venture. Two or more individuals joining together for one specific project as partners. A joint venture is of limited duration and if the members of the venture undertake another project, the association becomes a partnership.

Labor-extensive industry. A business with a low concentration of employees per acre.

Labor-intensive industry. A business with a high concentration of employees per acre.

Labor-oriented industry. A business that tends to locate near a low-cost labor pool.

Landlord. A lessor. A landowner who has leased his or her property.

Land use planning. The creation of long-term plans for large-scale development, usually in urban areas.

Lease. A contract for the possession and profits of real estate in return for rent. The property owner is the lessor, the tenant is the lessee.

Liability insurance. Insurance protecting a property owner or manager against damage to the person or property of another due to the owner's or manager's negligence.

Limited liability. When responsibility for a business's debts is restricted to the size of one's investment in it (as for corporate stockholders and limited partners).

Limited partner. The member of a limited partnership whose liability is limited to his or her investment in the business and who is not involved in managing the partnership.

Limited partnership. A business arrangement which limits certain partners' liability to the amount they invested. Usually a limited partner is not permitted to have a voice in managing the company; his or her role is primarily that of an investor. The limited partnership must have at least one general partner.

Management agreement. A written contract in which another person assumes the responsibilities for managing a property for the owner in exchange for a fee.

Management fee. Money paid for the performance of management duties.

Management plan. An outline of a property's physical and fiscal management that is directed toward achieving the owner's goals.

Market data approach. One of the three standard methods of appraisal; based on comparing similar properties. Also called the comparative analysis approach.

Marketing. All business activity involved in moving goods and services from producers to consumers.

Market-oriented industry. A business that tends to locate near industrial users and consumers of its products.

Market survey. The gathering of information about comparable properties and comparing it to data on the subject property to judge its advantages and disadvantages.

Mart building. A multi-story property that is a cross between a retail arcade and a loft building, used by wholesalers and jobbers to display sample merchandise.

Maximum percentage lease. A type of percentage lease that sets a ceiling on the amount of rent to be paid.

Merchandising. An aspect of marketing that creates a desire for a product by pointing out features in the item that will appeal to or benefit the buyer.

Merchants' association. An organization formed to advance the interests of shopping center tenants in planning advertisements, promotions, decorations, etc.

Minimum-guaranteed percentage lease. A type of percentage lease requiring the tenant to pay either a fixed minimum rental or a percentage of gross sales, whichever is greater.

Miniwarehouse. A self-storage facility open to private individuals and businesses on a rental basis.

Mobile home. A factory-manufactured dwelling often placed on a foundation and connected to local utilities in a mobile home park.

Money supply. The total amount of currency in circulation.

Mortgage. A document that details the terms of a real estate loan agreement and serves as the lender's security for the debt.

National Housing Act of 1934. The first significant housing legislation; created the Federal Housing Administration.

Negotiation. Dealings between two or more parties to reach an agreement on price, quantity, quality, or other terms.

Neighborhood. An area within which there are common characteristics of population and land use, usually bordered by some kind of landmark: main arterials, shopping districts, freeways, etc.

Neighborhood analysis. A study of a neighborhood's characteristics (e.g., population, growth trends, economic class) and comparing it to the broader economic and geographic area of which it is a part.

Neighborhood shopping center. A relatively small retail district, approximately 25,000 to 75,000 square feet, designed to provide convenience shopping for day-to-day consumer needs.

Net lease. A lease under which the tenant pays the rent and also certain expenses connected with the leased premises.

Net-net lease. A lease under which the tenant pays a rental amount plus all maintenance and operating expenses.

Net-net-net lease. A lease under which the tenant pays a rental amount plus maintenance and operating expenses, property taxes, and insurance.

Net operating income. A property's gross income less all operating expenses.

Non-competition clause. A clause in a lease giving a retail tenant an exclusive right to operate a particular business without competition from any of the other tenants.

Noncontrollable expenses. Items such as real estate taxes, insurance, and labor-union wages over which the property management has no control.

Nuisance rent raise. The rent raise a tenant will pay to avoid the expense and inconvenience of moving.

Operating budget. A projection of income and expense for the operation of a property over a one-year period.

Option to renew. A clause in a lease giving the tenant the right to extend the lease for an additional period of time on specified terms.

Percentage lease. A lease agreement (usually for retail property) where the rental is based on a fixed amount plus a percentage of the tenant's gross sales or net income.

Periodic costs. A type of fixed expense (e.g., property taxes) that occurs on a regular but infrequent basis.

Per-unit cost method. A method of computing management fees based on the direct costs of managing a specific number of units.

Physical life. Estimated time a building will remain structurally sound and capable of being used.

Planned Unit Development (PUD). A development designed for intensive use of the land, combining a high density of dwellings with maximum utilization of open space.

Preventive maintenance. A program of regular inspection and care allowing the prevention of potential problems or their immediate repair.

Principal. One of the parties to a transaction; in property management, the property owner who authorizes the manager to act on his or her behalf.

Profit and loss statement. An annual financial report of a property's actual net profit before taxes.

Property analysis. A complete description of a property, including its design, features, and physical condition.

Property management. A profession where someone other than the property owner supervises the property's operation, striving to meet the owner's objectives.

Property manager. An agent who administers real estate according to the principal's (owner's) goals.

Proprietary lease. A lease giving a cooperative shareholder the right to exclusive possession of a unit, usually for a long period of time (e.g., 99 years).

Prospect. A potential customer.

Publicity. A news or feature article in a newspaper, magazine, or other medium that attracts public attention to an individual or company.

Purchasing agent. The person in the management firm who supervises the purchase of goods and services.

Radius clause. A shopping center lease provision where a tenant agrees not to own or operate another outlet within a specified distance of the leased premises.

Real estate. The land and all things affixed to or appurtenant to the land, including buildings and other fixtures.

Real estate investment trust (REIT). An unincorporated business association, with a minimum of 100 owners, which is allowed to pass profits through to investors without paying corporate tax. The investors have limited liability.

Recession. A period of negative economic growth; the point in the business cycle when supply equals and begins to surpass demand.

Recruitment. The active process of obtaining new employees.

Referral. Obtaining new business using recommendations from satisfied clients.

Regional analysis. Studying the economic, demographic, and physical aspects of the area surrounding a property.

Regional shopping center. A large retail district, approximately 300,000 to 1,000,000 square feet, that offers a wide selection of merchandise and serves a large residential sector.

Rehabilitation. The process of lengthening a building's economic life by restoring its condition.

Rent. Compensation paid by the tenant or occupant of real property to the owner in exchange for the use and possession of the property.

Rent control. Government regulations or ordinances that limit the amount of rent that can be charged for a unit. Usually restricted to residential property.

Rent receipt. A record of rent received.

Rentable space. The floor area of an office building minus allowances for stairs, elevator shafts, duct work, and other areas not available to the tenant.

Rental center. A special leasing area in a real estate development, consisting of a display area, furnished models, and a closing area.

Rental inquiry card. A record of all prospects who call or visit a property.

Rental ledger. A written record of the tenants' names, units occupied, phone numbers, rental amount, security deposits paid, and other tenant information.

Rental price level. An indicator that moves up or down in response to supply and demand, indicating the economic strength of the real estate market.

Rental schedule. A list of the rental rates for units in a given building.

Resident manager. A person who is responsible for administering and maintaining a property and its staff and resources.

Retail properties. Developments where goods and services are sold directly to individuals and households.

Sale and leaseback. A form of real estate financing in which the owner of industrial or commercial property sells the property and leases it back from the buyer, normally under a triple net lease.

Security deposit. Money paid in advance by a tenant to cover possible damage to the property and ensure faithful compliance with the lease.

Slum. A core area of a city where there is severe overcrowding and deterioration.

Sole proprietorship. When a business is owned and managed by one person.

Space planning. The process of combining functional efficiency with a pleasant atmosphere in an office interior.

Special-purpose property. Hotels, resorts, nursing homes, theaters, schools, churches and other properties whose specialized design is only suitable for a particular kind of tenant.

Statement of disbursements. A listing of all of a property's expenses incurred during a specific operating period.

Straight percentage lease. A type of percentage lease that bases rental rate solely on gross sales.

Strip shopping center. A retail center designed as a straight line of stores, usually very narrow in proportion to its length.

Super-regional shopping center. A retail center covering more than 750,000 square feet.

Syndicate. An association of two or more people formed to make and operate an investment. This can be a corporation, real estate investment trust, or partnership.

Tenant. One who pays rent to occupy real estate.

Tenant union. An organization that represents tenant interests.

Time-share condominium. Ownership in vacation area residential property for an assigned period, usually two weeks.

Townhouse. A type of single-family home built as attached or semi-detached row houses.

Uniform Residential Landlord and Tenant Act. Legislation designed to regulate and standardize the relationship between residential landlords and tenants.

Urban renewal. A complete program for clearing slum areas and designing redevelopment projects.

Usable space. The floor area of an office building that tenants may use for office space.

Use clause. A provision in a lease limiting the uses the tenant may put the property to.

Utility. A public service, such as gas, water, or electricity.

Value. The amount of goods or services offered in the market place in exchange for a given product.

Zoning. Government regulation, through zoning ordinances and regulations, of the uses of property within specified areas.

Index

3 FEB 97

Equity

- Fiscal Policy - Put in effect Fed Govt.
  - Spending...
- Monetary Fed Reserve

CBD - Central Bus Dist. (Higher Occupancy

CPI - Consumer Price Ind.